2nd National Edition

STAND UP
to the IRS

How to Handle Audits,
Tax Bills and Tax Court

By Tax Attorney Frederick W. Daily
Edited by Robin Leonard

NOLO PRESS BERKELEY

YOUR RESPONSIBILITY WHEN USING A SELF-HELP LAW BOOK

We've done our best to give you useful and accurate information in this book. But laws and procedures change frequently and are subject to differing interpretations. If you want legal advice backed by a guarantee, see a lawyer. If you use this book, it's your responsibility to make sure that the facts and general advice contained in it are applicable to your situation.

KEEPING UP TO DATE

To keep its books up to date, Nolo Press issues new printings and new editions periodically. New printings reflect minor legal changes and technical corrections. New editions contain major legal changes, major text additions or major reorganizations. To find out if a later printing or edition of any Nolo book is available, call Nolo Press at (510) 549-1976 or check the catalog in the *Nolo News,* our quarterly newspaper.

To stay current, follow the "Update" service in the *Nolo News.* You can get free a two year subscription by sending us the registration card in the back of the book. In another effort to help you use Nolo's latest materials, we offer a 25% discount off the purchase of any new Nolo book if you turn in any earlier printing or edition. (See the "Recycle Offer" in the back of the book.)

This book was last revised in: **January 1995**

SECOND EDITION	
SECOND PRINTING	January 1995
ILLUSTRATIONS	Derick Daily
COVER DESIGN	Susan Wight
BOOK DESIGN & LAYOUT	Jackie Mancuso
INDEX	Mary Kidd
PROOFREADING	Anne Hayes

Daily, Frederick W., 1942-
    Stand up to the IRS / by Frederick Daily. -- 2nd National ed.
       p.   cm.
    Includes index.
    ISBN 0-87337-240-9
    1. Tax protests and appeals--United States--Popular works. 2. Tax auditing--United States--Popular works. 3. Tax courts--United States--Popular works. 4. United States. Internal Revenue Service.
I. Title.
KF6324.Z9D345 1994
343.7304-dc20
[347.3034]
                                     94-2699
                                     CIP

THANK YOU

Everyone who gave me thoughtful suggestions on writing, and then improving, my first book, *Winning the IRS Game*—your comments were considered and incorporated into *Stand Up to the IRS*.

My partner in life, Brenda, and my son and cartoonist, Derick.

Alan Rosenthal for his assistance with the (very tricky) bankruptcy issues in this book. Alan is an independent paralegal in San Francisco who completes forms for people filing their own bankruptcies.

My editor extraordinaire Robin Leonard, head Noloid Jake Warner and all the other nice people at Nolo Press.

Contents

1 Inside the IRS: What You Need to Know About IRS Operations

2 Filing Tax Returns: If You Haven't Filed and Other Concerns

3 Winning Your Audit

4 Appealing Your Audit

5 Going to Tax Court: No Lawyer Necessary

6 When You Owe the IRS: Keeping the Tax Collector at Bay

7 IRS Enforced Collection: Liens and Levies

8 Problems Resolution Program: A Friend at the IRS

9   Family, Friends, Heirs and the IRS

10   Fraud and Tax Crimes: Do You Really Have to Worry?

11   Small Businesses: When IRS Trouble Comes

12   Penalties and Interest

13

Help Beyond the Book: Tax Professionals and Tax Information

14

When You Owe State Income Taxes

15

Taxpayers' Bill of Rights

16

The 25 Most Asked Questions

Glossary

Appendix

INSIDE THE IRS: WHAT YOU NEED TO KNOW ABOUT IRS OPERATIONS 1

Chances are you will have a problem with the Taxman at least once in your lifetime. Nearly everyone faces an audit, receives a bill for back taxes or has some other serious problem with the IRS. If it's your turn, you need to understand how your adversary—the IRS—is organized. Later, when we cover specific tax situations, this knowledge will be a big help.

So, let's take a look at the Internal Revenue Service (IRS).

The IRS operates on four primary levels. The divisions within the various levels can have similar names, which makes dealing with the IRS more confusing than it should be. A chart of the IRS divisions you are likely to encounter appears a few pages ahead.

National. The IRS is a branch of the U.S. Treasury Department, with headquarters in Washington, DC, and is ruled by a Commissioner appointed by the President. Regional Commissioners and District Directors, also political appointees, oversee IRS operations. The IRS "brain" is its National Computer Center in West Virginia. There are two other computer centers—one in Detroit and one in Memphis. The National IRS office sets tone and policy, while procedures—especially collection procedures—are left to the ten regional Service Centers and the 63 District Offices. There are also numerous suboffices under the District Offices.

The IRS is divided into nine departments, but the only one that affects you directly is Compliance, which has five divisions—Examinations, Appeals, Collections, Criminal Investigation and International Operations.

Service Centers. Service Centers process annually about 200 million tax returns, more than half of which are individual income tax returns. Service Centers collect over one trillion dollars in tax payments each year from 125 million taxpayers and seven million organizations. The centers are located in Andover, Atlanta, Austin, Cincinnati, Fresno, Holtsville, Kansas City, Memphis, Ogden and Philadelphia. Each center has its own computer that endlessly mails out tax notices—collection notices (bills), audit notices and tax forms. Any tax bill dispute you have with the IRS probably originated

here. Contacts with the Service Center are usually by mail, or occasionally by telephone.

Tax Return Processing

From January to May, IRS Service Centers often operate around the clock receiving income tax returns, extension requests and tax payments. Many temporary workers are hired, trained on the job and paid little more than the minimum wage. IRS officials admit that many processing mistakes are caused by these seasonal employees.

The processing pipeline starts with machines opening tax return envelopes and removing tax returns and checks. Transcribers scan the returns for completeness and enter the key tax return data into a computer; the computer then checks for arithmetic accuracy. A second transcriber double checks the first transcriber's work up by re-inputting the same information into the computer.

Magnetic tapes of tax return data are sent to the National Computer Center, where each return is computer scored for its audit potential. About 10% of all individual (non-business) income tax returns are selected by the National Computer Center for further review. These files are sent back to the Service Centers. There, IRS classifiers (human beings) pick out about 10% of the 10% already selected for audit, based on their opinion of the probability of serious errors on the tax return. So, roughly, 1% of all tax returns filed are audited. (For more information on how returns are selected for audit, see Chapter 3, Section B.)

Automated Collection System (ACS). This program was developed in the 1980s to facilitate communication with taxpayers who owe money to the IRS. It is a highly computerized regional collection system staffed by personnel working by phone and mail. You may talk to an ACS person, but you will never meet one. The ACS computer and the National computer are not linked, which can and does cause problems in dealing with the IRS. The ACS collection information may not match what is in your National computer file.

District Offices. The U.S. is divided into 63 IRS Districts, each headed by a District Director. These offices sit in major cities with suboffices in smaller cities. You can bet one is near you. In the IRS organization, each District Office falls under a Service Center. They provide each other with information, although their sharing scheme is less than perfect and often contains glitches. If you ever meet with someone from the IRS, that person will most likely work out of a suboffice of a District Office.

Each District Office contains several divisions, four of which you may encounter—Examination, Collection, Criminal Investigation and Problems Resolution.

Let's look at the four IRS District Divisions in more detail.

- *Examination* division conducts audits ("examinations" in IRS-speak). The people who audit tax returns are called Tax Auditors if you meet them at a District Office, or Revenue Agents if they come to your home or business. I use the term "auditors" to refer to both.

- *Collection* division collects tax dollars. IRS collectors are called Revenue Officers. If your case goes to collection, you or your representative will meet with a collector face-to-face. The Service Center and Automated Collection System are also part of the collection apparatus.

- *Criminal Investigation* is the police force of the IRS, and its employees are called Special Agents. They work out of District Offices and Service Centers. Chances are slight that you will ever meet an IRS criminal investigator. If you do, you or someone you know is in trouble.

- *Problems Resolution Program* (PRP) employs the IRS troubleshooters (Problems Resolution Officers—PROs) to call on when you can't get tax problems solved through normal IRS channels. These officers are found at Service Centers and Regional and District Offices. (The Appendix contains a list of PRP addresses and phone numbers. This list is taken from IRS Publication 1320, Operation Link.) PROs hold powers to cut through red tape and get things done quickly.

The total number of IRS employees at all levels comes close to 125,000, making it our largest federal bureaucracy. The Examination division employs 25%, Collection 15%, and Criminal 3%. The other 57% make policy, run the computers, answer taxpayer inquiries and God only knows what else.

If you're confused about the structure of the IRS, don't worry—you're not alone. Read the following example, which should shed some light on the relationship of the various divisions.

Example

1. On April 15, Arnold and Aimee Tyson file their income tax return by mail with their *Service Center*.

2. The information on their return is transmitted to the *National Computer Center* for analysis and given a potential audit score. If the score is high enough (the Tysons' is), the return is screened at the *Service Center*. If the return is then deemed to have a high enough audit potential (the Tysons' does), it is sent to their *District Office*.

3. At the *District Office*, the return is scrutinized again. The Tysons' return is selected for examination (audit) and they are sent an examination notice.

4. The Tysons call to set up the appointment, and then go to the *Office Audit* with a *Tax Auditor*. (Or alternatively, a *Revenue Agent* comes to their business.)

5. The auditor is alarmed and suspects fraud. He refers their file to *Criminal Investigation* (a part of the *District Office*) to be investigated by an IRS *Special Agent*. The audit is suspended. (A criminal investigation is very rare.)

6. The special agent concludes that the Tysons made many errors and may even have committed fraud, but he's not confident he could make a criminal case against them. He sends the file back to the auditor.

7. The auditor concludes the audit and sends the Tysons an examination report. The report states that they owe the IRS taxes, interest and penalties. The Tysons disagree with the report.

8. The Tysons file an appeal request with their *District Office*.

9. The appeal is heard at the regional *Appeals Office*. The *Appeals Officer* upholds the auditor and the Tysons file a petition in Tax Court. (Tax Court is independent of the IRS.) The Tysons win a partial victory in Tax Court.

10. After their Tax Court hearing, the Tysons still owe the IRS some money. Taxes, interest and penalties are formally assessed in the Tysons' IRS records.

11. The Tysons receive their first series of computerized collection notices from their *Service Center*. They don't pay as they don't have the money.

12. The Service Center gives up. Now collection notices and telephone calls come from the *Automated Collection System* (*ACS*).

13. The Tysons still can't pay. The ACS sends the file to a *Revenue Officer* who works in the *Collection Division* of the *District Office*.

14. They try to work out some collection arrangement, but the collector is unreasonable and threatens to take their property. The Tysons seek help from the *Problems Resolution Office*.

15. With the help of a *Problems Resolution Officer*, they arrange a payment plan with the *Revenue Officer*. Payments are sent to the *Service Center*.

A. IRS Inefficiency

The IRS machinery moves slowly and often breaks down. If you don't already know how a bureaucracy operates, the IRS will give you a lesson. Internally, the IRS is very specialized, which can give you fits if you can't find the right department to deal with. Often when you have a tax problem, your first challenge is to locate the correct person to deal with. Because most IRS employees don't know (or care) how the IRS operates outside of their own small arena, this can truly be a vexing task.

Here are the major problems you will encounter in dealing with the IRS.

Bureaucracy. Civil servants in the IRS bureaucracy are not usually self-starters. For many, the IRS provides an escape from the long hours and competitive pressures of the private business world. Others are gaining work experience or biding their time until a better job comes along. All this results in a paint-by-the-numbers approach that can drive any taxpayer nuts. In contrast, you are highly motivated in IRS dealings—it's your pocketbook at stake. What's important is that you hang in there. Dealing with the IRS is not impossible, especially if you are armed with the information and strategies suggested in this book.

Computers. The IRS loves its computers, and would replace all its people with machines if possible. Sometimes your file gets lost in the computer—usually through human error. Often this is good—for example, if you want to delay dealing with the IRS. You will, however, usually want to get your file out of the computer and into human hands. Every individual taxpayer's IRS file is electronically stored by tax period and is accessed by Social Security Number (SSN), not by name. Returns filed by businesses with employees are accessed by Employer Identification Numbers (EIN).

This doesn't mean that anyone at the IRS can punch in your SSN and get a complete history of your tax account. The IRS has several different computer systems, which are not yet linked. For example, your local District Office cannot directly gain access by computer to all of the information on you at a Service Center or the National Computer Center.

IRS ORGANIZATIONAL CHART

The IRS structure is far more complicated (I'm sure you're surprised) than the chart below indicates. I have pared down the IRS to its four levels and the divisions you are most likely to encounter. I've also included the titles of the people who staff the offices in parentheses. The IRS publishes its own chart showing the entire organizational scheme, but you'll probably be more confused than educated if you try to read it.

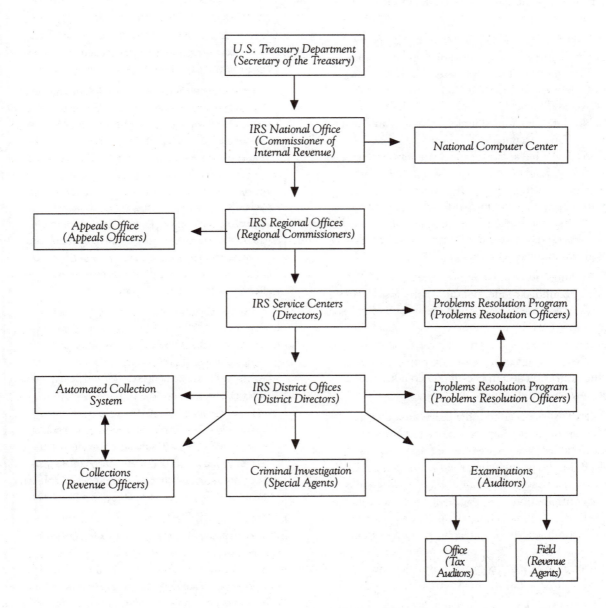

The ultimate computerization goal of the IRS is paperless tax returns. The IRS reasons that if all your income, deductions, exemptions and credits were electronically reported, a paper tax return becomes unnecessary. Information returns (W-2 and 1099 forms filed by employers, banks and the like) already make it possible for the IRS to prepare tax returns for non-filers. And new electronic tax filing (which I don't recommend for most folks) allows many taxpayers to have refunds processed quickly without a paper filing.

Confusion. Beyond the problems generated by poorly motivated people operating mindless computers is something I call confusion. Although it's hard to define with precision, believe me, it exists. Taxpayers tell many "Twilight Zone" tales about the IRS. Not long ago, for example, Jed was in an IRS office to sign a document. The agent said that she couldn't make Jed a copy of the document because the office was out of copy paper. When Jed called two weeks later to find out where his copy was, the agent told him that the budget for copy paper had run out, and that hundreds of reports would be held up for several more weeks. So much for our $5.5 billion tax administration system.

And how about this? A few years ago, an IRS collector confided to me that during the installation of a new computer system, one-third of his collection files were lost in the computer for over a year. He kept on collecting, but if any taxpayers had requested a printout of their tax accounts, he would have had to stop collection action because he couldn't prove that they owed the money.

Complexity. Americans have the dubious honor of having the most complex income tax laws in the world. The IRS was created to see that we follow the rules. But nobody, including the IRS, understands all of them. It's no wonder—given that the tax code is full of contradictions and hopelessly unclear provisions. Blame Congress. It is far easier to pass a tax law than to administer it, or to teach a taxpayer or tax professional how to apply it. Each major tax revision produces unworkable tax provisions which are revised or repealed in the next term of Congress.

If you think I am exaggerating, *Money* magazine each year asks 50 professional tax preparers to prepare a hypothetical tax return. Never, since this feature began, have two tax professionals come up with the same amount of taxes due on the same return. And in the most recent year, no preparer arrived at the "correct" amount as stated by the test's creator.

Requesting a Copy of Your Computer File

The IRS computer includes statements of account of all taxpayers, individuals and businesses. These accounts show the dates the IRS claims you filed your tax returns, any assessments of penalties and interest, and payments credited to your account.

You can obtain a copy of your IRS account by simply asking for your Individual Master File (IMF) transcript. If you are a business, request a Business Master File (BMF). Direct your request to the Taxpayer Service Representative (800-829-1040), or your local District Office (by telephone) or your regional Service Center (in writing). You must provide your Social Security number (and your spouse's if you're married) or your Federal Employer Identification Number, as well as the tax years requested —tax accounts are separated by tax periods. You may also need to send a photocopy of some form of identification, such as your driver's license.

Within days or a few weeks, you'll receive a copy of your IMF or BMF. Don't be discouraged if you can't easily decipher it. It's replete with IRS codes because it's not meant for public viewing. Read over the statement carefully and note all items you don't understand. Then call the Taxpayer Service Representative (800-829-1040), and ask for explanations of the items you're unclear about, or of any mistakes you find, such as payments not credited to your account or tax information relating to another taxpayer. If the Taxpayer Service Representative can't help you, call the Problems Resolution Office (see Chapter 8) or your tax professional.

If you simply want copies of tax returns you have filed with the IRS, complete Form 4506, Request for Copy of Tax Form (a copy is in the Appendix) and mail it in to your Service Center with a payment of $14.00 for each return requested. You cannot order copies of tax returns by telephone.

B. Rules of the Game—Tax Laws

Congress writes the tax laws, which become part of the Internal Revenue Code, or tax code for short. The tax code is amended every year. In the 1980s, there were five major revisions, including the Tax Reform Act of 1986. The present tax code was over 2,200 pages before the 1993 Clinton tax changes.

Part of the problem is that many tax laws are passed for purposes other than raising money. A *social goal* using a tax law, for example, is Congress's attempt to alleviate the housing problem by giving tax breaks to those who invest in low income housing. Similarly, an *economic goal* is found in allow-ing rapid tax writeoffs to buyers of new business equipment to stimulate manufacturing. And there are purely *political reasons* for tax laws. Many special interest groups, such as oil companies, horse breeders, broadcasters, insurance companies and even major league baseball clubs, have gotten tax laws passed that are designed to give them special treatment. These special provisions of the tax code outnumber the laws of general application.

C. Interpreting the Tax Code

Congress has given the IRS the power, in the first instance, to interpret the tax code through a series of IRS Regulations. These interpretations are expanded versions of tax code provisions with illustrations of how the law is applied in different situations. The Regulations are about four times the size of the tax code. The IRS also publishes Revenue Rulings, Rev-enue Procedures and Letter Rulings, which provide guidance in much the same manner as the Regula-tions. Not every provision of the tax code has a corresponding Regulation.

The IRS is not the final word on interpreting the tax code. The federal court system, composed of the U.S. Tax Court, federal District Courts, the U.S. Court of Federal Claims and U.S. Bankruptcy Courts, all have the power to decide, on a case-by-case basis, how Congress intended the tax laws to be applied. Any taxpayer or the IRS, unhappy with a court's tax decision, can appeal to a Circuit Court of Appeal, and in rare cases to the U.S. Supreme Court.

There are many thousands of situations where it is not clear exactly how the tax law should be applied. In these gray areas, disputes often arise between the IRS and the taxpayer. This is where the tax professionals (I call them Tax Pros) earn their keep—by fitting the tax code most advantageously to a client's case. Or put another way, if the tax case is analogized to the fence around Farmer Brown's cabbage patch, the perimeter has gotten so long and twisty that a self-respecting rabbit may have a decent chance of finding enough room to wiggle through or under it.

D. Self-Assessment of Income Taxes

The U.S. income tax system is based on a self-assessment theory. This means that you are respon-sible for reporting income and telling the govern-ment how much tax you owe. You assess your own income tax every time you file a tax return. This doesn't mean that the system is voluntary or that you have a legal choice whether or not to assess taxes against yourself.

The IRS' job is to determine whether or not you obeyed the self-assessment principle by:

- reporting all your income
- stating the correct amount of taxes due, and
- paying the taxes due.

If the IRS suspects that you have violated your self-assessment obligation, you may be audited or sent a bill for an additional assessment. Ignoring the bill or notice won't make it go away. In fact, it will probably make matters worse. It's at this stage that people conclude they have "IRS troubles."

E. Winning the IRS Game

If you file and pay your taxes on time and never get an IRS notice, then you are already winning the IRS game and probably don't need this book—at least not yet.

The rest of us who encounter the IRS up close and personal still have a chance to win, or at least to not lose disastrously. This means keeping your income and assets away from the IRS and staying out of jail. And this is one game where, despite your first grade teacher's lesson "it's not whether you win or lose it's how you play the game," you darn well want to win.

Great, but you won't win the IRS game unless you know the rules. This book tells you the most important rules—written and unwritten—and helps you develop a game plan.

Let's call the IRS team the "Goliaths" and your team the "Goodguys." On paper, the Goliaths look unbeatable, but on the playing field it comes down to the strengths and weaknesses of the individual players. Here's an analysis of the teams and players.

Goliaths have experience. You are a rookie, so even the weakest IRS team member is ahead of you. But he or she probably can't make it a runaway—remember, the IRS has a high rate of employee turnover. Score seven for the Goliaths in the first quarter, 7-0.

Goodguys have motivation and the advantage here every time. Coaches say that motivation is the key to winning. The Goliath player gets the same pay, win or lose, while the Goodguys are playing to keep their money. Score seven for the Goodguys in the second quarter. It's tied at the half, 7-7.

The game will be decided in the second half. You have to be prepared to go the distance. Know what you are doing and show strength and perseverance to the IRS. Don't beat yourself. Remember the words of Pogo, the comic strip philosopher: "We have met the enemy and he is us."

A Costly Victory. One way to lose is to play the IRS without bothering to learn the rules of the game, preparing or devising a game plan. You'll lose if you

ignore IRS contacts or respond incorrectly, miss deadlines or lie to IRS employees. Charlie is a prime example.

Charlie had been having IRS problems for five years when he called a Tax Pro. (Let's call her Sheila.) He had lost an IRS audit, an appeal and then in Tax Court. When the tax bills came he threw them away. Charlie believed he was right and he was sticking to his principles.

An IRS collector repeatedly warned Charlie that his house was going to be sold at auction to pay the tax bill. Sheila asked when the sale was to take place. "Tomorrow," Charlie replied. She agreed to try to help Charlie but made no promises—the game was just about over and he was behind by several touchdowns.

Sheila called the IRS and got a postponement of the sale for 30 days to give Charlie a chance to get a home equity loan to pay the taxes. He tried, but the bank didn't approve the loan. The IRS refused another postponement and sold the home for $92,000, well under its market value of $120,000. After paying the mortgage of $60,000 and taking $20,000 for the tax bill, Charlie was given the remaining $12,000—but his days in his home were numbered.

Happily, the story does not end here. Charlie had one more chance to save his home. Sheila pointed out that the tax code lets a taxpayer buy back any real estate lost at an IRS tax sale. The deadline is 180 days from sale, and full payment must be made with interest. During that time, Charlie found a mortgage company that loaned him $96,000 to pay off the auction purchaser. (Chapter 7, Section G.1.b, covers this in detail.)

The sad part is that if Charlie had sought tax advice at the beginning of the game, he would have been able to settle with the IRS for $7,000. By stubbornly refusing to meet the problem he almost lost his home. And, he cost himself $29,000 in taxes, penalties, interest, new mortgage financing and Tax Pro fees. Charlie needed to know the rules and needed a plan before playing the IRS game.

FILING TAX RETURNS: IF YOU HAVEN'T FILED AND OTHER CONCERNS

2

Over 50% of us file our annual federal income tax return before April 1 of each year. Most of the rest file in the first two weeks of April, but 5% get an extension to August 15 and 1% extend further to October 15.

According to the IRS, at least 3% of us don't file at all. (My guess is that the number is even higher, probably close to 10%.) Even if we accept the IRS' figure, at least five million of us are either illegally not filing tax returns or are filing beyond all extension dates. This number is so large that some non-filers may never get caught—but don't bet on it.

A. How Long Must You Worry About Not Filing a Tax Return?

The tax code sets out the time periods (statutes of limitations) in which the IRS must pursue non-filers.

Criminal. The government can only bring criminal charges against a non-filer within six years of the date the tax return was due. For example, after April 15, 1995, you can't be prosecuted for failing to file a 1988 tax return, which was was originally due on April 15, 1989.

Civil. There is no deadline, however, on the IRS for going after non-filers and imposing civil penalties. This means that while you can't be put in jail for not filing a 1972 tax return, you still owe the IRS a return—as long as you earned enough to have had an obligation to file. And fines (penalties and interest) on unfiled tax returns run forever.

IRS policy. Don't worry too much about that 1972 tax return. The IRS usually doesn't seriously pursue non-filers after six years. The Internal Revenue Manual section on Taxpayer Delinquency Investigations reads as follows:

> *Taxpayers failing to file returns due will be requested to prepare and file (them). All delinquent returns... will be accepted. However, if indications of willfulness or fraud exist, the special procedures for handling such returns must be followed.... Factors taken into account include, but are not limited to: prior history of noncompliance, existence of income from illegal sources, effect upon voluntary compliance and*

> *anticipated revenue in relation to the time and effort required to determine tax due. Consideration will also be given to any special circumstances existing in the case of a particular taxpayer, class of taxpayer or industry....*

> *Normally, application of the above criteria will result in enforcement of delinquency procedures for not more than six years. Enforcement beyond such period will not be undertaken without prior managerial approval.*[1]

Be aware that the IRS may still request a tax return from you for a period more than six years ago. But if you tell the IRS that you don't have enough information to prepare a return, the agency usually will drop the request.

B. Consequences of Not Filing

It is a crime not to file a tax return if taxes are owed. By contrast, there is no criminal penalty if you file but can't pay your taxes. In this situation, you'll owe interest and penalties, but you won't be sent to jail. So even if you don't have two dimes to rub together and owe a bundle of taxes, file your return.

If you ignore this advice and fail to file, in theory you can be fined up to $25,000 per year and/or sentenced to one year in prison for each unfiled year. But our justice system doesn't have enough jails to put away even 1% of the non-filers, so going to jail is highly unlikely.

The IRS looks for non-filers through its computerized Information Matching Returns Program. This tremendously effective operation matches information documents—W-2 wage statements and 1099 income reports from payors (such as your boss or the bank where you earn interest on your deposit account)—against tax returns on file of payees (taxpayers). If the computer search fails to find a return, the IRS initiates a Taxpayer Delinquency Investigation (TDI). A TDI is an IRS search for a taxpayer to find out why he didn't file a tax return.

---

[1]Internal Revenue Manual 0021; IRS Policy Statement P-5-133.

TDIs usually begin with computer-generated notices sent from your IRS Service Center. If you don't respond to the notices, your case is eventually turned over to the Automated Collection System (ACS) for telephone contact or more letters. If the IRS is really serious, your file is assigned to a Revenue Officer or Revenue Agent at your local District Office who goes out looking for you. (See Chapter 6 for more information on the Service Center, ACS, and Revenue Officer's and Revenue Agent's contacts with a taxpayer.)

If you're an independent contractor, earn investment or interest income, sell real estate or stocks, the IRS receives this information annually. The IRS Information Matching Returns Program will probably catch that you didn't file. The IRS is about 12 to 24 months behind in notifying the non-filers it discovers. So don't think that because you haven't heard from the IRS within a year or two after not filing you are home free. Ten years ago, 5% of the calls I received were from non-filers. Today, they make up 50% of my clients. The IRS *will* catch you— it's just a matter of time.

1. IRS Notifying Non-Filers

How the IRS contacts you is the key to how serious a problem you have. There are four ways you can be notified—and they are not mutually exclusive. If the IRS tries one method and you don't respond, it will no doubt try another.

- Written request from the Service Center—The computer spits out three written requests over a 16-week period. Most non-filers are initially contacted in this relatively non-threatening manner. (Threats do come if you ignore these notices.) These notices mean that you don't have to worry about criminal prosecution, at least for the years requested.

- Telephone call or notice from the Automated Collection System (ACS)—You will be given a deadline to get your returns filed, usually within 30 days. These notices don't differ much from the Service Center notices.

- Visit or call from a Revenue Agent or a Revenue Officer—Your case may be sent to your local

District Office. He will give you a deadline to file the missing returns directly with him, or will offer to help you prepare your return. If you don't comply, the IRS can legally prepare a return for you, based on any information it has and guesses it makes. In 1992, the IRS initiated a nationwide "Non-Filer Program" and reassigned 2,500 Revenue Agents to this project. The object is to bring everyone into the system in a "kindler and gentler" fashion. This is not a tax amnesty, as no penalties or interest on taxes are being forgiven for those who file. In fact, the IRS adds the maximum penalties and interest to the taxes found due.

- Visit by a Special Agent—This is the very worst way you can be notified. This means that your non-filing is the subject of a criminal investigation. (See Section B.3, below.) This is very uncommon, however, unless the IRS suspects you of not reporting hundreds of thousands of dollars in income.

IRS Questioning About Unfiled Tax Returns

Someone from the IRS may ask you point-blank if you filed income tax returns for the years in question.

This creates a dilemma. If you haven't filed but you answer "yes," you will have lied to the IRS, a crime punishable by up to five years in prison. But if you answer "no," you may have confessed to the crime of failure to file a tax return. The best response is to say you'll get back to the IRS after you check your records or speak with your tax advisor. You can't get into trouble with these magic words.

The IRS might also ask why you haven't filed all returns and how much income you had. Remember, if you answered the first question with "I'll get back to you," you won't have to answer these questions.

Regardless of your answer, the IRS will set a deadline for the filing of all tax returns. If you need time to get your records together ask for 60 to 90 days to "discuss" this situation with your tax advisor —which really means that you should start working on getting the returns prepared right away.

2. When the IRS Prepares Your Tax Return for You

As mentioned above, the IRS has the power to prepare and file tax returns for you whenever you don't file them.[2] In IRS-speak, this is called a Substitute For Return (SFR). Usually, it is not to your advantage to have the IRS do this. IRS preparers will give you only one exemption, no dependents and the standard deduction on your return. Beyond that, the IRS guesstimates your tax liability based on information it has, usually from W-2 forms and 1099 informational reports. This can result in a tax bill much higher than for a tax return you prepare yourself.

If the IRS prepares an SFR, it will mail you a copy to your last known (to the IRS) address and ask you to sign it, agreeing to the findings. Again, it may not be in your best interest to sign, even if the figures are accurate. Instead, prepare a return yourself. Send it to the IRS along with a copy of the return it prepared and sent you. Request that the return you prepared be accepted in lieu of the SFR prepared by the IRS. If your return looks okay, the IRS will accept it. The IRS may want to audit it first, however, this usually doesn't happen.

Another reason to prepare the return yourself has to do with the deadline the tax code gives for auditing your return. If the IRS prepares an SFR, the limitation on the number of years that the IRS has to audit that return is suspended—that is, the IRS will be able to audit it forever, unless you sign the SFR. (See Chapter 3 for information on audit time limitations.) But, if you prepare the return, the IRS normally will have only three years from the time you file it to audit you. (If the IRS believes you understated your income by 25% or more, the period is extended to six years.)

If you don't prepare your own return, the IRS will file the SFR as your tax return whether or not you sign it. Any taxes due, plus penalties and interest will then be formally assessed against you.

3. Non-Filing Is a Crime

Very few people are put in jail for not filing a tax return, but it can happen. A "willful failure to file" a tax return is a misdemeanor that can get you up to a year in jail and a $25,000 fine—for each year of non-filing.[3] If your failure to file is deemed to be part of a scheme to evade taxes you can be charged with a felony, a more serious tax crime, which carries a maximum punishment of five years in prison and a monetary penalty of $100,000—but rarely is anyone criminally prosecuted for this felony.[4] The distinction between the two offenses is that the felony requires a deceitful act beyond the non-filing, such as intentionally using a false Social Security number. The misdemeanor doesn't require any additional deceitful act.

If you are contacted by an IRS agent who specifically asks you about your non-filing, but does not ask you to file a return, start worrying. This probably means that your file is being sent to the IRS Criminal Investigation Division (CID). A CID referral does not guarantee you will be prosecuted, only that you might be. In fact, just a small percentage of CID cases result in criminal prosecutions; most are quietly dropped. But, you still have to get your past due returns prepared and filed. (Criminal Investigations and other criminal matters are covered in Chapter 10.)

In deciding whether or not to recommend prosecuting a non-filer, the CID, through its Special Agents, considers many factors. The most important considerations are:

- the number of years you haven't filed returns
- the amounts of taxes due
- your occupation and education
- your previous history of tax delinquencies
- if you are in a business which is largely done by cash, and
- how truthful you were during the investigation.

Certain types of non-filers, such as reputed crime figures and politicians, may be prosecuted regardless

---

[2]Internal Revenue Code § 6020.

[3]Internal Revenue Code § 7201.

[4]Internal Revenue Code § 7206 (1).

of any other factors. And lawmakers are held to a higher standard to maintain taxpayer confidence in the tax administration system.

If your non-filing case is referred to the CID, there is little you can do to influence the IRS agent's decision regarding recommending prosecution. If you try to talk your way out of it, you will only make matters worse. In short, if you suspect that the IRS is investigating you, see an attorney. If an agent calls you, don't consent to an interview—in fact, don't say anything except that you want to speak to an attorney. Then, find a tax or criminal attorney immediately and have no further direct contact with anyone at the IRS.

C. It's Better to File Before the IRS Contacts You

If you haven't filed a tax return for a year or more, it's never too late to catch up. The IRS has a policy of not normally prosecuting those who file *before* being contacted by the IRS.[5] Also, the IRS is more sympathetic in collecting the taxes owed from voluntary filers than from the ones they catch. This is because when you file your return on your own accord, the Service Center initially handles your file. If the IRS

---

[5]IR-92-114, instituted in late 1992.

has sought you out, your local District Office has the file. District Offices put a lot more pressure on tax-payers than do Service Centers.

Example

Uncle Jack worked in construction for 50 years. He bragged that he never filed a tax return or got an IRS notice. He changed addresses with the seasons and used many different Social Security numbers, none of which were his own. Because the IRS relies primarily on Social Security numbers to keep track of taxpayers, it never found Jack. (He didn't get Social Security benefits, either). If Jack was around today, the chances of him outrunning the IRS computer would be slim—better than beating the house in Las Vegas, but not by much.

1. Minimizing Trouble When Filing Late

To file a past year's return, you must use the tax forms for that year. Past years' forms may or may not be available at local IRS offices. Tax return preparers usually have forms going back at least a few years or can get them. Or, you can order old forms by calling 800-829-3676, the IRS Forms Distribution Center. Expect to wait several weeks for them.

Your form order will be entered into the national IRS computer. Now they have your number, and you should file once you receive the forms. Ordering forms won't necessarily trigger a delinquency investigation, but it could. To lessen this possibility, you can ask a friend who filed his return for the years in question to order the forms for you. Or ask a Tax Pro to order them.

When a return is filed on time, it is seen only briefly by a human being—to make quick data entries into a computer at the Service Center. Late returns, however, are hand-screened by IRS classifiers before the data is entered. Thus, take extra care in preparing late returns; consider having them done by a Certified Public Accountant, Tax Attorney or Enrolled Agent. (See Chapter 13 for more information on tax professionals.) The IRS classifier will be much more impressed by a professionally prepared return—so impressed he might pass it right through after seeing the preparer's signature.

2. Voluntary Filing to Minimize the Chance of a Criminal Investigation

The IRS won't provide any guidelines on voluntarily disclosing your non-filing of past income tax returns to minimize the risk of criminal prosecution. While the government policy is not to prosecute average citizens who make up the vast majority of these cases (the average non-filer has not filed for three to five years and owes less than $70,000), there is no assurance of this.

What about "non-average" filers? Some are public figures or suspected criminals. Others are taxpayers with five or more years of non-filing and hundreds of thousands in taxes owed. But they all stand out from the herd and should take every possible precaution to prevent prosecution.

Tax attorneys typically handle the cases of serious non-filers in one of three ways:

• The attorney writes the local District Director and makes the voluntary disclosure for her client. The lawyer then files the tax returns.

• The attorney calls the local chief of the Criminal Investigation Division and requests a meeting. There she discusses the case without naming the client and asks if the client would be prosecuted if she were to make a voluntary disclosure. If the chief says no, the attorney makes the disclosure. Legally, the chief cannot bind the government here, but I know of no one criminally prosecuted after making this kind of deal.

• The tax attorney prepares the returns for the last six years and files them with the Service Center, without contacting anyone first. The tax attorney gets a power of attorney from the client—a form authorizing the attorney to act on behalf of the client—and uses her address (not the client's) on the tax returns. This assures that any further contact about the late returns from the IRS comes to the tax attorney directly.

The advantage of these tax attorney approaches is the "attorney-client" privilege. Under this ancient legal doctrine, neither the IRS nor any other government agency can force your attorney to disclose anything you say. There is no accountant-client or tax preparer-client privilege—I guess their unions are not as strong as lawyers'.

D. What Will Happen When You File Late

The IRS can punish you for filing tax returns late by imposing civil penalties, criminal penalties or both, and by denying refunds due you.

1. Civil Penalties Added to Your Tax Bill

If your late tax return shows taxes due, you will be fined 5% per month, up to a maximum of 25%.

Example

Your return was due April 15 and you file on September 16 of that year or later. You will be charged 25% extra on the amount of taxes not paid on time. If you file on August 16, you will be charged 20% (four months times 5% per month). There is no daily proration of the penalty, so one day late costs the same 5% penalty as does 29 days. After five months, the late filing penalty stops increasing.

That's not all. In addition to the late filing penalty, the IRS can impose a late payment penalty of $1/2$% to 1% per month. And here's a little more bad news: interest is running all the while. Interest changes quarterly; as of September 1994, it is 8% per year, compounded daily.

This means that it is costlier to owe the IRS than most anyone else. In fact, IRS interest and penalties taken together amount to usury (charging an illegally high interest rate) in most states, but are perfectly legal for the IRS. And, interest is not a deductible item on your tax return, unless it's for a business tax debt. Penalties are never tax deductible. The lesson here is to pay the IRS as soon as you can even if you have to borrow to do it. Getting out of paying these penalties is not easy, but can be done under certain circumstances.[6] (See Chapter 12.)

---

[6]For thorough information on paying all kinds of debts, see *Money Troubles: Legal Strategies to Cope With Your Debts,* by Robin Leonard (Nolo Press).

The Mechanics of Filing a Late Return

You have two basic methods to get your late return to the IRS.

Hand filing. It's safer to hand file tax returns at a local District Office than to mail them in, and this is especially true with late returns. If you file in person, ask the IRS clerk to file-stamp a copy of the first page of the tax return. This shows irrefutably that the return was filed. And it is better than a post office return receipt or card which shows only that "something" was sent to the IRS on that date—but not what was sent. Take along your own extra copy for the IRS to stamp; the IRS won't make a copy for you.

Mailing. For some unknown reason, late filed returns are more likely to get delayed in processing or lost by the IRS than are current ones. If you plan to mail in your late returns, send them by certified mail, return receipt requested, to your Service Center.

---

2. Criminal Charges May Be Brought

As bad as the civil fines are, criminal penalties for not filing are much worse. As mentioned earlier, non-filing is a misdemeanor for which you can be sentenced to one year in prison and a $25,000 fine for each year you didn't file a tax return, for up to six years. You cannot be criminally prosecuted for non-filing after six years, although you can be civilly fined beyond six years. (See Chapter 10.)

3. Refunds Will Be Denied

If you file your return late, you can still get any refund due as long as you file within three years of the return's original due date (without extensions). For example, to still get your refund, a tax return for tax year 1992 (normally due on April 15, 1993) must be filed by April 15, 1995. For returns filed more than three years late, you will lose any refund due forever.

Example

Andy filed ten years of back tax returns at once. For the first four years he was due refunds, but in the later six years he owed taxes. His request to have the IRS offset the early years' refunds against taxes owed for the later years was denied because all of the refund years were beyond the three year cut-off. This isn't fair, but it's the law.

E. Requesting an Extension to File a Tax Return

The only good reason for filing your tax return by April 15 is if you need to get a refund check quickly. If you are getting large refunds, however, that is a sign that your wages are being overwithheld or you are sending in too much in estimated tax payments. It's okay to look at tax refunds as a kind of forced savings plan, as long as you realize that you are making an interest free loan to Uncle Sam. It may make more sense to adjust your withholding or quarterly estimated payments so that you owe the IRS rather than the IRS owing you. In the meantime, you can invest the money and collect the interest (which, of course, is taxable).

The alternative is to apply for an extension to file by August 15. Each year about six million taxpayers request extensions to file their tax returns.

To get an extension to file, complete Form 4868, Application for Automatic Extension of Time to File U.S. Individual Income Tax Return, and file it with the IRS by April 15 for the year your tax return is due. (This form changes each year. To get a current copy, visit your District Office or call 800-829-3676.) Your application is granted automatically. You then have until August 15 to file your return without incurring late filing penalties.

If you still need or want more time, you can request a second extension by filing Form 2688, Application for Additional Extension of Time to File U.S. Individual Income Tax Return. (This form, too, changes every year, so you'll have to visit your District Office or call the IRS for a copy.) You must file it in duplicate by August 15 and state "good cause" for needing more time. (Just saying that you don't yet have all records necessary to prepare your return is usually sufficient good cause to get the second extension.) The second extension is discretionary with the IRS, but the IRS usually grants it. The IRS will send you a copy of your request stating whether or not it was granted. If it is, you will have until October 15 to file your return.

If you live outside the U.S., you get an automatic two-month extension to file (to June 15). In the past, anyone outside the U.S. on April 15 could get the automatic extension. The IRS changed the rule in the early 1990s to disqualify "daytrippers" who were making short trips to Mexico and Canada just to get the extension. Even if you live outside the U.S., however, you do not get extra time to pay the taxes you owe.

Some Tax Pros contend that filing tax returns "on extension" decreases your chance of being audited. They reason that the IRS districts fill their annual audit inventories before the returns on extension are due. The IRS denies this, but at the same time the agency won't say that returns filed on extension have a higher audit frequency. At worst, extensions are a neutral factor; they can't hurt and just might help.

 An extension to file does not extend your time to pay taxes. You should make tax payments with your extension filing forms. If you don't pay all of your tax bill by April 15, you'll get hit with penalties and interest for the underpaid amount when you do file. It is possible, but very difficult, to get an extension of time to pay without incurring an underpayment penalty. To do so, you must file IRS Form 1127, Application for Extension of Time for Payment of Tax (a copy is in the Appendix) by April 15. Follow the instructions on the form, but don't get your hopes up.

Don't File a Tax Return During An Audit

Avoid filing an income tax return while an audit is in progress—unless you want to risk having the audit expanded to include that return. For example, in 1994 you are being audited for 1992. If the auditor finds errors she will want to know if you made the same mistakes in your 1993 return. If you have not yet filed for 1993, don't. She cannot force you to file or even provide her with any 1993 information. File a request for extensions until October 15 on Forms 4868 and 2688.

If the audit is still alive on October 15, consider not filing until it is completed. As long as you have paid all the taxes due and have no fraudulent intent, you won't incur any penalties or interest for not meeting the deadline. If you owe additional money, send in your payment with a letter stating that the payment is to be applied to the tax year on extension. Also note this on your check or other payment instrument. Some states impose late filing penalties whether or not you owe taxes, however, so you may want to file your state return on time.

And if you didn't read this in time and have already filed a return during an audit, politely refuse to give a copy to the auditor if she asks. It's not as easy for her to get it from the IRS Service Center as you might think. That's why she's asking you for a copy.

F. Filing a Return When You Can't Pay What You Owe

If you owe taxes, but don't have the money to pay the full amount, file a return and send what you can. Remember—you can incur up to a 25% civil penalty for not filing. For not paying, the penalty is initially only 1/2% per month of the tax you owe. Interest is also charged. Any partial payment will cut down on the penalty and interest owed.

Don't send a personal check. Anytime you send a partial payment, don't use a personal check. The IRS always records your bank account number with your payment. If you ever owe the IRS and it must resort to enforced collections, the agency can freeze this account to get the balance of the taxes owed—and cause your outstanding checks to bounce. (See Chapter 7.) Instead, use a money order, cashier's check or attorney's trust fund check to make payments if you anticipate any IRS collection problem.

Keep copies of the check or money order. Write your last name, Social Security (or employer ID) number, type of tax (income or payroll) and year of tax in the lower left-hand corner of the payment instrument. To make sure your payment is credited quickly, use the payment slip and envelope sent from the IRS Service Center.

G. How to Reduce the Chance of an Audit When Filing

There is no sure-fire way to audit-proof your tax return, but you may be able to reduce your audit risk. Here are some suggestions which may (or may not) work:

1. If you claim large deductions for unusual items, such as an earthquake, flood or fire loss, attach documentary proof to the back of your tax return. Copies of repair receipts, canceled checks, insurance reports and pictures are advisable. This won't stop the IRS computer from flagging your return. These attachments, however, should catch the attention of the IRS classifier who next screens computer-picked returns for audit potential. If she thinks your documentation looks reasonable, you won't get audited.

2. File but leave a few dollars unpaid. (This obviously won't apply to people due a refund.) The theory is that by owing a small amount, $100 or so, your file will be sent to the Collection Division before being considered for audit. The file stays there until the tax is paid. I don't know if this is true and the IRS denies it. I have filed returns for many clients at least three years overdue, who already owed taxes for other years, and very few were audited. One reason may be that taxpayers with returns this late are already being handled by the the Collection Division.

This reasoning assumes that your file can't be in two places at the same time, which is doubtful in this electronic age. Nevertheless, the worst harm that can come from leaving a small tax balance unpaid is the accruing of small amounts of interest and penalties.

3. Report side job income as "other income" on line 22 of your tax return. This should be tried only if this income is relatively small, and you are not claiming any business deductions against it. Technically, side job income is supposed to be reported on a Schedule C, "Profit or Loss from Business." But filing a Schedule C undoubtedly increases your audit chances.

4. Prepare your tax return by computer. A neat, computer prepared return looks more "official" to IRS classifiers and fits the IRS bias favoring computer processing. Most tax preparers now use computers. There are some good PC and Macintosh programs, such as *Turbo Tax* and *MacInTax*, which you can use to prepare your own return.

5. Don't use electronic filing or the IRS preprinted address label on your tax return. These enable the IRS to get your return into the processing cycle, including the audit cycle, more quickly than otherwise would happen. Anything that slows down the IRS machine can't be bad. On the flip side, however, using electronic filing or the label usually means that any refund due you will come faster. If you expect a refund but fear an audit, you'll have to weigh the pros and cons here.

6. Live in a low audit area. Your audit chances are radically different depending on where in the U.S. you live. For example, Nevada taxpayers are audited four times more than people in Wisconsin. While this might seem extreme just to avoid an audit, it might make sense if you travel most of the time or have several homes. If you have flexibility in choosing your tax reporting address, choose the one with the lower audit rate. If you're really interested in this, visit the IRS local office information reading room or your library and look at the statistics in the IRS Commissioner's Annual Report.

H. Amending Tax Returns

It is possible to change your tax return after you've filed it, even years later. You can even do this to correct a mistake, such as an overlooked deduction or loss, that would entitle you to a refund. Also, some provisions of the tax code require you to file amendments. For example, if you sell your home, make a profit and don't reinvest in another home within 24 months, you must amend the tax return for the year the home was sold. An amended return filing does not extend the time the IRS has to audit the first return.

To amend your return, you must file IRS Form 1040X, Amended U.S. Individual Income Tax Return. (A copy, with instructions, is in the Appendix.) To get a *refund*, you must file the amended tax return within three years from the date the first return was filed or within two years from the date you paid the taxes due on that return—whichever is later. For example, if you filed your 1992 tax return on April 15, 1993, you can file a 1040X any time up until April 14, 1996. If you filed an extension, you can add the extended period on as well. One exception: if you file an amended return to claim a refund based on a worthless security or bad debt loss, you have up to seven years after you first filed.

1. How to Amend a Tax Return

As mentioned, a copy of Form 1040X, Amended U.S. Individual Income Tax Return, with instructions, is in the Appendix. If any significant amount of money is involved, I suggest that you hire a Tax Pro to complete the form for you. You will want to attach documentation to support your changes.

You can hand deliver or mail the amended return. If you will hand deliver it, take the 1040X to the nearest IRS District Office and get a stamped copy as your filing receipt. If you use the mail, because of the strict time limits, send it certified, with postal return receipt requested to the Service Center where you now file your tax returns. (Addresses are in the 1040X instruction sheets.)

Don't forget to amend your state return too if your state has an income tax. Get the forms from its tax department. (Addresses and phone numbers of state taxing authorities are in the Appendix.)

2. Audit Alert for Amended Tax Returns

When filing amended returns claiming refunds, your audit likelihood increases greatly—and not just for the amended items but for the whole tax return. This is partly because 1040X forms are manually worked by IRS employees rather than just computer processed. You can be sure someone's eyes will fall on your amended form, which is never a good thing.

The IRS ordinarily has only three years to audit a return from the date it was originally filed. Filing an amended return for a refund very near the three-year audit deadline is a tactic worth considering. This gives the IRS very little time to audit your amended or original return, and it may simply pass it through.

This ploy can backfire on you, however, as the IRS does not have to accept an amended tax return. If you file an amended return near the three-year audit deadline, the IRS may be willing to accept it only on the condition that you agree to extend the time for audit beyond the three year deadline. Then you'll probably be audited. If you're considering this strategy, you may want to talk to a Tax Pro. (See Chapter 13.) Although filing an amended return for a refund near the three-year audit deadline works more times than not, a Tax Pro can point out pitfalls you may not see.

I. A Word About "Aggressive" Tax Filing

The question on everyone's mind at tax filing time is always, "What kind of deductions and tax things can I get away with and what can get me in IRS trouble?" The best answer I can give is that it depends on your particular emotional makeup. Are you very conservative? Or are you a risk-taker by nature? Most people have at least a little of each trait in their personality.

Aggressive tax filing means interpreting the "gray areas" of the law in your favor—and taking the chance that you will either not be audited or survive if you are. (You may want to peruse Chapter 3 first to find out what happens at an audit.)

Tax Pro litmus test. I have never met two Tax Pros who agreed on the meaning of "aggressive." The best way to find out how aggressive your Tax Pro is, is to run by her ideas on deducting certain expenses. For instance, if you are in business for yourself, ask a Tax Pro about deducting things such as business lunch expenses, a combined business and pleasure trip or health club dues. Or, if you don't own a business but do some investing ask her about financial publication expenses and trips to check out investments.

How the Tax Pro responds clues you into how aggressive that professional is. If she repeatedly says, "you can't do that," instead of offering advice on how to make your expense deductible, then she may be too government oriented—at least for my taste. On the other hand, if she says not to worry, deduct anything you want because chances are you won't be audited, she could get you into trouble down the road.

Comfort level. When I first interview a tax return preparation client I try to determine his "IRS comfort level." I ask outright how concerned he is about facing an audit, and if it happens, whether he will be able to document gray area deductions. (Again, I refer you to Chapter 3, Section D, specifically, for information on proving your deductions.)

I do not counsel tax cheating. But, there is a fine line between being aggressive and cheating. No reputable tax return preparer will sign a tax return for someone she believes is planning to file a work of fiction. And, if the preparer is not reputable, you don't want her name and identification number on your return. The IRS knows, or will eventually find out, about crooked tax preparers and may reward you with an audit for choosing one.

Finding and using a Tax Pro is covered in Chapter 13. Some things to look for and types of preparers to avoid are covered there. Don't take picking a tax preparer lightly.

J. Filing in a Nutshell— Kernels of Wisdom

1. Not filing a tax return is a crime if you owe taxes; most people, however, are fined but not prosecuted.

2. If the IRS asks you if you filed returns and you haven't, don't lie, but don't admit or deny either. State that you want to consult a Tax Pro or check your records.

3. Filing before the IRS catches you means that you won't be prosecuted.

4. The time limit for criminally prosecuting a non-filer is six years, but the time limit for collecting from a non-filer is ten years and the clock doesn't start until you actually file a tax return.

5. Penalties for late filing are substantial and rarely forgiven.

6. Don't file a tax return while you are being audited.

WINNING YOUR AUDIT 3

Don't File a Tax Return During an Audit

As I warned in Chapter 2, Section E, never file a tax return while an audit is in progress. You risk having the audit expanded to include that return. Instead, file requests for extensions until October 15.

If the audit is still alive on October 15, consider not filing until it is completed. If you've paid all taxes due, you won't incur any penalties or interest for not meeting the filing deadline. If you owe additional money, send in your payment with a letter stating that the payment is to be applied to the current tax year.

If you didn't read this in time and have already filed a return during an audit, politely refuse to give a copy to the auditor if she asks.

We call them "audits"; the IRS prefers "examinations." Whatever term you use, it describes one of life's most dreaded experiences—the IRS probing into your financial affairs.

The vast majority of tax returns are accepted by the IRS without question. But, while your chance of being audited in any one year is only about 1%, the odds of an IRS examination in your taxpaying lifetime are closer to 50%. As your income increases, so does your audit likelihood. If you regularly earn over $50,000 per year, expect to endure more than one audit. And when your time does come, expect it to cost you some money—five out of seven people who are audited owe additional taxes. A few people get tax refunds after an audit, but don't count on it. The amount of money the IRS assesses in audits is 32 times greater than the amount given back.

As a rule, your tax return cannot be audited after three years from its original filing date. If you filed before the due date, April 15, the three years starts running from April 15 of the year it was due.

There are a few exceptions, however:

- If you understated your income by 25% or more on your tax return, the audit deadline is extended to six years.

- If you file a fraudulent return, there is no time limit on an audit. Tax fraud is conduct meant to deceive the IRS, such as using a false Social Security number. A really big mistake, if done negligently, not intentionally, isn't fraud. The burden of proving fraud is always on the IRS. And the IRS seldom audits returns after three years even if fraud is evident.

- The audit time period (called a statute of limitations) starts to run only if and when you file a tax return. Non-filed tax years are always open to audit, until you file the return. If, however, you haven't filed and haven't heard from the IRS within six years of the due date of a tax return, you have probably escaped the audit net.

Audit notices are usually sent between 12 and 18 months after you file your return. Generally, if you haven't heard from the IRS within 18 months, you won't be audited.

The Internal Revenue Manual directs auditors to complete their audits within 28 months after you filed your tax return. Legally, the IRS has 36 months. The 28-month internal deadline is imposed, however, to allow sufficient time (eight additional months) for the IRS to process any appeal you might request. (Appeals are covered in Chapters 4 and 5.)

These internal IRS time limits usually work to your benefit. Audit cases are often delayed within the IRS for various reasons—backlogs, agent transfers, postponements and lost files. The older your file gets, the more anxious the IRS is to close it. Auditors can be fired for missing the 36-month deadline, known as "blowing the statute," but it still happens.

You can't stop an audit once it begins. Once the IRS sends an examination notice to your last known address, the audit has begun. It is all but impossible to stop an audit once started. Even if you die, your spouse or the executor of your estate is obligated to carry on the audit.

The Audit Burden Is On You—Not the IRS

An audit is the process by which the IRS determines whether you properly reported your income—all money you made—and took the correct deductions, exemptions and credits. If the IRS finds that you didn't, you will be assessed additional taxes, interest and, usually, penalties. An "assessment" is the formal entry of a tax liability in your records at the IRS Service Center.

To do its job, Congress has given the IRS wide powers to inspect your papers and financial records, and to ask you and others about your financial affairs.[1] The IRS will investigate the items listed on an audit notice checklist given to you or will scrutinize any other areas deemed question-able. And the law specifically places the burden on you to demonstrate that the information shown on your tax return is correct—think of the IRS as the "Show Me" state of Missouri.

Proving the correctness of your tax return may not be that easy to do. The IRS wins 80% of all audits, mostly because taxpayers can't properly verify the information on their tax returns. IRS auditors say that the biggest reason for this is poor recordkeeping, not taxpayer dishonesty.

Will the auditor discover the money I made from playing the organ at weddings?

I lost my records in a move last year—what am I going to do?

Was I entitled to claim my mother as an exemption?

Will the IRS question my home office deductions?

Is the IRS going to put me in jail if they find out I've been cheating?

These are common taxpayer concerns. So, let's look at what really goes on when the IRS decides to audit you.

---

[1]Internal Revenue Code § 7602.

The two primary issues in every audit are:

- Did you report all income?
- Were you entitled to the deductions, exemptions and credits claimed?

IRS Publication 17, Your Federal Income Tax (page 252), explains the audit process—from the IRS point of view. It's in the Appendix.

A. Do I Have to Learn Tax Law to Win My Audit?

To understand the audit process, we begin with the Internal Revenue Code (tax code). As mentioned in Chapter 1, the tax code contains thousands of pages of very fine print. Add to that IRS Regulations, Revenue Rulings, Letter Rulings, Manuals and Official Publications, all of which add another 100,000 pages of tax law. Finally, there are thousands of court decisions telling us how the tax laws should be applied in individual cases. The total number of tax law pages exceeds one million!

How will I ever understand the tax laws?

You won't. But that may not be as much of a disadvantage as you might think. Tax law is so volu-minous and complex, most IRS auditors don't know it well either. Moreover, the training and experience level of IRS personnel is declining while the law is getting more difficult to understand. This means that auditors of individual (non-business) tax returns normally stick to the most basic audit issues. A tax-payer with very high income or an intricate tax issue, however, may be assigned an auditor with more experience. But if you are well prepared and understand the audit process, you come out okay (experiencing the minimum damage) most of the time.

In a few hours, you can learn most of the tax law you'll need for your particular audit issues. The information is in this book and other sources mentioned in Chapter 13. And you can—and probably should—consult with a Tax Pro before taking on the auditor.

The truth is that you can often succeed in an audit without knowing any tax law at all. This is because many audit issues are factual, not legal. It's as important to know IRS procedures—the rules of the game and your rights in dealing with the IRS—as tax law. This book explains the rules to follow and a psychology for dealing with the IRS as well.

B. Audit Selection— Why Me, O Lord?

You just got an Examination notice from the IRS. Are you merely unlucky, or are there more sinister forces at work?

Don't Tell Others About Your Audit

There is nothing to be gained by telling your audit woes to the world. At best, your brother-in-law will be quick to tell you the outcome of his cousin's best friend's audit. Whatever you hear is probably wrong and in any case has absolutely nothing to do with your audit. The real danger in spreading the word is that the wrong person will hear about your audit. A competitor, ex-spouse or disgruntled employee may volunteer information to the IRS. Why risk having someone contact the IRS who would like to hurt you?

---

1. Computers and Classifiers

The IRS computer is to blame for 75% of all audits. Tax return data is sent to the IRS National Computer Center where it is analyzed by a computer program called the Discriminant Function. Each tax return is given a "DIF" score—the higher the DIF score, the more audit potential the return has. The DIF program is super secret—few people in even the IRS know how it works or how a return is given a particular score. Outsiders only know that hundreds of variables on a return are compared to the data in the Discriminant Function program.

About 10% of all tax returns—those with the highest DIF scores—are initially selected for audit consideration. IRS classifiers (human beings) then look at this batch of returns and decide not to audit nearly 90% of them. The remaining returns are sent to the local IRS District Offices where they are further screened. The survivors—less than 1% of all returns filed—are audited.

According to the IRS Manual, only "significant" items should be selected for audit. What is considered significant depends on the classifier's overall view of the return as well as particular items in the return which seem questionable. Factors that guide the classifier (and probably figure into the DIF scoring process) include:

- Comparative size of an item to the rest of the return. For example, a $5,000 expense on a tax return reporting $25,000 in income would be significant; the same expense on a $100,000 income return wouldn't be.

- An item on the return is out of character for the taxpayer. For instance, a plumber claiming expenses relating to a business airplane would cause suspicion.

- An item is reported at an inappropriate place on the return. For example, $2,000 of credit card interest reported as business expenses on Schedule C is very questionable because most personal interest is not deductible, but business interest is. The IRS might suspect that you improperly deducted personal interest as a business expense.

- Evidence of intent to mislead on the return. Filing a tax return with missing schedules or not providing all information asked for on the forms raises an IRS classifier's eyebrows.

- Your gross income. If you make over $100,000 per year, your audit likelihood is 1 in 20 versus 1 in 100 for the rest of the population.

- Inconsistency of related items on the return. For instance, if you list $50,000 in business expenses but only $10,000 in business income, inquiring minds will want to know how you paid your bills. Business losses which offset other income on your return will greatly increase your audit probability.

2.   Other Reasons for Audits

There are seven reasons that the other 25% of tax returns are selected for audit.

IRS special targets. Every year, the IRS decides that certain occupations need special scrutiny. Past favorites have included doctors, waitpersons and airline pilots. Also targeted are people working for or running cash businesses, such as bars and laundromats. If you are on this year's audit Hit List, you won't know about it until it is too late—and then there is nothing you can do anyway.

The IRS has clues for how you earn your income from the W-2 and 1099 forms filed by those who paid you money in past years. In addition, the IRS looks at the tax return box in which you state your occupation. Some people try to be creative here, such as the prostitute who was fined by the IRS for putting down "public relations" as her occupation. (The IRS discovered the truth when she mentioned her line of work during an audit.) Misstating the source of your income is illegal, even if you report it all.

Market Segment Specialization Program. The IRS is zeroing in on 31 different types of workers, including truckers, attorneys, morticians, gas station owners, auto dealers, insurance agency owners, telemarketers and check cashing services owners. This is a relatively new initiative, but it promises to be big in the IRS' future audit plans.

Prior audits. Previous IRS audits often beget new ones. If you were audited and the IRS made large adjustments, you have a higher chance than most of hearing from the IRS in the future—although it is not a certainty. Some people get slapped with an enormous bill after an audit, go back to their old sloppy tax reporting ways and never hear from the IRS again. Also, if a partnership or corporation is audited, it can lead to audits for individual partners and shareholders, and vice versa.

Criminal activity. If you are charged with a crime involving large cash transactions, such as drug trafficking, expect an IRS audit, if not a criminal tax investigation. The tax code requires that all income, from sources legal or illegal, be reported. The IRS does not care how you made the money as long as you report it.

If you'd prefer not to disclose the source of your income, you legally can file a "Fifth Amendment" tax return. This is a regular tax return on which you have written the words "Fifth Amendment" next to the line or lines reporting your income and on the line asking for your occupation. This keeps you out of criminal tax trouble. But, it also means an increased audit potential and possible other agency criminal investigations. For these reasons, never file a "Fifth Amendment" tax return without first consulting a Tax Pro, preferably an attorney.

Amended returns and refund claims. You may file an amended tax return at any time within three years of the date the original tax return was due and filed. (See Chapter 2, Section H.) While the IRS has discretion to reject an amended return, it usually accepts them. Most folks amend returns to claim an overlooked tax deduction resulting in a tax refund. A few others amend their returns to correct errors, which causes a higher tax bill. As you would expect, the audit likelihood for amended returns claiming refunds is fairly high—about one in three in my experience. And if your amended return is audited, the entire return—not just the items amended—is subject to examination.

TIP Filing an amended tax return does not extend the period of time that the IRS has to complete an audit of your return—three years from the original filing date. So, the closer to the end of the three year deadline that you file an amended return, the less time you have to worry about an audit. Amending tax returns can be tricky, and is best done with the help of a Tax Pro. (See Chapter 2 for information on filing an amended return and Chapter 13 for information on finding a Tax Pro.)

Informant's tips. Ex-spouses, disgruntled business associates, former employees and law enforcement agencies can all report you to the IRS. While an audit could result, it should put your mind at ease to know that fewer than 5% of all audits result from tattletales. IRS sources say that most tips, particularly anonymous ones, are not seriously followed up. The IRS prefers to rely on its computers for audit selection. Historically, the IRS has found that many tips are not provable and are motivated by spite.

Random selection. The IRS selects about 50,000 individual taxpayers at random every three years for a Taxpayer Compliance Measurement Program (TCMP) audit. Considering that over 100 million individual income tax returns are filed each year, your chance of being TCMP-selected are quite small.

TCMP audits are excruciating, line-by-line examinations of a tax return. The last TCMP instructions for auditors I saw was 12 pages and had 367 questions. You will be expected to show documentation for almost every item on your tax return, including birth certificates of children claimed as dependents and the deed to your home. The hours allotted auditors to do a TCMP audit are virtually unlimited. This is not because the IRS has reason to suspect anything is wrong—remember, TCMP audits are chosen randomly. It's because the IRS wants to know everything to add to its statistical database. And of course, the IRS wants you to spread the word far and wide about how tough the IRS is.

Always scan an audit notice for the letters TCMP. If you find them, consider seeing a Tax Pro who has been through a TCMP audit. Preparation for the audit may be beyond your ability to handle alone, especially if you have any skeletons in your tax closet. If you are really worried, see a tax attorney. If you have nothing to hide and would prefer to go it alone, bear in mind that you will need to provide documentation for every line of your tax return.

TCMP audit results are the key to future years' computerized audit selections. The results of these audits create statistical models and provide the basis for the computer program that "DIF" scores all tax returns and picks the majority of all tax returns that are audited. (See Section B.1, above.) For each three-year period following TCMP audits, all individual tax returns are judged against these norms.

The IRS suspended the TCMP audit program for a few years. A new round of TCMP audits is scheduled to begin in 1994, however.

> **An Auditor's Heavy Case Load Is Your Best Friend**
>
> Any IRS auditor will tell you she is overworked. But the IRS doesn't pay bonuses or overtime, so there is little incentive for her to break her back on any case. Her job performance is judged on how many files she closes a month. The Taxpayers' Bill of Rights forbids the IRS to evaluate auditors on the dollars produced from their audits.[2] Judging auditors on the number of files closed, however, probably produces much the same result.
>
> A heavy case load can work to your advantage. Auditors don't have the time to go over every tax return with a fine-tooth comb. Auditors often miss taxpayer errors that could have resulted in large adjustments in the IRS' favor.

C. Types of IRS Audits

There are three types of IRS audits: office, field and correspondence. About 55% of all audits are done at the IRS offices, 20% by correspondence and 25% in the field—usually at a taxpayer's business or a tax professional's office. There is also an automated correspondence procedure through the Service Center which, while technically not an audit, can produce the same result—a tax bill.

The type of audit you are selected for can be very important. In 1990, office audits resulted in additional tax and penalties averaging $1,965 per individual return, correspondence audits $3,817 and field audits a whopping $16,248. For those taxpayers who made more than $100,000 per year, field audits resulted in added taxes, penalties and interest averaging $35,295!

---

[2]There is some evidence, however, the auditors are still judged by their dollar production. Before the enactment of the Taxpayers' Bill of Rights, auditors were evaluated by their "yield"—the total dollar amount of the tax adjustment on an audit, divided by the number of hours the auditor spent on the examination. According to an IRS insider, this still goes on.

Your Rights During an Audit

IRS Publication 1, Your Rights as a Taxpayer, should be included with your audit notice. (A copy is in Chapter 15.) It very clearly explains the Taxpayers' Bill of Rights. The most important audit rights are to:

- Be treated fairly by IRS personnel. If you find some-one who is not professional, prompt and courteous, you have a right to speak to a supervisor.

- Have a representative handle your audit. He must be qualified to practice before the IRS and have your written power of attorney. With a few excep-tions, the IRS can't force you to appear or even con-tact you, if you send a representative in your place.

- Sound record the audit, although I don't recommend it. Most likely taping an audit would only cause the auditor to be unfriendly and work harder.

- Not have to submit to repeat audits. If you were audited within the last two years, and the IRS made little or no tax adjustments, you can't be audited for the same items again. The IRS can examine differ-ent items in your return. If you believe you're being re-audited for the same items, complain to the IRS appointment clerk or auditor. The no-repeat audit policy does not apply to examinations of business-related items on an individual's return or for previous Taxpayer Compliance Measurement Program audits. (See Section B.2, above.)

- Have proposed adjustments explained. Audit reports are vague, so you are entitled to ask the auditor for a detailed explanation. You can do this by phone or in person. If the auditor refuses, talk to her supervisor.

- Not be forced to incriminate yourself. You always have this Constitutionally guaranteed right when dealing with the government, even the IRS. For example, if you earn your living by robbing banks, the IRS can't demand that you give details, as long as you report the income. You cannot, however, lie to the IRS about the source of your income. In this case, you should state on your tax return, or during an audit that you are claiming the Fifth Amendment, but see a tax or criminal attorney before doing so. (See Section B.2, above.)

- Appeal your audit. See Chapter 4.

1. Office Audits—Hi Ho, Hi Ho, It's Off to the IRS We Go

Office audits are announced by a form letter either setting a time or requesting you to call to the IRS for an appointment. The letter often specifies documents you are requested to bring with you, usually receipts and canceled checks. It may list up to four areas the IRS wants to examine—such as rental property income, deducted interest expenses, deducted unre-imbursed business expenses and charitable contri-butions. At the audit, if you are questioned about non-listed items and you don't want to answer, just say that you are not prepared to discuss those issues. The auditor will probably drop it.

Thankfully, the IRS doesn't expect auditors to examine every item on a tax return. Remember—only "significant" items are selected by classifiers, although IRS Examination Group Managers may modify the list.

Don't Be Too Eager to Help the Auditor

During an examination, auditors frequently ask taxpayers for copies of additional returns or for information not related to the areas listed on the audit notice. Sadly, most audit victims respond or provide whatever is asked for, often needlessly providing the rope to be hung with.

The IRS cannot require you to furnish data not directly related to your tax return for the year under audit. If the auditor asks for something you don't think pertains, make her explain how it relates to the audit year. If you are given written notice that the audit has been expanded to other years, however, then you must submit information for those years.

Sometimes data on other years' tax returns—such as loss carryovers or depreciation of assets—do relate to the tax year under audit. In this case, show the auditor only the portion of the other year's tax return in question, not the whole return. Similarly, avoid letting the auditor photocopy your records unless you are certain there is nothing harmful in them. Tell her that you don't see why she needs copies and she will probably back down.

If you are asked if you filed all other years' tax returns and you haven't, reply that you will check your records and get back or simply shrug your shoulders. Don't lie. If you want to avoid this question altogether, hire a Tax Pro to go to the audit in your place. Unless you have told him otherwise, he can answer that as far as he knows you filed all tax returns when due. Unless the auditor has reason not to believe this answer, the auditor almost always just moves on.

Why and How to Delay an Audit

In general, the words to live by are, "don't hurry, be happy," and "an audit delayed is an audit well played." The more time an audit drags on, the better the result in most cases. This is because auditors are under pressure to close files, and they want your cooperation to do it. The later it gets, the greater the pressure. The main drawback with prolonging an audit is that interest and penalties are growing—but this may be insignificant next to the damage caused by a large tax adjustment.

There are two ways to delay an office audit:

- Make the appointment as far into the future as possible. Then, call a day or two before and postpone the audit. You can get one, or possibly two, postponements for almost any reason. Valid excuses include having to order copies of vital documents, such as canceled checks from the bank, your accountant going out of town, and the old standby of having been ill.

- On the day of the audit, leave some records at home. Then ask for time to furnish them later. Auditors have come to expect missing records and will routinely allow taxpayers two weeks or more to get them. If you want to push it to the limit, call right before the deadline and ask for a further extension.

After you get over the shock of reading "We have selected your federal income tax return for the year shown below to examine the items listed," you are expected to call the IRS phone number on the letter. The IRS does not award gold stars for calling as soon as you get the notice. In fact, delaying is a good strategy.

Even if you don't want to delay, when you call the IRS for an appointment, ask for the furthest date available so you have sufficient time to get your records in order. You probably won't get an appointment much beyond two months. If you need more time, ask to speak to the clerk's supervisor and try again. Federal law (the Taxpayers' Bill of Rights) requires that you be given a say in the appointment process.

In some IRS offices, the auditor might try to speak to you over the phone about the facts of your case prior to your appointment. If this happens, politely decline. Simply state that you aren't prepared to talk about it right now, period. Don't let her pressure you into going further.

It is possible (but seldom advisable), to have an office audit held at your home or business. If you are physically unable to go to the IRS or bring your records in, the IRS must come to you.

It may also be possible to turn an office audit into a correspondence audit. (See Section C.3, below.) Call the local office after receiving an audit letter and ask. You'll need a good reason for not wanting to come in, such as illness or living far from the IRS offices.

A. WHAT THE AUDITOR WILL DO

On the day of the office audit, arrive on time. Being late starts you off on the defensive. Auditors are usually on a tight schedule and tardiness puts them behind. The auditor, usually a woman, meets with you in a small, plain cubicle with a desk and a few chairs. Seldom are other IRS employees present unless a rookie is being trained.

The Internal Revenue Manual instructs auditors to handle the audit interview as follows:

(1) The initial interview is the most important part of the audit process. The first few minutes should be spent making the taxpayer comfortable and explaining the examination process and appeal rights....

(3) Sufficient information should be developed to reach informed judgments as to:

(a) financial history and standard of living

(b) the nature of employment to determine relationship to other entities and the existence of expense allowances, etc.; this could include the exchange of merchandise or services (bartering)

(c) any money or property received which was determined to be tax exempt and/or not taxable income, and

(d) the potential for moonlighting income.

(4) If warranted by issues on the return or responses to previous questions, the following information should be developed:

(a) the real and personal property owned, including bank accounts, stocks and bonds, real estate, automobiles, etc., in this country and abroad

(b) any purchases, sales, transfers, contributions or exchanges of personal assets during this period, and

(c) the correctness of exemptions and dependents claimed.

(5) Remember, the taxpayer is being examined and not just the return. Therefore, develop all relevant information to the fullest extent possible. If the appearance of the return and response to initial questions lead the examiner to believe that indirect methods to determine income may be necessary...they should be covered at this time.

The auditor will begin by asking a series of background questions—some will be innocuous, such as verifying your address and marital status. Others are more serious, like asking if you have filed all tax returns due. A complete list of questions is in IRS internal Form 4700, Examination Workpapers and Supplement, copies of which are in the Appendix. As Form 4700 highlights, the items in the next section are the areas covered in every audit.

B. THE PRIMARY ISSUES THAT WILL COME UP IN AN OFFICE AUDIT

An at office autdit, expect to be asked about the following:

1. Income. Did you report it all? Auditors are taught to look for wage earners with side jobs—the moonlighting electrician or homemaker who does child care at home. Also, they are alert to any income which was not subject to withholding, such as income from renting out part of your home, pensions and tips.

If you seem to be spending more than you earn, the IRS will want to know where the money is coming from. Specifically, the Internal Revenue Manual states:

Examiners must be alert to...omitted income. Some indications [are] apparent on the face of the return. If income...appears insufficient to meet the cost of living...examiners should ask questions....Two sources are moonlighting...and bartering. The reasons for failure to report...should be developed and the file documented accordingly.

*Observations: Taxpayers standard of living,…
neighborhood, house, furnishings, automobiles,…
clothing,…shopping places,…travel, entertainment
and recreational styles are good barometers,…as are
schools attended by the children….The observant agent
can draw a very good picture…by…these signs.*

The Manual instructs auditors to probe further
into living expenses if omitted income is suspected.
For example, the auditor may want to see your insurance policies to see if you have covered expensive
items like jewelry, furs, art and other such assets.
Auditors seldom go to this trouble, however.

2. Exemptions. Were you entitled to claim everyone listed on your return as a dependent? For instance,
if you support elderly parents, take expense documents
(canceled checks, bills and the like) showing their
income (such as Social Security and pension payments) and how much you spent on them. If you are a
divorced parent and claim your child as an exemption,
have proof of child support payments or costs paid
directly for the child's benefit. Also, try to get a copy
of your ex-spouse's return to show that she or he
didn't claim the exemption. If, however, you both
claimed the exemption, produce your divorce
agreement stating that you are entitled to it.

3. Theft and casualty losses. Were you legally entitled to claim losses here? You will need a list of items
lost plus documentation that the loss occurred—
copies of police reports and insurance claim forms are
good ways to prove losses to the IRS.

4. Charitable deductions. Can you verify charitable
deductions—particularly if the total exceeded $250?
For example, if you dropped $40 into the collection
plate every Sunday, you will need more evidence
than your own statement. Prove it by getting a letter
from your minister attesting to your church atten-
dance and copies of automatic teller withdrawal slips
made on Sunday mornings.

5. Employee business expenses. If you are a wage
earner, can you verify any unreimbursed employee
business expenses claimed on your return—especially
for car, travel, entertainment and home office? At a
minimum, you will need a statement from your
employer describing its reimbursement (or non-
reimbursement) policy—that it pays you back for
some expenses, but not for other items or above

certain limits. Have receipts and a diary. If you don't
have a diary, you can create one after the fact, but
you should tell the IRS that it is a reconstruction.
Note that the IRS is very picky in the employee
expense area.

6. Itemized deductions. Can you verify large itemized deductions on your Schedule A—such as
mortgage interest or medical expenses? You should
have mortgage company statements and medical bills
or canceled checks.

7. Previous audits. IRS records of previous audits
are spotty. A prior audit may not be noted in the
auditor's file. Thus, you will be asked if you've been
audited and how it came out. If you had to pay a
bundle, tell the auditor that you were audited, but
don't recall exactly how it came out. If she wants to
dig out the prior report, she'll do it. Don't do her job
for her by showing her a copy—which might point
her toward issues to probe in the new audit.

8. Other years' tax returns. Auditors usually ask to
see copies of your tax returns for the year before and
after the audit year. The reason is obvious—to see if
any adjustments are appropriate in those years. Don't
bring other returns to the audit, even if they are on
the list of items you are told to bring. Tell the auditor

that you don't have them with you, but will look for them or will ask your tax advisor about them. It takes time and paperwork for an auditor to get copies of tax returns from the IRS Service Center. If you don't give them to her voluntarily, she may not bother to request them. Even if she does, you will have delayed the process—always a plus.

C. HOW LONG IS AN OFFICE AUDIT APPOINTMENT?

In most IRS District Offices, office auditors are usually scheduled to meet four non-business-owning taxpayers or two small business owners each day. This varies among offices—depending on how busy the auditors are—but it's almost always true that their schedule puts pressure on them to keep moving. Auditors don't have time to scrutinize everything on your tax return. Most want to go through your documents and get you out of the office almost as much as you want to leave. Usually, one office appointment is all you'll be subjected to. If you need to furnish information to the auditor after the office appointment, you can usually just mail it in.

2. Field Audits—Look Out, Here Comes the IRS

If you get a letter notifying you of an audit from a Revenue Agent, not a Tax Auditor, the notice will either specify a date that the agent plans on coming to your business or home, or will ask you to call to set it up. This is called a field audit. The letter might include a list of items the IRS wants to look at, but Revenue Agents are not limited to the list. They can examine any and all areas of your tax return.

Field audit notices are sent to the self-employed or to people with issues deemed to be too complex for office auditors. But not all small business people are field audited; many are only office audited. The IRS tends to do field audits on self-employed business people knowing that they have more opportunities to cheat on their taxes than do wage earners. Small business owners are two to three times more likely to be audited than non-business owners. Corporation, partnership and fiduciary tax returns are usually field audited as well.

TIP   Always consider seeing a Tax Pro before a field audit. Field audits can be dangerous to your financial health; tax adjustments are eight times greater than with office audits.

Before calling the Revenue Agent to set up the appointment, decide when you want the audit held. You have the right to a convenient time and date for the audit. The IRS doesn't work evenings or weekends, but the Revenue Agent may be willing to start early or work late. Field audits take at least half a day and often much longer. The agent will want to hold the audit at your business. If you work out of your home she'll want to come there on the assumption that your records are located there.

Revenue Agents, to a far greater extent than office auditors, are trained to play detective to see if your lifestyle and business match your tax return. They have a minimum of 24 semester hours of college level accounting, plus ongoing IRS audit training. They pay attention to the home that you live in, your car and how prosperous your business appears. You could be in for a tough audit if you live in a $700,000 house and drive a BMW, but report only $20,000 annual income.

Field auditors have two main concerns:

- taxpayers who don't report all of their income—especially if they run a cash heavy business

- taxpayers who claim personal expenses as business-related, such as deducting a car for business which is used mostly for personal transportation.

A. THE PRIMARY ISSUES THAT WILL COME UP IN A FIELD AUDIT

A field audit will no doubt include a probe into the following:

1. Unreported business receipts. The auditor will be particularly concerned if your business or profession typically has a lot of cash transactions, such as a bar, laundromat or grocery store. Expect the auditor to ask you outright if you reported all your income. The IRS claims that it loses ten times more tax revenue from underreported business cash than from overstated deductions. The only reason that auditors dwell on verifying deductions during audits is that unreported income is much harder to find—but the IRS is always looking.

If you have been doctoring the books, don't go into an audit without talking to a Tax Pro first, preferably a tax attorney.

2. Bank deposits. This is closely related to unreported business receipts, but it bears separate mention. Did you deposit more money into your bank accounts than you reported as income? Some business owners take great pains to "skim" receipts, but then stupidly put that money into their bank accounts. Bank records can easily be obtained by the IRS from your bank, if you don't produce them voluntarily. Revenue Agents almost always perform a bank deposit analysis early on in a field audit. They simply add up all your deposits and compare them to your income.

TIP Do your own bank deposit analysis before the audit. Make notes on your bank statements that explain the source of the deposits. There can be any number of explanations when deposits exceed taxable income—loans, redeposits of bad checks, transfers between accounts, inheritances and gifts received, sales of assets and the like.

3. Business expense verification. The Revenue Agent will ask you to verify major business expenses you claimed (usually on Schedule C). The agent is on the lookout for disguised personal expenses—particularly auto, travel and entertainment. The tax law specifically requires strict recordkeeping in these three areas. Bringing a business diary will help immensely. If you didn't keep one, you can create one for the audit but you should tell the auditor it is a reconstruction.

4. Asset sales. Can you document your gains and losses from sales of property—particularly stocks and real estate? This can sometimes be a problem as you may have owned the stocks or property for many years before selling. You will need the original documents when you purchased the asset and receipts for improvements (on real estate) during your ownership.

Tax Basis of an Asset

If you're audited, you may be asked to verify your tax basis in an asset on your tax return. The basis is the figure from which the IRS calculates how much profit or loss you've made on the sale of an asset, and therefore if you owe taxes. Essentially, tax basis is the amount you paid. To this figure, add the cost of improvements and tax benefits, such as rollover of gains from prior house sales or subtract costs such as the depreciation taken on rental property. If you received gifts or inheritances, the tax basis is figured from the date of the original purchase, not from the time you received the item.

---

5. Real estate rental. Can you verify rental property expenses you claimed on Schedule E? If you are a landlord, you should have records of all income and expenses. If not, you must reconstruct records from canceled checks, deposits, receipts and notes.

6. Independent contractors versus employees. A big audit issue with the IRS in the 1990s is whether you properly classified people working for you as independent contractors or employees. This issue is covered in Chapter 11, Section C.

B. KEEPING THE AUDITOR AWAY FROM YOUR HOME OR BUSINESS

Avoid having an audit at your home or business, even if you have nothing to hide. Maybe you really earn only $20,000, but appear to live much better. It could be that you inherited a $700,000 house from your aunt, rebuilt your BMW from junkyard parts and made a few good investments. Assuming you can prove all this, you should have no problems with the IRS, right? Well maybe not. These are the kinds of things that can cause the auditor to dig deeper until she finds something.

Here are some tips on how to keep the IRS auditor away from your home or business.

Taxpayers' Bill of Rights. The Taxpayers' Bill of Rights gives small business owners the right to reject a field audit at the business if it is so small that an audit would virtually shut it down. In this case, request it to be held at the IRS office. If your request is denied, complain to the Revenue Agent's manager and then to the Problems Resolution Office. (See Chapter 8.)

Tax professionals. If you give a tax professional a power of attorney, he can insist that the field audit be at his office, not yours, as long as your records are there. (See Chapter 13, Section B.)

C. THE IRS' RIGHT TO VISIT YOUR BUSINESS

Even if the audit is held somewhere else, a Revenue Agent has a right to come to your business to verify data, such as inventory. She doesn't have the right to come inside your home, but she may disallow any home office expenses if you don't let her in. If the auditor wants to tour your business, schedule it when employees or customers are not present. Don't give the auditor a chance to talk with your employees, or even let them know that you are being audited. Remove things that might cause suspicion, like the picture of your boat, airplane or ski cabin.

When the auditor comes, you don't want him around any longer than is necessary for a quick look. If the auditor asks for any records during his inspection, say that your records are at your tax preparer's office. Auditors don't get search warrants to verify the truthfulness of your assertion. Let your conscience be your guide.

3. Correspondence Audits— Please Mr. Postman

Just as it sounds, this is an audit by mail from the IRS Service Center, or less often from an IRS District Office. The IRS requests that you mail information or documents instead of meeting with you. This method of auditing is used to verify such things as stock market transactions, real estate sales and itemized deductions. Amended tax returns are often audited by mail.

You should (almost) always cooperate with an audit by mail, being thankful that you weren't chosen for a field or office audit. Unless the documents requested are lost or non-existent, promptly send copies. Don't send originals—you won't get them back. It's possible to speak to the Service Center auditor to discuss your documents. You can write and ask the auditor to call you or look to see if a name and telephone number is listed in the IRS notice you received. As a precaution, send document copies by certified mail, return receipt requested.

If you have a problem with the IRS Service Center Correspondence Audit section—for example, the auditor is not satisfied with your supporting receipts and canceled checks—you can request that your file be transferred to your local IRS District Office to meet with an auditor. Just making this request may cause the IRS to reconsider any proposed adjustments. And sometimes, mail audits forwarded to local IRS offices are closed with no adjustments—without even contacting you. If you're given a meeting with an auditor at the District Office, consider it a "second chance."

4.   Automated Adjustment "Audits"

IRS Service Centers increasingly are using—or rather misusing—a procedure which is not an audit but can produce the same result: more tax liability for you. I call it an automated adjustment audit. The IRS sends you a Statement of Change to Your Account. The IRS calls them correction, matching or recomputation notices. (They are technically referred to as CP-2000 notices; a copy of one follows.) These notices often seek to impose thousands of dollars of taxes, penalties and interest against you with only vague explanations of why this is happening. What's worse, because this is not really an audit, your return can later be examined anew.

The IRS originally created this procedure to correct mathematical and obvious clerical errors in your tax returns—such as incorrect addition, wrong tax tables and the like—without having to audit the return. Unfortunately, the IRS zeal to computerize every function has turned this into an automated audit, which can be very difficult for many taxpayers to effectively deal with.

CP-2000 notices result from the IRS Information Returns Program, where the IRS computer tries to match information from 1099 income forms and W-2 wage statements to your tax return. If the program can't find the income on your return—such as $482 in bank interest—you will probably get a CP-2000 notice billing you for the additional tax, plus interest and a penalty.

A.   THE PROBLEM WITH CP-2000 NOTICES

Many CP-2000 notices are wrong—*Money* magazine asserts that 25% to 50% of these notices contain errors, such as a failure to see that the income was reported on a different section of the tax return than where the computer program looked. Few people

object, however, and Americans annually pay perhaps as much as $7 billion that they don't really owe.

If you don't agree with, or don't understand, an automated adjustment notice, you can contest it. Just follow these steps:

Call the IRS. Use the telephone number on the notice or try 800-829-1040 if you can't get through. State that you are requesting an "abatement" of a bill because it is wrong. Because this is the term the IRS uses internally, you should say "abatement" so that the IRS staff person you speak to understands what you want. Then explain why the notice is wrong or simply say that your records show that you don't owe the bill. What you want the person to do is to enter into the IRS computer that you do not agree with the notice. But don't stop there.

Protest in writing. Never rely on a phone call alone to straighten out an IRS problem. Furthermore, if you don't make a written objection within 60 days of a CP-2000 notice date, it will become final. There is no IRS form to use to contest it—you must write (preferably type) a letter to the Service Center. Make the letter simple and to the point, like the sample letter that follows. Service Center personnel have notoriously short attention spans and won't struggle through long-winded explanations or unclear handwriting.

Staple a photocopy (not the original) of the CP-2000 notice to the front of your letter. Mail it certified, return receipt requested. Make several photocopies of your letter and enclosures, as you may have to send the same things several more times. Never send anything to the IRS without keeping a copy for yourself. Use the IRS-coded return envelope you received with the notice to make sure it gets to the right department.

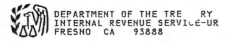

DEPARTMENT OF THE TRE   RY
INTERNAL REVENUE SERVICE-UR
FRESNO   CA   93888

TYPE OF   TICE: CP-2000
DATE OF THIS NOTICE: 02/19/92
SOCIAL SECURITY NUMBER:
TAX FORM: 1040   TAX YEAR: 1989

I...III.I.II.I.I.I.II.II...IIIII.I.I.III.II..III...IIIII.I

PLEASE RESPOND TO THIS NOTICE
BY COMPLETING THE LAST PAGE
AND SENDING IT TO US IN THE
ENVELOPE PROVIDED.

Edward & Mona Jackson
1234 Elm Street
Aurora, CO 66666

FOR GENERAL INFORMATION
PLEASE CALL US AT:

839-1040 LOCAL SF/OAKLAND
1-800-829-1040 ST. OF CA

NOTICE OF PROPOSED CHANGES TO YOUR 1989 TAX RETURN

WE ARE PROPOSING CHANGES TO YOUR 1989 TAX RETURN BECAUSE THE INFORMATION ON YOUR TAX
RETURN IS NOT THE SAME AS THE INFORMATION REPORTED TO US BY YOUR EMPLOYERS, BANKS, AND
OTHER PAYERS.

PLEASE READ THIS NOTICE CAREFULLY. IT EXPLAINS WHAT YOU SHOULD DO IF YOU AGREE OR
DISAGREE WITH OUR PROPOSED CHANGES. PAGE 2 SHOWS THE PROPOSED CHANGES TO YOUR 1989
ACCOUNT. WE PROPOSE TO INCREASE YOUR TAX. IF YOU AGREE WITH THIS CHANGE, YOU WILL
OWE US $316.

PLEASE COMPARE YOUR RECORDS WITH THE PAYER INFORMATION SHOWN ON PAGE 3 OF THIS NOTICE.
IF YOU AGREE WITH THE PROPOSED CHANGES ON PAGE 2:
- CHECK BOX A ON THE LAST PAGE OF THIS NOTICE,
- SIGN AND DATE THE CONSENT TO THE TAX INCREASE,
- ENCLOSE YOUR PAYMENT IN FULL, IF POSSIBLE, AND MAKE YOUR CHECK OR MONEY ORDER
  PAYABLE TO THE INTERNAL REVENUE SERVICE, AND
- RETURN THE LAST PAGE OF THIS NOTICE ALONG WITH YOUR PAYMENT IN THE ENCLOSED
  ENVELOPE.

IF YOU DO NOT AGREE WITH THE PROPOSED CHANGES ON PAGE 2:
- CHECK BOX B OR C ON THE LAST PAGE OF THIS NOTICE,
- ENCLOSE A SIGNED STATEMENT EXPLAINING WHY YOU DISAGREE,
- INCLUDE ANY SUPPORTING DOCUMENTS YOU WISH US TO CONSIDER, AND
- USE THE ENVELOPE ENCLOSED TO RETURN THE LAST PAGE OF THIS NOTICE WITH YOUR
  STATEMENT AND DOCUMENTS. PLEASE INCLUDE A TELEPHONE NUMBER, INCLUDING AN AREA
  CODE, AND THE BEST TIME TO CALL YOU.

IT IS IMPORTANT THAT WE RECEIVE YOUR COMPLETED RESPONSE WITHIN 30 DAYS FROM THE DATE
OF THIS NOTICE. YOU HAVE 60 DAYS IF YOU LIVE OUTSIDE OF THE UNITED STATES. IF WE
DO NOT RECEIVE YOUR RESPONSE WITHIN THIS PERIOD, WE WILL ISSUE A NOTICE OF DEFICIENCY
TO YOU FOLLOWED BY A FINAL BILL FOR THE PROPOSED AMOUNT SHOWN ON PAGE 2. YOU MAY
CONTEST THE NOTICE OF DEFICIENCY IN COURT IF YOU BELIEVE YOU DO NOT OWE THE ADDITIONAL
TAX.

PLEASE RESPOND TO US EVEN IF YOU DO NOT UNDERSTAND OUR COMPUTATION OR CANNOT PAY THE
PROPOSED TAX DUE. IF YOU DELAY YOUR RESPONSE, INTEREST ON ANY AMOUNT YOU OWE WILL
INCREASE. INTEREST STOPS ONLY WHEN YOU PAY THE TOTAL AMOUNT YOU OWE. IF YOU SIGN THE
CONSENT TO TAX INCREASE, FULL PAYMENT IS DUE WITHIN 15 DAYS AFTER WE RECEIVE YOUR
SIGNED CONSENT. IF WE DO NOT RECEIVE YOUR PAYMENT BY THEN, WE WILL SEND YOU A BILL.
THIS BILL WILL INCLUDE YOUR TAX, ANY PENALTIES, AND ADDITIONAL INTEREST.

IF YOU AGREE WITH THE CHANGES WE PROPOSE, YOU DO NOT HAVE TO FILE AN AMENDED TAX
RETURN. HOWEVER, YOU SHOULD REVIEW YOUR RECORDS AND RETURNS FILED AFTER THE YEAR
IDENTIFIED IN THIS NOTICE, TO MAKE SURE YOU REPORTED ALL INCOME CORRECTLY.

IF YOU DID NOT REPORT ALL YOUR INCOME CORRECTLY, YOU SHOULD FILE AN AMENDED TAX RETURN
(FORM 1040X) FOR EACH YEAR, AND PAY ANY ADDITIONAL TAX AND INTEREST YOU OWE. IT IS TO
YOUR ADVANTAGE TO CORRECT YOUR TAX RETURNS AND PAY ANY ADDITIONAL TAX AND INTEREST
AS SOON AS POSSIBLE TO AVOID PENALTIES AND ADDITIONAL INTEREST.

THE ENCLOSED PUBLICATION 1383 CONTAINS DETAILED INFORMATION ABOUT HOW TO RESPOND TO
THIS NOTICE. PLEASE KEEP THIS NOTICE FOR YOUR RECORDS. THANK YOU FOR YOUR COOPERATION.

NOTE: WE SEND INFORMATION TO YOUR STATE AND LOCAL TAX AGENCIES ABOUT ANY INCREASE
OR DECREASE IN YOUR TAX AS A RESULT OF THIS NOTICE.

00001966

CP-2000 (REV. 7/91)

SAMPLE CP-2000 NOTICE

```
FRESNO SERVICE CENTER                                         DO 94 02/19/92


               OUR PROPOSED CHANGES TO YOUR 1989 INCOME TAX
              (DETAILED INFORMATION FOR THESE CHANGES BEGINS ON PAGE 3)


   CHANGED ITEM(S)                  SHOWN ON        REPORTED TO      INCREASE OR
                                     RETURN        IRS BY PAYERS      DECREASE

   TAXABLE WAGES             $     91,875     $     92,788     $       913.00


   PROPOSED CHANGES IN ADJUSTED GROSS INCOME
                                    SHOWN ON         PROPOSED        INCREASE OR
                                     RETURN           AMOUNT          DECREASE

   MISCELLANEOUS DEDUCTION   $      2,330     $      2,312     $        18.00
___
   TOTAL INCREASE                                             $       931.00
___
   PROPOSED CHANGES IN TAX COMPUTATION
                                    SHOWN ON         PROPOSED        INCREASE OR
                                     RETURN           AMOUNT          DECREASE
    1.  TAXABLE INCOME       $    61,648.00   $    62,579.00   $      931.00

    2.  TAX                       13,238.00        13,499.00          261.00

    3.  TOTAL TAXES              13,238.00        13,499.00          261.00

    4.  NET TAX INCREASE..............................................    261.00

    5.  INCOME TAX WITHHELD        16,521.00        16,521.00            0.00

    6.  INTEREST FROM 4/15/90 TO 15 DAYS AFTER THE DATE OF THIS NOTICE.......   55.00

    7.  PROPOSED AMOUNT YOU OWE IRS.........................................$    316.00
```

CP-2000

SAMPLE CP-2000 NOTICE

FRESNO SERVICE CENTER   DO 94 02/19/92

AMOUNTS REPORTED TO IRS BUT NOT IDENTIFIED, FULLY REPORTED, OR CORRECTLY DEDUCTED ON
YOUR INCOME TAX RETURN FOR 1989.

   1. CHARLES SCHWAB & CO. INC.   ISSUED FORM W-2
                                         FOR TAXABLE WAGES $ 913
                                              SOCIAL SECURITY WITHHELD   68
      ACCOUNT NUMBER   SOCIAL SECURITY WAGES   913
      EIN 94-1737782
                                                                        0002

                         EXPLANATION OF CHANGES

DISCLOSURE AUTHORIZATION STATEMENT

IF YOU WISH TO AUTHORIZE SOMEONE, IN ADDITION TO YOU, TO DISCUSS THIS NOTICE
WITH US, PLEASE SIGN AND DATE THE AUTHORIZATION STATEMENT ON THE LAST PAGE OF THIS
NOTICE.   ALSO INCLUDE THE NAME AND ADDRESS OF THE PERSON YOU AUTHORIZE.

THE PERSON YOU CHOOSE MAY ONLY GIVE AND RECEIVE INFORMATION ABOUT THE TAX YEAR IN THIS
NOTICE.   HE OR SHE CANNOT SIGN FOR YOU, OR REPRESENT YOU IN AN INTERVIEW OR IN
U.S. TAX COURT.   IF WE NEED MORE INFORMATION, WE WILL ASK FOR IT THROUGH THE PERSON
YOU CHOSE.   PLEASE HAVE THAT PERSON:
            – WRITE TO US AT THE ADDRESS SHOWN ON THIS NOTICE,
            – SEND ANY SUPPORTING DOCUMENTS TO US, AND
            – GIVE US A TELEPHONE NUMBER, INCLUDING AN AREA CODE, AND THE BEST TIME TO CALL.

YOU MAY CHANGE OR CANCEL YOUR AUTHORIZATION BY SENDING A SIGNED STATEMENT TO THE RETURN
ADDRESS ON THIS NOTICE.   PLEASE STATE THE TAX YEAR FOR WHICH YOU WISH TO CHANGE OR
CANCEL YOUR DISCLOSURE AUTHORIZATION.

YOUR STATEMENT SHOULD INCLUDE THE NAME, ADDRESS, AND TELEPHONE NUMBER OF THE PERSON WHO
WILL NO LONGER BE AUTHORIZED TO DISCUSS THIS NOTICE AND THE NAME, ADDRESS, AND TELEPHONE
NUMBER OF ANY NEW PERSON YOU ARE AUTHORIZING.

MISIDENTIFIED INCOME

IF ANY OF THE INCOME SHOWN ON THIS NOTICE IS NOT YOURS:
– SEND US THE NAME, ADDRESS, AND SOCIAL SECURITY NUMBER OF THE PERSON WHO RECEIVED THE
  INCOME, OR SEND US A COPY OF THE INCOME TAX RETURN WHERE THE INCOME WAS REPORTED,
  IF YOU HAVE IT,
– CHECK BOX B OR C ON THE LAST PAGE OF THIS NOTICE,
– RETURN YOUR SUPPORTING DOCUMENTS AND THE LAST PAGE OF THIS NOTICE IN THE ENCLOSED
  ENVELOPE.

CHILDREN'S INCOME

IF THE INCOME BELONGS TO YOUR MINOR CHILD AND THE LAW DOES NOT REQUIRE YOUR CHILD TO
FILE AN INCOME TAX RETURN:
– SEND A SIGNED STATEMENT TO US EXPLAINING THIS, AND
– NOTIFY THE PAYERS TO CORRECT THEIR RECORDS TO SHOW THE NAME AND SOCIAL SECURITY NUMBER
  OF THE PERSON WHO ACTUALLY RECEIVED THE INCOME, SO THAT FUTURE REPORTS TO US ARE
  ACCURATE.

INTEREST PERIOD

INTEREST HAS BEEN FIGURED FROM APRIL 15, 1990 TO 15 DAYS AFTER THE DATE OF THIS NOTICE
ON THIS PROPOSED CHANGE ONLY.   IF A FULL PAYMENT WAS RECEIVED, INTEREST IS FIGURED FROM
APRIL 15, 1990, TO THE DATE OF THE PAYMENT.   WE ARE REQUIRED TO CHARGE INTEREST AS
PROVIDED BY LAW, ON THE UNPAID TAX FROM THE DUE DATE OF THE RETURN, TO THE DATE THE TAX
IS PAID.

MISCELLANEOUS DEDUCTIONS PERCENTAGE LIMITATION

YOU CAN ONLY CLAIM YOUR MISCELLANEOUS DEDUCTIONS THAT ARE OVER 2% OF YOUR ADJUSTED
GROSS INCOME ON LINE 31 OF YOUR TAX RETURN.   WE REFIGURED YOUR MISCELLANEOUS
DEDUCTIONS BECAUSE WHEN YOUR ADJUSTED GROSS INCOME CHANGED, YOUR 2% LIMIT CHANGED.

                         PAGE   3

                                                                    CP-2000

                    SAMPLE CP-2000 NOTICE

```
FRESNO SERVICE CENTER                          1989    DO 94          02/19/92
                                               FSC -
290*00261/806*      /764*        0*    /170*    /310*    /IN  .0055/680*    /   *    /
```

RESPONSE TO OUR PROPOSED CHANGES TO YOUR 1989 INCOME TAX

        PLEASE COMPLETE THE SECTION BELOW THAT APPLIES TO YOU AND RETURN THE ENTIRE PAGE
IN THE ENVELOPE WE ENCLOSED. BE SURE THE INTERNAL REVENUE SERVICE ADDRESS SHOWS
THROUGH THE WINDOW. IF YOU ARE MAKING A PAYMENT WITH THIS NOTICE, WRITE THE AMOUNT
OF YOUR PAYMENT ON THIS LINE $_____. PLEASE MAKE YOUR CHECK OR MONEY ORDER
PAYABLE TO THE INTERNAL REVENUE SERVICE.

CHECK ONE

A) []   TOTAL AGREEMENT, CONSENT TO TAX INCREASE - I CONSENT TO THE IMMEDIATE ASSESSMENT
         AND COLLECTION OF THE INCREASE IN TAX AND PENALTIES SHOWN ON THIS NOTICE, PLUS
         INTEREST. I UNDERSTAND THAT BY SIGNING THIS WAIVER, I WILL NOT BE ABLE TO
         CONTEST THESE CHANGES IN THE U.S. TAX COURT FOR THE TAX YEAR SHOWN ON THIS
         NOTICE UNLESS ADDITIONAL TAX IS DETERMINED TO BE DUE FOR THIS YEAR.

_____   _____ _____
   SIGNATURE   DATE   SPOUSE'S SIGNATURE
                                                             (REQUIRED IF YOU FILED A JOINT RETURN)

_____

B) []   PARTIAL AGREEMENT WITH PROPOSED CHANGES - I AGREE TO A PORTION OF THE PROPOSED
         CHANGES TO MY INCOME, DEDUCTIONS, TAXES AND/OR CREDITS SHOWN ON THIS NOTICE.
         I HAVE ATTACHED A SIGNED STATEMENT EXPLAINING WHICH ITEMS I DISAGREE WITH AND
         WHY I DISAGREE, ALONG WITH MY SUPPORTING DOCUMENTS.

_____

C) []   TOTAL DISAGREEMENT WITH PROPOSED CHANGES - I DISAGREE WITH ALL OF THE PROPOSED
         CHANGES ON THIS NOTICE. FOR EACH PROPOSED CHANGE, I HAVE ATTACHED A SIGNED
         STATEMENT AND SUPPORTING DOCUMENTS EXPLAINING WHY I DISAGREE.

_____

AUTHORIZATION STATEMENT
IF YOU WISH TO AUTHORIZE SOMEONE, IN ADDITION TO YOU, TO DISCUSS THIS NOTICE WITH THE
INTERNAL REVENUE SERVICE, PLEASE SIGN BELOW.
I AUTHORIZE_____
                   NAME   ADDRESS
TO GIVE AND RECEIVE INFORMATION FROM THE INTERNAL REVENUE SERVICE ABOUT THIS NOTICE.

_____   _____
   SIGNATURE OF TAXPAYER   DATE
                                                                              CP-2000
. . . .

PLEASE DO NOT DETACH

PLEASE BE SURE OUR ADDRESS SHOWS THROUGH THE WINDOW


```
INTERNAL REVENUE SERVICE
FRESNO SERVICE CENTER
FRESNO CA   93888
```

                                    PAGE   4

SAMPLE CP-2000 NOTICE

B. BE PATIENT IF YOU DON'T HEAR FROM THE IRS IMMEDIATELY

Don't be surprised if you keep getting Service Center bills in spite of your letters. It takes a month or more to get your response into the system to stop the computerized cycle. Respond to later IRS notices with a photocopy of your earlier letter. Never ignore IRS letters and never send originals. If notices keep coming after 90 days, call the Problems Resolution Office at the Service Center or at your local District Office. (Telephone numbers are in the Appendix.) Tell the Problems Resolution Program that the Service Center has not answered your letters and ask for help.

Consider calling a Tax Pro for advice, although it is seldom cost-effective to hire one for this type of problem. Many Tax Pros will talk to you for a few minutes on the phone free of charge. If the erroneous IRS bill is for a large amount, it may be worth your money to consult with a Tax Pro for an hour.

If all else fails and the IRS won't cancel the bill, it must send you, by certified mail, a Notice of Deficiency. You can then contest the tax by filing a Petition with the Tax Court. (See Chapter 5.)

Even if the IRS eventually proves to be correct, by sending letters, requesting help from the Problems Resolution Program and filing a Petition in Tax Court, you will have greatly delayed the final tax bill. This gives you an extra six months or more to get the payment together.

D. How an Auditor Approaches an Examination

The tax code gives the auditor many tools to pry into your financial affairs. The basic tools in the auditor's kit are the interview, summons, IRS and other government files, and contacts with third parties who have knowledge of your finances.

Interview. The questions the auditor will ask in the interview are covered in Section C.1.a, above. Your answers provide grist for her mill. She already has your tax return to build on—it shows where you live and work, and gives clues as to your assets. She

adds the answers to her questions, which I should remind you are given under penalty of perjury, to her file. Also, you will be asked to bring documents to the audit—your bank statements and canceled checks are on the top of the list of what the auditor wants to see. A U.S. Supreme Court Justice once said that a person "can be defined by the checks he writes." The IRS knows that.

If You Don't Give the Auditor What She Asks For

When you don't give the auditor information that she has requested, she has three choices:

Drop it. You'd be surprised how many auditors back off or are forgetful. They are working on many other cases. If they have most of the information requested from you, they may let it slide.

Go further without your cooperation. Auditors call, write or issue summonses to third parties (such as your bank) for records of your transactions. Auditors can summons you to appear before them and provide information. If you don't, you can be brought before a federal judge. He can put you in jail until you comply. But don't worry much about this. I have never seen anyone put in jail for not producing records at an audit.

Issue an Examination Report anyway. The auditor can issue the report based on the information she has and her guesstimates for the missing income or expense data. By far, this is the most likely consequence of your not cooperating with an auditor.

Summons. If you don't show up or ignore an audit notice, an auditor can order your appearance at an audit by a summons. It is unlikely you will ever get a summons, but if you do, see a tax lawyer.

Letter to Dispute a Service Center Adjustment

Hamilton and Jill O'Brien
SSN: 123-45-6789
(Married couples—use the first spouse's number on your tax return)
123 Elm St.
Ukiah, CA 90000

June 16, 1993

IRS ADJUSTMENTS/CORRESPONDENCE
IRS Service Center
Fresno, CA 93888

REQUEST FOR ADJUSTMENT
Re: IRS Notice Dated 6/2/93

To Whom It May Concern:

I am responding to your notice of 6/2/93, a copy of which is attached.

[Choose 1, 2 or 3 below followed by your explanation. If none fits your situation, explain in your own words.]

1. **Math errors.**

    The notice is wrong. I did not make any math errors in my tax return. Here is how I made the calculations: $10,432 - $3,190 = $7,242.

2. **Matching error (CP-2000 Notice).**

    a. The 1099 form filed by _Apex Industries_ was wrong and the company has prepared a letter stating the correct amount, which is attached to this letter.

    b. The W-2 form filed by my former employer is incorrect in that I made $_42,815_ in 1991, not $_49,815_.

3. **Partially corrected errors.**

    a. I responded to your notice of 5/2/93 but you did not fully correct your error. Enclosed is a copy of my letter of 5/9/93 with a full explanation.

    b. In your letter to me of 5/2/93 you said that the tax bill of $666 was corrected to $222 (copy enclosed), but I just got a notice dated 6/2/93 for the $666 again.

Please abate the taxes, penalties and interest in the amount of $_1,612_.

We can be reached at 707-555-0562 anytime.

Sincerely,

Hamilton O'Brien

Jill O'Brien

Hamilton and Jill O'Brien

Enclosed: Copies of IRS notices,
          prior correspondence

Third party summons. An auditor can issue a summons to get information from banks, employers, business associates and any other third party. Auditors routinely summons records when you don't cooperate, or when the auditor wants verification of information you have given. You are supposed to be notified when a third party summons is issued and you have a right to object. Practically speaking, however, you can't stop a third party summons. Never tell another person not to comply with an IRS summons of your records—that is illegal.

IRS files. Your previous tax returns, audit reports and tax account history can be checked by auditors using IRS records. The auditor might first ask you for this information. As discussed above, you don't have to give these items to an auditor. Because a lot of IRS information on you is not accessible by computer, it isn't all that easy for an auditor to get this data otherwise. He may have to request items from IRS record storage facilities, which could take months to process. As a rule, auditors don't go to this trouble unless they mistrust you or feel that a large adjustment (tax bill against you) will result.

Other government and public records. IRS offices have direct computer access to the Treasury Enforcement Communication Systems (TECS) computer, which has all kinds of data on you. (Information on TECS is secret, so I'm not sure of the precise data in the files.) The auditor can also get information from the Social Security Administration, Passport Office and Postal Service. Auditors can get local and state public records showing ownership of vehicles, boats, airplanes, real estate and business entities you might be involved in. Private databases and credit reporting agency files contain a wealth of personal data about all of us, and are available to the IRS. As a rule, office auditors don't make these inquiries, but field agents, who conduct audits at homes or businesses, often do.

Contacts. Auditors can make contacts by letter, call or visit to people who have dealt with you, such as a call to the secretary of a church where you claimed a charitable contribution. You cannot legally object to these contacts. If the auditor reveals audit information about you to the third party, however, you can complain to your local District Director that your right to privacy has been violated. I doubt if this will help your audit, though.

E. Preparing for an Audit

In preparing for an audit, begin by taking the following four steps:

1. Thoroughly review the tax return being audited. Make sure you understand how you, or your tax preparer, arrived at the figures.

2. Find all records to substantiate the return and organize them logically and clearly.

3. Identify problems with the return or your records. You may want to consult the preparer of your tax return or another Tax Pro.

4. Research tax laws for guidance. Be ready to legally back up your deductions and other tax benefits claimed.

You have two goals in the audit:

To minimize the financial damage. Because the odds are great that your audit will end with a tax bill, your goal should be damage control—keeping your liability as low as possible. But, don't go in with a defeatist attitude—if you owe no money try to prove it. Just don't have unrealistic expectations. In a recent year, audits resulted in $19 billion in additional taxes and penalties, and about $600 million in refunds—a ratio of 32 to 1 against you.

To prevent expansion. Office audits are initially limited to the items checked on the audit notice. If the auditor sees other problems, however, she will pursue them. This often happens when a taxpayer shows the auditor a document that he wasn't even obligated to show her, or makes a slip of the tongue. Don't show the auditor anything not specifically related to the items and year under audit. For example, if you must produce your check register or business diary, first remove the portions that overlap into other years.

Audits are often expanded into other tax years. An auditor may examine any "open" tax year and she is encouraged to do so. Open years are those within three years of when a return was filed.

Example

In November 1994, Noreen is audited for 1992. The auditor could expand the examination to 1991 and 1993; Noreen filed those tax returns timely. The auditor could not expand the audit any further back, as Noreen filed her 1990 on April 15, 1991, more than three years before the audit date.

Remember not to show the auditor copies of tax returns for years other than the one being audited. If the IRS expands the audit, you may or may not be sent any official written notice. The auditor must at least tell you that the audit has been expanded, however.

F. Who Should Attend the Audit?

You may bring someone with you to the audit. If you do, the auditor may ask you to sign a form allowing the other person to be present. This person cannot represent you, however, unless he is an Enrolled Agent, CPA or attorney. Chapter 13 contains information on bringing a Tax Pro with you or sending a Tax Pro in your place.

In addition, you may want any of the following people to attend:

- your tax return preparer—to explain how the return was prepared.

- an employee—your bookkeeper, accounts payable supervisor or similar employee who has knowledge of your business records can help you explain them.

- your spouse—only one spouse needs to attend an audit when a joint tax return is being audited, but if both spouses have financial knowledge, provided different information on the return or can substantiate that information, both should show up. If only one is being audited, the other can attend to offer emotional support.

- another family member or friend—you can bring a friend or relative to offer moral support, translate if your English isn't very good, wipe your eyes with a handkerchief or do whatever would help you get through the examination.

Not Cooperating in an Audit—When You Have Something to Hide

It may be in your best interest not to cooperate in an audit. For example, if your bank records show deposits in great excess of your reported income or you claimed phony deductions, it may be wiser to suffer the consequences for not going to an audit than submitting. Cooperating or blurting something out because you're tense could earn you a visit from the Criminal Investigation Division (CID). Never say "I guess you caught me, ha, ha," or "I didn't think you would find that account." On hearing such things, auditors are instructed to stop an audit and refer the case to CID. (See Chapter 10.)

When you don't cooperate, the IRS will take one of three actions:

Conduct the audit without you. The IRS may also examine tax years not covered by the initial audit. The auditor may look at all "open" years—returns due and filed within the past three years. And if the auditor suspects you committed fraud, he may go back as far as six years. At the conclusion, the IRS will issue a report disallowing all items listed as questionable. A month or so later you'll receive a bill from the Service Center.

Contact you again. If the IRS wanted a field audit, you may be contacted by the auditor and asked why you are not cooperating. Eventually, she'll give up and issue a report, which will probably disallow most of your deductions and exemptions. A tax bill will follow.

Serve a summons and order you to appear. It's unusual for an auditor to go to this extreme, but it can happen. A summons is a legally enforceable order and you could be held in contempt of court—and even jailed—if you ignore it. See a tax attorney before not complying.

Even if you ignore the audit, you can contest the outcome by an appeal or a Petition to the Tax Court. (See Chapter 4.) The strategy is to skip the audit so as to limit the types of adjustments the auditor will make. On appeal, you pick the items to contest and let the other adjustments stand.

G. How to Act at an Audit

The Internal Revenue Manual says that the taxpayer interview is the most important phase of an audit. You, the taxpayer—not just your tax return—are under examination. Your actions and behavior are being observed and noted by the auditor. Does it look like you are being evasive—trying to hide something? Do you become visibly shaken when some items are being discussed?

Dress Like Yourself

Dress according to your occupation and station in life. Anything else may make you uncomfortable—and an audit is uncomfortable enough already. Use your common sense—don't wear expensive clothes and jewelry if you work at Burger King, and don't dress like a fry cook if you are a dentist. If you are a bus driver coming from work, wear your uniform. Don't try to look like someone you are not. It's simple really—be yourself.

---

1. Mum's the Word

People under stress often talk too much. The IRS is well aware of this principle of human behavior, so auditors are trained to listen and to create silence. They examine records without speaking, with the hope that you will volunteer information. Don't. Take this advice seriously. I can't overemphasize it. Auditors get much damaging information from taxpayers who blurt out answers to questions that weren't even asked. For example, one taxpayer volunteered that he always deducted clothing expenses because he had to come to work dressed. The auditor made adjustments in the other years available for audit (within three years of when the return was filed) as well.

The five best responses to a question posed by an auditor are:

- Yes.
- No.
- I don't recall.
- I'll have to check on that.
- What specific items do you want to see?

Again, don't say more. As a rule, you can't hurt yourself when your mouth is shut.

2. Don't Offer Any Favors to the Auditor

Auditors are trained to watch out for, and report, all offers of favors of any kind. Some taxpayers are from countries where bribing government officials is the norm. IRS employees are closely watched and are among the cleanest of all officials anywhere. An offer of a favor, say tickets to a ball game, may be ignored. But any suggestion of an outright bribe will get you a visit from the Criminal Investigation Division and a very thorough audit. Don't try it.

3. Try to Get Along With the Auditor

When you meet an auditor, be polite and possibly offer some chit-chat about something harmless, such as the weather, traffic or local sports team, to break the ice. Office auditors are under time pressures and may not respond. Field auditors, on the other hand, are encouraged to get to know you; they will chat.

It doesn't hurt to show an interest in the auditor as a person. Ask friendly questions—How long have you been with the IRS? How does someone get to be an auditor? How long have you worked in this area? Everyone likes to talk about their favorite subject—themselves. If the auditor responds, it may get him to like you or at least it will reduce the amount of time he spends examining your return.

In short, don't go in with an anti-IRS attitude. You are not happy to be there, but make the best of it. Remember what Grandma told you about catching more flies with honey than with vinegar.

What about turning this advice on its head and taking a defiant, aggressive attitude into an audit? This is not my style, but it might work with auditors who are timid, or so unused to being challenged that they will give in to get rid of you. One Tax Pro suggests that you continually ask the auditor why he wants to know whenever he asks a question. Obnoxious or peculiar behavior, or even bad B.O. may work. Similarly, some taxpayers give an auditor an unheated or poorly lighted, dirty and noisy storeroom to conduct a field audit. If the offensive approach works, let me know. I am always open to new ideas, especially if they work.

A. WHEN THE AUDITOR IS UNREASONABLE

You may run into an auditor intent on giving you a hard time. She may be impolite, hostile or rude. Worse, she may disallow your deductions unless you produce ironclad documentation in triplicate. Perhaps you did something to upset her, she is having a bad day, or all of her days are bad and everyone upsets her.

The important thing to understand is that you don't have to take guff from an auditor. Ask her politely to lighten up. If she doesn't, tell her you are too upset to continue and want to recess the audit to another day. If she balks, tell her that you want to consult a Tax Pro before continuing. She must grant you that right. You don't have to consult the Tax Pro, but the audit is finished for the day.

Threatening to leave—or having a recess—can have positive results. The auditor may well change her tune and try to be more accommodating. She doesn't want to have to see you again if she can help it, as she already has a backlog of cases. Because her performance is judged by how many files she closes, she won't want anything to delay her. In the end, she is looking for your agreement to close the case. If you have a second meeting, the auditor may be in a better mood. She also knows that a Tax Pro won't put up with her lack of courtesy or professionalism. And it's even possible that your file will be transferred to another auditor for the next meeting. Remember—you never know what is going on in the auditor's life. If she seemed unhappy, it might not have had anything to do with you. She may have been ill, or in the process of quitting, getting fired or transferring to another IRS department.

B. ASKING FOR A NEW AUDITOR

If the recess didn't help and the auditor continues to abuse you, demand to see her Group Manager. Tell him that you are not being treated respectfully and professionally, and that you want a different auditor. While chances are slim that you'll be granted your request, the auditor you have should start treating you more civilly.

Have You Seen This Auditor Before?

The Internal Revenue Manual prohibits an examination by an auditor who has examined your tax return within the previous three years—if that audit was concluded and your case was closed. If you recognize the auditor from your recent past—this might happen if your local office has only a few auditors—and you don't want to deal with her again, complain to the Group Manager or District Director.

4. Getting a New Auditor When You Didn't Ask for One

While auditor changes rarely happen in office exams—even when requested—they are not unusual in field audits. This is because office audits are finished in days or weeks, but field audits often drag on for months. The original auditor may be transferred, promoted, sent for training or special assignment, take maternity leave, quit or be fired.

If your case is assigned a new auditor, you may be contacted by the old auditor before she leaves. She may be anxious to close your file and ask you to agree with her proposed adjustments. She may even send you an examination report to sign. This could be a chance to negotiate a favorable audit settlement. Look over the report carefully and call the auditor to discuss the items you want to negotiate. Your leverage is that she wants to close your file. If she gives in, have her produce a revised report for you to sign. (See Section G.6, below.)

If the auditor doesn't contact you before she leaves, her replacement soon will. He probably doesn't want to do a tremendous amount of work on a half-done case, so his goal may be to close the file as soon as possible. This can be a godsend.

Example

An auditor found that Laura had taken an improper business deduction for three years running—totaling $120,000. After the auditor raised the issue, Laura asked for time to do further investigation and research. In reality, she knew she was dead in the water. She had no valid explanation and was stalling in hope of a miracle. She got one. The auditor was transferred. The new guy was lazy, stupid or overworked, but he never noticed the glaring error. Laura sure didn't bring it up and dodged the bullet. The case was closed without the adjustment.

It's Unfair to Have to Produce Records Twice

If you've already shown records to an auditor, it's reasonable to object to producing them again. The longer the audit has been going on, the louder you should complain. If the auditor saw them before, she should have taken better notes. If there is a new auditor, it isn't your fault that the old one didn't finish—yet you are being punished. The IRS can hardly disagree with this logic.

Even if you aren't successful, you will put the auditor on the defensive, which is always a good idea. You may be able to take control of the situation. Act indignant, tell the auditor what the records show and produce a few items to back it up. If appropriate, suggest a few small adjustments and propose an immediate settlement.

If the auditor still wants to look at the records, demand to speak to her manager and renew your complaint of unfairness. She might agree with you and direct her auditor to avoid repetition and speed up the outcome—so she doesn't have to be bothered with you again. If you have a serious basis for your complaint, for example, the records are voluminous and took a lot of your time to gather, go further. Ask to see the manager's boss, usually a Branch Chief. The squeaky wheel gets the grease, so if you really become a pest, you might get your way. It never hurts to try.

---

5. Hold Your Ground—Even When Your Documentation Fails You

It is a good idea throughout the audit to directly ask the auditor if she has found any problems. Her response gives you the chance to argue, explain or request time to find papers. Why do this? Because most auditors will give you 15 to 30 days to send in additional documents. It is easier to get auditors to see things your way before they have written their report than after. If you don't ask, you won't know until the audit report comes. Just keep asking if everything is okay or if the auditor needs anything else. Some auditors will stay mum, knowing that they can hide behind the final report and never have to face you again. But some auditors will explain what they are thinking about and will agree to compromise or even back down.

A. PROVING YOUR DEDUCTIONS

You must prove that you prepared your tax return properly to win your audit. The IRS is not required to prove that you are wrong. You will be required to present proof at the audit. Proof should be in writing, but auditors have some discretion to accept oral explanations as well.

If you deducted business expenses or expenses that helped you produce income, the expenses must be "reasonable and necessary" as well as verifiable. This means that even if your expenses are legally allowed, if they are unreasonably large or extravagant, they won't pass muster. For example, you owned a hot dog stand and claimed $20,000 in entertainment expenses. The auditor would disallow this amount as unreasonable, even if you could substantiate it. This is not usually grounds for disallowance, practically speaking.

Documents to Bring to the Audit

With an audit notice is a list of documents the IRS requests you bring to the audit. And, you may want to show the auditor items not on the list if you need to explain or reconstruct missing records. (See Section G.5.b, below.) IRS Publication 552, Record-keeping for Individuals, shows how the IRS wants you to keep your records. Don't be concerned if you haven't followed all the suggestions. As long as you can show your income and expenses to the auditor in some understandable manner, you are okay.

Here are specific documents to bring:

Canceled checks and receipts. Take only the checks and receipts relating to the areas listed in the audit notice. Don't let the auditor rummage through all your checks and receipts. One reason is that if it appears you are spending more money than you are reporting, the auditor may become suspicious.[3]

Books and records, if you operated a business. You aren't required to have a formal set of books as long as the auditor believes your records reflect your true income and expenses. Many successful businesses have no records beyond the check register. A check register may take the place of a set of books, if it's backed up by canceled checks and receipts.

If your business has no records of any kind, you can be fined by the IRS for "failure to keep adequate records," although this is seldom done. And the auditor is allowed to make up missing records by guesswork. For example, she may double the gross receipts you say you made by "guesstimating" the volume of your business. This forces you either to come up with your own records or to accept her figures.

(continued)

---

[3]In 1992, the IRS adopted a new policy in line with modern electronic business and banking. The IRS will now allow an account statement from a financial institution showing a check has cleared instead of the canceled check itself. (IRS Revenue Procedure 92-71.)

Appointment books or business diaries. If you claimed travel or entertainment expenses, you will need some writing showing dates and times the expenses were incurred, their business purpose and who was visited or entertained. If you have no diary, you can write one up in preparation for the audit, but tell the auditor it is a reconstruction if she asks.

Auto logs. Auto logs aren't required by law, despite what some auditors say, but they will help you prove auto expenses. Again, you can create one after the fact, but be up front about it. Repair and maintenance receipts should have odometer mileage written on them and your diary may have notations of trips and expenses.

Escrow papers. These will help if you claim rental property depreciation and need to show the cost basis of the property.

B. IF YOU DON'T HAVE DOCUMENTATION

Myth: If you can't prove a deduction in writing, it won't be allowed by the IRS auditor.

Fact: Courts repeatedly tell the IRS that taxpayers can't be expected to keep flawless records. The Internal Revenue Manual instructs auditors to consider oral explanations, reconstructed records when the originals are missing and approximations of expenses, and to allow for missing receipts for expenses under $25 each.

Here are the real audit rules when you don't have records:

Substantial compliance. If your records are otherwise complete, the auditor can overlook a few missing documents. If she insists, vigorously argue that you are in "substantial compliance" and are entitled to the benefit of the doubt. Substantial compliance means that you have produced enough documentation to show that you obeyed the tax reporting laws even though your documentation is not complete.

If you lost your canceled checks or bank records, order copies well in advance of the audit. The charges for this service may be high, so only order copies of major expense items. Expect a wait of at least several weeks for the bank to pull up these records off of its microfilm. If need be, ask the auditor for a delay so you can get your records.

Oral explanations. Whatever reason you give the auditor to justify missing documents must be given consideration, if reasonable. Records may have been lost in an earthquake or hurricane, thrown out by a child or housekeeper, or lost in a move, but "burglars stole them" or "aliens with ray guns vaporized them" is not going to fly. It is important that you establish and maintain credibility with the auditor, so keep your imagination on a reasonably short leash.

Reconstruction. Gaps due to missing documents may be filled by reconstructing them. Tax Court decisions recognize that expenses were incurred even if records are lost. Therefore, you may be able to establish expenses by recreating records from other sources or by indirect means.

For example, if you rented an office, paid some expenses in cash, but lost your paid receipts, you can reconstruct your rent expenses with a letter from your landlord or a witness statement from someone who saw you make the rent payment. Or if you can deduct a portion of your electric bill as a home office expense, but you lost three months of receipts, take the average of the other nine and use them to approximate the missing three.

If you can't come up with any documentation of an expense, write it yourself. Be up front with the auditor; tell her you prepared it as a reconstruction of the expense. For example, write a rent receipt on a paper with the date, landlord's name, address and amount of payment.

 There are legal restrictions on the reconstruction of expenses. The tax code is more restrictive for proof of a few types of expenditures, such as travel and entertainment. You can reconstruct "travel and entertainment" records only if they were lost in a casualty, such as a fire.[4] But a business dinner, for example, might be allowed if you can show an entry in your business diary, or a signed statement from the person entertained.

---

[4]Internal Revenue Code § 274(d); IRS Regulation 1.274-5T(c)(5).

Cohan Rule. An old, well-known tax case has saved many an audit victim with missing records. George M. "I'm a Yankee Doodle Dandy" Cohan was nailed for not having receipts in a 1920s IRS audit. George fought the IRS to the U.S. Court of Appeals, which held that a taxpayer can make an approximation of expenditures for tax purposes as long as he can reasonably show that some amount was spent.[5]

The Cohan Rule has its limits. First, you must make some showing of why the records are not available. They may have been lost, destroyed or be in such small amounts and from transactions in which receipts are not normally given, such as cab fares or tips. And the rule can't be applied to approximate travel and entertainment, as mentioned above.

🖋️ In reality, the Cohan Rule is useful as a bargaining chip with which you can confront the auditor. If she says "no deduction without documentation," cry the Cohan Rule. Her eyebrows will likely raise in surprise, and she may back down, at least part of the way.

Small expenses. Small business-related expenses don't require substantiation if they are less than $25. Under IRS regulations, an entry in your business diary is sufficient.[6] But the expense itself must seem reasonable and necessary to the auditor.

6. Negotiating With the Auditor

The IRS has a guiding principle for all auditors—settle the audit case at the lowest IRS level, if possible. The IRS wants you to accept its auditor's report. It does not want you clogging up the appeals and Tax Court process.

This goal, however, is inconsistent with another directive given to auditors—do not negotiate with taxpayers. In reality, indirect deal-making with auditors is common. The key to doing this is to understand that you cannot successfully negotiate based on the *amount of taxes due*—for example, don't ask the auditor to take 50 cents on the dollar. But you can

negotiate *specific adjustments* to particular items to produce a lower audit bill. Here are two examples.

Missing documentation. If your documentation is lacking, you have what the IRS calls a substantiation or verification problem. Suppose you claimed a storage rental expense of $50 per week and lost your receipts. The auditor says she will disallow the $2,600 item for lack of verification. The manager of the storage facility writes a letter attesting to your regular payments, but the company records have been lost as well. Try proposing a compromise. Suggest a disallowance of 25% to get the audit over with. If the auditor agrees, or offers a 50% disallowance, you have just negotiated a fairly decent settlement—and you've learned a lesson about keeping your records.

Questionable legal ground. You may have perfect records, but a shaky legal position. For instance, suppose you spent $5,000 to replace a deck and $5,000 for a new roof on rental property you own. On your tax return, you deducted both items as "repairs." The auditor claims that these are "capital improvements" that must be deducted over the life of the improvements. Assuming the auditor is right, and each has a ten-year estimated life, you would be limited to deducting only 1/10 of the cost ($1,000), for each of the next ten years.

To propose a compromise, you can suggest that one item is an improvement (perhaps the deck) but

---

[5]*Cohan v. Commissioner of the Internal Revenue*, 349 F.2d 540 (2nd Cir. 1930).

[6]IRS Regulations § 1.274-5T.

the other is a repair (the roof, which was leaking like a sieve). You could then deduct all $5,000 for the roof and $500 for the deck. While you wanted to deduct $10,000, deducting $5,500 is much better than the IRS' initial position that you deduct only $1,000.

Adjustments in Your Favor— Taking the Offensive

Auditors must make any adjustments in your favor whenever they are found during an audit. Even the most hard-nosed auditor knows that taxpayers occasionally make mistakes in the government's favor or overlook tax benefits on their returns. This is a good reason to see a Tax Pro before meeting with an auditor—to find out if you missed any deductions or can find anything else in your favor to show the auditor. [7]

If you or your preparer were overly conservative—for example, you decided not to take a certain expense as a deduction because you had no receipts—then claim it at the audit. It just might be accepted by the auditor, and nothing ventured, nothing gained.

Don't, however, bring up any favorable items until the auditor has completed her review and decided on any changes for the IRS. At that time present your positive adjustments. If you show them to her earlier she might try to counter by coming up with offsetting adjustments that she otherwise would have passed by. After she is locked in to her position, things can only get better if she accepts any of your new, positive change items.

---

7. Ending the Audit

Although you will want to delay the start of most audits (see Section C.1, above), once it begins you will probably want to finish up as quickly as possible.

This is especially true when a problem lurks that the auditor has not yet found. The longer she looks, the greater the chance of discovery. If the auditor hasn't yet looked at your bank statements and found the $10,000 deposits you don't want to explain, you want out of there ASAP.

You are more likely to have control over ending a field audit than an office audit. While "mum's the word" in an office audit, you will have to interact somewhat in a field audit. A Revenue Agent (a person who does a field audit) can sometimes be maneuvered into closing a file *if* she falls into one of two types:

Bored, unhappy or unexcited. As soon as the audit begins, tell the auditor that you know that audits usually produce adjustments. Say that you would appreciate it if she finds them quickly and gets it over. If she gets the idea that you won't fight, she might take you up on your offer. This is especially true if you point out any obvious errors in your return or records—such as $6 + 6 = 13$—that she will almost surely find anyway. Many auditors have a kind of psychological tax adjustment quota or level, which once reached allows them to be more ready to close your file.

Example

Alison had taken a very questionable tax position on a $2,000 deduction. In going over her return, the auditor hadn't yet reached the item. Nearing the end of a full day of the audit, Alison pointed out that there was a $350 deduction that could not be substantiated. Because the auditor had already found $300 in other items to disallow, Alison thought he might be satisfied with one more sizeable adjustment and end the audit. She was right. The auditor took the bait and said that another day would not be necessary. Even if she had not kept the auditor away from the $2,000 item, by volunteering the $350 item, Alison came across as reasonable. Such good deeds are often rewarded later by an auditor, in the event certain documents are missing.

Overly conscientious. Some auditors—usually the ones straight from IRS basic training—come on strong, looking at every little thing and laying down the law like a Marine drill instructor. When this

---

[7]In Chapter 13, Section D.2.a, I suggest some publications that might help you identify deductions you may have missed. Be sure to review that material before you go into an audit.

happens, drop the "nice guy" approach, get your back up and argue over every item that he looks at, even when you know you are wrong. Let him know two can play his game and that you won't be steamrollered. If you know serious problems are ahead due to questionable items or missing documents, demand an end to the audit for that day. Say that you want to consult a Tax Pro. He won't like being slowed down, but he knows he must grant your request.

At your next meeting, the auditor should at least be more reasonable, if not anxious to conclude the audit. If not, threaten to call in the auditor's manager. I guarantee that this will cause the auditor to adjust his attitude. He can better use his time working on other files where the taxpayer does not stand up to him instead of putting more time into your case.

8. IRS Pressure on an Auditor to Finish— Extending the Deadline

As stated at the beginning of the chapter, legally the IRS does not have forever to audit you. The deadline is three years after your return is due (April 15) or actually filed, whichever is later. If the IRS suspects fraud or underreporting of income by at least 25%, the period is extended to six years—but this is rarely ever done.

The IRS Manual suggests that an auditor is to complete the audit within 28 months after the date you filed the return. If an auditor hasn't completed her work within 28 months, you will be asked to extend the deadline by signing IRS Form 872, Consent to Extend the Time to Assess Tax. When asked, you have three options:

- sign the consent form
- don't sign, or
- negotiate the terms of the extension.

I recommend the second or third approach in most cases.

The auditor usually asks you to sign an open-ended extension agreement, meaning that an audit adjustment can be made on any item, at any time in the future. Counter by asking that the term be

limited to specific items—those on which the auditor says she needs to do more work. Also ask that the period of extension be no longer than six months. These perfectly reasonable limitations on the auditor narrow your risk and assure finality in the audit.

If you don't sign the Form 872 extension, one of two things will happen.

1. The auditor will issue the Examination Report, and a Notice of Deficiency simultaneously. This means that you cannot appeal the report within the IRS but can only contest it by filing a Petition to the Tax Court. (See Chapter 5.)

2. The auditor may slip up and let the three-year audit deadline pass—meaning that no assessment will ever be made. This doesn't happen very often. The IRS gets very upset with auditors who blow the deadline. But it does happen and it's like winning the lottery.

H. Finishing the Audit

At the end of your first, and hopefully last, meeting with the auditor, ask her again to specify exactly what adjustments she intends to make. While she may not be willing to commit without further review of your file, she surely has a pretty good idea. Try to pin her down. If you disagree, you can argue your case on the spot or ask her for time to get more documents together.

If the IRS Loses a File

Audit files sometimes get lost in the IRS bureaucratic maze for many months. When found, an unfinished audit file could be assigned to a new auditor who will not want to work on a half-done case and will look for ways to close out the file rapidly. Even better, the three-year deadline for auditing your return may expire before the file resurfaces. This means that the IRS forever loses its right to make adjustments, and you are in the clear.

1.   Receiving the Examination Report

When the auditor completes her work, you will be handed or mailed IRS Form 4549, an Examination Report. It shows adjustments to your tax liability for the years under audit, and for any other "open" years into which the auditor expanded the examination. It also provides a brief, categorical explanation for each change, such as "You did not prove the amount shown was a rental expense." A sample is shown below.

From your point of view, the Examination Report falls into one of three categories:

Win. Instead of a Report, you will receive a "no change" or even a "refund" letter. These require no explanation—you've won.

Lose. The Report makes changes—you owe more taxes, plus interest and maybe penalties. You didn't have good documentation or what you had was not accepted. Or perhaps the auditor didn't buy your legal entitlement to the tax benefits claimed.

Draw. A mixed bag—some of your documents were accepted, but others weren't. Or maybe your legal position was shaky on one or two items but strong on another.

2.   Understanding the Examination Report

The total amount of taxes, penalties and interest added by the audit is shown on your Report. Each change is listed, the tax code section cited and a general explanation given. As stated, most explanations are vague. You are usually not specifically told how you failed to prove your case. If you don't know, call the auditor and ask. She must tell you where you failed. (See the Examination Report on the following pages.)

3.   Your Options After Getting the Examination Report

You have three choices after you receive the Report.

1. Agree. The IRS hopes you will sign, date and return a copy of the Report along with IRS Form 870, Consent to Proposed Tax Adjustment. This is referred to by the IRS as an "agreed" case.

By signing Form 870, you agree to the immediate assessment of the tax deficiency found, plus any penalties and interest listed on the Examination Report. You give up your right to appeal or go to Tax Court. Theoretically, you could pay, change your mind and sue the IRS for a refund in court, but this seldom makes sense.[8]

A Report even if signed by you is not final until approved by the auditor's manager and Audit Review staff. Occasionally, a signed Report will be kicked back to the auditor for correction of obvious errors or to further develop issues. If this happens, the auditor may contact you. You can't complain about being audited twice because the first audit is not officially concluded—even if you signed the Report.

You can, but, you don't have to pay the tax bill when you sign the Report. Beginning in 1992, auditors are allowed to offer a payment plan to most taxpayers who owe less than $10,000 as a result of an audit. You have your choice of a 12-, 24- or 36-month plan. Before you automatically choose the longest period, you should know that interest and late payment penalties still accrue on the unpaid balance. (Interest and penalties on late tax payments add 13% as of January 1994.) Unlike debts over $10,000 (see Chapter 6), you do not have to reveal your finances to the IRS to get one of these audit payment plans.

You may just wait until a bill comes from the Service Center. Sometimes, the bill is less than the audit report figure because a penalty was dropped or a computation error corrected. If the bill is more than the amount on the Report, you can complain; if it is less, let your conscience be your guide. If you pay the lesser amount, no one may ever notice. Don't be surprised, however, if you are later billed for the difference.

---

[8]Although most tax lawsuits are filed in U.S. Tax Court, a "refund" case must be brought in a U.S. Federal District Court or the U.S. Court of Claims. (See Chapter 5, Section C.)

Internal Revenue Service
District Director

Department of the Treasury

Date: 11/18/92

Tax Year Ended: 1990

Person to Contact: Mort Meyer

Contact Telephone Number: 213-555-7878

Contact Address:

> Ruth McMillan
4388 West Berkeley Bowl
Burbank, CA 90300

INTERNAL REVENUE SERVICE - OE 2106
11500 W. Olympic Blvd., Suite 510
Los Angeles, CA 90064

Dear   Ms. McMillan

    Enclosed are two copies of our report explaining why we believe adjustments should be made in the amount of your tax. Please look this report over and let us know whether you agree with our findings.

    If you accept our findings, please sign the consent to assessment and collection portion at the bottom of the report and mail one copy to this office within 30 days from the date of this letter. If additional tax is due, you may want to pay it now and limit the interest charge; otherwise, we will bill you. (See the enclosed Publication 5 for payment details.)

    If you do not accept our findings, you have 30 days from the date of this letter to do one of the following:

    1. Mail us any additional evidence or information you would like us to consider.

    2. Request a discussion of our findings with the examiner who conducted the examination. At that time you may submit any additional evidence or information you would like us to consider. If you plan to come in for a discussion, please phone or write us in advance so that we can arrange a convenient time and place.

    3. Discuss your position with the group manager or a senior examiner (designated by the group manager), if an examination has been held and you have been unable to reach an agreement with the examiner.

    If you do not accept our findings and do not want to take any of the above actions, you may write us at the address shown above or call us at the telephone number shown above within 30 days from the date of this letter to request a conference with an Appeals Officer. You must provide all pertinent documentation and facts concerning disputed issues to the examiner before your case is forwarded to the Appeals Office. If your examination was conducted entirely by mail, we would appreciate your first discussing our findings with one of our examiners.

(over)

District Director, Los Angeles District

Letter 915(DO) (Rev. 1-88)

SAMPLE EXAMINATION REPORT

The Appeals Office is independent of the District Director. The Appeals Officer, who has not examined your return previously, will take a fresh look at your case. Most disputes considered by Appeals are resolved informally and promptly. By going to Appeals, you may avoid court costs (such as the United States Tax Court filing fee of $60), clear up this matter sooner, and prevent interest from mounting. An Appeals Officer will promptly telephone you and, if necessary, arrange an appointment. If you decide to bypass Appeals and petition the Tax Court, your case will normally be assigned for settlement to an Appeals Office before the Tax Court hears the case.

Under Internal Revenue Code section 6673, the Tax Court is authorized to award damages of up to $5,000 to the United States when a taxpayer unreasonably fails to pursue available administrative remedies. Damages could be awarded under this provision, for example, if the Court concludes that it was unreasonable for a taxpayer to bypass Appeals and then file a petition in the Tax Court. The Tax Court will make that determination based upon the facts and circumstances of each case. Generally, the Service will not ask the Court to award damages under this provision if you make a good faith effort to meet with Appeals and to settle your case before petitioning the Tax Court.

The enclosed Publication 5 explains your appeal rights.

If we do not hear from you within 30 days, we will have to process your case on the basis of the adjustments shown in the examination report. If you write us about your case, please write to the person whose name and address are shown in the heading of this letter and refer to the symbols in the upper right corner of the enclosed report. An envelope is enclosed for your convenience. Please include your telephone number, area code, and the most convenient time for us to call, in case we find it necessary to contact you for further information.

If you prefer, you may call the person at the telephone number shown in the heading of this letter. This person will be able to answer any question you may have. Thank you for your cooperation.

Sincerely yours,

District Director

Letter 915(DO) (Rev. 1–88)

SAMPLE EXAMINATION REPORT

Report of Individual
Income Tax Examination Changes

Department of the Treasury
Internal Revenue Service

Name of Taxpayer	Year	Form	Filing Status	In Reply Refer To:
Ruth McMillan	1990	1040	Single	OOO IRS 222

Authorized Representative	Date of Report	Social Security Number	Examining District
	11/18/92	123-456-7890	000-00

Income and Deduction Amounts Adjusted

Explanation Number (See attached)	Item Changed	Amount Shown on Return or as Previously Adjusted	Corrected Amount of Income or Deduction	Adjustment Increase (Decrease)
6102	Net Operating Loss	23226	0	23226
5605	Sch-C Rentals Loss	13757	0	13757
5605	Sch-C Acting Loss	17246	0	17246
0101	Gross Receipts Rentals	—	—	—
0101	Gross Receipts Acting	—	—	—
8203	S.E. Tax	—	—	—
8133	Negligence	—	—	—
8120	Substantial Understatement		—	—

A. Adjustment in income and deductions — increase (decrease) (See explanation of adjustments attached.)		54229
B. Adjusted gross or taxable income shown on return or as previously adjusted		17660
C. Corrected adjusted gross or taxable income		71889
D. Tax figured	Tax Rate Schedule	16261
E. Tax credits (general business, child and dependent care, foreign, etc.) (If adjusted, see explanation attached.)		—
F. Other taxes (self-employment, alternative minimum, tax from recapture of investment credit, etc.) (If adjusted, see explanation attached.)	S.E. Tax	667
G. Corrected tax (line D less line E plus line F)		16928
H. Tax shown on return or as previously adjusted		4197
I. Deficiency (increase in tax before credit adjustments—line G less line H)		12731
J. Overassessment (decrease in tax before credit adjustments—line H less line G)		—
K. Adjustments to prepayment credits		—
L. Balance due — this does not include any interest charges (line I or J as adjusted by line K)		12731
M. Overpayment—this does not include any interest due you (line I or J as adjusted by line K)		—
N. Penalties, if any (See explanation attached.)	Negligence § 6653 (a)(1)	636.55
	Substantial Understatement § 6661 →	3182.86

Although this report is subject to review, you may consider it as your notice that your case is closed if you are not notified of an exception to these findings within 45 days after a signed copy of the report or a signed waiver, Form 870, is received by the District Director. If you agree, please sign one copy of this report, and return it in the enclosed envelope. Keep the other copy with your records.

Consent to Assessment and Collection - I do not wish to exercise my appeal rights with the Internal Revenue Service or to contest in the United States Tax Court the findings in this report. Therefore, I consent to either:
   (1) The immediate assessment and collection of the balance due shown on Line L, plus any interest due on this tax, and also any penalties shown on line N, or
   (2) The overpayment shown on line M, plus any interest and adjusted by penalties shown on line N.

Your signature	Date	Spouse's signature, if a joint return was filed	Date

(See notices on the back)

Form **1902-B** (Rev. 1-87)

SAMPLE EXAMINATION REPORT

FORM 886-A (REV APRIL 1968)	EXPLANATION OF ITEMS	SCHEDULE NO. OR EXHIBIT A
NAME OF TAXPAYER Ruth McMillan		YEAR/PERIOD ENDED 1990

6102 You did not sustain a net operating loss in the tax year within the meaning of section 172 of the Internal Revenue Code because your loss was attributable solely to non-business expenses. Therefore, there is no net operating loss carryback or carryover, and your deduction claimed is disallowed. Taxable income is increased accordingly.

0101 Although not adjusted. Gross Receipts are an open Audit issue.

8203 We have adjusted your self-employment tax due to a change in your net profit from this self employment.

5605 Since you did not establish that the business expense shown on your tax return was paid or incurred during the taxable year and that the expense was ordinary and necessary to your business we have disallowed the amount shown.

DEPARTMENT OF THE TREASURY - INTERNAL REVENUE SERVICE
† U.S. GOVERNMENT PRINTING OFFICE 1983-381-541/5140

FORM 886-A (REV. 4-68)
Page____

SAMPLE EXAMINATION REPORT

FORM 886-A (REV. APRIL 1968)	EXPLANATION OF ITEMS	SCHEDULE NO. OR EXHIBIT B
NAME OF TAXPAYER Ruth McMillan		YEAR/PERIOD ENDED 1990

8138 Since all or part of the underpayment of tax you were required to show on your return is due to negligence or intentional disregard of rules and regulations, you are being charged a penalty under Internal Revenue Code Section 6653(a). For tax returns due, without regard to extensions, after December 31, 1988, this penalty is 5% of the underpayment. The interest on the penalty is calculated according to Internal Revenue Code Section 6601(e)(2)(B) from the due date of the return (including extension) until the additional tax is paid.

8120 Since there is a substantial understatement of income tax you are liable for a penalty of 25 percent of the amount of any underpayment attributable to such understatement. This applies to tax not assessed prior to October 21, 1986. In addition, interest is figured on the penalty from the due date of the return (without regard to extensions). See Internal Revenue Code Section 6661 and 6601(e)(2).

DEPARTMENT OF THE TREASURY - INTERNAL REVENUE SERVICE
+U.S GOVERNMENT PRINTING OFFICE 1980-381-541/5140

FORM 886-A (REV. 4-68)
Page____

SAMPLE EXAMINATION REPORT

2. Argue. Examination Reports are not cast in stone. If you want to fight the Report, call the auditor. Tell her what findings you disagree with. Ask what additional proof it would take to get her to change the Report. Request two weeks or more to get a missing document or reconstruct a record. Most auditors will ask that you mail the proof to them. Pushing for another appointment may be better—it forces them to face you again, and shows that you are serious about contesting the Report's findings. If she is not cooperative, ask to speak to her manager. If you are successful, you'll be sent an amended Examination Report.

If your new documentation doesn't help, ask the auditor if you can see her workpapers on your case— these are the notes the IRS requires an auditor put in a file. Workpapers should explain and justify any changes made to a tax return. If the auditor shows you her notes, ask her to fully explain them—and the conclusions she drew—if it isn't obvious.

Don't be surprised if the auditor refuses to show you her workpapers. Many auditors don't like to show taxpayers their notes. If she refuses, tell her you know you are entitled to see them under the Freedom of Information Act, and if she won't show them to you, you will make a formal request for them. (Chapter 4, Section B.2, explains how to make a Freedom of Information Act request.)

If you don't get anywhere with the auditor, ask to meet with her manager. Generally, the manager will agree to meet with you. I call this an "informal appeal." Managers usually, but not always, back their auditors. They also have a strong motive to close files handled by auditors in their group with an "agreed" notation, so they may try to appease you.

When you meet with the manager, don't criticize the auditor, as the manager may then concentrate on defending his employee instead of considering your position. Instead, raise some substantive issues that will allow the manager to compromise. Even if this doesn't work, the manager's explanations may make the IRS' position clearer to you or point out the weaknesses in your case. As a last resort, if she won't budge, calmly say that you are disappointed and that you don't want to appeal, but you don't know what else to do.

(For an example of compromising with an auditor's manager, see the Case History below.)

3. Do nothing. You don't have to respond to an Examination Report. If you ignore it, in a month or two you will probably receive an IRS "30-Day Letter." This is your formal notice that your case is considered "unagreed" and that you have 30 days to start an appeal. The appeals process is covered in Chapter 4, and is also described in IRS Publication 5, Appeal Rights and Preparation of Protests for Unagreed Cases. A copy of Publication 5 is in the Appendix; you should receive a copy with your Examination Report.

The IRS does not have to allow you to appeal within the IRS—it is discretionary. In any event, the IRS must eventually send you a "90-Day Letter," formally known as a Statutory Notice of Deficiency. This letter may not arrive for months after the audit was completed. To get your attention, the IRS sends it by certified mail. To contest the audit results now, you must file a Petition in the U.S. Tax Court within 90 days. (See Chapter 5.) If you don't, the Examination Report becomes final—your right to contest the audit without first making full payment has ended.[9] The taxes, penalties and interest found due in the audit are then officially assessed against you.

In about 60 more days, you will get a Notice of Tax Due. This is the beginning of the IRS collection effort. (See Chapter 6.)

Opening a Closed Audit

There are procedures for reopening a closed audit either by you (see Section I.2, below) or by the IRS. Fortunately, the IRS rarely reopens closed audits. If it does in your case, however, see a Tax Pro to find out if the IRS is acting properly under its own procedures, or do a little legal research yourself. (See Chapter 13.)[10]

---

[9]You can also contest by paying the tax bill and filing a claim with the IRS for a refund. Refund claims are always denied. You can then file a "refund suit" in U.S. District Court or the Court of Claims. (See Chapter 5, Section D.)

[10]The relevant laws are Internal Revenue Code § 7605(b); IRS Regulation 601.105; Revenue Procedure 85-13; IRS Policy Statement P-4-3.

CASE HISTORY OF AN INFORMAL AUDIT APPEAL

Mr. Ky, a Vietnamese immigrant and San Francisco restaurant owner, was audited. When he received the Examination Report, Ky was so distraught he considered jumping off the Golden Gate Bridge. Ky had fallen victim to a dishonest tax return preparer who guaranteed his clients they would never have IRS problems. His clients almost always got tax refunds, and he charged a percentage of the refund received.

One day, the office of the bogus "tax advisor" was raided and his records seized by the IRS. All of his clients got audit notices. Ky was understandably suspicious of anyone calling himself a tax expert, so he decided to handle the audit himself. He wanted to come clean knowing he would have to pay some additional taxes.

The auditor knew Ky was selected as part of a special IRS project involving the crooked tax preparer. At the meeting, things went from bad to worse. Ky spoke broken English and produced records written in his native language. The auditor became irritated and impatient.

The Examination Report came quickly, disallowing most of Ky's business deductions and finding a great deal of unreported income. The resulting taxes, with heavy fraud penalties and interest added, came to $79,500. To pay meant Ky would have had to sell his business and lose everything he had worked for in the ten years he had been in America.

Ky finally sought a Tax Pro. During their meeting, the Tax Pro became convinced that Ky should not owe anywhere near $79,500. The Tax Pro called the auditor's manager and made an appointment to meet her in two weeks. He then found a Vietnamese-American accountant to convert Ky's records and notes into a more conventional set of books. The accountant acted as an interpreter and helped the Tax Pro take sworn statements from Vietnamese people who had worked in the restaurant. These books and statements created a true financial picture of the business, in clear English.

When the Tax Pro met with the auditor's manager, he presented the statements and records. In less than an hour they had agreed on a total tax of $13,000 and no harsh fraud penalty. After the tax bill came, Ky negotiated an installment payment agreement with the IRS Collection Division. Ky did not jump off the Golden Gate or any other bridge. His family now owns two restaurants in San Francisco.

I. Serious Audit Problems

Everyone considers being audited to be a problem, however, a few uncommon—yet serious—audit problems merit special discussion.

1. The Auditor Suspects You of Fraud

Tax fraud is covered in Chapter 10.

2. You're Billed for an Audit You Didn't Know About

Many taxpayers receive bills from phantom IRS audits. Yes, the IRS is required to notify you of an audit of your tax return. Theoretically, if the IRS doesn't let you know about an audit, your return can't be audited. In reality, however, the IRS is only required to mail a letter to your last known address. The IRS blithely assumes that notices sent to the address on the tax return selected for audit meets the requirement—even if you filed a later return with a new address.

The Tax Court, however, has said the IRS must update its files regularly and send notices to the address on your most recent tax return or other address that you have provided.[11] The IRS Service Center is allowed three months to process a change of address after it receives notification.

If you don't answer an audit letter and it is not returned to the IRS by the Post Office, the IRS usually proceeds without you. Exemptions and deductions are disallowed in whatever manner the auditor wishes.

TIP   To make sure you get all IRS notices, file IRS Form 8822, Change of Address, whenever you move. (A copy is in the Appendix.) The IRS does not recognize a Post Office change of address form.

The unfairness of the IRS' willingness to go ahead with the audit when you don't get the audit

---

[11] *Abeles v. Commissioner of the Internal Revenue*, 91 U.S.T.C. 1019 (1991).

notice is underscored by what happens next. The IRS usually sends a 30-day letter informing you of your appeal right to your old address. And next out is the Notice of Deficiency giving you 90 days to object in Tax Court. This letter is always sent by certified mail, but the law does not require that you actually receive it—only that the IRS can prove that is was sent. The IRS doesn't seem to care if you get any of these notices. Its position is that as long as the notices were sent to an address in the IRS records, the audit was legitimate. Hardly fair, but you can fight back.

There are three ways to fight a phantom audit.

Audit reconsideration. If you receive a mysterious tax bill, immediately call and write to the Service Center that sent it. State that you never received notice of the audit and you are requesting an audit reconsideration. If you get no response within 30 to 60 days, which is likely, call the Taxpayer Service Representative (800-829-1040) or the Problems Resolution Officer (PRO) at your local IRS office. (See the Appendix for telephone numbers and locations.) Make an appointment with him, or send the notices to him by fax or mail. Ask the PRO to send your file to the Examination Division for an audit reconsideration. This will give you an opportunity to meet with an auditor and have a full hearing, like any other audit.

You do not have a right to an audit reconsideration—it is discretionary with the IRS, so be nice when you ask for it. The IRS also has an audit re-examination procedure which it may grant you. This differs from an audit reconsideration in that a re-examination can open up your entire file for audit—and not just the items that were initially charged in the phantom audit. Again, it is discretionary with the IRS how to handle your request.

Petition the Tax Court. If your reconsideration request is denied, file a Petition to the Tax Court, stating that a Notice of Deficiency was not sent to your last known address as required by law. (See Chapter 5.)

Offer in Compromise. If your reconsideration is rejected and you lose in Tax Court, you can still make a formal Offer in Compromise. This is an offer to pay a small percentage of the amount the IRS

claims is due, based on a doubt as to your liability for the tax bill. (See Chapter 6, Section E.) The IRS may treat your Offer as it would treat an audit reconsideration and reopen your case.

3. Jeopardy Assessments

The IRS has a "shoot first, ask questions later" power to make quick tax assessments against you without an audit. This is called the jeopardy assessment procedure. The tax law normally requires a formal assessment of taxes against you at the IRS Service Center before the IRS can legally collect. The jeopardy assessment process gives the IRS legal authority to immediately grab your assets without notice. You do have a right to a hearing, but not until after the jeopardy assessment is made.

This extraordinary use of power must be personally approved by the local District Director or Director of Foreign Operations. Thankfully, this procedure is used sparingly and only in the following circumstances:

- you appear to be planning to hide out or depart the U.S.

- you are concealing, dissipating or removing property from the country, or transferring it to other persons, or

- your financial solvency is endangered.

Jeopardy assessments are most frequently made against persons arrested with large amounts of cash—especially suspected drug dealers. If you are ever faced with a jeopardy assessment, see a tax lawyer right away.

J. Audits in a Nutshell— Kernels of Wisdom

1. In an audit, you must convince the IRS that you reported all of your income and were entitled to any credits, deductions and exemptions that are questioned.

2. Delaying the audit usually works to your advantage. Request more time whenever you need it to get your records in order or for any other reason.

3. Keep the IRS from holding the audit at your business or home.

4. Give the auditor no more information than she is entitled to, and don't talk any more during the audit than is absolutely necessary.

5. Don't expect to come out of the audit without owing something—the odds are against you.

6. Don't give copies of other years' tax returns to the auditor; if you do and she sees something she doesn't like she will make adjustments in these years too.

7. The IRS must complete an audit within three years of the time the tax return is filed, unless the IRS finds tax fraud or a significant underreporting of income.

8. If you have something to hide, don't provide evidence to the auditor, but don't lie either. The adjustments she may make could be less damaging than if you had given her what she asked for. If in doubt, see a Tax Pro.

9. If the audit is not going well, demand a recess to consult a Tax Pro.

10. Ask to speak to the auditor's manager if you think the auditor is treating you unfairly.

11. Read IRS Publication 1, explaining the Taxpayers' Bill of Rights, prior to your audit.

12. Research tax legal issues by using free IRS publications and commercial tax guides.

13. If you are still unclear about the tax law or how to present your documents to an auditor, consult a Tax Pro before the audit.

14. If you are missing receipts or other documents, you are allowed to reconstruct records.

15. Don't bring to an audit any documents that do not pertain to the year under audit or were not specifically requested by the audit notice.

16. It is possible to negotiate tax issues with the auditor but not the amount of taxes to be paid.

17. If the subject of tax fraud comes up during an audit, don't try to handle it yourself.

18. Field audits are more intensive than office audits. They are used mainly when there is business income; you should consult a Tax Pro before a field audit.

19. When you get the Examination Report, call the auditor if you don't understand or agree with it. Meet with her or her manager to see if you can reach a compromise.

20. If you can't live with an audit result, you may appeal within the IRS or go on to Tax Court.

APPEALING YOUR AUDIT 4

Y ou tried to get the auditor to be reasonable but she just wouldn't see things your way. In fact, you received a costly Examination Report. You spoke to the auditor's manager in an effort to win an informal appeal. Again, you didn't have any luck. You are not ready to give up, though. What's next?

A formal appeal, that's what. The IRS has a single-level administrative procedure for appealing "unagreed" Examination Reports to an IRS Regional Appeals Office. Take advantage of this procedure. Your rights are described in IRS Publication 5, *Appeal Rights and Preparation of Protests for Unagreed Cases.* (A copy is in the Appendix.)

Less than one in ten audited taxpayers appeal. Many more taxpayers should. The procedure is neither difficult nor time consuming, and your chance of achieving at least *some* tax reduction is excellent. And you rarely need to hire a Tax Pro to appeal. Despite this, however, most taxpayers are either too discouraged or intimidated to appeal.

Appeals of other IRS action. In addition to audits, many other IRS decisions may be appealed, as discussed throughout this book.

The Odds of Winning an Appeal

Most auditors privately refer to the Appeals Office as the IRS' "gift shop." There is even an IRS in-joke that appeals officers work on the 50% rule—they like to cut auditor's adjustments by half.

IRS statistics show that the auditors are exaggerating—but not by much. The average appeal results in a 40% decrease in taxes, penalties and interest imposed by the auditor. So, even the IRS confirms that it pays to appeal. The only mystery is why more audit victims don't.

A. Pros and Cons of Appealing an Audit

There are three solid reasons for appealing and two relatively insignificant reasons not to.

PROS

- Appealing is simple and costs nothing unless you use a Tax Pro—which is not required.
- Appealing, in the majority of cases, results in some savings, although rarely a total victory.
- Appealing delays your audit tax bill for months, buying you time to raise the cash.

CONS

- The Appeals Officer can raise issues the auditor missed—but this almost never happens. Nevertheless, if you are afraid that a particular item will be discovered and you'll owe a lot more in taxes, you can skip the appeal altogether and go directly to Tax Court where new issues can't be raised. (See Chapter 5.) You should consult a Tax Pro before skipping the appeal, however. (See Chapter 13.)
- Interest on the tax bill continues to run while you are appealing, but this is a small item as compared with the likely tax savings resulting from most appeals.

B. How to Appeal an Audit

After the audit, the IRS sends an Examination Report with proposed adjustments—additional taxes, penalties and interest. If you don't sign and return a copy of the Report within a few weeks, the IRS usually sends a 30-Day Letter explaining how to protest the Report.

The IRS Can Reject Your Request for an Appeal

The IRS is not legally required to give you an appeals hearing after an audit—and sometimes it doesn't. Instead of a "30-Day Letter" stating your right to appeal, you may get a "90-Day Letter" telling you that the only way to challenge the audit is to file a Petition to the Tax Court. (See Chapter 5.)

If you don't get an appeals hearing and do file a Tax Court Petition, your case will be sent to the Appeals Office anyway—for at least the four-month period following your filing. (Never try to understand the logic of the IRS.) You will probably be offered a hearing at this point, or you can request one. If you don't settle in the Appeals Office, your file will be sent to the District Counsel's Office and assigned to an IRS lawyer.

"Protest" is the official term for appealing an IRS determination. You must protest within 30 days of the date on the appeal notice letter—not the date you received it. As discussed in Chapter 3, Section, H.3, you can appeal informally by arranging a meeting with the auditor's manager. You can try this before, or the same time, you send your protest letter. Meeting informally with the manager does *not* extend the 30-day deadline to file a formal appeal.

If you can't file your protest in the time allowed, you can request an extension for another 30 to 60 days to appeal. Requests are usually granted orally, but don't rely on a phone call. Send a confirmation letter as soon as you hang up the telephone. Don't delay. If the IRS denies your extension, you might lose your chance to appeal.

There is no IRS form for protests—the IRS probably doesn't want to encourage appeals, given that it has forms for everything else. You must write a protest letter—unless the amount contested is less than $2,500. In this situation, an oral request to the auditor is sufficient, but follow it up in writing anyway.

1. Writing the Protest Letter

If the audit bill you are protesting is between $2,500 and $10,000, a simple letter stating you disagree with the Examination Report is all that is technically required. For amounts over $10,000 you must file a more formal written protest containing:

- your name (or names, if husband and wife) and Social Security number(s)
- a statement that you are appealing an Examination Report
- the findings in the Report that you disagree with, including penalties and interest
- a brief explanation why the Report is wrong—although not required, you can attach copies of any documents supporting your explanation
- your signature(s) and date under a penalty of perjury clause, and
- copies of the 30-Day Letter and Examination Report.

Regardless of the amount at stake, I recommend that you file the slightly more detailed written protest. It's not hard to do and helps you focus your objections to the audit report. Send your letter (simple or detailed) to the local IRS District Director, certified mail, return receipt requested. Also send or give a copy to the auditor. Use the address on the Examination Report or the letter accompanying it.

Make the protest letter short and sweet. Stick to the facts and don't criticize the auditor or the IRS—whether justified or not. Blowing off steam may make you feel better but it only detracts from an otherwise valid appeal.

Below is a sample protest (appeal) letter.

This sample letter is a skeleton type of protest letter, giving only the bare bones of your appeal grounds. Some Tax Pros recommend very detailed protests with copies of all documents you want to be considered. This can be difficult to do if you are not a tax expert, so go with the minimal approach. Then either send in the details to the Appeals Officer before the hearing or bring them to the hearing.

Sample Protest (Appeal) Letter

August 15, 1994

District Director
Internal Revenue Service
P.O. Box 44687 (Stop 11)
Indianapolis, IN 46244

PROTEST OF MICK RODRIGUEZ
SSN: 555-55-5555
111 Elm Street
Bloomington, IN 47000

Dear Sir/Madam:

I wish to appeal from the Examination Report of 8/1/94, a copy of which is attached. I request a hearing. The tax years protested are 1991 and 1992.

The adjustments that I disagree with are [fill in something like, "the disallowance of business expense deductions shown on my Schedule C of $12,999, and penalties and interest in the total amount of $848"].

The adjustments were [again fill in your explanation, like "incorrect because the deductions I took were legitimate expenses of my music business, and I was trying to make a profit"].

Under penalty of perjury, I declare that the facts presented in this protest and in any accompanying documents are, to the best of my knowledge and belief, true, correct and complete.

Sincerely,

Mick Rodriguez

Mick Rodriguez

Copy to Auditor
Enclosed: Copy of 30-Day Letter &
          Copy of Examination Report

TIP Consult a Tax Pro if you are unsure about preparing your protest. You can get advice on writing the Protest and preparing your case for the appeals hearing. The Tax Pro can tell you what evidence—documents and statements—the appeals officer will look for. (See Chapter 13.)

2. Requesting the Auditor's File

Under the federal Freedom of Information Act (FOIA), you are entitled to a copy of almost everything in your IRS auditor's file—meaning her notes and workpapers which show how she arrived at her conclusions. There may be nothing new in the file, but you may mine a gold nugget using the FOIA. You never can tell. For instance, the file may contain a Report Transmittal form with confidential information—such as fraud suspected by the auditor or a criminal referral. This matter can legally be edited out of your copy, but if it is, it may be apparent or you may be told that "something" has been kept from you. You can draw your own conclusions.

Certain things, notably the DIF score—the computer score that probably caused the audit in the first place—are protected from disclosure by law. This is no big deal, as the DIF number won't mean anything to you anyway. (DIF scores are covered in Chapter 3, Section B.1.)

To get your IRS file, you must send a separate letter to the FOIA Disclosure Officer at your IRS District Office. (See sample, below.) Ask for copies of your audit file and offer to pay for copying charges. Hand deliver your letter or send it by certified mail, return receipt requested. Enclose a photocopy of your driver's license or birth certificate with your letter.

Allow four weeks or more for a response. If you don't hear from the Disclosure Office, start calling. Technically, the IRS does not have to make copies for you, although it usually will. Instead, you might be told you have to come into the office to look at the file. If the date of the appeals hearing is approaching and you haven't yet received or had a chance to review your file, ask for an extension. If it's granted, send the Appeals Officer a letter confirming the extension.

Sample FOIA Letter

August 15, 1994

District Director/Disclosure Officer
Internal Revenue Service
P.O. Box 44687 (Stop 11)
Indianapolis, IN 46244

FOIA REQUEST OF MICK RODRIGUEZ
SSN: 555-55-5555
111 Elm Street
Bloomington, IN 47000

Dear Sir/Madam:

Under the Privacy Act of 1974, 5
U.S.C. 552A, and the Freedom of
Information Act, 5 U.S.C. 552, I
request a copy of all files relevant
to the audit of my tax return for
years 1991 and 1992.

I agree to pay reasonable charges for
copying the requested documents, up to
$25. If the charges exceed this
amount, please contact me for further
authorization.

If you determine that any portion of
these files are exempt, please
identify the portion claimed exempt
and the specific exemption which
justifies your refusal to release
them.

Sincerely,

Mick Rodriguez

Mick Rodriguez

Appeals Officers Are Negotiators

IRS Appeals Officers are usually senior IRS employees with accounting or legal backgrounds. Many have been promoted up from the ranks of auditors. But, Appeals Officers have only one job—to settle cases. You might think that their work involves raising money for the U.S. Treasury, but that's not the case.

Appeals Officers are trained to be flexible and are given discretion in dealing with taxpayers that auditors don't have. Proof of this lies in IRS statistics showing 70% of appeals cases are settled amicably with taxpayers. Appeals Officers' job performance is judged by their success in compromising with taxpayers—not how often they uphold IRS auditors!

C. How the Appeals Office Works

The IRS Regional Appeals Office is completely separate and independent from the local District Office that handled your audit. It probably won't be in the same city or building. Cases are viewed by Appeals Officers from a fresh perspective—most of the time. (Some are lazy and just rely on work done by auditors, but most review files anew.) Your auditor plays no part in the appeal, other than the fact that her file is before the Appeals Officer. Auditors' files often lack detail or notes, however, which can limit the understanding of the Appeals Officer.

An Appeals Officer is aware of legal precedents on recurring issues, like what kinds of documentation are needed to verify travel and entertainment or home office expenses. This means that unless your case is very unusual, the Appeals Officer will almost surely know how it stacks up legally. What an Appeals Officer usually wants to know are *the facts* of your situation—especially anything which might cause a judge to rule for you if you take the case to Tax Court. Or put bluntly, the Appeals Officer will try to settle with you if, after considering the facts and applying the law, he believes you have *some* chance of winning in court. If you can supply a decent reason to compromise, he will.

IRS and Tax Court Resources Are Not Unlimited

The IRS doesn't want taxpayers going to Tax Court if it can be avoided. It is not a fear of losing so much as a policy of keeping the Court's docket manageable. No one wants your "small potatoes" case to use up any more government resources than is necessary. After all, the same court that will try your case (if it isn't settled) will hear IBM's, Exxon's and GE's IRS problems.

Unlike IRS auditors, Appeals Officers have discretion to weigh the "hazards of litigation." This means they can consider the IRS' chances of losing if an audit is contested in court. In doing this, Appeals Officers know that almost 50% of all taxpayers win at least partial victories by going to Tax Court. Appeals Officers do not have authority, however, to settle cases based on "nuisance" value alone. In other words, they are forbidden to settle just to get rid of you.

Most of the money allocated to the IRS in the federal budget during the last decade has gone into computerization and hiring of collectors. The number of auditors, Appeals Officers and attorneys has hardly grown at all. At the same time, however, the number of tax disputes continues to rise. So again, there is pressure on the Appeals Office to settle with taxpayers.

D. Preparing for an Appeals Hearing

After notifying the IRS of your wish to appeal, you have at least two months—and probably longer—to prepare for the hearing. In some backlogged IRS regions, you may wait a year or more before your appeal is heard. Use this time to review everything you presented to the auditor, to make your Freedom of Information Act request (see Section B.2, above), to get more documents and to check out the tax law.

Start by considering if there are better ways to organize and present your documents than you did at the audit. Audits are frequently lost because the taxpayer's records were not fully presented or understood. Try some creativity—for example, don't limit yourself to printed documents. A musician once presented an audio cassette of his group and a tape player. Although his offer to play the tape was declined, the appeals officer seemed impressed that he brought it. Charts, graphs and drawings are also ways to effectively make your point. Appeals Officers, like everyone else, like to look at photographs. (Remember, a picture is worth a thousand words.) No matter what your case is about—a disputed home office deduction or a chartered sailboat fee you deducted as a business expense—bring a snapshot or two to show the Officer.

Also, make a list of IRS-challenged items. Staple receipts to canceled checks and lists. Write full explanations on separate sheets for each disallowed deduction. Put these items into separate folders or a three-ring binder with dividers. Organize this material with subheads.

Example

Jenny's audit focused on the use of her home as her office. The auditor rejected several of her expense deductions, claiming that they were not related to her business. In preparing for her appeals hearing, Jenny organized her receipts and other supporting documents into the following categories—rent payments, utilities and telephone, cleaning, maintenance and repairs.

If you can't organize the documents yourself, get an accountant or bookkeeper to help you. If you were missing documents at the audit, look harder for them. Get copies of checks from banks and duplicate receipts from businesses you dealt with. You can also reconstruct records of missing documents. (See Chapter 3, Section G.5.)

Statements from people with knowledge about your disallowed expenses also help. For example, if you hired a handyperson to make repairs on your rental property who insisted on being paid in cash and has since left town (and you can't find the receipts for the labor and materials), get a statement from a tenant like the following:

I, Clara Burton, declare that for most of 1992, I was a tenant in an apartment owned by Alexander Woolf, located at 123 Hannah Road, Appleton, Wisconsin.

Early in the spring of 1992 we had a bad storm. The rain caused plaster to fall from the ceiling in my apartment and ruin the carpet. All the damage was repaired by Joe Williams, who did a good job.

I moved out to be closer to my job in November of 1993. I now live at 456 Dover in Appleton, Wisconsin. My phone number is 555-1290.

Under penalty of perjury, I declare that the statements of fact contained in this declaration are, to the best of my knowledge and belief, true, correct and complete.

Dated: _6/20/94_   _Clara Burton_
                              Signature

SAMPLE WITNESS STATEMENT

E. Presenting a Case to an Appeals Officer

Rehearse what you are going to say several times before the meeting. Write an outline of the points you want to make. List the documents and other evidence you want to present. Then try it out by explaining your case to your friends or family. Ask if they understand it clearly. Their responses may direct you to weaknesses that you can work on before the hearing.

A Formal Appeals Hearing May Not Be Necessary to Make a Deal

One of the larger cases I ever settled on appeal I did without ever meeting the Appeals Officer. We had trouble arranging our schedules, so I sent him my research and documentation. After several lengthy telephone conversations, we settled a $250,000 audit bill.

The Appeals Officer conceded that my client was correct and agreed that it would not be in the IRS' best interest to go to Tax Court (where an unfavorable precedent might be set.) The result was a total victory for my client. This was unusual, but if it is very difficult for you to meet with an Appeals Officer, ask if you can have your appeal heard by telephone. If the nearest appeals office is hundreds of miles away, it's worth a try.

You will be shown into a small meeting room or office. Seldom will anyone other than the one Appeals Officer be present. You won't have to face the auditor again, if that worries you. The Appeals Officer won't tape the hearing. You have the right to make an audio recording, but I don't recommend it. Taping might put the Appeals Officer on the defensive and do more harm than good.

Some Appeals Officers sit back and wait for you to present your case, while others run the show by asking you questions. Unless the Appeals Officer directs otherwise, start with a brief statement outlining your case. Here's an example:

I believe that the auditor was incorrect in finding that I was not entitled to claim a part of my apartment as a home office deduction on my tax return in 1992.

I can show that my home office is legitimate by my testimony and with the following documents:

- *floor plan of my apartment showing the space used exclusively for my home office,*

- *business diary showing that I spent more than 50% of my working hours at my home office, and*

- *bills and canceled checks for the expenses I incurred in running my home office.*

After you make your opening comments, show the Appeals Officer the documents that you brought, one at a time. Carefully explain how each receipt or witness statement backs up your case. Tell why some documents are missing and how other proof fills in the gap. Or argue that you are in "substantial compliance" if a few of the needed documents are missing.

If you bring witnesses (usually their statements are all that is needed) ask if they may be allowed to speak first, and then ask the Appeals Officer if they can leave.[1] He may want to question them too, but Appeals Officers don't like to discuss settlement if other people are present. The IRS is not anxious for the word to get around that taxpayers can make deals if they don't like how audits turn out.

As soon as you have presented your case, start negotiating a settlement. Most Appeals Officers wait for you to make the first move. Tax penalties are often knocked out by Appeals Officers if they believe that any tax mistakes you made were honest ones. So your first request might be to have any penalties the auditor proposed removed.

Unless you honestly feel that the auditor was completely wrong, next offer to agree to at least 10% of the adjustments that the auditor made. Remember, talk in terms of *adjustments* not tax dollars. If you can show the Appeals Officer that there is at least a small chance that you would be successful in Tax Court, the Appeals Officer is likely to agree to a settlement.

For example, if the auditor disallowed 80% of the $2,000 you claimed in business entertainment expenses ($1,600), first argue that your records support your position. If the Appeals Officer won't budge, offer to accept a disallowance of 10% ($200) instead. Typically the Officer may come back by offering to meet you halfway, or better, with a 45% ($900) disallowance. This process is an art, not a science. Remember, the definition of a good compromise is both sides accepting less than what they want—so be flexible.

Most settlements are formalized on IRS Form 870, Consent to Proposed Tax Adjustment, which is

prepared by the Appeals Officer. Agreeing does not bar you from changing your mind. If you want, you can later pay the tax bill and sue in a regular federal court for a refund. If you paid first, you give up your right to go to Tax Court. (See Chapter 5, Section D.) Also, under certain limited circumstances, the IRS could reopen the audited year, but this rarely happens.

CASE HISTORY OF AN APPEAL

Mick was a telephone company executive by day and a rock musician by Saturday nights. For 20 years he played in local bands. He had his dreams, but never got close to the Big Time. Mick enjoyed performing and was happy— at least until the IRS entered his life.

In recent years, raises and bonuses allowed Mick to buy new musical gear and a Ford van to haul it. He became more enthusiastic about his music, formed his own group and hired an agent. Following his accountant's advice, Mick reported his musical income and expenses on his tax returns as a sideline business. Mick's business showed net losses in two years. These losses were used to offset Mick's income from his regular job on his tax returns, thereby lowering his total tax bill.

Sideline business and the tax code

A sideline business loss can produce a tax writeoff for Mick as long as the IRS believes that he is trying to make a profit. The tax code provides one test for determining if a profit motive exists—if a business does not make money in at least three of the five past years, it is presumed to be not for a profit and is considered a hobby. Hobby losses cannot be deducted for tax purposes. As it turned out, Mick had made a small profit in two of the last four years he had been reporting musical activities on his tax returns.

While this three-of-five-years legal presumption is not final, it puts the burden on Mick to show he was trying to make a profit. The issue would never arise unless Mick was audited.

Guess what?

Mick was audited. IRS audit classifiers are on the lookout for businesses that show losses. This is especially true if business losses offset income from another job—in effect creating a "tax shelter." The IRS hunts tax shelters like wolves pursue sheep.

---

[1] It is highly unusual to bring witnesses to an Appeals Hearing. For help in deciding whether or not to do so—and for guidance in preparing your witnesses if you decide to bring them—see Chapter 5, Section B.7.a.

The consequence of an auditor not finding a business was really run to make a profit is a disallowance of all expenses in excess of income. For example, if your Amway distributorship brought in $1,000 and you claimed $3,000 in expenses, the IRS could disallow your $2,000 tax loss—unless it was convinced that you were seriously trying to make a profit. In this type of case the IRS has frequently said that the real motive in this type of business was social—entertaining friends and getting home products for personal use. Dabbling in a side business is not good enough.

In the year audited, Mick's music income was only $300 but he claimed $12,300 in business expenses. (Small wonder he was picked for audit.) His largest expenses were the new van and music gear. Under the hobby loss rules, the auditor decided Mick's music expenses were primarily for his personal pleasure, and only incidentally for profit.[2] She disallowed the $12,000 tax loss. This meant added taxes, penalties and interest of $4,500. To make matters worse, she then said she was going to audit two more years and make the same adjustment.

Mick argued that he had worked hard to make a musical career, that he had been getting local jobs, that his band's reputation was on the rise and that one hit record would make him millions and the IRS plenty of taxes. The auditor, apparently not a music fan, was unmoved. A meeting (informal appeal) with her manager did not change things.

Mick got the Examination Report and then a 30-Day Letter to appeal. He decided to appeal—he had clearly been trying to make money in music, even though his efforts had been largely unsuccessful. Mick knew he had enough to show an appeals officer a justification for compromising the audit result.

The legal principle in Mick's favor is that the profit motive, not the actual result, distinguishes a business from a hobby. The intention to make a profit is sufficient under the tax law, even if the probability of financial success is small or remote.[3] At least Mick had some income.

---

[2]Internal Revenue Code § 183.

[3]Dreicer v. Commissioner of the Internal Revenue, 78 U.S.T.C. 642 (1982). See also, Cornfield v. U.S., 797 F.2d 1049 (D.C. Cir. 1986).

Research for Mick's Appeal [4]

The IRS disallowed Mick's deduction of his music equipment as a business loss. The Examination Report said only that the business expense was not established. Mick called the auditor to ask what tax code section she relied on to reach her decision. The answer was IRC § 183.

Mick looked at the Master Federal Tax Manual index under tax code section 183 and "losses," and found the subhead "business." It directed him to a page which defined a business as "a pursuit or occupation carried on for profit, whether or not profit actually results." The guide has an excerpt from a Tax Court case which stated that an activity may be for profit although the investment is not expected to generate profits for several years under the current level of activity. This meant that Mick's musical activities are not disqualified as a business just because he lost money. Mick photocopied this page.

Next he opened J.K. Lasser's Your Income Tax and found more specific information. The index lists "Hobby as a Sideline Business," which leads to the following: "If you show a profit in three or more years the law presumes you are in an activity for profit. The presumption does not necessarily mean that losses will be automatically allowed; the IRS may rebut the presumption." Reading further, Mick saw this as significant because it mentioned tax code § 183 on which the auditor based her decision. Mick made another photocopy.

In two years of his tax returns since claiming his music business, Mick was still using his old equipment. And, he did claim any vehicle expense on his return. The tax result was in year one he showed a profit of $100, and in year two, a $200 profit. In year three, however, Mick bought the van and the new equipment. These purchases caused sizeable losses in years three and four. The appeals hearing took place in year five, for which a tax return was not yet due. So Mick cannot rely on the three-year presumption of profit rule. Mick had only two profitable years.

If Mick's appeal hearing were held after he filed a tax return for year five, it could be prepared in such a way as to show a profit—for example, by not taking the vehicle

---

[4]Researching tax issues is covered in Chapter 13, Section D. Briefly, you have two alternatives—see a Tax Pro or do it yourself. If you're going to do the research yourself, follow the advice from Chapter 13.

and equipment depreciation expense deductions. In this case we could go into the hearing with the benefit of the three year presumption of profit rule—that is, Mick made money in three of the last five years. This fact would give us a position which could be strong enough to give him an outright win.

Mick's Appeal Hearing

After Mick filed his protest requesting an appeal, the IRS set a conference date. Several months later Mick and an Appeals Officer met at the Appeals Office. No one else was present. Mick went directly to the most favorable facts of his case. He showed a contract from a talent booking agent who, in two years, had gotten his group one job. He also presented a flyer and event calendar showing the group had performed in public twice during the audited year. He omitted the fact that one appearance was at a charity benefit where no performers were paid. He also gave the Appeals Officer a publicity photo and his diary showing band rehearsals.

The documents were not strong enough evidence to win his case, but they got Mick "in the door." The goal was to give the Officer justification for compromising, not to win outright. In a half hour, Mick finished presenting the evidence and said, "Let's settle the case. I will accept a 25% disallowance of my losses." In other words, Mick was offering to let the IRS reduce his losses from the $12,000 adjustment the auditor made to $3,000.

The Appeals Officer replied that he was thinking more like a 75% disallowance, from $12,000 to $9,000. Mick was in! The Officer had accepted the possibility that a court might find that Mick was trying to make a profit. They took a break.

After the break, Mick commented on the photo of the Little Leaguer on the Officer's desk. He had a similar picture at home, and Mick and the Appeals Officer talked about their kids awhile. The Officer seemed relieved not to talk taxes for a bit. At 4:30, near IRS quitting time, Mick said that he'd agree to split the difference, and accept a 50% disallowance (from $12,000 to $6,000) of his losses and no penalties.

He also requested the Appeals Officer not to recommend the other two open years for audit. The Officer agreed. While this did not guarantee those years would not be audited—Appeals Officers don't have this authority— their recommendations carry great weight and their

reports are routinely approved. Several weeks later, Mick received a settlement letter.

Mick's case is typical of how IRS appeals are handled— and settled. If Mick hadn't appealed, he would have owed the IRS $4,500, plus he would have been audited for two other years. The potential tax disaster was over $13,000. The settlement made with the Appeals Officer cost Mick about $2,000.

Epilogue

Mick's appeal didn't require great knowledge of tax law. It did involve several hours of preparation as well as a basic understanding of the IRS appeals process. Evidence of Mick's profit intent was shown; a settlement was proposed and negotiated. The great majority of appeal issues—be they home office deductions, entertainment expenses or business auto usage—can be handled successfully in this same manner.

F. Should You Hire a Tax Pro for Your Appeal?

The pros and cons of working with tax professionals (Tax Pros) are outlined in Chapter 13. The information here supplements what is in that chapter.

Most Appeals Officers respect an experienced tax representative. Furthermore, the Officer and Tax Pro may have had prior dealings with each other. A Tax Pro knows what Appeals Officers are looking for and can make their job easier by getting straight to points.

Whether or not you should hire a Tax Pro is often an economic decision. Don't consider hiring a Tax Pro, especially a tax lawyer or CPA, unless you are contesting at least $5,000 in taxes. Depending on the complexity of your case, many Tax Pros will charge upwards of $1,500 for an appeal, although Enrolled Agents may charge less. If you hire a Tax Pro, first ask her how much IRS appeals experience she has had and how the appeals came out.

Hiring a Tax Pro also depends on the intricacy of the case and how comfortable you are at arguing and negotiating. For example, if you lost your audit because of inadequate records and you have since located or reconstructed them, going ahead on your own may make great sense. If your case seems to turn on a point of law, however, such as whether or not your business is subject to employment tax reporting, having professional help may be the better approach.

 A pre-appeals consultation with a Tax Pro is a good idea—even if you do the appeal yourself.

Types of Cases Appeals Officers Won't Hear

There are certain issues that the IRS appeals officers are prohibited from hearing under IRS policy. These issues center on refusals to comply with the tax laws based on moral, political, Constitutional, religious and similar grounds. The issues are often raised by what the IRS terms "tax protestors." A word to the wise: If you fit into this category, think long and hard about what you are doing. Get good professional advice before getting in over your head with the federal government. The arm of the law is indeed long.

G. If You Don't Settle on Appeal

If you and the Appeals Officer haven't reached a settlement by the end of your conference, maybe he needs further convincing. Ask him directly what else you can provide to change his mind. He may reply that he needs further documentation or supporting legal precedent. Then, ask for time to get this together and sent to him, before his decision becomes final. Do everything possible to get him what he needs. If in doubt how to do this, see a Tax Pro.

If you don't reach a settlement, you will receive in the mail a written notice of denial of your appeal. With the letter comes a Notice of Deficiency advising you of your right to file a Petition to Tax Court within 90 days. If you ignore the notice, after 90 days the proposed taxes, penalties and interest will become final. Then, you'll get a tax bill from the IRS Service Center several months later.

If you want to keep up the fight, see Chapter 5, on going to tax court.

H. Appeals in a Nutshell— Kernels of Wisdom

1. The IRS usually allows you to appeal its decisions to the IRS Appeals Office.

2. Appeals are often successful in reducing liabilities, but seldom are auditors totally reversed.

3. Many appeal issues are simple enough for you to handle without hiring a Tax Pro, but a consultation with one is a good idea.

4. Start an appeal by writing a protest letter and sending it to the local IRS District Director.

5. Collection of your tax bill is delayed for many months when you appeal.

6. When you appeal, make a Freedom of Information Act request for the auditor's records.

7. The IRS Appeals Office is independent from the IRS audit department and wants to settle to keep you from going to Tax Court.

8. To get a settlement, you must show the Appeals Officer that you would have some chance of winning if you went to court.

9. Negotiate tax issues, not tax dollars, in an appeal.

10. Prepare for an appeals hearing by careful record organization and basic tax law research. I suggest that you consult a Tax Pro.

11. If you don't appeal or don't win your appeal, you can go to Tax Court.

GOING TO TAX COURT: NO LAWYER NECESSARY

5

Y ou lost your audit and were not able to reach a settlement with the IRS on appeal. What's your next option? You have two choices—you can accept your fate or you can go to Tax Court.

According to the IRS, 15% of all taxpayers who appeal an audit—over 30,000 taxpayers per year—file a Petition in Tax Court after losing their appeals. Taking your case on to Tax Court is usually not difficult and in many cases can be done without a lawyer. And your chance of winning—at least partially reducing an audit bill—is excellent. Once you file a Petition in Tax Court, the IRS knows you mean business and will often compromise with you for less than the tax claimed due. Over 80% of Tax Court cases filed settle before trial!

Technically, it is not necessary to have appealed within the IRS before going to Tax Court, but it's a good idea. Remember—the job of the Appeals Office is to settle. Also, you can file a Petition in Tax Court to do more than just protest an audit. You can also contest an automated (mail) adjustment notice you receive from an IRS Service Center. (See Chapter 3, Section C.4.)

And even if the IRS doesn't settle before going to court, you have a good chance of having your tax liability reduced once you talk to a judge. More than 50% of all petitions filed in Tax Court bring *some* tax reduction. In cases under $10,000 (called Small Cases), 47% of all taxpayers win at least partial victories. In cases over $10,000 (called Regular Cases), 60% come out ahead. Of course, Tax Court isn't a total panacea—the chance of a complete victory over the IRS is only 5%.

Filing a Petition in Tax Court also buys time. Just filing will delay an audit bill for at least a year. You can use this time to get your finances in order without worrying that the tax collector will seize your assets.

There is a minor drawback in filing a Petition in Tax Court—interest, and sometimes penalties on the taxes you owe, accrues until your case is finally concluded. The only way to stop the clock is to deposit with the IRS the taxes the agency claims you owe. You do this by sending a check for the amount you owe. You designate the money as a "deposit," not a payment of the audit bill, and write "deposit" both

on the check and in a letter accompanying the check. If you win, your money is returned.

When Not to Go to Tax Court

You can be fined for filing a Petition to Tax Court without legal grounds. This is not normally something to worry about, however. You can almost always find a legitimate reason for disagreeing with an audit report. Only by filing a Petition that is clearly frivolous or done for the sole purpose of delay do you risk a fine.

In addition, if you file a tax-protester type of petition, you may get coded into the IRS computer system in the same category as "dangerous and potentially violent" taxpayers. In "IRS computerese," these people are called PDTs. While people who refuse to pay taxes in protest of government policy or because they don't believe the tax system is Constitutional are regularly fined for filing frivolous petitions, hardly anyone else is.

So don't let the fear of a fine keep you from going to Tax Court unless you are tax protester or are being foolish—like the man who deducted the costs of keeping a mistress as a business expense on the theory that she made him more "productive."

A. Tax Court Facts

In large states, Tax Court hearings are held monthly throughout the year (except summer) in major cities. In small states, the Tax Court may meet only once or twice a year for a week or two in the state's largest city. Sessions are usually held at the local federal building. (The cities in which the Tax Court sits are listed in the Appendix.)

The President appoints Tax Court judges for 12-year terms. Judges are lawyers and come from senior IRS legal staffs and, to a lesser extent, from private law firms. Special (temporary) judges also regularly serve as Small Case judges. Although many Tax Court judges are ex-IRS employees, they are not especially pro-IRS. They do not like to see the IRS cut corners in audits or mistreat taxpayers. Tax Court is completely independent from the IRS. You will get as fair and impartial a hearing in Tax Court as you would in any other federal court.

After you file your Petition, it will be at least six months until you are called for trial. While most Small Cases (see immediately below) are decided within one year, Regular Cases take much longer. In 1993, the Tax Court had a backlog of 30,000 cases—it moves rather slowly.

B. Small Tax Cases—People's Court

There is a small case division of the Tax Court, designed for cases in which the IRS claims that amount of taxes and penalties owed *for any one tax year* is $10,000 or less. If you've been audited for three years and the amount the IRS claims you owe for each year is $10,000—meaning the total is $30,000—your case will still qualify for the small case division. A case that qualifies for the small claims court-type handling is called a Small Case and is given an "S" designation.

You must specifically elect to be treated as an "S" case. This election is automatically made as part of the Tax Court Petition. (A copy of the Petition is in the Appendix.) The filing fee for "S" cases is currently $60, and normally you'll have no further court costs. No jury trials are allowed in Tax Court. Judges can rule on the spot, although they usually

mail their rulings to you. You cannot appeal the decision in an "S" case.

With "S" cases, Tax Court operates much like a small claims court. It's a lot like "People's Court" without the TV cameras—you simply tell the judge your story, show your evidence and are not expected to know legal procedures. Even if you lose, you have the satisfaction of knowing that you had your day in court.

1. Preparing and Filing a Small Case Petition

The Appendix contains a blank Tax Court Petition, a Designation of Place of Trial and an Election of Small Tax Case Procedure and Preparation of Petitions booklet. Call the Clerk of the Tax Court (202-606-8754) and ask for a current set of forms.[1] Unlike many other government departments, the Tax Court office is very responsive and efficient. There is no charge for these items, which will be sent promptly. Keep in mind, however, that you have only 90 days after receiving the Notice of Deficiency to file your Petition. Don't wait until day 83 before contacting the Clerk. If you don't have time to get a current Petition, see a Tax Pro or use the one in the Appendix. The Tax Court will most likely accept an out of date Petition form, but it won't accept a late filing.

2. Completing the Tax Court Forms

First, read the Election of Small Tax Case Procedure and Preparation of Petitions booklet in the Appendix. Also, look at the completed sample Petition, below. Next, make several photocopies of the Petition and Designation of Place of Trial before you begin in the event you mess up any of the forms.

Below are a completed sample Petition and line-by-line instructions. (Completing the Designation of Place of Trial is self-explanatory.) Don't worry if you make minor errors—the Tax Court will usually over-

---

[1] If you want to write to the clerk, the address is Clerk, U. S. Tax Court, 400 Second St., NW, Washington, DC 20217.

look them. Type your Petition and Designation of Place of Trial if possible. Printing by hand is allowed, but unclear handwriting invites misinterpretations.

Top. Type your name. If a joint tax return was audited, type in your name and your spouse's name exactly as they appear on the tax return.

1. In the first blank, type in all years in which adjustments were made. In the next blank, enter the date that appears in the upper right-hand portion of the Notice of Deficiency (90-Day Letter). In the third blank, enter the city and state from which the IRS sent you the Notice of Deficiency. That information is on the front of the IRS notice.

2. Type your Social Security number. If a joint tax return was audited, type your spouse's number as well.

3. In the first column, type in the years you are contesting. You will normally want to contest all years in which adjustments were made. In the second column, list the exact amount of the tax that you are disputing for the corresponding year. This need not be the entire amount of the adjustment made by the IRS. For example, if the adjustment includes tax on $120 of interest from Xavier Bank that you forgot to report, you wouldn't contest that part.

   In the third column, list the penalty which you are disputing for the corresponding year. This amount will be separately listed in the Notice of Deficiency, marked "penalty" or "addition to tax." You will want to contest all penalties, even if you admit that you owe the tax or portion of the tax (such as the tax on the $120 of unreported interest income) found during the audit.

   The fourth column applies only if you are seeking a refund for an overpayment of taxes for the corresponding audited year, which is unlikely to be the case. For example, if you found additional deductions before your audit, raised them with the auditor and had them rejected, you will want to request your refund in Tax Court. You will have to recalculate income tax liability for the year and type in your requested refund. You may want to have your tax preparer help you come up with this figure.

4. Specify the findings in the Examination Report with which you disagree—don't automatically contest everything. For example, you wouldn't list the $120 of unreported interest income from Xavier Bank.

   TIP In "S" cases, don't be overly concerned with using precise legal terms. The Tax Court doesn't expect you to sound like a tax lawyer. Just make sure your point is clear. For instance, it's enough to say: "I disagree with the $1,200 deduction disallowed by the IRS. I incurred this expense as the rent I pay on the portion of my apartment I use for my home office." The form also asks you to state why you disagree with the adjustments, but this isn't really necessary.

   Bottom. Sign and date the Petition. If a joint tax return was audited, both spouses must sign and date. Also, type your address and phone number.

   After you prepare the Petition, fill out the separate Designation of Place of Trial form. A list of cities in which Tax Court trials take place is found on pages 4 and 5 of the Small Tax Case Procedure and Preparation of Petitions booklet in the Appendix. Type your name (your spouse's as well if a joint tax return was audited) and the city which hears cases nearest you. Then sign and date the form. Again, both spouses must sign if a joint return was audited.

3. Filing the Tax Court Forms

The following information is accurate as of January 1994, and the IRS has not announced any proposed changes. To be safe, however, call or write the Clerk of the U.S. Tax Court (address and phone number are in Section 1, above), to verify this information.

- Make five photocopies of the following forms:
   - ✓ Completed Petition
   - ✓ Completed Designation of Place of Trial
   - ✓ Notice of Deficiency (90-Day Letter) you received from the IRS.

- Put aside one photocopy each of the Petition, Designation of Place of Trial and Notice of Deficiency for your own records.

UNITED STATES TAX COURT

(FIRST)   (MIDDLE)   (LAST)

Andrew & Malia   Lawrence

(PLEASE TYPE OR PRINT)   Petitioner(s)

V.

COMMISSIONER OF INTERNAL REVENUE

Respondent   Docket No.

PETITION

1. Petitioner(s) disagree(s) with the tax deficiency(ies) for the year(s) __1989, 1990__
as set forth in the NOTICE OF DEFICIENCY dated __September 17, 1992__, A COPY OF WHICH
IS ATTACHED. The notice was issued by the Office of the Internal Revenue Service at
__Austin, Texas__

(CITY AND STATE)

2. Petitioner(s) taxpayer identification (e.g. social security) number(s) is (are)
555-12-3456; 555-56-7890

3. Petitioner(s) dispute(s) the following:

Year	Amount of Deficiency Disputed	Addition to Tax (Penalty) if any, Disputed	Amount of Over-payment Claimed
1989	$2,766	$632	
1990	$ 517	$109	

4. Set forth those adjustments. i.e. changes, in the NOTICE OF DEFICIENCY with which you disagree and why you disagree.

For 1989, we disagree with the disallowance of $1,710 in expense against Andrew's

royalty income. As a writer, Andrew incurs significant travel expenses to research

and promote his books. For 1990, we disagree with the disallowance of our $325

donation to the Church of Questionability as a charitable contribution. The Church of

Questionability is a legitimate religion with a 501(c)(3) non-profit corporation status.

Petitioner(s) request(s) that this case be conducted under the "small tax case" procedures to provide the taxpayer(s) with an informal, prompt, and inexpensive hearing. A decision in a "small tax case" is final and cannot be appealed to a Court of Appeals by the Internal Revenue Service or the Petitioner(s). If you do not want this case conducted as a "small tax case" place an "X" in the following box.

Andrew Lawrence   10/4/92   33678 Johnson Drive
SIGNATURE OF PETITIONER   DATE   (PRINT) PRESENT ADDRESS-STREET

Austin,   Texas   78700   (512) 555-6629
CITY   STATE   ZIP CODE   AREA CODE TELEPHONE NO.

Malia Lawrence   10/4/92   Same as above
SIGNATURE OF PETITIONER (SPOUSE)   DATE   (PRINT) PRESENT ADDRESS-STREET
(IF NAMED IN A NOTICE OF DEFICIENCY)

CITY   STATE   ZIP CODE   (   ) AREA CODE TELEPHONE NO.

SIGNATURE, NAME, ADDRESS, TELEPHONE NO., AND TAX COURT BAR NUMBER OF COUNSEL, IF RETAINED BY PETITIONER(S)

☆ U.S. GOVERNMENT PRINTING OFFICE 1992-321-839   T.C. FORM 2 (REV 4/92)

SAMPLE TAX COURT PETITION

- Attach the original Notice of Deficiency to the original Petition, and attach the four remaining copies of the Notice of Deficiency to the four remaining copies of the Petition.

- Make out a check or money order for $60 payable to "Clerk, U.S. Tax Court."

- Enclose the original and four copies of the Petition and the Notice of Deficiency, the original and four copies of the Designation of Place of Trial, and your check or money order in a large envelope. Send to Clerk, U.S. Tax Court, 400 Second St., NW, Washington, DC 20217, by U.S. mail—certified and return receipt requested, or by Express Mail—the U.S. Post Office's overnight mail service. Do not use a private delivery service such as UPS.

To timely and legally file your Petition to the Tax Court, the envelope must bear a U.S. mail postmark and must be dated within 90 days of the date on the Notice of Deficiency. If it arrives after day 90, that's okay as long as the postmark is within 90 days. And bear in mind that 90 days does not mean three calendar months.

Within seven days of receiving your Petition, the Tax Court will send you a confirmation of receipt and assign you a case number. If you ever write to or call the IRS or the Tax Court about your case, you will have to refer to your case number. You don't need to do anything else now, unless the IRS files and sends you a written response, called an Answer, stating that you committed fraud. In this (highly unlikely) event, you must file a legal paper called a Reply. You should consult a tax attorney before filing a Reply.

4. Meeting With the IRS Before Your Court Hearing

During the four-month period after you file your Petition, your case may be sent to the IRS Appeals Office. If you haven't met with an Appeals Officer, you may now. (See Chapter 4 on handling an audit appeal.) The Appeals Office wants to keep the IRS out of court if possible, and thus has an incentive to try to settle your case. (If you already had an appeals conference and weren't able to settle, your case may

go directly to the IRS attorney who will represent the IRS in Tax Court.)

If you don't settle now with the Appeals Officer, your case will be sent to the IRS District Counsel's office. You will receive a notice from the court of your trial date and location.

Before the trial, the IRS attorney may ask you to come to her office to discuss the evidence that both sides plan on presenting in court. Bring copies of the documents and declarations that you plan to use to prove your case and show them to the lawyer. She'll do the same. If you plan on bringing witnesses to court, you must provide the attorney with their names. She must do likewise. You don't need to worry about anything going wrong at this meeting. The IRS attorney won't raise new issues or try to trap you into saying something harmful to your case.

TIP This is another chance to compromise without trial. You and the IRS lawyer can settle your case at any time—up to, during and even after the trial—as long as the judge has not rendered a decision. Present your case to the lawyer just as you did with the Appeals Officer. If you have new information or documents, show her. Carefully review Chapter 4, Section E, before going to the meeting.

5. Settlement Before Trial Is Likely

Most cases settle before the trial. It is not unusual for an IRS lawyer to initially turn down a settlement and later change her stance. She may have reviewed the case and decided you have a better chance to win than first thought. Or, the lawyer might find that an IRS witness is not available or an IRS document has been lost, and that her case is weaker than first believed.

If you agree to a settlement, the IRS District Counsel's Office will prepare a document called a Stipulated Tax Court Decision. This paper is signed by you, the IRS attorney and the Judge. Signing means you don't have to appear in court. You may not understand what you are signing fully, as it is a fairly technical document. If you don't understand it, ask to have it explained, or have it reviewed by a Tax Pro before you sign it.

6.   Stipulations for Tax Court

If you don't settle before the trial, the IRS lawyer may ask you to agree in writing to certain undisputed facts about your case. Then the IRS lawyer prepares a court document called a Stipulation of Facts. Tax Court rules require both sides to agree (stipulate) to as many facts as possible before coming to court. The purpose is to save the judge's time. Any facts not agreed to in a written stipulation must be proven in court. Judges get upset if you have refused to agree to obvious facts.

Written stipulations cover routine things like identification of your tax return, the fact that the signatures on various documents are yours and that your bank or other records are genuine and are accurate reflections of your deposits and withdrawals. If there are items in the stipulation that you don't agree with, ask the IRS lawyer to delete them. Or, see a Tax Pro before you sign.

7.   Preparing Your Case for Trial

By now, you should have the facts of your case down cold. You may have already told your story to an auditor, her manager, the Appeals Officer and the IRS lawyer. But Tax Court is a whole new ballgame. You are not limited by what went on with the IRS before you came to court. You are given a "de novo" (brand new) hearing.

Begin preparing for Tax Court several months before your trial date. Make an outline of what you want to prove and a list of your documentary evidence backing up each point. While you're preparing, keep in mind that you have the legal burden of proving your case. This simply means that you must convince the judge that the IRS is wrong—the IRS doesn't have to prove it is right.

A. YOUR TRIAL NOTEBOOK

One way to arrange your materials is in a "trial notebook"—a three-ring binder or a series of files. After you've gathered it all together, practice your presentation in front of family or friends. Be sure that you are making your points clearly and your documents are understandable. Rehearsing gives you confidence in court.

Your trial notebook should contain the following:

Opening statement. The first item in your notebook should be an opening statement, which you will make at the beginning of the trial. This is your summary of what the case is about and an outline of what you intend to show the judge to prove that you are right and the IRS is wrong. It should be brief and to the point. Tell it to the judge as if you were speaking to a friend. Here are two samples:

> *Your Honor, the IRS auditor found that I was not serious about making money in my side business of an Amway home products distributorship in 1992. She said that the presentations I made in my home were really social gatherings and she therefore disallowed my $2,492 in losses. I will show the court that I always had a profit motive and that I operated in a business-like manner, even though my business showed a loss in 1992.*

> *Your Honor, the Examination Report is incorrect in finding that I was not entitled to take my two children, Tammy and Jimmy, as exemptions on my 1993 tax return.*

> *I will testify that the children lived with me for the greater part of 1993. I will show the court copies of school records showing that the children were in school next door to my home, and that my address was their home address. I will present canceled checks showing that I paid for their clothing, medical care and other needs in 1993. My next door neighbor, Corrine Busybody, will testify that the children were living with me.*

Your testimony. Anytime you speak to the judge, you will be "testifying." Before going to court, you will want to summarize the testimony you will give. For example, in proving that you tried to make a profit with your Amway distribution, you might write as follows:

> *I first started selling Amway products in 1988. In the first two years, I made small profits. In my home presentations, I strictly followed the guidelines given*

to me by Amway. Although the business lost money, I did make sales at the February, May, June and October presentations.

Evidence. Lucky for you, "rules of evidence" don't apply in Small tax cases. You can forget all about the TV lawyers who are forever objecting on the grounds of "hearsay," "relevancy" and other similar legalese. Small Case judges want to get to the bottom of the dispute and will generally consider anything you want to show them, regardless of legal technicalities.

It's helpful to arrange your papers in your trial notebook in the order you want to show them to the judge. Insert the originals and two sets of copies, one to give the court and one for the IRS attorney.

The most common evidentiary documents are canceled checks, receipts, bills, photographs, tax returns and witness statements. (A sample witness statement is in Chapter 4, Section D.) But be creative. Bring anything of relevance. Continuing with the Amway example, to show your profit motive, you might prepare to bring to Tax Court the following evidence:

* Schedule C (Business Income and Expense Form) of your 1988 and 1989 tax returns showing your profit for those years
* the Amway home presentation guidelines
* a videotape your husband made of one of your presentations, and
* records of sales made at the presentations.

Witnesses. Most Small tax cases require the oral testimony of only one person, you. Written witness statements (declarations or affidavits) are usually satisfactory to the judge instead of bringing witnesses to court. In some cases, however, live witnesses can be quite helpful. If you're going to bring people to court to testify, list their names in your trial notebook. Next to each name, summarize what the witness will say.

In preparing for the trial, review with each witness what she plans to tell the judge. For example, to bolster your claim that you tried to make a profit in your Amway side business, ask your neighbor and friend Scarlet to testify. Scarlet should be prepared to state that she attended Amway parties at your home, that they were business-like with only slight social overtones, that she bought some of the products and that you stored your Amway inventory in a special room in your house.

Written Statements or Live Witnesses?

In deciding whether to use live witnesses or their written statements, consider the following:

Persuasiveness. A person whose testimony will be extremely supportive of your position—such as a stranger (a friend of a friend) who attended your Amway presentation and thus has no motive to lie — should testify in person if possible. She is likely to be much more persuasive in person than on paper.

Convenience. Don't seriously inconvenience someone and require her to be present. For instance, if someone who attended your Amway presentation is an airline pilot who is scheduled to be 40,000 feet above ground when your case is heard, her written statement will be sufficient.

Cost. Some witnesses are expensive to bring to court. For example, suppose your Tax Court hearing will focus on work done on rental property you own and deducted as a repair. The IRS disallowed the deduction, saying that it was an improvement that has to be deducted over its expected useful life, in this case five years. You want to bring to court the contractor who did the work, and have him testify that your rental property was in need of serious repair. Remember that you must pay witness fees, often by the hour. If his hourly rate is high, and he must sit in the hall for a while awaiting his turn to testify, his fee will add up. You could just bring his statement in declaration or affidavit form.

Harm. If you're concerned that your witness might say something harmful to your case, then just provide her statement. Remember, the IRS attorney will get to ask her questions in court.

If you are not sure a witness will show up or she needs an official court paper to get off from work, you can get an order for her appearance—called a subpoena. You can get a subpoena from the Tax Court clerk in Washington. (Address and phone number are in Section B.1, above.) Be sure to make your request at least two weeks before the trial. You can also get one at the last minute from the local Tax Court clerk once your trial session has begun.

The subpoena must be "served" on—meaning given to—the witness. Because there are strict rules of what constitutes "proper" service, this is best done by the U.S. Marshall's office in your IRS district. Anyone over 18 and not a party to the case, however, can serve the subpoena. By law, you or your spouse can't do it. You must also give the witness money to cover her "witness fee" and mileage for the distance from her house to the Tax Court. Ask the clerk for the current witness fee and mileage rate when you request the subpoena.

Legal authority. If legal research is necessary to prove your case, include in your notebook copies of cases or other legal authority you or your Tax Pro found to support your case. (See Chapter 13 for information on doing legal research.) Many Tax Court cases are factual, rather than legal disputes, so legal research won't be necessary.

Closing statement. The last item to include in your trial notebook is your closing statement. This is the "summing up" presentation you will want to make at the end of the trial. Like the opening statement, it should be brief and to the point. Here's a sample:

Your Honor, you have heard the evidence and can understand why I disagree with the IRS. I do not believe I owe the government any amount of money as a result of the audit or my tax returns for 1990 and 1991.

I explained how I have tried to make money in the music business for many years. I showed the court my receipts and canceled checks for all of my music expenses. I showed flyers I had printed to promote my appearances. I presented the declaration of my booking agent, Irving R. Schwartz, stating that he made valiant efforts to get me into more nightclubs.

It should be clear to your honor that I always had a profit motive. I operated in a business-like manner, and not as a hobby, as the IRS contends. Therefore, my business losses should have been allowed by the auditor, and I should owe no additional taxes for 1990 and 1991.

Thank you for hearing my case.

TIP Show your trial notebook to the IRS attorney whenever you meet to discuss your case. If it is well organized and shows that you are serious about your Tax Court case, there is a good chance the IRS attorney will offer you a settlement.

B. YOUR FIRST DAY IN COURT

On the date that you're scheduled to have your trial, show up in court on time. You'll probably see lots of other petitioners in the court room. The court clerk will take roll call. When your name is called, respond that you are present.

The clerk or judge may assign you another date and time to come back for your actual court trial, usually in that week or the next one. Or you may be put on telephone notice—told to call in or expect to receive a phone message giving you the precise date and time of your hearing. If the date is impossible for you or your witnesses, ask the judge to change it. Your request may not be granted, but most judges are understanding.

If you live far from the Tax Court trial city, call the court clerk or IRS lawyer before your trial day. Ask for permission to not come to court until the day your case will actually be heard. Whether or not you will be granted this request depends on the policy of the judge assigned your case. Again, most judges try to be accommodating so it doesn't hurt to ask. You might also make the request if you will have a hard time getting more than one day off work.

C. YOUR TRIAL DAY

On the day of your actual trial, don't put on fancy clothes or airs. Be yourself. If possible, come early and watch another Small Case trial. You probably won't learn anything helpful to your case, but the experience should put you at ease. If you and your spouse were audited for a joint return, only one of you is required to attend the trial. It makes a better impression on the judge when both of you show up, however.

Should You Bring a Tax Pro to Court?

If you get cold feet at the last minute, you can bring a representative (Tax Pro) to court with you. The Tax Pro usually must be a lawyer—but you can also bring an Enrolled Agent or CPA who is admitted to practice before the Tax Court. (See Chapter 13.) If your Tax Pro is not allowed to practice in Tax Court, she may nevertheless sit with you and advise you during the trial with the permission of the judge. She just cannot speak directly to the judge on your behalf.

Again, representatives are not necessary in most Small tax cases, although you might want to consult with one before trial.

Court sessions are held during normal business hours—no evenings or weekends. Most Tax Court proceedings take place in a city's Federal Building. But because the Tax Court has only a few permanent facilities outside Washington, DC, the room won't necessarily be a courtroom, and may not even be in a courthouse.

The judge will sit on his wooden throne (the bench) or at the end of a conference table. It's hard to generalize about Tax Court judges—each is an individual. Most are patient and will give you all the time you need. Judges are assigned randomly and there is no way you can pick a particular judge, or request a different one once he's assigned. It's doubtful you'd ever know a Tax Court judge anyway, unless you live in the Washington, DC area. Address the judge as "your honor" or "judge."

Also present will be the judge's clerk, a court reporter (stenographer) and the IRS lawyer. The clerk will call your name. Simply answer that you are present and ready for trial.

If you're not ready for the trial, ask that your case be "continued" (postponed). But you must have a very, very good reason, or your request will be denied. A very good reason is a serious illness, a death in the family, a fire that destroyed your records or an accident involving a crucial witness on his way to court. Any lesser excuse won't do. The judge came from Washington, DC to hear your case and he wants to hear it, come hell or high water.

Once your case is called for trial, you will be summoned forward to sit at one of the two tables in front of the judge (or at a large conference table). The IRS lawyer will probably already be ensconced at one of the tables, so finding your spot won't be difficult. Bring your trial notebook and all papers with you. If you have witnesses, bring them with you to the table or have them sit nearby and tell the judge that they will be testifying; then introduce them.

Although Tax Court trials are open to the public, few spectators attend. You can bring friends and loved ones for support, but they cannot sit with you at your table unless you have permission from the judge. Rarely are Tax Court trials publicized. They are far removed from the drama of "L.A. Law."

Courtroom Tips

Keep in mind the following while you are in Tax Court:

- Stand when you speak, unless you are sitting at a conference table with the judge close by or the judge tells you to remain seated.

- Don't read your statements to the judge. Reading is artificial and boring. Just speak in your own words.

- Be as brief as possible, but fully explain yourself.

- Be polite. Never interrupt the judge or the IRS lawyer.

- Be well organized. Don't fumble with your papers.

The judge will not know much about your case before your trial begins. He will have before him only your Petition, the IRS' Answer (if any) and Stipulation of Facts (if any). *The judge doesn't work for the IRS and won't have IRS files, or anything that you submitted to the auditor or Appeals Officer.* This means you must start from scratch in educating the judge about your case.

To begin the trial, the judge will put you and your witnesses (if any) under oath to tell the truth. You will then be asked to present your evidence.

Ask the judge for permission to give a brief "opening statement." It's rare that the judge will deny your request. Your opening statement should be the first item in your trial notebook. Try not to read it word for word—you'll appear stiff and unbelievable.

Next, tell the judge your full story and show your evidence. When you present your documents, give one copy to the judge and one copy to the IRS attorney. You won't get these documents back, so don't give the judge your originals. (The judge may want to see the originals to compare them to the copies, however, which is why you should bring the originals to court.) Also give the judge copies of the legal authority (if any) you have in your trial notebook.

After you give your documents and legal authority to the judge, you will want your witnesses

to testify. To get their story, you must ask them questions. In the example of the Amway distributor whose losses were not allowed by the IRS, here are the questions to ask Scarlet, the neighbor and friend:

Are you familiar with my Amway business?

Did you come to my home for presentations?

How were those presentations conducted?

How many other people were present?

Were you a customer in 1992?

How many times have you bought Amway products from me?

Did other people buy products at the presentations you attended?

Have you seen where the products are stored in my house?

Do you know if I have a home office?

After you and the IRS have presented your documents, testimony and witnesses, you can sum up your case. Now is the time to present your closing statement, the last item in your trial notebook.

The typical Small Case trial lasts less than two hours, although you will be given more time if you need it. Try not to be nervous. The judge doesn't expect you to be a lawyer or tax law expert.

8. Awaiting the Judge's Decision

While the judge may announce a decision at the end of your trial, don't count on it. Usually, you'll get a ruling in the mail about a month or two after the trial. Many judges don't like to state their decisions in court to avoid debates with sore losers.

Judge's rulings don't usually explain why you won or lost in Small Cases. Unlike Judge Wapner's court, seldom are detailed explanations given in Small Case decisions. Futhermore, the decisions won't show the exact amount you owe the IRS.

9. The Tax Bill

Assuming you owe something, you will get a tax bill after the judge makes a decision.

Interest is not calculated by the judge, but will be added to a bill sent to you several months later from the Service Center. You don't need to pay right away. There is no right to appeal from a Small Case decision. Win or lose, the audit game is over.

C. Regular Tax Court Cases—Over $10,000 at Stake

If the taxes and penalties from an audit total over $10,000 *for any one audited year*, your case is called a Regular Case. This means that you will not qualify for the simplified Small Case procedures. Usually you should not represent yourself in a Regular Case, but it still might be possible.

Like an "S" case, one judge hears the testimony and takes the evidence. But, the normal procedure calls for the judge to take your case back to the headquarters of the Tax Court in Washington, DC where the judge presents it to all of the 22 other Tax Court judges for consideration and decision. You and the IRS attorneys must submit formal legal briefs, which are usually anything but brief. They are very detailed and technical in nature, and require the hand of (an expensive) tax attorney. Briefs recite evidence, supporting legal theories and tax law precedents.

In two situations, it might make sense for you to handle a dispute of over $10,000 before the U.S. Tax Court without a tax attorney.

1. Bench Decision

As an alternative to the (believe me) horrendous procedure of brief writing, you may request that the judge issue a "bench" opinion or decision in a Regular Case. This means that you want your over-$10,000 case to be treated pretty much like a Small Case (no briefs and only one judge decides). Disposing with briefs is discretionary with the judge

hearing a Regular Case. He will grant your request only if he is satisfied that the facts and legal principles are clear. Many judges grant this request because it saves the court work. If the IRS objects, however, the judge is not likely to issue a bench decision. If your request is rejected and you don't submit a written brief, you are not likely to win.

2. Not Contesting Amounts Over $10,000

If your audit bill is over the $10,000 threshold for Small cases, you may still be able to fit into the "S" category. The catch is that you must agree to give up (waive) your right to contest any amount over the $10,000. For example, if the IRS claims you owe $12,000 for 1992 and $9,500 for 1993, you can proceed as a Small Case if you contest only $10,000 in 1992 (giving up $2,000). You can, of course, contest all $9,500 for 1993.

D. Still Other Courts—Big Bucks and Lawyers Only

Instead of going to Tax Court, you have the option a taking your tax dispute to a U.S. District Court (there is one in a big city near you) or the U.S. Court of Federal Claims in Washington, DC. Like cases over $10,000 in Tax Court, you will need to know tax law, legal procedures and the rules of evidence. Only an attorney can represent you here (no CPAs or Enrolled Agents), but you can represent yourself. I highly recommend against self-representation in these two courts.

Only 5% of all tax disputes come to a District Court or the Court of Federal Claims. Unlike Tax Court, you must pay the tax before suing here. Then you must file IRS Form 843, Claim for Refund and Request for Abatement, after paying the tax. (A copy is in the Appendix.) Once your claim is officially denied, you can sue. The IRS usually denies this type of refund claim. You have six months after the denial to file your lawsuit, which, not surprisingly, is called a Refund Suit.

If the IRS claims you owe a lot—$50,000 or more—and you have firm legal grounds and enough money to pay first, see a tax attorney. Consider filing a lawsuit in a District Court or the Court of Federal Claims. Statistically, you might have a better chance of winning in these courts than in Tax Court, but it's worth considering only when big bucks are at stake.

The advantage of going to one of these alternative courts lies in our somewhat inconsistent judicial system. The Tax Court, District Courts and the Court of Federal Claims all have the power to decide tax cases, and sometimes decide the same tax issue differently. Because their decisions are published in books found in law libraries, it is no secret how a court may rule on a given issue. Although judges can change their minds, and the makeup of courts changes over time, courts are very reluctant to go against their own precedents. This means you can choose the court that has been most kind to your situation in the past. Perhaps of greater importance is that you can ask for a jury trial in a District Court. If a jury is upset with the IRS or the tax law, it can give you a break.

There is another reason why some people sue in a District Court or the Court of Federal Claims. The government attorneys in the District Court and Court of Federal Claims do not work for the IRS and are often more reasonable in settling cases than are the IRS' Tax Court lawyers. In choosing between the District Court and Court of Federal Claims, most people base their decisions on finances only—it's cheaper to send your lawyer to a local District Court than to pay to send her to the Court of Federal Claims in Washington.

Bankruptcy court. Bankruptcy judges also have the power to decide tax disputes for cases pending in their courts. I have seen some very favorable tax decisions made in bankruptcy courts. Of course, you must file bankruptcy first to get a tax case heard. If bankruptcy is a serious option for you, see both a bankruptcy and a tax lawyer, or the rare one who specializes in both.[2]

---

[2]For information on bankruptcy, see Chapter 6, Section F. Also, for detailed information, including the forms and instruction for filing a Chapter 7 (straight liquidation bankruptcy), see *How to File for Bankruptcy*, by Elias, Renauer and Leonard (Nolo Press).

E. Appealing to Higher Courts

Small cases heard in Tax Court cannot be appealed to higher courts. All other cases—Regular cases heard in Tax Court, as well as cases brought in District Courts and the Court of Federal Claims—can be appealed to a U.S. Circuit Court of Appeals. A lawyer is needed to handle this highly technical process, and you can expect to pay legal fees of upwards of $10,000. Your statistical chance of winning is about 10%. If you lose, you can ask the U.S. Supreme Court to hear your case, but your chances of success are roughly equivalent to winning first prize in your state's lottery.

F. Tax Court in a Nutshell— Kernels of Wisdom

1. Filing a Petition to Tax Court is easy and costs $60. Forms are in the Appendix.

2. If you are contesting $10,000 or less in taxes and penalties for any one tax year, you qualify as a Small Case. You can handle it without a lawyer.

3. The chance of getting a tax bill reduced in Tax Court or a settlement before trial are 50-50, but only 5% of all taxpayers win outright.

4. If you file a Petition without an arguable case or just to delay collection, you can be fined—but this is rarely done.

5. Prepare for a Small Case in Tax Court like you would prepare for an appeals hearing.

When You Owe the IRS: Keeping the Tax Collector at Bay 6

According to the IRS, 15% of all taxpayers owe back taxes at any given time. And this figure includes only people who have actually filed tax returns. As mentioned in Chapter 2, many people required to file tax returns haven't.

There are several possible reasons for owing the IRS back taxes:

- You didn't file a tax return; the IRS prepared a return for you and sent you a bill.

- You didn't pay your income taxes in full when you filed your tax return.

- You believed you paid your taxes in full when you filed your return, but you later received a bill or adjustment notice from the IRS. (See Chapter 3, Section C.4.)

- After an audit, the IRS found that you owed additional taxes; you signed the audit report in agreement.

- After an audit, the IRS found that you owed additional taxes; you didn't sign the audit report, but you neither appealed nor filed a Petition in Tax Court.

- After an audit, the IRS found that you owed additional taxes; you appealed and lost, and did not file a Petition in Tax Court.

- After an audit, the IRS found that you owed additional taxes; you filed a Petition in Tax Court and lost.

No matter which of these categories you fit into, one thing is clear—you have a problem with the IRS. Let me tell you what passes for humor there: An auditor recently told me (with a straight face) that the IRS now requires a basic humanity test for all applicants. Those who flunk are hired by the Collection Division.

He may have been joking, but you won't laugh if an IRS collector calls. He'll probably be the toughest bill collector you'll ever face, with the possible exception of Louie Loanshark's boys. Unlike other creditors, the IRS has no legal obligation to take you to court before seizing your car, home or paycheck. Similarly, you can lose your business, bank accounts and even your pension in the blink of an eye. As far as the IRS is concerned, your income tax obligation takes priority over all other debts. If the IRS records

a notice of tax lien, your credit rating may be ruined for years. In short, the IRS tax collector can make your life seem like a bad dream.

Luckily, this doesn't have to happen to you. If you deal with the IRS—in particular, if you correctly respond to IRS notices—chances are good that you'll keep your property and survive the worst of what the IRS throws at you.

The IRS Collection Division has one objective—to collect the maximum amount of taxes from you with the minimum amount of effort. To accomplish this, the IRS has established an extensive collection system, both computerized and staffed. (I'll get into the details, below.) The IRS first tries to collect by sending you computer-generated notices from the Service Center. If that doesn't work, the IRS Automated Collection System (ACS) kicks in, sending you more computer-produced notices. If the IRS still doesn't get its money, it assigns a human being from its Collection Division—a Revenue Officer—to come after you and your property.

Dealing With an IRS Tax Bill You Owe

No matter what stage of the collection process you find yourself in, you have five ways to deal with a tax bill you unquestionably owe:

- pay in full

- pay a monthly installment agreement with the IRS

- reduce, eliminate or pay the debt through bankruptcy

- reduce the debt and pay it through an IRS offer in compromise, or

- have the IRS determine that you are temporarily unable to pay and suspend collection.

While reducing your bill through an offer in compromise, going into bankruptcy or having the IRS determine you are temporarily unable to pay seem like the most attractive options, most taxpayers don't qualify for them. Thus, paying in full is the best way for most people to deal with a tax bill. This stops the accrual of interest and penalties, and gets the IRS off your back. But for many taxpayers, paying through an installment plan is the most practical option. Therefore, much of this chapter deals with how to get a fair monthly payment deal with the IRS. In 1993, over one million taxpayers were on the installment plan.

Statute Of Limitations On Collections

Luckily the IRS does not have forever to collect a tax debt. The tax code limits the IRS to ten years from the date the tax was assessed against you to collect it. After that time, the slate is wiped clean, unless by your act or agreement you have extended the period of time the IRS can collect from you. For example, filing an offer in compromise or a bankruptcy action will automatically suspend the clock on the ten-year period.

You may jump to the conclusion that paying your IRS debt over time (or some other way) is your best option. But that is not always true, so read this entire section before making your decision on how to deal with the tax collector.

First, do you really owe all the IRS says you owe?

Before you agree to pay any amount to the IRS, make sure the bill is correct. You are entitled to a full explanation of why you owe any IRS bill.

Here are some suggestions for making sure your bill is correct—or for possibly reducing it.

- Review your tax returns (or have a Tax Pro look at them) to see if you may have missed any deductions, loss or contribution carryovers or similar items. If you find any, you can amend your tax return and reduce your bill.

- Review the bill to make sure you have been credited with all payments, including any wage or bank levies and any refunds taken. It is common for the IRS to incorrectly apply payments and credits to your account.

You can find out how the IRS calculated your bill and credited your account by getting a transaction register (computer printout). Call 800-829-1040 or your local IRS office. Be warned: these printouts are in code and not easy to understand—most likely you will need an explanation from the IRS. Call the 800 number again, go to your local IRS office or ask a Tax Pro for help. Compare your canceled checks, prior tax notices, bank and wage levy notices with the IRS printout. If it doesn't match up, immediately bring this to the attention of the IRS.

- Almost all old tax bills include amounts for penalties and interest. It may be possible to have some or all of these unwanted additions canceled, or "abated" in IRS terminology. See Chapter 12 to determine whether or not you qualify and how to go about asking the IRS for an abatement.

Where IRS Collection Efforts Are Headed

Despite its fierce image and extraordinary powers, the IRS, by its own admission, is a lousy bill collector. At last report, the amount of income taxes reported owed but uncollected exceeded $130 billion! Add to that amount the taxes the IRS estimates are owed, but unreported and the total easily doubles.

The IRS claims it has neither the personnel or computer power to do better. Congress has responded with increased funding. By the mid-1990s, the IRS Collection Division is scheduled to have a multi-billion dollar computer system. Supposedly, the IRS will be able to instantly track down tax delinquents and seize their bank accounts and wages much more quickly than they can now. The IRS plans to expand its reliance on computers, not people. A disturbing thought.

A. When You Can't Pay With Your Tax Return

If you don't have the funds to pay your taxes when you file your return, send in as much as you can and request a monthly payment plan for the balance. You also have to fill out Form 9465 Installment Agreement Request (the one-page form is in the Appendix) and staple it to the *front* of your tax return.

On Form 9465, you must tell the IRS how much you think you can pay every month. You cannot, however, use Form 9465 to request a payment period longer than 36 months. For that, you will have to negotiate a plan by telephone or by meeting with an IRS Revenue Officer.

The IRS is supposed to let you know within 30 days whether or not your request was approved. If you owe less than $10,000, you should easily be able to get an installment agreement with Form 9465 without furnishing personal financial information. For amounts over $10,000, go on to Section B.

Like your VISA or MasterCard, the IRS charges interest (and penalties) for the luxury of paying over time. (As of December 1993, the interest and penalties combined total 13%.) Speaking of bank cards, the IRS is considering allowing payment of tax bills using a credit card. There are some IRS credit card pilot programs in various parts of the U.S. now.

B. Understanding Service Center Tax Bills and Notices

If you owe more than $10,000 (and therefore can't request a payment plan using Form 9465) or you owe less but don't submit Form 9465 when you file your tax return, you will get a bill from the IRS.

IRS collection efforts begin at the regional Service Center where you file your tax returns. The IRS stated mission of the Service Center Collection Branch (SCCB) is to:

- resolve collection cases at the earliest possible time
- increase the IRS collection "yield" and cash flow

- reduce field cases
- ensure taxpayer compliance, and
- provide effective service to the public.

Once your tax return has been posted to your account, the IRS sends you a "CP" balance due notice. If you never file a return, the SCCB sends you a Tax Delinquency Account (TDA) notice. This first notice is a non-threatening "Request for Payment" or "Notice of Federal Taxes Due."

If you don't pay up, how the IRS contacts you again depends on the kind of tax you owe—personal or business.

Individual Income Taxes. Beginning five weeks after sending the first CP notice, the IRS sends one to four more notices over a period of 26 weeks. This time table may vary, depending upon the type of tax owed. The notices are called CP 500 notices because of the numbers (following the date of the notice) in the upper right hand corner. The notices are as follows:

- 501—Reminder of Unpaid Tax.
- 502—Overdue Tax. (The IRS often skips this one and goes directly to 503.)
- 503—Urgent-Payment Required. (You may be sent several duplicate mailings of this notice.)
- 504—Final Notice. The 504 "pay up or else" notice is sent by certified mail to let you know the IRS is getting serious. But to say this is a "final" notice is misleading. It *is* probably the final notice you will get from the Service Center, but not from the IRS. A 504 notice only means the IRS *may* start enforced collection—seize your bank account or wages—at any time. You have no way of knowing if the IRS will really start grabbing your property at this point, so don't panic—yet.

With the 504 notice, the IRS sends Publication 594, Understanding the Collection Process. (A copy is in the Appendix.) It tells you what the IRS can do if you ignore the 504 notice.

TIP At any time during the "500" notice cycle, you can slow down the IRS by requesting more time to pay in full, or asking by sending Form 9465 (see above).

In response to your request, the IRS may send you Form 433-F asking for financial information (See Section D.3, below).

If you still don't pay within ten days of receiving the 504 notice, your file will be sent to the Automated Collection System (ACS) discussed at Section C, below.

Business Taxes. The above discussion pertains only to individual income taxes owed. If you owe business taxes, collection on your account may be accelerated. Usually, the IRS shortens the notice cycle from 26 weeks to 15 weeks.

Special Circumstances. If you did not file a return and the IRS is sending notices regarding your Taxpayer Delinquency Account, the IRS may omit the 500 series notices. Instead, your file goes directly to the ACS if you didn't file or the account has a large balance due—usually somewhere between $10,000 and $100,000. Also, the IRS may speed your file to the ACS if the SCCB believes your account is currently uncollectible, or that you are deceased, filing for bankruptcy or incarcerated.

1. Delaying the "500" Notice Cycle

If your goal is simply to buy more time, respond in writing to each "500" notice. Send a letter with the bill saying that you can't pay right now. You don't need to give an excuse; just ask for 60 more days to pay. This is the maximum time period which can be entered into the Service Center computer to suspend the collection cycle. When the next CP notice comes, respond by requesting another 60 days. If you are able, send a small payment with each of your request letters to show that you are trying. This should buy you an unofficial short term payment plan which might be all you need.

Sometimes, making 60-day delay requests throws a monkey wrench into the system. Taxpayers have been known not to hear from the IRS again for as long as a year. It all depends on the efficiency (or lack thereof) of your particular Service Center. Most are slow and unresponsive.

2. Service Center and Property Seizures

Even if you ignore the first few "500" series notices, you should respond to the 503 and 504 notices. Remember that ten days after the IRS sends the 504 notice, it has the power to grab your property, although it rarely does at this point. The IRS usually leaves levying to the ACS and local Revenue Officers. (See Sections C and D below.)

Nevertheless you should take seriously the IRS' power to seize property after a 504 notice is sent. At this point, the IRS computer may automatically send a levy notice to any financial institution holding funds under your Social Security number or name, or to any employer known to have paid you in the past. This levy notice requires these third parties to freeze your account or pay the IRS most of your wages. (Liens and levies are covered in Chapter 7.)

C. IRS Automated Collection System (ACS)

As mentioned above, if you don't pay your tax bill during the 500 series notices, your file will be sent to the IRS Automated Collection System (ACS). The ACS has the authority to collect most overdue tax bills, solicit tax returns from people who haven't filed and issue orders seizing property. Much of the ACS internal workings are a mystery to Tax Pros. One reason is, unlike most of the Internal Revenue Manual, the ACS section has not been made public under the Freedom of Information Act.

According to the IRS, the ACS is a computerized telecommunications system which maintains delinquent accounts and delinquency investigations. An ACS account is a balance due account or delinquency account which has gone through all notice routines at the Service Center Collection Branch.

The ACS computer automatically analyzes accounts which require telephone contact, dials the calls and resequences your phone number for call back if the IRS gets no answer or a busy signal.

According to me, the ACS is the IRS' dunning and telephone harassment apparatus. I have visited ACS facilities (chances are you never will—they are not open to the public) and have found 150 or more clerks sitting in front of computer monitors and wearing telephone headsets. They follow scripts demanding payment from tax debtors and respond to calls or faxes requesting payment plans or more time to pay. The ACS also sends out taxpayer letters, levies and tax liens, all on computer generated forms.

How Long Your File Stays With the ACS

Unless your case has enough "points"—under a secret IRS "Q" scoring system for collection accounts—it can theoretically stay under the jurisdiction of the ACS for as long as is left on the statute of limitations to collect the debt (ten years from the date the tax was first assessed against you). The chief factor is the amount you owe. Other factors are your past history of tax delinquencies and the number of years of taxes you owe.

As your case ages and gets near the end of the statute of limitations for collection, even small balances accumulate "Q" points. If the score gets high enough, your file will leave ACS and be sent to the local District Office for handling by a Revenue Officer. (See Section D, below.)

Unfortunately for taxpayers, ACS computer data is often inaccurate. For example, the ACS frequently requests tax returns from women who have changed their names after getting married or from people who have moved and file tax returns at other Service Centers.

1. Delaying the ACS Collector

If you want to slow down the ACS, you must ask for time. To suspend the computerized collection process, a collector must enter an appropriate "freeze code" into the computer. There are many freeze codes, but the precise details—such as the code designations, the exact number of codes and when they can be used by ACS collectors—is not public information. I do know, however, that requesting more time to pay, filing for bankruptcy or asking for a suspension of collection due to a hardship (see Section H, below) all have different freeze codes. Of course, the collector still must punch the code number in, which makes getting a freeze far from automatic.

When a freeze code is entered into the computer, collection activity on your account is put on hold for the time specified for that code number—up to one year. No action will be taken on your case during that period. After the time period elapses, the computer automatically pulls the case back up for further review and contact by the IRS.

Short term hold. You can get a short term hold— one week to 60 days—usually by just asking for it. First, make your request over the telephone. Also, follow up with a written response to the ACS. Just photocopy the notice you were sent, write on it that you need (up to) 60 days to get the money to pay, and send the notice back—a separate letter is not necessary. You may be able to get a second 60-day freeze in this same manner.

Long term hold. If you really can't afford any monthly payment amount, you want the collector to enter a code that will classify your account as "currently not collectible" and suspend collection activities for 12 months or more. You must convince the collector you are truly down and out—no assets, no job or very meager income, and you survive mostly through welfare or the kindness of others. (See Section H, below.) If you keep giving excuses, you may come up with one that causes the collector to enter a long term hold code. But, ACS collectors are tough, and not known for being sympathetic.

Three Other Ways to Stop the ACS Collector

If asking for a hold doesn't delay the tax collector for long, you can try one of these tactics:

- **Question the accuracy of the tax bill.** Because tax bills are difficult to decipher, you don't need to say anything other than you disagree with the bill. If you raise a doubt in any IRS tax collector's mind, he must exercise "reasonable forbearance"—that is, he can't take further steps to collect until he verifies the bill's accuracy. This could take him several days or several months. If he refuses your request, ask to talk to his manager. If this doesn't work, call the Problems Resolution Officer. (See Chapter 8.) [1]

- **Submit an Offer in Compromise.** The IRS usually suspends all collection activities while the offer is pending, often a period of several months or as long as a year. (See Section E, below.)

- **File for bankruptcy.** This immediately stops all IRS collection activities. (See Section F, below.)

---

2. Calling the ACS Collector and Arranging Installment Payments

ACS collectors can be unreasonable. Before you deal with an ACS collector, first have a plan of action. If the ACS collector calls you and you're not ready to speak with her, give a polite excuse, such as you're late for a doctor's appointment, the baby is playing with matches or you work nights and are sleeping now, and promise to call back. Don't answer any questions asked by an ACS collector, other than your name, until you have made your plan.

If you owe less than $10,000, you should get a payment plan for up to 36 months, without much

problem. Just ask for it. But if you owe more than $10,000 or less and can't pay it off within 36 months, you will have to negotiate with the ACS collector.

You need to make a comprehensive list of your assets, debts, income and—most importantly—your living expenses. The collector will be looking for information from IRS Form 433-F, Collection Information Statement. (A copy is in the Appendix.) Use it to organize the information, especially your expenses. You'll probably need it some time during the collection process. (Follow the instructions in Section D.3, below.) Your goal is usually to convince the collector to give you time to pay your taxes. Her goal, however, is getting you to pay the full tax bill as soon as possible.

Once you've compiled your financial data, call the ACS. Have in front of you a notepad, pencil, the tax bill and your Form 433-F information. Most ACS offices take incoming calls up to 6:30 p.m. (and make outgoing calls until 8:00 p.m.). Of course, getting through may be a different story. The best times seem to be Tuesdays, Wednesdays and Thursdays, early morning or lunchtime. Expect to call numerous (as many as 20) times before you don't hear a busy signal. Once someone finally answers, you may be put on hold. Expect a long wait—set aside snacks, the remote control, reading material or your knitting.

When a collector finally comes on the phone, write down her name. You may get only a first name or a pseudonym, as most ACS collectors do not give their real names out of fear of harm from irate tax-payers. This person may be on an ACS collection team of five to seven members. Make notes of important points throughout the conversation. If you ever have to call back you may not be able to talk to the same person, but you will probably speak to another team member. The IRS claims that you will get the same result no matter to whom you speak, but this is not always true. If you don't like a particular ACS collector, you can get off the phone, call back later or the next day and hope that a different collector answers.

ACS collectors sit all day long listening to every excuse in the book—and some that aren't. They hear so many cries of anguish and screams of rage they become cynical and unsympathetic. Nevertheless, without lying, you want to accent the negative—how

---

[1] If anyone questions your right, refer them to the Internal Revenue Manual 0018; IRS Policy Statement P-5-16.

hard your life is, your large expenses and low income, and the like. If you don't, the collector is likely to conclude that you are in better shape than may be the case. If the collector becomes rude or bullying, ask to speak to her supervisor. If all else fails, try begging or crying. You may be assigned another team member or the supervisor may personally handle your case.

The telephone collector will first ask you a series of scripted questions to discover where you work and bank. Her purpose is to identify assets (called "levy sources") the IRS can seize if you do not voluntarily pay the tax bill. Don't lie—about your assets or anything else. If you're asked a question you don't want to answer, such as whether or not you have any sideline income (you may not want to get into it with the ACS), gracefully end the conversation—use a prepared excuse, such as your child just turned on the gas stove. Call back later. You may not be asked the question again. If you are, try another excuse and call back a third time.

The IRS telephone collector will also ask about specific assets, such as bank balances and equity in your home or other real estate, and about your cash borrowing power. Remember—her goal is to get you to pay the full tax bill at once. If she thinks that you can, she will demand payment within a week or two. You won't be offered an installment plan.

If she concludes that you can't pay now, she will ask questions to see if you qualify for a monthly payment plan, called an Installment Agreement (IA). If you owe more than $10,000, you'll be asked about your family's income and living expenses— what you spend for rent or mortgage, food, transportation bills and most everything else.

After the questioning, the collector may ask you to send substantiating documentation, such as rent receipts or pay stubs. She may demand that you complete an IRS collection statement form—similar to Form 433-F. If she does, follow the instructions in Section D.3, below, for completing the form. Sometimes the ACS will orally agree to an installment agreement without any written information.

TIP Negotiating Installment Agreements with the ACS. Be prepared to negotiate a monthly amount with the ACS collector if you owe

more than $10,000 or owe less but can't pay it in 36 months. You should make the first offer—an amount you think you can afford. Make this offer a little low, as the ACS collector may well ask for a higher amount. More than likely, the ACS collector will insist that you cut back on some of your expenses. Be firm in holding your ground if the expenses are really necessary to your survival.

Example

The ACS collector questioned Yung's assertion that his family's monthly grocery bill totaled $600, feeling it was too high for a family of four. Yung explained that they did not eat extravagantly, but that his two children were lactose-intolerant diabetics on special costly diets. Then the collector challenged his high car expenses. Yung justified the costs, pointing out that his 1974 Dodge has 150,000 miles on it and requires constant work to keep it running.

If you agree to a payment plan with the ACS, the collector will send a written agreement for your signature. Sign it, make a copy for your records and return the original as soon as you can. Sometimes it takes weeks or months for the payment agreement to be sent. Regardless of when the agreement arrives, you must start making payments whenever you and the ACS collector agreed you would start. If you haven't yet received the written IA when you send in a payment, enclose a letter stating that you are paying "per a telephone conversation with Carol on 12/29/94 in which I agreed to pay $350 per month beginning 1/15/95." Send your payment to the ACS office.

Keep in mind that interest (and usually late payment penalties, too) continue to accrue on tax debts paid through installment plans. For example, if you owe $20,000 and agree to pay $400 per month, $200 or more of the $400 may be going to interest and penalties and only $200 toward your tax debts. If this sounds like it will take forever for you to pay—and you picture yourself on a treadmill with only a faint light at the end of your tunnel—then you may want to consider other options. (See Sections E and F, below.)

3. Requesting That Your File Be Sent to the District Office

If you can't get anywhere with the ACS, or you don't want to deal with them (because, for example, the bill or notice is wrong), request that your file be transferred to your local IRS District Office. There, your case will be handled by a Revenue Officer. (See Section D, below.) There are several other reasons why you might want your file transferred from the ACS:

- Once ACS collectors know where you live, work or bank, they may garnish your wages or seize your bank accounts at any time, without further notice. (See Chapter 7.)

- Revenue Officers can grant longer payment plans than can ACS collectors, even for *indefinite* periods of time. You will, however, have to disclose more details of your financial life to a Revenue Officer than to an ACS collector—who is more likely to accept information you give her without verifying it.

- If you've had (or have potential) tax problems, such as many years of non-filing of returns, you may want to avoid talking to the ACS.

How do you get your case out of the ACS? ACS collectors do not grant transfer requests in the absence of special circumstances. Just asking probably won't do it. Reasons that may work include telling the collector that you don't agree with the tax the IRS claims you owe, and that you want to meet with a Revenue Officer for a full explanation. Very few of us understand tax notices, so you won't be lying. ACS staff are supposed to transfer a file whenever a taxpayer questions the correctness of taxes on a notice.

If the collector refuses to send your file to your local IRS office, ask for her supervisor. Unless your complaint is clearly phony, you should get your way. Keep asking for a transfer if you don't first succeed. The more you owe, the easier it will be to get a transfer—that is, the ACS will grant transfers to people owing $50,000 more readily than those owing $5,000.

You can (and should) make the same transfer request in writing in response to the ACS notices you receive in the mail. Write that you don't under-

stand how the tax bill was computed and therefore don't agree with it. Ask to meet with someone from your IRS District Office for an explanation and to discuss payment.

D. Revenue Officers—Front Line Collectors of the IRS

If you owe more than $10,000 and if the IRS Service Center and ACS have tried—and failed—to get you to pay, or you've requested that your file be transferred to your local IRS office, your case will end up with a Revenue Officer. These tax collectors follow a four-step process:

1. They make a surprise visit to your home or office.

2. They either ask you questions on the spot or set up an interview to collect financial information. If you owe less than $10,000 and can pay it all with interest and penalties within 36 months, you can request a monthly payment plan. In all likelihood, your request will be granted.

can request a monthly payment plan. In all likelihood, your request will be granted.

3. If you owe more than $10,000, Revenue Officers will record your financial information on detailed IRS financial forms, which you'll be asked to verify and sign.

4. They try to collect what you owe the IRS in one or more of the following ways:

   - demand immediate payment

   - request that you obtain a bank loan

   - demand that you sell assets

   - propose an installment payment agreement (*only* if you have filed all past due tax returns)

   - begin enforced collection (seize your wages, bank accounts and other assets), or

   - report your file as currently uncollectible.

These steps are all discussed in detail, below.

1.   The Surprise Visit

One popular method used by Revenue Officers to catch delinquent taxpayers off guard is what I call the "ambush." The Officer simply comes to your home or work, unannounced. If you aren't there, he'll leave a card requesting that you call back within a few days.

If he finds you at home or work, or if you call back, he will start asking questions or set a time for you to be interviewed at the IRS office. His first area of concern is your current finances. Don't lie, but avoid giving financial information unless you are completely prepared. Say that you have to check your records. Then he'll ask if you've filed your tax returns. If you have, no problem. If you haven't, don't lie. You can need to "check" with a Tax Pro, but don't say yes if you haven't filed your returns.

More likely than not, the Revenue Officer will set an appointment for a collection interview. He may, however, want to talk to you in person or on the phone before the interview. Before giving him any information, ask him if he intends to get financial data from you at the meeting.

After he says yes (and he will say yes because that is the purpose of the meeting), request that he

send you a copy of the collection form. It will be Form 433-A, Collection Information Statement for Individuals and if you are self-employed, Form 433-B, Collection Information Statement for Businesses. He will go over the forms with you during the interview. (Both forms are in the Appendix.)

By requesting the 433 series form(s) before the interview, you can delay the collection process a bit. Explain that you want the form(s) to work on so that you can be as accurate as possible during the interview. He can't argue with that. If he sends the form(s), fill them in before you go to the meeting. (See Section D.3, below.) If he forgets or won't send them, use the forms in the Appendix.

2.   The Collection Interview— Meeting the Collector

According to the Internal Revenue Manual, the first taxpayer interview *is the most important event in the collection process.* The Revenue Officer plays detective. Know that he is trained to act sympathetic in order to gain your confidence and cooperation. But, you will quickly discover that after the honey comes the vinegar.

Legally, you can't be forced to answer the questions of the Revenue Officer. But if you do not give the information requested, you risk rapid "enforced collection" action—seizure of your property and wages. How you perform at the collection interview generally will determine how successful you will be in dealing with any IRS collection problem.

If You Refuse to Divulge Financial Information

In general, you don't have to give the IRS financial information about yourself. While lying to a collector is a crime, refusing to give information is not. If you don't cooperate or you only partially cooperate, the IRS has three options:

- Seize known assets or wages, rather than look for assets you refuse to talk about—the most likely outcome of your lack of cooperation.

  Revenue Officers can locate assets without your cooperation. They can check public real property and motor vehicle records, and contact financial institutions. The IRS has a hard time finding out-of-state deposit accounts and real estate, however.

- Forget about you and your property, and instead go after other tax delinquents—you should be so lucky.

- Issue a summons for you to appear and produce information—a summons is a legal order to appear and bring records or give information. The IRS doesn't like to use this power because of the paperwork and trouble. If you get a summons and don't want to meet the IRS, see a tax attorney. If you ignore a summons, you risk a court hearing and jail.

The IRS purpose for the interview is to prepare Forms 433, which detail your finances. These forms reveal much more of your history and lifestyle than a typical financial statement.

The IRS has several versions of Form 433:

- 433-A, Collection Information Statement for Individuals.

- 433-B, Collection Information Statement for Businesses—this form is used with business owners and self-employed persons.

- 433-F, Collection Information Statement—for Service Center and ACS collections. (See Sections A and B, above.)

To negotiate with a Revenue Officer, all taxpayers must complete Form 433-A. All business owners and self-employed taxpayers must submit both Forms 433-A *and* 433-B.

A Revenue Officer will push hard to get all questions on the 433 forms answered. All 433 forms are divided into two main parts—(1) assets and liabilities, and (2) income and expenses. You will probably have little problem stating your assets, debts and income. The expense part usually gives taxpayers problems. Most of us know how much our car and house payments are, however, we have no idea how much we spend on groceries or at the cleaners. But the IRS expects you to know these costs during the collection interview.

After the interview, the Revenue Officer will ask you to immediately sign the financial disclosure forms. Don't be coerced into signing, even if you are desperate to get out of the IRS office. If you haven't prepared your figures ahead of time, you will probably underestimate your living expenses by 10% to 40%. (Precise instructions for completing this form are in Section D.3, below.) In turn, this gives the false impression that you have a lot of money left over after paying your monthly expenses. Then the Revenue Officer will demand you pay the IRS all of this "left over" money *plus* whatever amount he deems as unnecessary living expenses.

Tell the Revenue Officer you want to go over the forms in your home or office with your records at hand. Make this request even if you got the forms in advance and filled them out before the meeting—if nothing else, you can buy a little time. This is far less nerve-wracking than coming up with figures at the IRS office. If he gives you a hard time or asks what part is incorrect, tell him that you want to go over your records or talk with your tax advisor first. If he still balks, tell him you want to discuss the matter with his supervisor. He probably will relent without calling in the boss.

TIP If it's too late—you've already signed the 433 form without the chance to review your expenses, you may still be able to revise it. Tell the Revenue Officer that some of your original figures were incorrect and you have further information to make them right. Then show him the correct numbers.

Defending Your Expenses to the Revenue Officer

The IRS will give you credit only for "necessary" and "proven" living expenses. Be prepared to defend your expenses to a tax collector. Bring your canceled checks, rent or mortgage receipts, apartment leases, repair bills, insurance notices, medical bills and anything else to the interview. If the Revenue Officer disallows certain expenses, they will not be considered to determine how much is left to pay your tax bill on a payment plan.

If the IRS questions your claiming expenses like entertainment, turn the tables. Ask the Revenue Officer if she doesn't find an occasional movie necessary for her mental health. If you make this a little personal, but in a non-confrontational way, she might agree.

Revenue Officers are always concerned with your present monthly installment payments—such as credit card and department store bills. They will allow you to pay only the minimum amount due each month unless you can show they are for necessities.

3. Filling in IRS Forms 433-A and 433-B

The key parts of 433 forms are "assets" and "monthly expenses." Let's go over these.

Assets. This reveals your property and its value. The IRS wants this information so if you don't voluntarily pay, the IRS can seize your property or require you to sell or borrow against it. Some property is easy to value, such as cash, listed bonds and stocks. Other asset values can only be estimated, like your furniture, boats and automobiles. As long as your estimates are believable, the lower the value you place on your property, the less interested the IRS will be in seizing it or requiring you to sell or borrow on it.

Here are some suggestions for valuing specific items:

Cars. Line 24 of Form 433-A (Line 21 of 433-B) asks for a list of your vehicles. Start with the lowest value shown in *Edmund's Used Car* or *Kelly Blue Book*, which the IRS refers to as well. (These books should be available at your local library or bank.) Reduce the value substantially if the car has a lot of miles on it or needs work.

Example

Marcia owns a 1990 Honda which she drives to work. It has a current market value of $10,000. She enters that in the first column. She owes her credit union $9,000, which goes into column two. But the car needs some transmission work that will cost about $700. The amount for column three, equity in asset, would be $300.

Market value	$10,000
Loan	− 9,000
Repairs needed	− 700
Equity	$ 300

[Note: The IRS would not consider seizing Marcia's Honda for two reasons. First, the $300 equity would be wiped out by the costs of seizure and sale. Second, IRS policy discourages seizing vehicles needed for work transportation.]

Personal items. Value your appliances, furniture and fixtures at garage sale or thrift shop prices, which are extremely low. A sofa you bought five years ago for $1,000, for instance, would be worth only $100 or less today. On the form, you can group items. For example, "furniture—$250 total" is sufficient.

TIP ➤ The IRS never verifies the values of personal items like household goods or wearing apparel. And, the IRS can't get into your home to see these items unless you are foolhardy enough to invite them in—which you don't have to do.

Real estate. Call several real estate agents. They'll be happy to tell you the fair market value of your property if they think there is any chance you might list it for sale. Or check ads in the paper for similar properties. Discount that value by about 15–30% for purposes of Forms 433-A and 433-B. This is realistic, as you would have to pay closing costs, sales commissions, fix-up fees and other expenses if you were forced to sell the property. Also, real estate agents tend to be overly optimistic in their valuations, hoping you will list the property for sale with them.

Expenses. If you have trouble negotiating a fair installment agreement, the snag will likely be a disagreement with the IRS over your "necessary living expenses." I cannot overemphasize how important it is for you to show the Revenue Officer exactly where your money goes—every penny of it.

IRS Forms 433-A and 433-B are biased in favor of the IRS—the forms omit spaces for listing many basic costs incurred by all of us. For instance, there are no spaces for clothing or cleaning expenses. (Does the IRS see us as a nation of nudists or is this an implied threat to take the shirts off of our backs?)

Let's go over some specific lines in the expense section of Form 433-A that often cause problems.

Rent (Line 42). Here, consider two things. First, when you list your rent, be sure to factor in any anticipated rent raises. Second, be ready for the Revenue Officer to tell you that you could find a place to live for less. Tell him that this would mean paying a mover, putting up deposits, taking your children out of their schools, increasing your commuting expenses or any other additional expenses you can come up with. Usually the Revenue Officer will back down. The IRS tells very few people that they have to find cheaper shelter in order to get an installment agreement approved.

Groceries (Line 43). IRS offices generally use locally determined guidelines for grocery expense limits. But collectors usually won't disclose the limits, probably hoping you will claim less than the IRS' meager guidelines. Good luck. In some places, the limit is as low as $100 per person per month for groceries—hardly generous. If anyone in your family has special dietary needs or you have voracious teenagers, make sure the IRS knows it. And, be prepared to back up your expense with grocery receipts. Don't forget to include non-food items that many of us buy at the grocery store—toiletries, paper goods, soap and the like.

Allowable Installment Payments (Line 44). Expect the Revenue Officer to let you make your car and mortgage payments in full. But collectors generally do not allow any more than the monthly minimum payment on your credit cards. If you use your cards to pay for necessities, you must be able to prove this (billing statements or receipts will work fine) in order to get higher amounts allowed.

Utilities (Line 45). The IRS may challenge your telephone long distance expenses. So, if you have a sick mother or another need to keep in touch with someone, explain this to the Revenue Officer. Cable TV expenses are usually allowed unless you have expensive premium channels.

Transportation (Line 46). Few of us keep good track of what we spend to get around town. It is important to compute how much you spend on your car or other mode of transport. Total up your car expenses—repairs, maintenance, gasoline, commute costs (parking and tolls)—for the last year and divide by 12 to get the monthly average. The age and kind of vehicle you own are important—especially if your car is old and needs constant repairs. If you know you need to replace the tires or muffler soon, factor in these costs. Add to the cost of having a car the amount you spend each month on other transit costs. Car owners who sometimes also take cabs and public transit—or send their kids on the bus to school or music lessons. Don't forget these expenses.

In general, it is hard to overestimate the costs of operating a car, so give yourself a cushion. If the Revenue Officer objects, point out that if you don't have a car that runs, you can't get to work. And, if you don't work, you can't make your tax payments.

Insurance (Line 47). Some Revenue Officers are reluctant to allow life insurance premium payments. If you have dependents and health problems, argue that life insurance is not a frill but a necessity. The IRS will usually back down. As long as you can show bills for homeowner's, auto, renter's, disability and health insurance you shouldn't have a problem getting these expenses accepted.

Medical (Line 48). Don't forget about the money you lay out for prescription and over the counter medications. Have receipts to show if asked.

Estimated Tax Payments. (Line 49). This is *extremely important* if you or your spouse has self-employment income. Estimated tax payments are the tax payments that all self-employed people are required to make every three months. List the amount you should be paying even if you are not currently doing so. Any installment agreement you make with the IRS will include a stipulation requiring you to keep current on all future tax payments. If you don't know the amount of estimated tax payments you should currently be making, ask the IRS or your Tax Pro to come up with the figure for you. Once the IRS approves your installment agreement, you must make all estimated tax payments on time or risk the agreement being declared in default.

Other Expenses (Line 51). This is where you are likely to get the most flack from the IRS. Don't try to cram everything else you spend money on in the paltry three lines on the form. Instead, on Line 51 write "see attachment" and the use total amount. That figure is from a list of items on a separate sheet of paper you stapled to your Form 433-A. (See the completed example, below.)

Other necessary expenses to list include (you can use the Expense Checklist worksheet which follows to make sure you don't miss anything):

- Taxes—Those not deducted from your wages, such as property taxes or any back state taxes you may be paying off.

- Home maintenance—Even if you rent your home you still spend some money keeping it up.

- Clothing and cleaning.

- Meals out—This is especially important if your work prevents you from eating all your meals at home.

- School activities and lunches for the kids—Don't forget any babysitting and child care expenses.

- Student and personal loan payments—If you owe a close family member, be prepared to show a promissory note or other evidence that it is a legitimate debt.

- Entertainment—Expect an argument from the Revenue Officer, but argue back that you are entitled to rent a few videos once in a while or take the family to McDonald's. Make the Revenue Officer feel like a scrooge if he hardballs you here.

- Charity—Again, expect a fight. If you are devoutly religious, tell the Revenue Officer that you couldn't live with yourself without dropping something in the plate on Sundays. If you are helping out an aged relative with $50 a month, list this too—the IRS person may be sympathetic if he is in a similar situation.

- Personal items—You can try to slip in the booze and cigarette expenses along with haircuts. Generally the IRS will allow some amount, albeit little ($10–$25).

- Pet food and care—I know that pets are expensive, but well worth the cost to many of us. But, pets are not a necessity of life to the IRS. If the collector is a pet lover, however, you will probably be allowed some expense for pets. Or, if your grocery bills show pet food costs, the IRS collector may just pass it by.

- Professional fees—Have you hired an attorney, accountant or other tax professional to straighten out your tax or other legal problems? Don't forget to include those bills here.

- Contingency expenses—No one can predict all expenses they will have to bear. For that reason, always argue that you are entitled to an "emergency" fund to cover unforeseen events.

EXPENSE CHECKLIST

The below expense checklist gives a far truer picture of your monthly living expenses than does Form 433-A or Form 433-B. Go through this list and then transfer the information to the form. If a particular item doesn't fit on the IRS form, use a separate sheet of paper.

Everyone's expenses are different; don't feel confined by this list in making yours. Remember to add up expenses that don't recur monthly (such as a doctor's visit or auto repair) and divide by 12 to get a monthly average amount.

Housing
- Rent or mortgage payment $_____
- Second mortgage payment $_____
- Home equity loan payment $_____
- Repairs and upkeep $_____
- Electricity and gas $_____
- Water and sewer $_____
- Telephone $_____
- Garbage $_____
- Cable $_____

Food
- Groceries $_____
- Meals out $_____
- School lunches $_____

Clothing $_____
- Replacement and mending $_____
- Laundry and cleaning $_____

Medical
- Doctors and dentists $_____
- Medications $_____
- Hospital bills $_____

Transportation
- Public transportation $_____
- Gas $_____
- Maintenance $_____
- Parking and tolls $_____

Insurance
- Homeowner's or renter's $_____
- Motor vehicle $_____
- Health $_____
- Life $_____
- Disability or other $_____

Taxes (not deducted from wages)
- Property $_____
- Income-federal $_____
- Income-state $_____
- Other (such as back taxes) $_____

Installment payments
- Motor vehicle $_____
- Credit cards $_____
-           $_____
-           $_____
-           $_____
-           $_____
- Department stores $_____
-           $_____
-           $_____
-           $_____
- Gasoline companies $_____
-           $_____
- Student loan $_____
- Personal loan $_____
- Other installment payments $_____

Family expenses
- Child support $_____
- Alimony $_____
- Child care $_____
- Educational expenses $_____

Bills for professional services
- Accountant $_____
- Attorney $_____
- Tax Pro $_____
- Other $_____

Other
- Payment to help relative $_____
- Personal items $_____
- Household and cleaning $_____
- Charitable contributions $_____
- Entertainment $_____
- Recreation $_____
- Subscriptions $_____
- Miscellaneous $_____

TOTAL MONTHLY EXPENSES $_____

Form **433-A**
(Rev. January 1994)

Department of the Treasury — Internal Revenue Service

Collection Information Statement for Individuals

NOTE: Complete all blocks, except shaded areas. Write "N/A" *(not applicable)* in those blocks that do not apply.

1. Taxpayer(s) name(s) and address	2. Home phone number	3. Marital status
John J. Kwong 555 Penny Lane San Francisco, CA 94000 County San Francisco	(415) 555-9010	Divorced
	4.a. Taxpayer's social security number 555-55-5555	b. Spouse's social security number N/A

Section I. Employment Information

5. Taxpayer's employer or business *(name and address)*	a. How long employed	b. Business phone number	c. Occupation
ABC Company	ten years	(415) 555-6500	Marketing
	d. Number of exemptions claimed on Form W-4 one	e. Paydays 1st, 16th	f. *(Check appropriate box)* [X] Wage earner [ ] Partner [ ] Sole proprietor

6. Spouse's employer or business *(name and address)*	a. How long employed	b. Business phone number	c. Occupation
N/A		( )	
	d. Number of exemptions claimed on Form W-4	e. Paydays	f. *(Check appropriate box)* [ ] Wage earner [ ] Partner [ ] Sole proprietor

Section II. Personal Information

7. Name, address and telephone number of next of kin or other reference	8. Other names or aliases	9. Previous address(es)
Florence Kwong, mother 8 Retirement Village St. Petersburg, FL 33700 813-555-0438	N/A	34 Port Meyers Lane Sarasota, FL 32000

10. Age and relationship of dependents living in your household *(exclude yourself and spouse)*

Martin Kwong, 12 years old, child

11. Date of Birth ▶	a. Taxpayer 5-17-53	b. Spouse N/A	12. Latest filed income tax return *(tax year)* 1993	a. Number of exemptions claimed two	b. Adjusted Gross Income $22,222

Section III. General Financial Information

13. Bank accounts *(include savings & loans, credit unions, IRA and retirement plans, certificates of deposit, etc.)*

Name of Institution	Address	Type of Account	Account No.	Balance
Bigbux National Bank	100 Easy Street San Francisco, CA 94000	checking	5-5-00005	$20
Realgood Credit Union	555 Blue Bonnet Way San Francisco, CA 94999	savings	7-777770	$75
		Total *(Enter in Item 21)*		$95

Cat. No. 20312N

Form **433-A** (Rev. 1-94)

COLLECTION INFORMATION STATEMENT FOR INDIVIDUALS (FORM 433-A)

Section III - *continued*   **General Financial Information**

14. Charge cards and lines of credit from banks, credit unions, and savings and loans

Type of Account or Card	Name and Address of Financial Institution	Monthly Payment	Credit Limit	Amount Owed	Credit Available
Visa	Bison Bank, P.O. Box 295003 Butte, MT 70000	$550	$5,000	$5,000	$0
Mastercard	Elk Savings & Loan, 123 Big Animal Way, Carson City, NV 80000	$333	$3,000	$3,000	$0
Totals *(Enter in Item 27)* ▶		$883	$8,000	$8,000	$0

15. Safe deposit boxes rented or accessed *(List all locations, box numbers, and contents)*

Bigbux National Bank, location listed above, box #5. My will and other personal papers.

16.	**Real Property** *(Brief description and type of ownership)*	**Physical Address**
a.	N/A	
		County _____
b.		
		County _____
c.		
		County _____

17.	**Life Insurance** *(Name of Company)*	Policy Number	Type	Face Amount	Available Loan Value
	Forever Life	9999999	term	$50,000	None
	Total *(Enter in Item 23)* ▶				$0

18. Securities *(stocks, bonds, mutual funds, money market funds, government securities, etc.):*

Kind	Quantity of Denomination	Current Value	Where Located	Owner of Record
N/A				

19. Other information relating to your financial condition. If you check the yes box, please give dates and explain on page 4, Additional Information or Comments:

a. Court proceedings	[X] Yes [ ] No	b. Bankruptcies		[X] Yes [ ] No
c. Repossessions	[ ] Yes [X] No	d. Recent transfer of assets for less than full value		[ ] Yes [X] No
e. Anticipated increase in income	[ ] Yes [X] No	f. Participant or beneficiary to trust, estate, profit sharing, etc.		[ ] Yes [X] No

Form **433-A**   **page 2**   (Rev. 1-94)

Section IV.   Asset and Liability Analysis

Description	Current Market Value	Liabilities Balance Due	Equity in Asset	Amount of Monthly Payment	Name and Address of Lien/Note Holder/Obligee	Date Pledged	Date of Final Payment
20. Cash			$100				
21. Bank accounts *(from Item 13)*			$ 95				
22. Securities *(from Item 18)*			$ 0				
23. Cash or loan value or Insur.			$ 0				
24. Vehicles *(model, year, license, tag#)*							
a. 1993 Honda, 5-5JJT	$8,000	$7,500	$500	$250	Highfinance Co., 180 Main St., Oakland, CA 94777	2/2/93	2/98
b.							
c.							
25. Real property *(From Section III, item 16)* N/A a.							
b.							
c.							
26. Other assets							
a. Furniture	$1,000	$0	$1,000				
b. Personal effects	$ 500	$0	$ 500				
c.							
d.							
e.							
27. Bank revolving credit *(from Item 14)*							
28. Other Liabilities *(Including judgments, notes, and other charge accounts)* a. Visa		$5,000		$550	See above	1993	
b. Mastercard		$3,000		$333	See above	1993	revolving
c. Dr. Hurt		$4,000			32 Main St., San Francisco	1992	revolving
d.							
e.							
f.							
g.							
29. Federal taxes owed		$20,000					
30. **Totals**			$2,195	$1,133			

Internal Revenue Service Use Only Below This Line

Financial Verification/Analysis

Item	Date Information or Encumbrance Verified	Date Property Inspected	Estimated Forced Sale Equity
Personal Residence			
Other Real Property			
Vehicles			
Other Personal Property			
State Employment *(Husband and Wife)*			
Income Tax Return			
Wage Statements *(Husband and Wife)*			
Sources of Income/Credit *(D&B Report)*			
Expenses			
Other Assets/Liabilities			

Form **433-A**   page 3   (Rev. 1-94)

COLLECTION INFORMATION STATEMENT FOR INDIVIDUALS (FORM 433-A)

Section V.

Monthly Income and Expense Analysis

Income			Necessary Living Expenses	
Source	**Gross**	**Net**		
31. Wages/Salaries (Taxpayer)	$ 2,400	$ 1,839	42. Rent (Do not show mortgage listed in item 25)	$ 600
32. Wages/Salaries (Spouse)			43. Groceries (no. of people __2__)	400
33. Interest - Dividends			44. Allowable installment payments (IRS use only)	
34. Net business income (from Form 433-B)			45. Utilities (Gas $ _45_ Water $ 20	
35. Rental Income			Electric $ _30_ Phone $ 35)	130
36. Pension (Taxpayer)			46. Transportation	125
37. Pension (Spouse)			47. Insurance (Life $ 50 Health $ work	98
38. Child Support			Home $ N/A Car $ _48_)	
39. Alimony			48. Medical (Expenses not covered in item 47)	35
40. Other			49. Estimated tax payments	
			50. Court ordered payments Alimony	150
			51. Other expenses (specify)	
			see attachment	275
41. Total Income	$ 2,400	$ 1,839	**52. Total Expenses** (IRS use only)	$
			53. Net difference (income less necessary living expenses) (IRS use only)	$

Certification   Under penalties of perjury, I declare that to the best of my knowledge and belief this statement of assets, liabilities, and other information is true, correct, and complete.

54. Your signature	55. Spouse's signature (if joint return was filed) N/A	56. Date 5/23/94

Additional information or comments:

   I am being sued by my dentist, Dr. Hurt, for $4,000 in past bill. In 1987, I filed a Chapter 7 bankruptcy; I received my discharge in 1988. My son has an eye disorder and needs an operation which will cost $10,000. The operation is deemed "experimental" and therefore my health insurance (through my job) won't pay for it. My company is cutting back in my department; I may be laid off or have my salary frozen within the next six months.

Internal Revenue Service Use Only Below This Line

Explain any difference between Item 53 and the installment agreement payment amount:

Name of originator and IDRS assignment number:	Date

Form **433-A**   page 4   (Rev. 1-94)

*U.S. Government Printing Office: 1993 — 301-643/92172

ATTACHMENT TO FORM 433-A
----

page 4, line 51, other expenses:

Parking at work	$25
Cable TV	20
Clothing replacement	20
Cleaning & laundry	22
Bus pass for son	8
School lunches for son	37
Entertainment	52
Toiletries, hygiene	31
Haircuts	19
Church	20
Postage for job (not reimbursed)	21
TOTAL, line 51	$275

4. Signing Form 433-A or 433-B— Proceed With Caution

As mentioned before, if you didn't prepare Form 433-A or 433-B in advance of your IRS interview, don't let the IRS do it. Instead, take the forms home and complete them. Once *you* (not the IRS) list your expenses, you add your John Hancock. Ask the Revenue Officer if you can mail it back, but he may insist that you bring it in person.

5. Protecting Yourself After Making Financial Disclosures to the IRS

You went through a collection interview, telling the IRS everything. Now the IRS collectors know where you work, bank, live and more. The IRS asks for next of kin, so it can track you down if you run. In short, the IRS is in great shape to seize your wages and assets. What can you do to protect yourself if you are worried about an aggressive Revenue Officer?

[TIP] Financial information must be true on the date that you give it, whether orally or on an IRS form. You do not commit to the IRS that you won't change jobs, sell assets or switch banks the next day. In fact, switching banks is a good idea. After disclosing your bank or brokerage accounts on Form 433-A or 433-B, reduce the balances to a minimum. Take the excess funds and open a new account at a different bank.

Bank accounts are not automatically reported to the IRS. If you have an interest-bearing account, however, it will be reported to the IRS after the end of each year. If you live in a small town, open the account outside the area or in another state. If you don't, a local bank "canvas" by a Revenue Officer might find your account. In large metropolitan areas with many banks, this is not likely to happen.

Deposit all further income and pay all bills from the new account, with one exception. If and when you start paying taxes, pay the IRS out of the old account or with money orders. The reason is that whenever you pay the IRS, the agency records your bank account number in its computer. Don't give the IRS your new account number after going to such efforts to keep it from the agency.

If a Revenue Officer requests an updated Form 433-A or 433-B, you must disclose the new accounts. Updates usually aren't requested more than once a year. Then you will have to start the account-moving process over again. Bank account moving is only a short term solution to dealing with IRS collectors who you fear might seize your accounts without warning. You can run, but you can't hide.

6. Proposing an Installment Agreement

After reviewing your financial disclosures on Form 433-A (and possibly Form 433-B too), the Revenue Officer will proceed in one of the following ways:

- demand immediate payment
- request that you obtain a bank loan (the Internal Revenue Manual mentions only bank loans, so don't worry about the IRS asking you to take out a loan from a finance company or relative if you don't qualify for a bank loan)
- demand that you sell assets
- propose an installment agreement
- begin enforced collection (seize your wages, bank accounts and other assets), or
- report your file as currently uncollectible.

If you have assets that can be sold or borrowed against, the IRS will insist that you proceed with one of the first three alternatives. If you don't, the last three are the collector's options. Enforced collection—the lien and levy process—is covered in Chapter 7. Reporting your file as currently uncollectible is discussed in Section F, below.

Discussion of the remaining option, proposing an installment agreement (IA), follows. When you don't have assets or borrowing power to pay your back taxes immediately, an IA is the most widely used payment alternative. Many taxpayers who owe back taxes are paying through IAs. Although you don't have an absolute right to an IA, the IRS must consider your proposal and negotiate with you in good faith.[2]

---

[2]Taxpayer's Bill of Rights and Internal Revenue Manual 5331.1.

You will *not* be eligible for an IA unless *all* your tax returns have been filed. If you are self-employed and are behind on the current quarterly estimated taxes, you won't get an IA until you become current. If you own a business and owe payroll taxes for the current quarter, you'll have to pay up. If you can't, stall the IRS until the quarter is over. Then propose an IA. (See Chapter 11, Section B.3.)

An IA May Give the IRS Longer to Collect From You

The tax code imposes a ten-year time limit on the IRS to collect taxes after they first become due. If you were billed after filing your return, this period starts on the date you filed. If you were audited, the ten years runs from the date the IRS assessed additional taxes.

Sometimes, as a condition of granting an IA, the IRS will require that you allow the ten-year period to be extended. You will be required to sign Form 900, Tax Collection Waiver. The extension period may be fixed (such as one-year) or open-ended, which gives the IRS forever to collect from you. When the Revenue Officer hands you Form 900, tell him that you want to talk to your tax advisor before signing. This stalling tactic may work. Often the IRS forgets to ask for the form later, and you are home free. If the IRS insists (and doesn't forget), go ahead and sign the form.

You can cancel your waiver by giving 90 days written notice to the IRS. As you might imagine, however, if you cancel your waiver, the IRS most likely will immediately revoke your installment agreement. The IRS has you over a barrel—no waiver, no installment agreement.

A. NEGOTIATING A MONTHLY PAYMENT

If you owe more than $10,000 or can't pay the amount you owe in three years or shorter, your request for an IA begins with an IRS collector analyzing Form 433-A or 433-B. (Remember—

business owners and self-employed people must submit both.)

The Revenue Officer uses the information on the forms to determine the amount you can pay. Beyond that, however, there are no hard and fast rules. Payment amounts are at the discretion of your Revenue Officer. If you deal with eight different Revenue Officers, you might end up with eight different IAs!

Nevertheless, here are some strategies for negotiating an installment plan.

- When you hand the completed Form 433-A or 433-B to the Revenue Officer, immediately propose a payment plan you can live with.

- You must offer to pay at least the amount on line 53 of Form 433-A—income less necessary living expenses. This is the cash you have left over every month after paying for the necessities of life. If possible, offer slightly more than the amount on line 53. Tell the Revenue Officer that you will cut back on expenses to make up the difference. For example, if line 53 is $189, offer $200. Don't, however, promise to pay more than you can afford just to get your plan approved. Promising the IRS more than you can deliver is a serious mistake. Once an IA is approved, the IRS makes it difficult for you to renegotiate it.

  If your line 53 shows $0 or a negative number, you're not in a position to negotiate a payment plan. At this point, your best bets are either submitting an Offer in Compromise (Section E, below), asking for a suspension of collection activities (Section H, below) or filing for Chapter 7 bankruptcy (Section F, below).

- Give a first payment when you propose the agreement—and keep making monthly payments even if the IRS hasn't yet approved your IA. If you don't have the funds, postdate a check or a series of checks and give them to the Revenue Officer to hold. Making voluntary payments demonstrates your good faith and creates a track record. For example, if you pay $200 a month for three months before your IA is approved, the Revenue Officer may be inclined to believe that this is the right amount.

B. WHAT HAPPENS AFTER PROPOSING YOUR INSTALLMENT AGREEMENT?

A Revenue Officer doesn't have authority to accept an IA proposal over $10,000 on his own. He can only recommend it to his manager. Most taxpayers who request them, however, get IAs. (See Section D.6.c, below, for information on what happens if the IRS rejects your IA.)

If the IRS accepts an IA, you may wait several months before receiving a written agreement on Form 433-D, called Installment Agreement.

Some Revenue Officers keep proposed IAs in their files for several months before giving them to their bosses just to see if the taxpayer will keep her promise. This is another reason to make the monthly payments while you are waiting to hear from the IRS.

How and Where to Make Installment Agreement Payments

Until your IA is approved, send your payments to the local IRS office in care of the Revenue Officer handling your case. After your IA is accepted, you will be directed to send payments to your local Service Center. The IRS will either send you a payment slip and envelope to mail back every month or, if you specifically request it (and your employer agrees), will automatically take the funds from your paycheck.

If you send the payments directly, write your name and Social Security number in the lower left hand corner of your check or money order. Photocopy each payment instrument and payment slip for your records, in the event the IRS ever denies receiving a payment. If you don't want the IRS to know where you keep your bank accounts, pay with cashier's checks or money orders, not from your checking account.

C. IF THE IRS REFUSES YOUR INSTALLMENT AGREEMENT PROPOSAL

Before a Revenue Officer will accept an IA, he must believe that the information on your 433 forms is truthful, your living expenses are "necessary" and the IRS is getting the maximum amount you can pay. As stated above, many IA proposals are accepted by the IRS. When the IRS won't agree to installment payments, it is for one of three reasons:

- Your living expenses are not all considered necessary—The IRS may deem your expenses "extravagant." For example, if you have hefty credit card payments, make any charitable contributions or send your kids to private school, expect the IRS to balk. Although everyone's expenses are different and reasonable people would disagree on what is necessary and what is extravagant, the IRS is rather stingy here.

- Information you provided on Form 433-A or 433-B is incomplete or untruthful—The IRS may think you are hiding property or income. For example, if public records show your name on real estate or motor vehicles that you didn't list, or the IRS received the W-2 or 1099 forms showing more income than you listed, be prepared to explain.

- You defaulted on a prior IA—While this doesn't automatically disqualify you from a new IA, it can cause your new proposal to be met with skepticism.

If your IA proposal is first rejected, you can keep negotiating. Ask to speak to the Revenue Officer's manager. Just making this request is sometimes enough to soften the Officer up. But, if you talk to the manager, don't criticize her employee or start yelling. She will get defensive, which does not help you achieve your goal. Keep your cool and if the manager believes you are trying to be reasonable, she may take over the case or ask the Revenue Officer to reconsider.

TIP   If you get nowhere with the manager, you can go over her head—everyone at the IRS has a boss. You can complain to her immediate boss, the Collections Branch Chief, and then to the District Director. Squeaky wheels sometimes do get greased. Again, just *talking* about going up the ladder may cause a change in the attitude at the lower rungs and get you a fair payment plan.

If going to the manager and her higher ups doesn't work, contact a Problems Resolution Officer

(PRO). (See Chapter 8 for information on how to contact a PRO.)

D. IRS REVOCATION OF AN INSTALLMENT AGREEMENT

Once you receive your written IA, supervision of your plan moves from the Revenue Officer to the Service Center. Normally, the only concern is that you make your monthly payments. You and the IRS are bound by the terms of the agreement for at least one year, unless:

- You fail to file your tax returns or pay taxes that arose after the IA was entered into. Although IRS computers don't continue to review your finances, they do monitor you for filing future returns and making promised payments.

- You miss a payment. Under the terms of all IAs, payments not made in full, and on time, can cause the IA to be revoked immediately. In practice, the IRS usually waits 30–60 days before revocation—at least on the first missed payment. You may be given a warning or a chance to reinstate the agreement, but the IRS isn't obligated to do so and don't count on it.

- Your financial condition changes significantly— either for the better or worse. The IRS usually won't find out about this unless you tell. The IRS may review your situation every year or two, however, and require you to submit a new Form 433-A or 433-B in order to continue your IA.

- The IRS discovers that you provided inaccurate or incomplete information as part of the negotiation, such as omitting certain valuable assets.

E. IF YOU CAN'T MAKE AN INSTALLMENT PAYMENT

If you can't make a monthly IA payment, call the Taxpayer Assistance number at 800-829-1040. If you negotiated with a Revenue Officer, call her.

Explain your problem and ask either for more time to pay or that collection be suspended. You'll need a good excuse, like losing your job, becoming disabled or a similar mishap. If you don't get anywhere with the Taxpayer Service Representative or the Revenue Officer, and the IRS says your IA will

be considered in default (meaning the IRS can begin grabbing your property), call the Problems Resolution Office. A PRO official can keep your agreement from being revoked. (See Chapter 8 for information on the PRO.)

If your IA is revoked. You may have to start negotiations over from scratch. The IRS may grant a reinstatement, but don't count on it. Remember, installment agreements are discretionary with the IRS. If the IRS is willing to reopen your case, you'll need a good excuse for defaulting the first time and more documentation of your living expenses. And while you are trying to get a new IA, the IRS can start seizing your bank accounts and wages.

Making an IA When You Also Owe State Taxes

Often you will find yourself owing both the IRS and your state tax department. If you do, you should negotiate payment plans with both agencies at the same time. Otherwise, any deal you make with one may not leave you with anything to pacify the other. See Chapter 14 for information on negotiating installment plans with both taxing authorities.

E. Offer in Compromise—Settling Tax Bills for Pennies on the Dollar

It is sometimes possible to wipe your tax slate clean at an enormous discount. There is no bottom limit on what the IRS will accept, if you know how to make your offer. There are cases where the IRS has accepted as little as 5% of an outstanding tax bill— including interest and penalties—and called it even. This procedure is called the Offer in Compromise.[3]

New IRS Policy. The Offer in Compromise law is not new. In the past, however, as it was not favored by the IRS, few Offers were made and even fewer

---

[3] Internal Revenue Code § 7122.

were accepted. In fact, in some IRS Districts, officers were forbidden to even mention that the IRS made deals with taxpayers.

In mid-1992, this changed. The IRS, in a dramatic about face, started encouraging its collectors not only to tell tax delinquents about the Offer law and procedure, but also to help taxpayers prepare offers. The approval process was streamlined, and the number of IRS personnel with authority to approve Offers greatly expanded.

1. Do You Qualify for Consideration of an Offer?

There is no legal right to have a valid tax bill reduced by the IRS. It is entirely discretionary with the IRS. You only have the right to submit an Offer in Compromise, and to have the IRS give it consideration.

To qualify for consideration of an Offer in Compromise, you must show the IRS that *either* of the following is true:

- There is some doubt whether or not the IRS can collect the tax bill from you, now or in the foreseeable future (called "doubt as to collectibility").

- There is some doubt whether or not you owe the bill (called "doubt as to liability"). This second ground is rarely applicable in tax collection cases, so the rest of this section deals only with "doubt as to collectibility."

Key to an Offer in Compromise. The Internal Revenue Manual states that an Offer must reflect "all that can be collected from the taxpayer's equity in assets and income, present and prospective."

The IRS is not giving away the store. If you have sufficient assets or income to pay a tax bill in full, having an Offer accepted by the IRS is not in your future. For instance, if you have $50,000 in the bank the IRS will not reduce any tax bill that is less than $50,000. Why should it when it could easily seize the bank account?

In brief, to compromise a tax bill, you must show the IRS that it doesn't have much of a chance to collect full payment from you today or in the foreseeable

future. Keep this concept clearly in mind as you read the rest of this section.

How Much to Offer? The amount of money you owe has no bearing on the amount of money the IRS will accept in an Offer. A $100,000 tax bill may be settled for $5,000 for one taxpayer and for $75,000 for another in a different financial situation. There are no set rules—each taxpayer's Offer is considered individually. The only true legal limitation is that the IRS cannot compromise a tax bill which is under $500.

2. Who Should Submit an Offer in Compromise?

Anyone owing the IRS can submit an Offer in Compromise to reduce that bill. Don't take this to mean you should submit an Offer just for the heck of it. The Offer in Compromise is a formal legal process—you can't just call up the IRS and ask for a deal. You must complete IRS forms and bare your financial soul. Before you go to the effort of making an Offer, determine if you realistically qualify. If your Offer is rejected, the financial disclosures you made provide a roadmap to your assets for the IRS collector.

Before 1992, fewer than one of every four Offers submitted were accepted. The new procedures improve the odds, but let me repeat—there is no fire sale going on at the Treasury Department. The majority of folks continue to have Offers rejected because they either don't qualify or didn't strictly follow IRS procedures in the Offer process.

If you read this section carefully, and act accordingly, you are a giant step ahead of everyone else who wants to make a deal on a tax bill with the IRS.

3. What the IRS Is Looking for in an Offer

Specifically, your Offer will not qualify for serious IRS consideration unless it meets two tests:

1. The money offered must be more than the amount the IRS could collect if it seized your property and sold it today—after paying off debts on the property, such as mortgages.

    AND

2. The Offer is for more money than the IRS could get from you in an installment agreement over the next five years or the remaining period of time left to collect its debt (whichever is less).

These tests are cumulative, meaning that you must add the amounts for each to come up with an acceptable Offer. (See the example, below.)

To get a complete picture of your finances, the IRS insists that you submit a completed Form 433-A (and Form 433-B if you have any self-employed income) with your Offer in Compromise. The 433 forms are divided into two parts:

- Assets and Liabilities, and
- Income and Expenses.

In completing the 433 forms, a married person must include financial disclosures for his or her spouse—even if the tax bill is a separate debt. If you owed the IRS before your marriage or if you file separate tax returns during the marriage, you still must list financial information for your spouse. This doesn't strike me as fair, but the IRS is trying to prevent you from channeling your property or income away from the IRS and to your spouse.

Instructions for completing the forms are in Section D.3, above. The forms are in the Appendix.

A. FIRST TEST: YOUR OFFER MUST BE GREATER THAN THE NET VALUE OF YOUR ASSETS

You must offer to settle your tax bill for at least the total equity value of all of your property, plus $1. For Offer in Compromise purposes equity value is the "quick sale value" of your property—personal or real—less your debts against it.

Example

Darlene has no assets except her home which has a quick sale value of $125,000. She owes Barney's Bank $77,000 on a first mortgage, Friendly Finance Company $33,000 on a second mortgage and her county $4,000 for back property taxes. Her equity value is $11,000, as follows:

Quick sale value		$125,000
First mortgage	$ 77,000	
Second mortgage	+33,000	
Unpaid property tax	+4,000	
Total debt		−114,000
Equity value (value less debt)		$ 11,000

So, Darlene would have to pay a minimum of $11,001 to the IRS to meet the "asset" test in an Offer in Compromise. But Darlene can't stop here. She must add to that amount the figure she comes up with under the second part of the test.

That the IRS uses quick sale value is a break for you. A quick sale value is less than the fair market value of an asset. As a result, you will show less equity in your property. The quick sale value, however, is not as low as a "forced sale value"— another way of valuing property.

Here's how the three values compare:

Jake's home has a fair market value of $100,000. If the house was foreclosed and sold at a Sheriff's forced sale, it would bring $70,000. The IRS pegs a quick sale value at approximately mid-way between fair market and forced sale value, or $85,000. If Jake had a mortgage on his home of $65,000, using a quick sale value of $85,000 his equity would be $20,000.

Also, to minimize your 433 assets, you get to take certain exemptions from your total assets. Your family's clothing, $1,650 of furniture and personal effects, and a few other items are legally exempt from IRS collection and not included in the asset test for an Offer in Compromise. (Publication 594, Understanding The Collection Process, in the Appendix, has a full list of exemptions.)

Your total equity shown on the IRS 433 forms is called your "net realizable equity." If your Offer in Compromise is for less than this amount, plus $1, it will be rejected.

B. SECOND TEST: YOUR OFFER MUST BE MORE THAN THE IRS COULD COLLECT THROUGH AN INSTALLMENT AGREEMENT

The IRS must compare the amount offered with how much it could collect if you were granted a monthly payment plan. (See Section C for discussion of installment agreements.) This is not an easy figure to come up with for several reasons.

The IRS collector must first treat your Offer as if it was a request for an Installment Agreement. Therefore, the Revenue Officer must collect all of the financial data required on IRS Form 433-A (and if you are a business owner or self-employed, Form 433-B). Then, the Revenue Officer estimates the maximum monthly payment that could be squeezed out of you. He plugs the monthly amount into a formula to determine what five years of monthly payments would equal. (It is not the monthly payment times 60. It is a complex formula based on the present value of money and the length of time the IRS has to collect from you—not necessarily the full five years.) The example below should make this more clear.

When You Owe for Several Years

Once taxes are assessed against you, the IRS has only ten years to collect that tax bill. If you owe for several different years, the IRS may have assessed the taxes against you at different times and therefore each bill would have a different ten-year period.

You can find out exactly how much time remains for each assessment by asking the IRS for the date of each assessment or by looking at your IRS - furnished Individual Master File computer printout. You can get a copy by calling 800-829-1040. Once you figure out each assessment date, calculate the number of months left to collect from you. If the number exceeds 60, use 60 for the Offer in Compromise test. Otherwise, use whatever number you came up with.

Example

The IRS assessed a tax against Franklin on August 15, 1990. The IRS legally has ten years, until August 14, 2000, to collect the bill. If Franklin submits an Offer in Compromise on August 15, 1994, the IRS has 72 months left to collect the tax. But for purposes of an Offer in Compromise, Franklin should use 60 months in the calculation.

Now that you know how much time on which to base your installment agreement portion of the Offer in Compromise test, you must determine the present value of a hypothetical stream of installment payments. You can figure it out with a calculator using the "PV" function.

Or, if you are like me and are not very handy with calculators beyond adding and subtracting, you can use the IRS' present value tables. They are in the Internal Revenue Manual, MT 5700-34, page 5700-239. Because few people have the IRS Manual lying around, go to the IRS office and ask for a copy of these tables. If you are working with a Revenue Officer get one from her. (Stay with me—I promise this will become clear in the example below).

The IRS present value tables assume different interest rates ranging from 7% to 12% and periods from one month to 120 months (ten years). Why the tables go up to ten years is beyond me—the IRS limits its calculations under this test to 60 months.

To come up with the figure representing how much the IRS could get from you in a hypothetical installment plan, you must plug the following figures into the IRS tables:

- the IRS interest rate at the time you make your Offer (it is 7% as of the time of this writing January 1994), and

- how many months the IRS has left to collect, or 60 months, whichever is less.

Example 1

Dan is a factory worker who owes $58,000 in back taxes for a tax bill exactly 60 months old. He is 59, is working in a depressed industry and will be lucky if the company holds out until he is of retirement age. He was divorced last year and has $5,000 equity in his assets. He makes $25,000 per year and based on his 433-A Collection Information Form, he could pay the IRS no more than $275 per month. The IRS interest rate is 9% at the time Dan makes an Offer. The IRS legally has five more years (60 months) left on the statute of limitations to collect from Dan.

IRS analysis: Dan's Revenue Officer will multiply $275 times 60 (months) to get $16,500. This is the amount the IRS would presumably get if Dan entered into an installment agreement and paid in full. The Revenue Officer than checks the IRS' present value tables for 9% interest. $16,500 paid over the next five years is worth today $13,246.75. Adding this figure to the $5,000 in assets, plus $1, means Dan's offer should be at least $18,247.75.

Example 2

Assume the same facts as in Example 1, except that the factory has closed down and Dan is unemployed with poor prospects of getting another job. He would like to start his own business but can't get a bank loan because of his tax problem. Because Dan can't afford to pay anything under an installment agreement, the first test does not apply. The IRS collector would look solely to Dan's $5,000 equity in his assets. In this case, the minimum Offer the IRS would consider is $5,001.

TIP I have seen the IRS ignore the payment plan test and apply just the asset test in accepting Offers in Compromise. But I have never seen vice versa. Therefore, if you have assets, you might first offer an amount based on the equity value of your assets plus $1. But be prepared to up your offer based on the second test which includes an amount for monthly payments.

C. OTHER FACTORS IN QUALIFYING YOUR OFFER

Before 1992, the IRS could also take into account any number of factors which might cause your fortunes to rise—including the chance that you would inherit money from a rich uncle or you would quit waiting tables and become a brain surgeon. It is now unclear whether or not these conditions are still considered in evaluating (and turning down) an Offer.

The IRS has always favored Offers from people with bleak future financial prospects due to mental or physical infirmities—including drug or alcohol addiction and the HIV virus. There does seem to be a heart somewhere at the IRS, no matter how small or hard it is, if you can prove a medical disability. If this is your unfortunate situation, play it to the hilt. With your Offer in Compromise, include financial data *and* statements from doctors and other medical records clearly indicating that your disability prevents you from earning much of a living—both now and in the foreseeable future.

TIP This isn't written anywhere in the Internal Revenue Manual, but in my experience, Offers of less than $5,000 are not accepted, regardless of the amount of taxes owed.

In sum, Offers that stand the best chance are from those people who can demonstrate poor health, lack of earning capacity and no rich relations. As the Rolling Stones sang, "Paint It Black."

Do You Need a Tax Pro to Submit an Offer?

If you follow the instructions here to the letter, I think your chances are almost as good in getting an Offer accepted as if you had hired me to do it for you. If you are really serious about getting an Offer accepted, do as much as you can to get the Offer together and then consult or hire a Tax Pro experienced in Offers in Compromise to do the rest. If she has had prior dealings with local IRS collection personnel, she may know how to sell your Offer better than you could. This is not to say that the IRS in general gives any special consideration to Tax Pros—it doesn't. But a Tax Pro is less likely to make a mistake in the process than you are, and will not get emotional in dealing with the IRS.

4. Structuring Your Offer in Compromise

You can propose payments under an Offer in Compromise in one of three ways—lump sum, installments or a combination. In general, lump sum offers have the best chance of acceptance, although the IRS won't reject a decent installment or combination Offer. For example, Ralph owes $100,000, and wants to offer $10,000 to call it even. Ralph could offer the IRS:

- $10,000 lump sum full payment
- $1,000 monthly for ten months (or $500 for 20 months), or
- $4,000 lump sum and $1,000 per month for six months (or $500 per month for 12 months).

The IRS would also probably require Ralph to pay interest on the unpaid balance under an install-ment offer until it paid in full.

5. Future Income Agreements May Be Required by the IRS

As a condition of accepting an Offer, the IRS may require you to forfeit income tax refunds and make additional annual payments of a percentage of any increases in your income for up to six years.

Example

Sandra made an Offer to settle a $27,000 tax bill for $8,000. The IRS accepted, on one condition—that in addition to the $8,000, Sandra pay 20% of all income increases she experiences during the next four years. Sandra earned $20,000 the year her Offer was accepted. This means if Sandra makes $25,000 the next year, she would owe the IRS another $1,000 (20% of $5,000). The IRS required her to sign Form 2261, Future Income Collateral Agreement.

TIP Future income conditions can be negotiated with the IRS. For example, Sandra could argue that 20% was too much of any increase in income because she has large medical bills to pay and that 10% would be more fair. Or, she could offer to "buy out" the future income condition by adding $1,000 to her Offer. The IRS wants finality in making deals and doesn't like to worry about moni-toring future income agreements. It may be easy to negotiate with the IRS here.

6. Pros and Cons of Making an Offer in Compromise

Making an Offer in Compromise has its advantages and disadvantages.

A. ADVANTAGES

The obvious advantage is that if your Offer in Com-promise is accepted, you'll save a heap of money. If your Offer includes installment payments, interest continues to accrue, but only on the amount you're paying under the Offer in Compromise—not the original amount owed.

Also, even if your Offer is ultimately rejected, your stress level will be reduced while the Offer is pending. This is because the IRS normally doesn't take wages or seize property during this time. No law requires that the IRS stop its enforced collection action, but it is the IRS's policy to do so unless the offer is frivolous.

Finally, once an Offer in Compromise is accepted and you've paid the amount agreed to, the IRS will remove the tax liens placed on your property within 30 days. Your credit rating will improve instantly.

B. DISADVANTAGES

There are some conditions to and disadvantages of making an Offer in Compromise. First, from the time you make your Offer in Compromise and until it is accepted, you must file all tax returns and make all tax payments that are due. This includes payroll taxes and estimated tax payments. If making those payments will be a struggle, consider filing for bankruptcy—not making an Offer in Compromise—to halt IRS collection activities. (See Section F, below.)

Second, you give the IRS extra time to collect the taxes you owe. As mentioned above, the IRS normally has ten years to collect taxes, interest and penalties. If you make an Offer in Compromise, the IRS gets to add the time that the Offer is under consideration *plus one year* to the ten-year period. If your Offer includes installment payments, the extra year doesn't start to run until your last payment is due.

Example

Seven years after the IRS assessed taxes against him, Kiichi submitted an Offer in Compromise. A year later, his Offer was accepted. The Offer called for him to make $500 monthly payments for 30 months. Kiichi made most of the payments and then stopped. At the end of the Offer period, he still owed $1,500. The IRS has a total of five more years to collect the balance—three years left in the original ten (remember, Kiichi submitted his Offer seven years after the taxes were assessed), the one year that his Offer was pending, and the extra one year from the date his payments stopped.

Third, if your Offer in Compromise is accepted, you give up any tax refunds for the years covered by the Offer (assuming you plan to make installment payments) and for the year in which the Offer is made. As part of your Collateral Agreement, the IRS also may insist that you give up future year's refunds —for a set number of years—as well.

Fourth, you cannot later contest, either in court or to the IRS directly, any taxes you proposed paying or eliminating through the Offer, even if your Offer is rejected.

Fifth, in making an Offer in Compromise, you must thoroughly disclose your assets. If your Offer is rejected, the IRS knows everything there is to know about your finances. Of course, if you tried to get an installment agreement before making your Offer, the IRS will already have this information.

Sixth, while your Offer is pending and the IRS is investigating your assets, it may decide to audit you. This is not common, however.

 Seventh and possibly the greatest disadvantage of all, if you default on making the payments required under your Offer in Compromise, the original amount owed, plus penalties and interest, is reinstated in full. And if you fail to file or pay any taxes due for five years after your Offer is accepted, the same thing happens—the deal is nullified and your original tax debt is reinstated.

7. Making an Offer in Compromise

Your offer *must* be presented on Form 656, Offer in Compromise, a blank copy of which is in the Appendix. As mentioned, you also must submit a completed Form 433-A and maybe Form 433-B, which are also in the Appendix. To make sure these forms are the most current ones, call the IRS (800-829-1040) or visit the Collection Division at your District Office.

Also, it's a good idea to visit your District Office and tell a Revenue Officer that you intend to submit an Offer in Compromise, and ask that no collection action be taken while you prepare the Offer. Your request will probably be granted.

If a Revenue Officer has already been assigned your file, enlist her support in recommending your Offer. She may not comment or may even say no. But if she says yes, her recommendation greatly helps your case. While your Offer is pending, your file moves to the IRS Special Procedures section. Chances are the Revenue Officer will be working with the Special Procedures staff in investigating your financial disclosures.

A. COMPLETING THE FORMS

The instructions for completing Form 433-A and 433-B are in Section D.3, above. As you're filling out the form, remember the suggestions in Section E.3, above.

A completed sample of Form 656 is below. A blank copy, with IRS instructions, is in the Appendix. Here are some additional instructions. The numbers refer to the corresponding paragraph numbers on Form 656.

1. List all taxes owed, specifically by year and type of tax—such as "income" or "employment." Be sure to add the words "plus statutory additions." This makes sure all penalties and interest are included in your Offer.

2. Enter the amount you propose to pay and how you intend to pay it—in a lump sum, installment payments, or a combination of the two.

9. Simply type "Doubt as to collectability of the full amount of tax, penalty and interest owed." Don't say anything more. This means there's a doubt as to whether or not the IRS could collect, not whether or not you owe the bill.

   Personal and business taxes. If you plan to make an Offer in Compromise to cover your personal tax liability *and* taxes owed by your corporation or partnership, you must make separate Offers for each —you can't combine two Offers on one Form 656.

B. SUBMITTING DOCUMENTATION

After you have filed your Form 656 Offer, the IRS will want evidence supporting the information on your Form 433-A and 433-B (if applicable). Be prepared to submit copies (never the originals) of:

- your income tax returns for the last two years

- deeds and mortgage papers to all real estate you own

- titles to motor vehicles, boats, planes and the like

- bank statements of all your accounts for the last six to 12 months

- life insurance policies (the IRS may want to see if you have cash value to borrow against)

- sources of non-wage income, such as unemployment, worker's compensation, a disability policy or a retirement or pension plan

- unpaid notes, bills and other evidences of your debts

- evidence of your major living expenses, such as your rent receipts, and

- doctor's statements and evidence of your medical problems.

   The IRS is always impressed by paper, so lay it on.

C. MAKING A DEPOSIT WITH YOUR OFFER

The IRS does not require that you include any payment with your Offer; however, to do so will create a good impression. If possible, submit about 10% of your total Offer. For example, if you are offering $10,000, a deposit of $1,000 shows good faith. Even if you can't afford that much, make a token payment, such as $100.

   If your Offer is rejected, you will get your deposit back. The IRS is not allowed to keep your money unless you sign a release letting the IRS keep it. You will not be paid interest for the time the IRS has your money.

D. AWAITING THE IRS' ANSWER

If the IRS finds your Offer defective—you didn't fill the forms in correctly—it will probably send your Offer back to you within a week or two. Simply make the corrections and refile. Don't get discouraged, as this is very common.

   If, however, you list more equity in your assets than you have offered, the IRS will quickly reject your Offer as "frivolous."

Form **656**
(Rev. Sept. 1993)

Department of the Treasury—Internal Revenue Service

Offer in Compromise

▶ See Instructions Page 5

(1) Name and Address of Taxpayers	For Official Use Only	
Martin Kuhn 4999 Wallace Berry Lane Ocala, FL 39000	Offer is (*Check applicable box*) ☐ Cash (*Paid in full*) ☐ Deferred payment	Serial Number (*Cashier's stamp*)

(2) Social Security Number 000-99-888	(3) Employer Identification Number	Alpha CSED Ind. _____

To: **Commissioner of Internal Revenue Service**

Amount Paid
$

(4) **I/we** (includes all types of taxpayers) **submit this offer to compromise the tax liabilities plus any interest, penalties, additions to tax, and additional amounts required by law (tax liability)** for the tax type and period checked below: (Please mark "X" for the correct description and fill-in the correct tax period(s); adding additional periods if needed.)

☐ Income tax for the year(s) 19_____, 19_____, 19_____, and 19_____

☒ Trust fund recovery penalty (formerly called the 100-percent penalty) as a responsible person of _____
Nopay Industries _____ (enter business name) for failure to pay withholding and Federal Insurance Contributions Act taxes (Social Security taxes) for the period(s) ended 12 / 31 / 90 , 3 / 31 / 91 , 6 / 30 / 91 , 9 / 30 / 91 (for example - 06/30/92)

☒ Withholding and Federal Insurance Contributions Act taxes (Social Security taxes) for the period(s) ended 12 / 31 / 90 , 3 / 31 / 91 , 6 / 30 / 91 , 9 / 30 / 91 (for example - 06/30/92)

☐ Federal Unemployment Tax Act taxes for the year(s) 19_____, 19_____, 19_____, and 19_____

☐ Other (Be specific.) _____

(5) **I/we offer to pay** $ _____ $22,000 _____ .

If you aren't making full payment with your offer, describe below when you will make full payment (for example – within ten (10) days from the date the offer is accepted): See the instructions for Item 5.

$2,000 is paid with this Offer; the balance to $20,000 to be paid in five monthly installments of $4,000 each to begin one month after I receive notice of the acceptance of this Offer.

As required by section 6621 of the Internal Revenue Code, the Internal Revenue Service (IRS) will add interest to the offered amount from the date IRS accepts the offer until the date you completely pay the amount offered. IRS compounds interest daily, as required by section 6622 of the Internal Revenue Code.

(6) **I/we submit this offer for the reason(s) checked below:**

☒ Doubt as to collectibility ("I can't pay.") You must include a completed financial statement (Form 433-A and/or Form 433-B).

☐ Doubt as to liability ("I don't believe I owe this tax.") You must include a detailed explanation of the reason(s) why you believe you don't owe the tax.

IMPORTANT: SEE REVERSE FOR TERMS AND CONDITIONS

I accept waiver of the statutory period of limitations for the Internal Revenue Service.	Under penalties of perjury, I declare that I have examined this offer, including accompanying schedules and statements, and to the best of my knowledge and belief, it is true, correct and complete.	
Signature of authorized Internal Revenue Service Official	(8a) Signature of Taxpayer-proponent *Martin Kuhn*	Date 7-8-94
Title	Date	(8b) Signature of Taxpayer-proponent	Date

Dispose of prior issues.

Part 1 IRS Copy

Cat. No. 16728N

Form **656** (Rev. 9-93)

SAMPLE FORM 656

If the IRS deems your Offer legitimate and "processable," it will take between four and 12 months to review and investigate it. During that time, deal with the IRS as you normally would. You must make payments under an existing installment agreement while you are awaiting an answer unless you can show the Revenue Officer that it is impossible for you. When it's time to file your next return, do so or make sure you file an extension, and pay whatever taxes are due.

The IRS works in mysterious ways. Sometimes, Offers to pay 10% of the tax bill are accepted, while 80% Offers are turned down. Consider the following two cases.

Leroy and Mary were in their late sixties and had filed for Chapter 7 bankruptcy (liquidation) several years before. Unfortunately, most of their income tax debts did not qualify for discharge and so they still owed the IRS $35,000. They were now retired and living modestly on Social Security. The IRS collection notices and threats kept on coming. This was particularly upsetting to Leroy, who had a bad heart.

Leroy and Mary submitted an Offer in Compromise to pay $3,500 cash, which Mary's sister promised to give them. An IRS Special Procedures staff employee came to Leroy and Mary's home to investigate their lifestyle. (This is standard IRS procedure.) The couple emphasized their frugality and Leroy's genuine health problems. Almost a year later they received a letter saying that the Offer had been accepted and that no collateral agreement was required. Leroy and Mary paid the IRS and the IRS removed its $35,000 tax lien. A very happy ending.

■

Louis and Juanita owed the IRS $51,000 as a result of a failed business venture. Louis worked sporadically in the Merchant Marine and Juanita was a nursing home attendant. Together they earned $35,000 per year. An aggressive IRS Revenue Officer threatened to seize their home if they didn't make payments of $1,500 per month. This was clearly impossible, as they had four children and a mortgage. They offered $500 per month. The offer was rejected.

Louis and Juanita's increased their Offer to $15,000 cash, plus $5,000 a year for five years—a total of $40,000. To their dismay, the amended Offer was also rejected. The IRS concluded that Louis and Juanita had

$59,000 of equity in their home. For this reason, any Offer for less than the full amount—$51,000—would be rejected under IRS guidelines.

After their two Offers were rejected, Louis and Juanita applied and were turned down for a second mortgage loan. The only way they could use the home's equity to pay the IRS was to sell their house.

Before taking this drastic step, they asked the Special Procedures Officer to recommend to the Revenue Officer a monthly installment agreement of $500—even though the Revenue Officer had rejected their request for a $500 monthly installment agreement in the past. They explained that Juanita was depressed and that their marriage was in trouble because of the stress of dealing with the IRS. He understood Louis and Juanita's financial and personal situation very well and agreed to make a recommendation. The Revenue Officer finally said yes, months after his obstinacy caused the Offer to be submitted in the first place. Another happy ending.

8.   If Your Offer Is Rejected—Keep Trying

The IRS must give you a rejection letter if your Offer is not accepted. The IRS usually rejects Offers in Compromise for one of two reasons:

- public policy, which means that you are a notorious character—for example, you've been convicted of a serious crime, or
- the Offer is too low.

Most rejected Offers fall into the "too low" category. If so, ask the IRS what amount would be accepted. An officer must tell you, either orally or in writing, at the time he notifies you that your Offer is inadequate.

You are also entitled to a copy of the report which lists the factors that caused the rejection. Ask the Revenue Officer or Special Procedures Officer for a copy. If he won't give it to you, make a request under the Freedom of Information Act. (See Chapter 4, Section B.2.)

After finding out why your Offer was rejected, try again. You don't need a new 656 Form if you write within a month or two. Instead, write a letter if the new Offer is not radically different from your old one and if your financial circumstances have not appreciably changed. State that you wish to change your Offer by increasing the amount of cash offered from $10,000 to $15,000, or whatever is appropriate.

To submit a significantly different Offer, or if more than a few months have elapsed, complete another Form 656. The Revenue Officer or Special Procedures Officer might help you come up with a way to make your Offer acceptable.

TIP Looking at Offers in Compromise which were accepted might give you an idea of what kinds of proposals the IRS goes for. Some Districts accept far more Offers than others. Go to your local District Office Collections Division and ask to see all Offers that were accepted within the last year. It's a good idea to call the IRS first and tell them you are coming. Accepted Offers are a matter of public record, for one year, although these Offers won't have any direct bearing on yours.

How to handle a summary rejection. A summary IRS rejection is a quick denial without looking into the merits of your Offer. The IRS can summarily reject an Offer in Compromise for three reasons:

- it is so inadequate as to be frivolous
- you haven't filed all past tax returns, or
- you didn't submit complete financial information.

If this happens, correct the problem and try again.

9. Appealing a Rejected Offer in Compromise

If your Offer in Compromise is rejected, you can try to negotiate further or appeal within the IRS. You must make your appeal request within 30 days of a turn down. You can appeal following any Offer rejection—if you don't appeal after the first, you can after the second. (In fact, if you want to appeal but the 30 days have passed, you can submit a second Offer and appeal after it is denied.)

This appeal procedure is similar to appealing an audit. Follow the letter in Chapter 4, Section B.1, but substitute the following for the first three paragraphs.

I wish to appeal from the rejection of an Offer in Compromise submitted June 20, 1994, and rejected on January 7, 1995. I request a conference.

That's it. You will also be sent Publication 931 when your receive your rejection notice. Review it carefully, as it describes the appeal process.

You have nothing to lose and an appeal usually delays the collection process further. The appeals conference is your last stop—no one else will review your request for an Offer in Compromise. You cannot go further within the IRS; nor can you file a petition in Tax Court for a denied Offer in Compromise.

F. Using the Bankruptcy Code to Stop the IRS

Bankruptcy is a technical (and widely misunderstood) legal procedure for debt relief, including tax debts. It is definitely not for everyone, but it might be just the answer to your prayers. The theory behind bankruptcy is that victims of financial misfortune should be offered a chance for a "fresh start." Only you can decide the moral or ethical implications yourself. My job is to point out that bankruptcy may be an option and show you how it works.[4]

---

[4]For more information on Chapter 7 bankruptcy, see *How to File for Bankruptcy,* by Elias, Renauer and Leonard (Nolo Press). For more information on Chapter 13 bankruptcy, see *Chapter 13 Bankruptcy: Repay Your Debts,* by Robin Leonard (Nolo Press).

There are several types of bankruptcies that can help with a tax bill:

- You may be able to erase most consumer debts in a Chapter 7 "straight bankruptcy," although tax debts qualify for erasure in only limited circumstances.

- You can repay your debts, including your tax debts, in a bankruptcy repayment plan through Chapter 11, Chapter 12 or, in most cases, Chapter 13.

1.   Effects of Filing for Bankruptcy

There are several effects of filing for bankruptcy.

A.   THE AUTOMATIC STAY

One of bankruptcy's most alluring features is the "automatic stay." The moment you file your bankruptcy petition with the bankruptcy court clerk, an automatic court order stops virtually all your creditors. The automatic stay prevents federal and state tax collectors from seizing your property and issuing lien notices.

There are restrictions on the automatic stay, however. For example, it does not stop a tax audit, the issuance of a tax deficiency notice, a demand for a tax return, the issuance of a tax assessment or the demand for payment of such an assessment.

B.   YOUR PROPERTY

When you file for bankruptcy, a person called a trustee is appointed by the court to oversee your bankruptcy case.

Bankruptcy is not designed to send you from the bankruptcy court to a welfare office. You are entitled to keep a reasonable amount of specific items (called "exempt property"). The particular items and the value of each exempt category is determined by state, not federal law. But most people who file for Chapter 7—no matter where they live—find that all their property is exempt, and lose nothing.

In a Chapter 11, Chapter 12 or Chapter 13 bankruptcy, you do not have to turn over any property for your creditors.

C.   YOUR CREDIT RECORD

An unavoidable consequence of bankruptcy is that it remains on a credit record for ten years. But bankruptcy doesn't seem to hurt your credit standing as it did in the past. Some lenders welcome those coming out of bankruptcy shortly after the proceedings are finished, especially people who filed for Chapter 13. In fact, in some parts of the country, court trustees work with local creditors to help people who complete Chapter 13 repayment plans get credit. And if tax lien notices already appear on your credit report, a bankruptcy might not make things any worse—at least it shows you are making an effort to handle debt problems.

2.   Taxes and Chapter 7 "Straight Bankruptcy"

Chapter 7 is what most people think of as bankruptcy—wiping out debts completely. Chapter 7 is a relatively simple process. You must complete several forms describing your income, expenses, property and debts.

Chapter 7 typically requires only one visit to the bankruptcy court for something called the Meeting of Creditors. Any creditors (including the IRS) can attend and ask questions about your forms. Rarely does any creditor appear, so don't worry about having to face the IRS or anyone else.

Unfortunately, some types of debts cannot be erased ("discharged" in bankruptcy parlance) in Chapter 7 bankruptcy:

- certain tax debts
- recent student loans
- child support, and
- debts incurred by fraud.

What follows is very technical. But read it carefully—the knowledge can be very rewarding.

A. DISCHARGING INCOME TAXES

For bankruptcy law purposes, federal income taxes fall into two categories—*secured* taxes (the IRS has filed a notice of tax lien) and *unsecured* (no notice of tax lien has been filed). We'll discuss each below.

Unsecured federal income taxes can be discharged only if four conditions are true:

- You neither filed a fraudulent return nor attempted to evade paying taxes.

- The liability is for a tax return (not a Substitute For Return) actually filed at least two years before you file for bankruptcy. This is the *two year rule*.

- The tax return was due at least three years ago (including any time for extensions and when due dates are automatically extended because of weekends and holidays). This is the *three year rule*.

- The taxes were assessed at least 240 days before bankruptcy filing. This is the *240 day rule*.

State Income Taxes

Some states have different rules for discharging state income taxes. For example, California imposes a 300 day rule, instead of a 240 day rule for discharging state income tax liabilities.

Certain actions extend the above time limits:

- If you filed any *bankruptcy* in the past—even if the case was kicked out of court the next day—the time the case was pending *plus* an additional six months is added to all three time requirements.

- If you made an *Offer in Compromise*, the time your offer was pending *plus* an additional 30 days is added to the 240-day requirement.

- If you requested a *Taxpayer Assistance Order* (see Chapter 8), the time your request was pending is added to all three time requirements.

Examples

1. On March 15, 1994, Fred owes income taxes for a 1989 tax return which was filed and taxes were assessed on April 15, 1990. Result: All three time tests are met, the taxes are dischargeable if Fred files a Chapter 7 petition.

2. Same facts as above only the tax return was a 1990 return filed on April 15, 1991. Fred is one month short of the "three year" test. No discharge.

3. Same facts as number two, except Fred's 1990 tax return was audited and additional taxes were assessed on September 15, 1993. Fred now flunks the "240 day" test, as well as the three year test. No discharge.

4. Same facts as number three, except Fred filed the 1990 return late, on August 15, 1992. Now Fred flunks the "two year" test by five months, and both the other time tests as well. No discharge.

TIP The time that you are in an IRS installment plan does not extend the three Chapter 7 time limits. So, if you can make monthly installment payments, you can get the IRS off your back until the tax debts qualify for Chapter 7 discharge under the three time tests.

You cannot turn your nondischargeable tax debt into a dischargeable debt by borrowing money or using your credit card to pay the taxes—and then file for bankruptcy to discharge the loan or credit card debt. The Bankruptcy Reform Act of 1994 specifically says a loan or credit card debt used to pay nondischargeable taxes is also nondischargeable.

B. DISCHARGING PENALTIES AND INTEREST

The above rules apply only to the "raw" tax liability, not to penalties and interest on the taxes due. The rules for discharging penalties and interest are less stringent than for discharging the underlying taxes.

Penalties. Even if a tax cannot be discharged in bankruptcy, any penalty on that tax may be. As a rule, tax penalties are dischargeable when they relate to a dischargeable tax *or* when the event giving rise to the penalty occurred more than three years prior to filing the bankruptcy.

Example

Joan is audited for her 1990 tax return on November 1, 1993 and additional taxes and penalties are assessed. If she files a Chapter 7 petition on May 10, 1994, she flunks the time test on the audit taxes. But the penalty on the tax may be discharged because the event giving rise to the penalty (the filing of the 1990 return) is more than three years old.

Interest. Interest on taxes is dischargeable only if the taxes are dischargeable. Otherwise, interest continues to accrue while you are in a Chapter 7 bankruptcy.

C. DISCHARGING SECURED INCOME TAXES

A tax debt is *secured* if the IRS has a legal claim to any property owned by you at the time you file for Chapter 7 bankruptcy. For the IRS, this interest is secured by filing a Notice of Federal Tax Lien with your county recorder's office. The lien is valid for ten years plus 30 days.

A tax lien "survives" bankruptcy. Assuming your taxes are dischargeable—all taxes in excess of the value of your property are wiped out. But because the lien is still there, the IRS can collect from you up to the value of the property you owned when you filed for bankruptcy. As a practical matter, secured tax liens usually cause the most problems with real estate, not personal property.

Example

Sarah's only asset is a car worth $1,000. The IRS records a lien notice for a $6,000 tax debt which is dischargeable. Sarah files for Chapter 7 bankruptcy and gets rid of her personal liability for the entire $6,000 tax debt. But the lien remains and is worth $1,000. The only way the IRS can collect is to force the sale of her car.

D. DISCHARGING OTHER TAXES

Other (non-income) types of taxes are not dischargeable in a Chapter 7 bankruptcy. Assuming you did not file a fraudulent return nor had a willful attempt to evade paying taxes, the following rules apply:

Trust fund taxes. Trust fund taxes are not dischargeable in Chapter 7 (but may be partially dischargeable in a Chapter 13).

Payroll taxes. If you were required to collect or withhold the tax, these taxes never are dischargeable in Chapter 7.

Social Security funds. If you were required to collect or withhold the tax, these taxes never are dischargeable in Chapter 7.

Sales taxes. If you were required to collect or withhold the tax, these taxes never are dischargeable in Chapter 7.

3. Taxes and Chapter 13 Payment Plans

Chapter 13 is the most widely utilized type of bankruptcy to deal with tax debts. In a Chapter 13, you devise a repayment plan for the bankruptcy court's approval. If the court okays it, you make a monthly payment to the trustee. The trustee splits payments among creditors, including the IRS. Payments are generally made over three to five years.

Interest and tax penalties do not accrue while you are in a Chapter 13. Interest and tax penalties on the taxes due up until the date a Chapter 13 is filed, however, must be paid in your Chapter 13 plan.

It is much easier to qualify a tax debt under Chapter 13 than under Chapter 7. For taxes to be included in a Chapter 13 plan, you must meet three conditions:

- You must have a fairly steady stream of income so that the court knows you will be able to make regular payments. The income may be wages, Social Security or pension benefits or independent contractor income.

- The total of unsecured debts—debts such as credit cards, medical bills and taxes where the IRS has not filed a tax lien notice—cannot exceed $250,000.

- The total of secured debts—such as mortgages, car and equipment loans and existing property subject to a tax lien—cannot exceed $750,000.

DISCHARGEABILITY OF TAXES IN BANKRUPTCY

This chart is designed to determine whether or not a specific tax debt was discharged in bankruptcy. You can use it to determine whether or not a specific tax debt can be discharged in bankruptcy. Source: Internal Revenue Manual MT5700-8.

#1

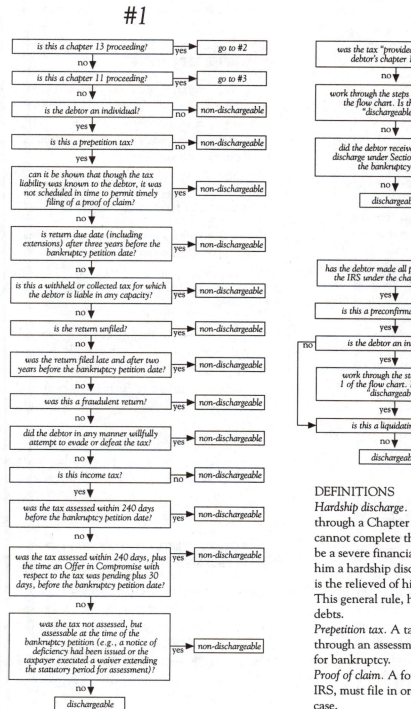

#2

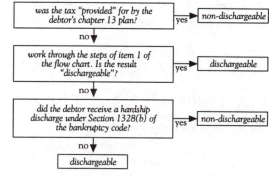

#3

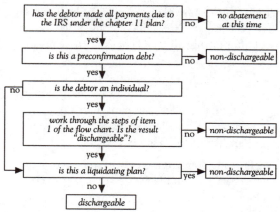

DEFINITIONS

Hardship discharge. If, in trying to repay debts through a Chapter 13 bankruptcy, a debtor cannot complete the plan because to do so would be a severe financial burden, the court can give him a hardship discharge. In general, the debtor is the relieved of his obligation to repay his debts. This general rule, however, does not apply to tax debts.

Prepetition tax. A tax liability that arose— through an assessment—before the debtor filed for bankruptcy.

Proof of claim. A form a creditor, including the IRS, must file in order to get paid in a bankruptcy case.

If You're Not Sure How Much a Debt Is Worth

The above dollar limits apply only to debts which are "noncontingent and liquidated." This means that your obligation to pay is definite and fixed in amount. If you may owe an unspecified amount—for instance, someone has filed a lawsuit against you for $2 million but there hasn't yet been a determination—you can still file for Chapter 13.

A. FILING FOR CHAPTER 13

To file for a Chapter 13 payment plan, you must complete several forms disclosing all your assets, liabilities, income and expenses. And, you must submit a proposed payment plan to the bankruptcy court. Unless you intend paying every unsecured creditor back in full, you must pay a trustee all of your net monthly disposable income for at least three years (five years tops). Disposable income is whatever is left over after paying all your "necessary expenses."

TIP Just how much is necessary for your rent, clothing and other expenses is discretionary with each bankruptcy judge. But bankruptcy judges are seldom as stingy as IRS collectors when you are trying to work out an IRS installment agreement.

Going to court. You will have to go to bankruptcy court at least twice if you file for Chapter 13 bankruptcy. The first time is for the Meeting of Creditors. Any creditor (including the IRS) can attend and ask you questions about your papers. Rarely does any creditor appear, so don't worry about having to face the IRS or anyone else. Creditors usually just file written claims to be paid. If a creditor named in your petition doesn't file a claim, you don't have to pay that creditor—ever.

The second court appearance is for a Confirmation Hearing. Either your creditors or the court-appointed trustee can object to your proposed repayment plan. The IRS usually can't object as long as the plan provides for full payment of all non-dischargeable taxes. The IRS, however, will ask the judge to require you to file any delinquent tax returns as a condition of allowing your Chapter 13 plan. And

you must keep current on tax returns filings and payments for as long as you are in Chapter 13.

It seldom happens, but a Chapter 13 plan can be rejected by the court if it is deemed to be proposed in "bad faith." The only people with tax debts who usually have to worry about this are tax protesters.

B. CHAPTER 13 PAYMENTS

Once your plan is confirmed by the court, you make monthly payments to the trustee. The trustee in turn takes a percentage off the top for her fee and pays your creditors, including the IRS, the balance in accordance with your plan.

C. IF YOU CAN'T MAKE YOUR PAYMENTS

If you can't make your payments under a Chapter 13 plan, the trustee has several options:

- modify your plan (reduce the amount your unsecured creditors receive)

- temporarily suspend your payments

- convert your case to Chapter 7, which will eliminate your unsecured dischargeable debts, but may not help you with your tax debts

- grant you a hardship discharge of your dischargeable debts—again, this may not help you with your tax debts, or

- dismiss your case, in which case the IRS (and all your other creditors) can restart their collection efforts and add back the penalties and interest that stopped while you were in bankruptcy.

D. TYPES OF CHAPTER 13 PLANS THAT CAN BE PROPOSED

Chapter 13 is designed to be flexible enough to fit the financial circumstances of each individual debtor. The types of Chapter 13 plans bankruptcy courts regularly approve are:

- *Standard payment plans.* The monthly payments are fixed over the life of the plan—for example, $300 per month for 36 months.

- *Step-up plans*. Your monthly payments increase over time, in anticipation of rising income or decreasing expenses. Payments may start low—such as $100 in the first year and then go to $200 per month in the second year, and so on.

- *Balloon plans*. This type of plan can be used if a regular or stepped-up plan won't satisfy the debts that must be paid, such as non-dischargeable taxes. A balloon plan usually runs five years. The last payment (60th) pays off the balance in full.

A balloon plan is often used by a homeowner who hopes her property value will rise during her bankruptcy case and that she will be able to refinance or sell to make the balloon payment. A debtor who does not own real estate might have a tough time convincing a judge to approve a balloon plan.

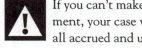 If you can't make the final balloon payment, your case will be dismissed and all accrued and unpaid tax penalties and interest will be resurrected.

- *Variable payment plans*. Monthly payments are varied to match seasonal or other uneven income streams. For example, a roofer can make lower payments in the rainy season or a schoolteacher may pay less in the summer.

E. ADVANTAGES OF CHAPTER 13 IN DEALING WITH THE IRS

There are nine good reasons for filing for Chapter 13 bankruptcy to deal with a tax problem.

1. Chapter 13 bankruptcy forces an installment agreement on the IRS. The IRS must accept a plan approved by the bankruptcy judge.

2. The IRS cannot take any collection action while your Chapter 13 is in place. Thus, Chapter 13 is a way to get around an unreasonable IRS Automated Collection staff person or a Revenue Officer who won't agree to a fair installment agreement. And, the monthly amount you'll pay the IRS in Chapter 13 will be lower than what the IRS would want under an installment agreement.

3. If the IRS has not filed a Notice of Federal Tax Lien, interest stops accruing. If the IRS has filed a notice, interest accrues only on the amount of your tax debt equal to the value of your property (assuming it's less than your full tax debt). If you pay under an installment agreement, interest continues to accrue.

Example

John owns property worth $30,000 and owes the IRS $90,000. The IRS has recorded a tax lien notice. In John's Chapter 13 bankruptcy case, interest accrues only on the $30,000 secured portion of the tax debt.

4. Tax penalties stop accruing the day you file for Chapter 13 bankruptcy. With an IRS installment agreement or when awaiting a decision on an Offer in Compromise, late payment penalties on tax debts continue to accrue on the unpaid balance.

5. Penalties on your tax debts are treated like any *unsecured* debt, such as credit cards. If your plan calls for a payback of 0% or 10% or 50% or 75% or whatever percentage of your unsecured debts (the payback amount will depend on your disposable income and what the judge thinks is reasonable), that's the percentage of the tax penalties you have to pay. (This is not the case, however, with Trust Fund Recovery Penalties, which must be paid in full.)

6. *Not all taxes must be paid in full in Chapter 13.* Generally, taxes that are dischargeable under Chapter 7 can be reduced or wiped out (see #5, above on how debts are reduced or wiped out in Chapter 13) under Chapter 13 as well. But, even taxes that are not dischargeable under Chapter 7 may be reduced in a Chapter 13 plan, at the discretion of the bankruptcy judge.

   For *income* taxes to be eligible for a reduction in a Chapter 13, your taxes must meet the Chapter 7 bankruptcy Three Year and 240 Day rules, but not the Two Year rule. (See Section F.2.a, above, and the below example, for an explanation of these rules.)

   Example

   Gail finally gets around to filing her 1988 income tax return on January 10, 1994, and is assessed $10,000 in taxes on January 25, 1994. Gail wants to file for bankruptcy to help her pay her taxes or reduce the amount she owes. Gail meets the three year rule, but not the two year or the 240 day rules for Chapter 7 bankruptcy. But, if Gail waits 240 days after January 25, her tax debt for 1988 will qualify for reduced payment of whatever percentage her unsecured creditors are receiving in her Chapter 13 plan. That could be as little as 0%, depending on what her bankruptcy judge approves.

   If Gail owns valuable property, the IRS may file a Notice of Federal Tax Lien when it formally assesses taxes against her. This makes the debt secured, meaning it must be paid back in full plus interest. But if Gail files her Chapter 13 before the IRS records the lien notice, she's in luck. The automatic stay prevents the IRS from filing a lien notice.

7. The IRS sometimes slips up and you can wipe out your tax debt without paying a penny. All creditors listed in your bankruptcy papers are notified by the court when you file. Each creditor (including the IRS) must return a claim form to the court by a certain date. If a creditor messes up—even the IRS—it loses the right to make a claim on the debt in bankruptcy, and is barred forever from collecting outside of bankruptcy. But you must complete all payments under the Chapter 13 plan. If you don't, the tax debt will reappear, with interest and penalties added on for the time you were in bankruptcy.

   Exception for secured taxes. If the IRS recorded a Notice of Federal Tax Lien, the amount of the tax debt secured by your property survives bankruptcy, whether or not the IRS files a claim.

8. You can dismiss your Chapter 13 filing for any reason before your plan has been approved. You can then file a new Chapter 13. You will have to pay another filing fee and do more paperwork. Why would you want to do this? Sometimes, a creditor (including the IRS) who filed a claim the first time around, will not realize that it must file a new claim in the new case. If the creditor doesn't, it is out of luck.

9. If the IRS is about to take drastic collection action (seizure of your assets), filing under Chapter 13 (or any other type of bankruptcy) stops the IRS cold. Even if you don't intend on following through with a Chapter 13 plan, filing buys time in dealing with the IRS.

F.   CHAPTER "20"—A WINNING COMBINATION

As discussed above, there are advantages and drawbacks to filing for Chapter 7 or 13 to deal with tax debts. Newer tax bills and payroll taxes can't be wiped out in a Chapter 7. And, while all tax debts can be included in a Chapter 13 plan, most of the time your tax debt will have to be paid at least partially or in full.

It is possible, however, to use the best features of both types of bankruptcies using what is referred to as a Chapter 20. Technically, there is no such animal—

it is simply a Chapter 7 bankruptcy followed by a Chapter 13 bankruptcy.

Here's how it works. You file for Chapter 7 to get rid of all your dischargeable unsecured debts (such as credit cards and hospital bills). You can also eliminate some taxes—typically older, non-payroll taxes. Once your case is over—that is, you have your discharge—you immediately file for Chapter 13 to pay in installments, your taxes (and any other debts) not eliminated in Chapter 7.

4.   Chapter 11 Bankruptcy

Chapter 11 is the most complex type of bankruptcy. Most Chapter 11 cases involve large businesses trying to reorganize their finances before their creditors force them to liquidate. Chapter 11 is extremely expensive (you usually pay lawyers and bankruptcy court fees every month). And, interest on your tax debts continues to accrue during a Chapter 11 case. You have six years to pay off your taxes in Chapter 11.

5.   Chapter 12 Bankruptcy

Chapter 12 is a repayment plan available only to debtors for whom the bulk of their debts come from operating a family farm. Tax debts in Chapter 12 are treated exactly as they are in Chapter 13.

6.   Final Word on Bankruptcy and Taxes

Bankruptcy as a strategy for dealing with tax bills may sound promising but it won't work for everyone. First, bankruptcy is a major blotch on your credit history which stays for ten years.

Second, bankruptcy will help only certain people with certain types of debts. For example, if you have sufficient nonexempt assets to pay your tax bills, Chapter 7 won't help. Nor will it do you good if your tax debts are payroll taxes.

If your income is too low to fund a repayment plan, Chapter 13 won't be of use. Nor will it help you

if your unsecured debts exceed $250,000 or your secured debts are over $750,000.

G. Protecting Your Assets From the IRS

It is illegal to transfer assets to defeat the IRS once it has started trying to collect a tax debt from you. Many people, however, have successfully transferred their assets to other entities or family members in legal ways through advance planning.

Before assuming that moving your property beyond the reach of the IRS is the way to go, keep in mind the following:

- Once you legally transfer property, it may be very difficult, if not impossible, to get it back,

- These strategies are not foolproof—the IRS might challenge a transfer and get the asset. If the transfer takes place less than two years before the IRS assesses the tax debt against you, the IRS may claim it was a fraudulent transfer.

- See an attorney to make sure you do the transfer right and do not commit fraud on the IRS or other of your creditors.

Here are a few of the most common ways people try to protect their assets from their creditors, including the IRS:

Transfer ownership of assets to a corporation that you own or control. You can lease back to yourself any corporate-owned property such as autos. You can also work for your corporation and control your salary. If you keep the salary low, you may be able to negotiate an IRS installment agreement that you can live with. The IRS could seize your stock interest as an asset, but it seldom goes after small corporation shares because they are not readily saleable to anyone else.

Put property into a Limited Family Partnership with other members of your family. But, don't simply put property into joint tenancy with family members—that won't stop the IRS.

Transfer property to a trust for a spouse or other family members. A children's trust, for example, can own assets used in your business. But, putting property into a revocable living trust won't offer any protection, because you maintain control over the trust. And, the IRS considers the use of off-shore trusts very suspiciously.

Putting life insurance policies into an insurance trust. This generally safeguards them from IRS seizures.

Fully fund your pension plans and 401(k) accounts. The IRS can legally take the accounts, but IRS policy discourages it. You can borrow back half of the money held by a 401(K) plan to reduce the amount that could be seized by the IRS from the account.

Transfer property to family members outright. If you are going to leave property to your children anyway, and you fear a future IRS tax bill, this might be a way to save the property for your heirs.

There are also ways to protect your assets by sophisticated estate planning devices. See an attorney if you want to learn more.

H. Suspending Collection of Your Tax Bill

If your finances are bleak—you have no job, little or no money, and no immediate prospects—you can ask a Revenue Officer or other IRS collector to "53" your case. If he agrees, it means that he recommends to his supervisors that your tax account balance be deemed "currently not collectible."

The collector will fill in IRS Form 53. (You can't do this; only IRS personnel have access to Form 53.) If approved, this data then is entered into the IRS computer at the Service Center. Once your account has been declared a "53," you won't hear from the IRS concerning your bill for up to one year. The IRS stops bothering you, but interest (and sometimes penalties) still accrue. At the end of your "53" period, the computer brings your account back up and you must start the process over again.

The IRS doesn't take the "53" procedure lightly. A highly convincible collector may agree to "53" your account just by talking to him over the telephone, but that's unusual. You will probably be required to complete one of the series of Form 433s

(See Section D.3, above) which lists your assets, liabilities, income and expenses. The IRS may want other documentation, too, such as statements from doctors explaining that you are disabled and cannot work. You must persuade the IRS that you are almost destitute—that even a $25 a month installment agreement is beyond your means.

Having your case classified as "currently not collectible" doesn't really solve your tax problem. It does, however, let you delay dealing with it. If you're hoping to beat the IRS by filing for bankruptcy or waiting out the ten-year collection limit, having collection on your file suspended under the "53" process buys time. When your debt is in "53" status, IRS time limits for collecting or discharging tax debts in Chapter 7 bankruptcy are running in your favor.

I. Collections in a Nutshell— Kernels of Wisdom

1. The IRS has far greater powers than any other bill collector. The agency has the power to take your wages, bank accounts and other property without first granting you a hearing.

2. The IRS collection process starts with computerized form letters, which should not be ignored. If you can't pay, request more time.

3. Avoid giving bank account and employment information to the IRS over the phone. If you don't want to deal with the ACS, request that your file be sent to the local District Office to meet with a tax collector to work out a payment arrangement.

4. Treat a collector with respect but remember you have rights. Read IRS Publication 1. (See Chapter 15.)

5. Never lie to an IRS employee about your assets or anything else. It is a crime.

6. Carefully prepare your financial information before speaking with the tax collector. Make sure you don't understate your living expenses.

7. If you can't pay your taxes all at once, you can propose an installment agreement. If you get an agreement approved, keep to it.

8. It is possible, but never easy, to reduce your tax debts through an Offer in Compromise.

9. Bankruptcy may work to cancel tax debts or let you pay over time without interest and penalties accruing.

10. If you are in dire financial straits, ask the IRS to suspend collection for hardship.

IRS Enforced Collection: Liens and Levies

7

If you and the IRS can't negotiate a satisfactory solution to your outstanding tax debt, you are likely to face IRS enforced collection—the lien (notice) and levy (seizure) process.

As a result of computerization and "get tough" policies, IRS property and wage seizures have more than doubled in the last decade. Levies are used on over half of all taxpayers behind in paying their income taxes. The percentage would be higher, except that the other half probably changed jobs or moved their assets before the IRS could seize them, or had no assets in the first place. The average IRS levy brings in about $1,600, mostly from individual bank accounts.

A. Liens and Levies— What Do These Terms Mean?

There is an important difference between a tax lien and a tax levy.

1. Tax Liens

If the IRS sends you a tax bill and you don't contest or pay it, the IRS has the right to inform the public that you owe taxes. This is done by recording a Notice of Federal Tax Lien at your county recorder's office (where real estate transactions are recorded). The lien is placed on public record where you live or own real estate (or both). Or, in states without county recording systems, it's recorded at your Secretary of State's office.

Just as a recorded mortgage tells the world that you owe the bank money on your home, a recorded Notice of Federal Tax Lien tells anyone interested enough to search public records that you owe the IRS. And like a mortgage, if you ever sell your real estate, the tax lien must be paid out of the proceeds. Or, the tax lien remains on the property after it is transferred to the new owner if the transfer doesn't generate any sales proceeds.

The practical effect of a recorded tax lien is to scare off potential lenders or buyers and to warn others that you are a tax deadbeat. The tax lien

notice will be picked up by credit reporting agencies, such as TRW, Equifax and TransUnion.[1]

The tax lien notice shows up in all counties (or your state) where recorded by the IRS. It attaches to all real property you own at the time it's recorded and to all real estate you acquire in the future. The only way the lien can be neutralized is for the IRS to file a Satisfaction of Lien (see immediately below and Section B) or a Certificate of Release (Section C). The original notices—and the Satisfaction or Release—both show up on your credit file and can stay for up to seven years from the time the lien was originally recorded. The satisfaction does not cause the tax lien to be erased.

The IRS files one million tax lien notices against seriously delinquent taxpayers each year. By law, the agency should notify you and give you one last chance to pay before filing a Notice of Federal Tax Lien. But this doesn't always happen. For instance, if you've moved, the warning notice may be sent to an old address and never received. And, once the lien notice is recorded, the IRS must send you a copy of it. Again, if the IRS uses an old address, you may first find out about the lien notice when you apply for credit and the lien shows up on a credit report.

Tax liens are not easily removed once recorded, unless you pay the taxes, penalties and interest in full. If the IRS doesn't file a Satisfaction or Certificate of Release, the lien notice remains on the public record for ten years from the date the taxes were first assessed against you.

If the IRS hasn't collected from you by the end of the ten years, the IRS must file a Satisfaction of Lien within 30 days of the expiration with the same public agency (or agencies) it recorded the Notice of Federal Tax Lien. If the IRS forgets to file the Satisfaction, contact the Collection Division of your local District Office and insist that it be done and that you be sent a copy.

Below is a flow chart from the Internal Revenue Manual instructing IRS personnel when to file a Notice of Federal Tax Lien. Although the IRS

---

[1]For information on credit ratings, rebuilding your credit after a financial setback (such as owing the IRS) and many other debt and credit issues, see *Money Troubles: Legal Strategies to Cope With Your Debts*, by Robin Leonard (Nolo Press).

IRS PERSONNEL CRITERIA USED IN DECIDING WHETHER OR NOT TO FILE A NOTICE OF FEDERAL TAX LIEN

Source: Internal Revenue Manual 5355.11

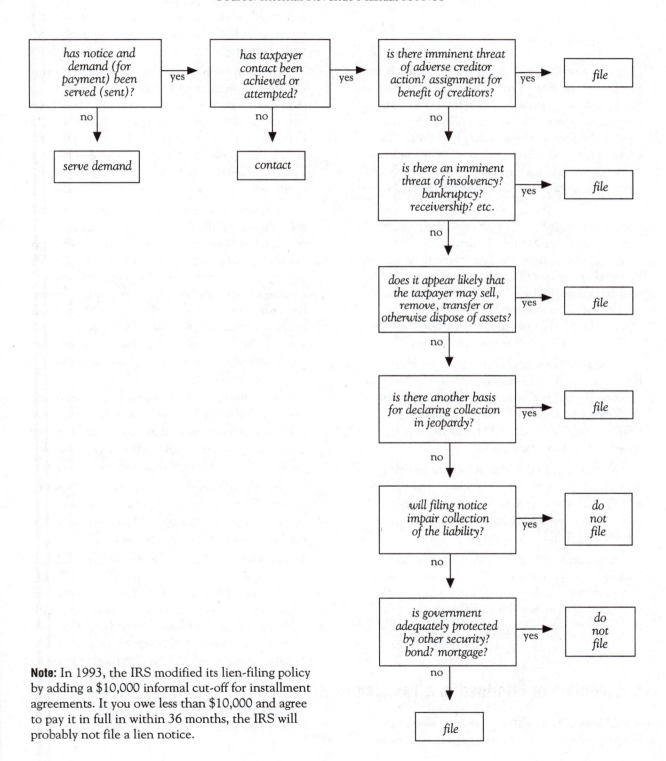

Note: In 1993, the IRS modified its lien-filing policy by adding a $10,000 informal cut-off for installment agreements. It you owe less than $10,000 and agree to pay it in full in within 36 months, the IRS will probably not file a lien notice.

does not always file a tax lien notice, as the chart shows, personnel are directed to file notices in most cases.

2. Levies

A recorded tax lien is a notice to the world that you owe taxes. The IRS cannot collect any money by just filing a tax lien. Instead, the IRS must seize your property—by way of a levy—to collect what you owe. Usually this means taking money held for you by others, such as your bank, stockbroker or employer. Although the IRS usually records a tax lien notice before seizing property, the IRS is *not* required to do so.

Before the IRS seizes your money or property, you must be sent a Notice of Intent to Levy. This gives you 30 days from the date on the notice to pay in full what you owe. The notice is either mailed to your last known address (so you may not get it if you've moved) or delivered to you by a Revenue Officer. Again, the law requires only that the IRS send the notice—not that you actually receive it.

The government collects only about 3% of the total income tax owed through IRS levies. The IRS seizes taxpayers' assets over 2.5 million times per year. Any type of personal property you own—wholly, partially or jointly with others—may be seized and sold to satisfy your tax bill.

The likelihood that the IRS will seize your property often depends on where you live in the U.S. For instance, for some unknown reason, a delinquent taxpayer in Los Angeles is six times more likely to suffer a levy than his counterpart in Chicago.

If you are unemployed, have only the clothes on your back and no money in the bank, you are a poor levy target for the IRS. If and when your financial situation improves you'll have to worry about the IRS' property seizure power.

B. Avoiding or Eliminating a Tax Lien

A tax lien can be the kiss of death on your credit rating. Lenders shy away from extending credit to people with tax problems. As discussed in Chapter 6, the best way to deal with a tax lien is to avoid one in the first place. Unfortunately, this is easier said than done. As shown on the IRS tax lien chart, above, the IRS usually files a tax lien if you don't respond to the tax bills you're sent or work out some arrangement within nine to 18 months after the first bill arrives.

For many people, a tax lien is just one of many black marks on their credit report and won't make their situation any worse. For others, it is best to try to keep the IRS from recording a tax lien. If you are in the latter group and receive a letter from the IRS stating that it intends to record a Notice of Federal Tax Lien, contact a Revenue Officer or Problems Resolution Officer at your local District Office.

You want to convince the IRS that you fall into the category, "Will filing notice impair collection of the liability?" One way is to argue that a tax lien will kill your credit rating and destroy your chance of getting a loan to pay the tax bill. Some Revenue Officers seem to understand this fact of life, but many have had no experience in the real world of financial matters. Unfortunately, others don't seem to care. If you face this kind of Revenue Officer, ask to speak to his supervisor or contact a Problems Resolution Officer. (See Chapter 8.)

A Notice of Tax Lien does not affect all of your property. For instance, it will not impair your right to sell personal property, such as your car, boat or computer system. Normally, tax liens cause problems mostly to those taxpayers who own real estate.

If you can't convince a Revenue Officer not to record a Notice of Federal Tax Lien, you will probably want to take all possible steps to get rid of the lien quickly. Your three options are:

1. **Pay in full.** The best way to deal with a tax lien is to round up the money and pay the tax bill in full. Then the IRS must record a Satisfaction of Lien within 30 days of receipt of payment. Frequently, however, the IRS forgets. To find out if the Satisfaction has been filed, check with your local IRS office Collection Division or get a copy of your credit report from a credit reporting agency, such as TRW, Equifax or TransUnion. If the Satisfaction of Lien has not been filed, call your local IRS District Office to speak with a Revenue

Officer or Problems Resolution Officer. (See Chapter 8.) Insist that she file a Satisfaction of Lien and send you a copy.

2. **Request a discharge of some of your property.** If you can't pay in full, and your own several assets which are tied up by a tax lien, there is another option available. You can request that the IRS discharge (release) one item of property, typically real estate, from the tax lien. The IRS will likely do this on condition that you show that the discharge will help you raise funds to pay the tax bill. For example, you own two pieces of real estate, and can't sell either because of the tax lien. You want to sell one and use the proceeds to pay the IRS. The IRS will go along with you, if you use a title or escrow company to handle the transfer of funds from the closing directly to the IRS.

3. **Ask the IRS to subordinate its lien.** Another option if you own real estate covered by a tax lien and can't pay in full is to borrow against the property. No lender will make a mortgage loan to someone with a tax lien unless the IRS agrees to subordinate its lien to a new loan. Subordination means to allow another person's interest to come before yours. In this case, the IRS would be allowing a lender's loan to come before the IRS' tax lien. The IRS will agree to a subordiantion only if it will get something from it. The loan money must go directly to the IRS through an escrow agent. If the loan doesn't cover the full amount of the tax bill, the tax lien remains. If the IRS later seizes your property to pay the balance, it would have to pay off the lender.

 Bankruptcy doesn't wipe out a tax lien. If your tax debts qualify for a discharge under any type of bankruptcy (see Chapter 6, Section F), the lien will remain. If you owned any property going into bankruptcy, that property is still subject to the lien. The IRS could take that property after your bankruptcy is over. Or, the more likely scenario is that the IRS would ask you to pay over the value of the property rather than seize it. And, in many cases, the IRS doesn't try to enforce the lien after bankruptcy—the IRS just goes away.

C. When the IRS Files a Tax Lien in Error

The IRS occasionally messes up and files a Notice of Federal Tax Lien when you don't owe anything. You may have already paid the bill but the money was not properly credited to your account. When this happens, under the Taxpayers' Bill of Rights you are entitled to a Certificate of Release which states that the lien was filed in error.

Call the person who signed the Notice of Tax Lien or the Lien Unit of the Collections Division at your local IRS office. If you don't get an immediate response, call a Problems Resolution Officer (telephone and fax numbers are in the Appendix). Demand that a Certificate of Release be issued and recorded right away, and that a copy be made for you. Deliver or mail photocopies to the "big three" credit bureaus—TRW, TransUnion and Equifax. Get their phone numbers from the Yellow Pages and call to find out where to send the copies of the Certificates. This should minimize the damage to your credit rating caused by the IRS error.

Suing the IRS for Collection Actions

It is possible to sue the IRS in U.S. District Court for damages if it fails to release a tax lien or takes other "unauthorized collection" actions.[2] To win in court, you must prove that you suffered direct economic damages from the IRS' behavior. Before suing, you must first try to solve the problem using channels within the IRS. Your litigation costs are recoverable too, but not any costs of fighting the IRS before suit is filed.

Don't get too excited about suing the IRS. The law makes it tough to prove your case or to recover any big money. And, judges are reluctant to award attorneys fees and costs even when you win. Few lawyers are willing to take this kind of case on a contingency basis, where the fee is a percentage of amount recovered.

---

[2]Internal Revenue Code § 7430; IRS Regulation 1.7430.

D. Property the IRS Can't (or Won't) Seize

If you don't pay your tax debt, the IRS may begin seizing your property. With a few exceptions, the IRS can take almost anything you own to pay your tax debt. Certain property is exempt, however, and IRS policies keep the agency from taking some other things you own. Despite this apparent generosity, the exemption list is hardly lavish. The full list is in the Appendix. (See Publication 594, Understanding The Collection Process.) Exempt property includes:

- non-luxury items of clothing (you might lose your furs)
- school books
- personal effects and furniture under $1,650 in total value
- books and tools of your trade under $1,100 in total value
- unemployment or worker's compensation benefits
- certain annuity, pension and disability payments
- income a court has ordered you to pay for child support, and
- a portion of your wages (see sidebar).

    In addition to the above exemptions, IRS policy discourages—but does not prohibit—Revenue Officers from seizing the following items of property:

- most retirement plans, IRAs, 401(k) plans and Keogh accounts, and
- your principal residence—a Revenue Officer must obtain approval of the boss of her IRS district, before grabbing your house.

    TIP   As a last resort, the IRS will seize retirement funds or a home from uncooperative taxpayers, but this is left to the discretion of the District Director. Lucky for you, this job is somewhat politically sensitive. If you contact your Congressional Representative's local office and enlist the help of a sympathetic staff person, your Congressperson may persuade the IRS not to take your house or pension fund. Usually the Problems Resolution Officer investigates these matters on behalf of the IRS District Director.

If the IRS Wants Your Wages

The IRS can legally take most, but not all, of your wages. The amount that you get to keep is determined by the number of your dependents and the standard tax deduction you're entitled to. For example, a married couple with two children get to keep about $300 per week, while a single taxpayer with no dependents gets only about $116. (See Publication 1494 in the Appendix to figure out the exact wage levy exemption amount.) The IRS gets the rest.

    If the IRS wants your wages, it sends a "wage levy notice" to your employer, who must immediately give you a copy. On the back of the notice is an exemption claim form. (See Publication 594, Understanding The Collection Process, in the Appendix.) You should fill out, sign and return this simple form to the IRS office that issued it within three days after you receive it. Your employer shouldn't pay anything to the IRS until you have your chance to file your exemption claim.

    If you don't file the claim form, your employer must pay you only $116 per week and give the rest to the IRS. If your employer ignores the IRS wage levy notice and pays you anyway, he is liable to the IRS for whatever amounts were wrongly paid to you.

    Once the wage levy takes effect, it continues until either the taxes are paid in full or the collection period (ten years from when the taxes are assessed) expires. If you'd prefer not to lose pay to the IRS, you can:

- try to negotiate with the IRS to release the levy (see Section F, below)
- file for bankruptcy (see Chapter 6, Section F), or
- quit your job.

E. Avoiding a Levy (Seizure of Property Other Than Wages)

There are several ways to avoid an IRS levy of your property.

Transfer your assets. Under some circumstances, to keep the IRS from levying on your property, you can transfer it (give it away, sell it or a combination of both). But you must convey it to other people or entities (such as a corporation) *before* the levy process begins.

People who owe the IRS frequently transfer property to other family members. They also transfer property to partnerships, trusts or corporations. This often slows down or discourages IRS collection action. (See Chapter 6, Section G.)

 Transfers designed to deliberately evade the IRS' collection attempts are illegal. Before you transfer title, get some legal advice to make sure the transfer is effective and you are not violating laws against concealing assets from the IRS.

One alternative is to sell your property at its actual value, not merely give it away or sell it for peanuts. If you retain partial ownership in property that the IRS seizes and sells, the IRS must compensate the other joint owner for her share—but only if you can show that she legitimately paid for her interest. If you can show this, the IRS may back off.

For instance, if you *sell* your sister one-half of your rental building, the IRS will be discouraged from seizing it because the IRS will have to pay your sister for her share. Of course, the IRS can go after the money you received from her if you haven't spent it. If you *give* her one-half of your building, however, the IRS can ignore the transfer. The IRS can do this under the theory of "transferee liability." This means that liability for your tax debt is transferred to your sister to the extent of the value of the property transferred.

And, if you don't retain any ownership in the property, the IRS can ignore the transfer if it was sold for less than its full value. The IRS can go directly to the recipient of the property and take it away. For example, if you sell your $10,000 Cadillac to a friend for $100, the IRS can still grab it.

TIP The IRS doesn't always discover or challenge a property transfer. And, even if the IRS finds the transfer and wants to get back the property (assuming it was given away or sold for less than its value), the transfer will greatly slow down the tax collector. You can gain time to raise money to pay or negotiate further. Warning: the IRS can push for criminal prosecution of tax debtors who transfer property *after* the levy process has begun. So don't make transfers once the IRS has issued a Notice of Intent to Levy.

(More information on transferring property is in Chapter 6, Section G.)

Keep mum about your assets. Unless the IRS issues a collection summons—a legal order requiring you to appear at an IRS office—you don't have to reveal your assets. Of course, if you've tried to negotiate an installment plan or have otherwise been dealing with the IRS, the IRS may already know what property you have. But if you've thus far avoided the collector, you don't have to tell all. Even if you get a summons, you still might be able to avoid making disclosures. Before keeping mum, however, speak to a tax attorney. It is a felony to lie to the IRS. It is not a crime to not answer questions or to ask to speak with your tax advisor first.

Keep your property out of sight. To avoid a levy, you can resort to the obvious—keep vehicles and other items of value away from your home or work. It is illegal to actively conceal assets from IRS collectors, so be careful how you do this. You may not think that keeping a car in a friend's garage is concealing it, but the IRS might argue otherwise. Don't over worry about this, however, as rarely are ordinary people prosecuted for concealing assets from the IRS. Drug dealers and crime figures are another story, however.

Move your bank accounts. See Chapter 6, Section D.5.

Rent, don't own. If you lease property, such as real estate, cars, furniture and equipment, you aren't the legal owner and the IRS can't seize them. The only exception is if your rental agreement allows you to purchase the property and you have built up a large amount of equity, which rarely is the case.

Deposit money into retirement accounts. As stated above, the Internal Revenue Manual strongly discourages tax collectors from seizing pensions and other retirement funds, and then only from exceptionally uncooperative taxpayers. So, if you owe a lot to the IRS and the levy process hasn't yet begun, consider fully funding your retirement plan.

File for bankruptcy. Filing for bankruptcy stops all IRS seizures immediately. (See Chapter 6, Section F.) Bankruptcy, however, may bring only temporary relief from the tax collector. And, many tax debts survive a bankruptcy discharge intact, meaning that you still owe the debt when your bankruptcy case is over.

F. Getting a Levy Released

If the IRS seizes your property, getting it back may not be easy. By this stage in the collection game, the IRS is very serious. But don't give up the fight. Contact the Revenue Officer named on the levy notice or ask for his manager. Request an immediate appointment—no later than the next day or two. At your meeting, try one or more of the following approaches to get your property returned:

- *Request more time to pay.* You will need a convincing story showing how you intend to get the money. Whether or not the IRS will grant your request and release the levy depends on how believable your story is. Try getting the money to pay in full, even if it means maxing out on your credit cards, taking out a home equity loan, borrowing from Uncle Mack who never liked you, or doing something else equally distasteful.

- *Propose an installment agreement (IA).* Read Chapter 6, Section D.6. This is a particularly good option if you haven't already tried for an IA, but instead have had your head buried in the sand.

- *Submit an Offer in Compromise.* (See Chapter 6, Section E.)

- *Cry hardship.* A tax collector can remove the levy if he believes it imposes a significant economic hardship. You will probably have to agree to a payment arrangement. Revenue Officers have a lot of leeway in deciding what constitutes a hardship. At minimum, he should release a levy if you show that it keeps you from having a roof over your head or feeding the kids. If the Revenue Officer refuses, go to the Problems Resolution Office. (See Chapter 8.)

- *Show that the seized property has very little value or that you have only a small equity in it.* Equity is the market value of an item less debt against it. If an IRS sale is likely to bring in a small amount of money, you might persuade the IRS to give the item back. For example, argue against the IRS selling your old car because it's worth only $200. The IRS has a policy against seizures made solely to teach you a lesson. If a Revenue Officer ever does this, go to her manager or the Problems Resolution Office. (See Chapter 8.)

> **TIP** An especially good argument is that the seized item has little equity *and* that the seizure would cause a hardship.

- *File for any type of bankruptcy.* A judge may order the IRS to return the property to you. (See Chapter 6, Section F.)

G. When the IRS Levies on Your Property—What You Can Do About It

When the IRS seizes your property, it physically takes custody of personal property (cars, boats, equipment). It seizes real estate by posting a notice on the property and serving (hand delivering or mailing) a copy of the notice on you. The IRS then can legally sell the seized property to the highest bidder at an auction about 40–45 days after the seizure. The IRS must publicly announce the details—date, location and time—of the sale in a local newspaper at least ten days in advance. The IRS also sends you notice of the auction and posts the sale information at the local District Office.

Prior to the auction, the IRS Revenue Officer handling your case sets a minimum bid price for your property and must inform you of it. Technically, you have the right to disagree with the IRS bid price. If you do, you must present written proof (such as an appraisal), within five days after the agency notified you, showing that the bid price is unfairly low. Unfortunately, this right doesn't amount to much. As long as the bid price set by the IRS equals the taxes you owe, it won't be considered too low.

Anytime before the sale, you may be able to get the levy released, thereby getting your property back, by:

- paying the taxes in full
- in the case of real estate, selling it yourself and entering into an escrow arrangement with the buyer that provides for payment of taxes out of the sales proceeds
- posting a bond with the IRS, which is so difficult to do that it's not really an option, or
- negotiating an installment agreement (IA) with the IRS. You should act quickly and call the Revenue Officer handling your case or his manager. Ask for an immediate meeting. Then proceed as described in Chapter 6, Section D.6. If the Revenue Officer and his manager reject your offer, call the Problems Resolution Office. (See Chapter 8.) If an IA is granted, you get your property back.

If you aren't successful with the IRS collector, the auction will take place. It's usually held at the nearest federal courthouse building, and is open to the public. You may attend if you want, but you aren't required to. But you'll probably want to know if your property sells. If no one bids the IRS' minimum bid price, the IRS has two options—either bid on the property for the minimum bid amount or release the levy and give the property back to you. If the IRS releases the levy, this may be only a temporary reprieve. The IRS may quickly relevy, reset the minimum bid price and reschedule the auction.

The winning bidder must be prepared to give the IRS a cashier's or certified check for the full amount, or make a deposit and pay the balance within a day or two after the auction. The IRS will apply the payment to the taxes, penalties, interest and costs of seizure and sale.

 If the sale proceeds don't cover your total IRS debt, you are still liable for the balance. If sale proceeds exceed the amount you owe the IRS, you must ask the IRS give you the overage. Submit your request in writing to the Revenue Officer handling your case. If you don't, the IRS will keep the balance in your tax account and credit it to your future taxes.

1. Levies of Real Estate

If the IRS levies on your home or other real estate, it must post a Notice of Seizure on the property. The IRS must also hand deliver a copy to you, if it knows your whereabouts. You *don't* have to move out after receiving the notice and the IRS won't ask you to leave. Although the IRS might show up later with an appraiser, you're *not* obligated to let anyone come inside your house until after it has been sold at auction.

After posting and serving you with the Notice, the IRS publishes the date, time and location of the auction in a local newspaper. It also posts that information on the federal building bulletin board or in the IRS' office public area. The sale usually is set for about 45 days after the seizure notice is posted.

TIP You can have a friend, a relative or your attorney bid for you at the sale. This is worth considering if you don't want the IRS to know that you have the money to pay your tax bill. But, if you don't have the money—which is usually the case—a wealthy trusted friend or relative can buy the house and rent it back to you. When you become financially secure, you can buy it back from her.

A. WHO GETS THE PROPERTY?

The highest bidder (buyer) at the auction gets an IRS Certificate of Sale. This is not the same as a deed to your property. If you are living in the house, the buyer cannot enter against your will. If you don't leave voluntarily, he must bring an eviction proceeding to get you out.

B. GETTING YOUR PROPERTY BACK

Once the auction is over, all is not necessarily lost. You can defeat the eviction proceeding by buying back (redeeming) or maybe by telling the judge that you intend to redeem your property.

Under federal law, you can redeem your property anytime up until 180 days after the IRS sale. You must pay the buyer (not the IRS) unless the IRS was the high bidder or the property did not sell. If you redeem your property, make sure that the buyer (except if the buyer was the IRS) gives you a Quitclaim Deed.

The buyer can require payment in full in cash, a cashiers check or certified check. You can ask her to accept a promissory note and mortgage if you don't have the full amount—but don't count on anyone doing this for you. To make sure the buyer understands that you are legally redeeming your property, notify her over the phone and in writing using certified mail. Then tender payment before the 180 days elapse. On the 181st day, you are out of luck.

Example

Georgina's house sold for $100,000 at an IRS auction to cover her back income taxes. She desperately wants title to her house back and 90 days after the auction, she found a bank willing to lend her the money to redeem it. She must pay the buyer of the Certificate of Sale as follows:

Prorated interest (90/365) * 20%	$4,932
Bid price	+ $100,000
Total needed for redemption	$104,932

Immediately notify the IRS of your redemption. Call and write to the Revenue Officer who seized the property and send a certified letter to the local District Director. If you don't tell the IRS, it may mistakenly issue a deed to the auction buyer at the end of the 180 days.

If the buyer refuses to accept your payment, call and write to the District Director and the Revenue Officer who seized the property. Tell them that the buyer is refusing to comply with the law. Insist that the IRS not issue her a deed and contact her on your behalf. If you do not get immediate action, contact the Problems Resolution Office. (See next chapter.)

2. Levies of Businesses

As explained above, the IRS has the power to take just about anything. If you are a partner or a sole proprietor of a business, the IRS can, and probably will, levy on its bank accounts for your tax debts. The IRS might also collect your accounts receivable by notifying your customers on credit to make further payments to the IRS instead of to your business. If you're in a partnership, the IRS can go after the business' assets, even if only one partner is having IRS problems.

If your business is a corporation, the IRS can seize your stock, but not the assets of the company for your individual tax debts.

Before levying on assets located inside your business, however, the IRS will ask your permission. If you refuse, the IRS can seize only property from *public* areas of your business. If you own a restaurant, for example, the IRS can take the tables and chairs, but not the kitchen equipment. To get the non-public area items, the IRS must get a court order, which can take days or weeks. This gives you time to negotiate or raise money to pay your bill. If you begin removing assets from the business while the IRS is awaiting the court order, however, it can seize the items immediately.

As a practical matter, the IRS rarely seizes a small business' inventory or fixtures. It is usually not worthwhile—auctions for used business equipment and inventory typically bring only pennies on the dollar. The IRS also realizes that if the auction doesn't cover the complete tax bill, the chance of collecting the balance is reduced severely if you're put out of business.

Payroll tax exception. The IRS will vigorously seize assets and padlock your doors if your business is behind in payroll tax deposits. This is doubly true if you are pyramiding your liabilities—you owe past quarterly payroll taxes and are not making current payroll tax deposits. In this case, the IRS will shut you down, just to keep the problem from getting worse. For more information on a business' obligation to pay payroll taxes, see Chapter 11, Section C.

3. Levies of Joint Tax Refunds

If the IRS takes a joint income tax refund when only one spouse owes back taxes, the other spouse can get her share of the refund money back. She must file an amended tax return, Form 1040X and attach an Injured Spouse Allocation, Form 8379. (Both forms are in the Appendix.)

On these forms, the injured spouse lists her separate income, deductions, exemptions and credits. The IRS computes the amount due and sends out a refund check if she qualifies.

PROBLEMS RESOLUTION PROGRAM: A FRIEND AT THE IRS   8

You've tried to solve your problem with the IRS, but no one seems to want to help—your letters and calls have fallen onto closed ears and the collectors are about to take the shirt off your back. So who can you call? The IRS Problems Resolution Program (PRP), that's who!

The PRP is for taxpayers to use whenever normal IRS channels have failed. Problems Resolution Officers (nicknamed PROs) staff these offices which are found at Service Centers and District Offices. (A complete list of addresses and phone numbers is in the Appendix.) If you qualify for the PRP's services, PROs have the power—mandated by Congress—to cut through red tape and help you.

The IRS claims that 46% of all requests for help from the PRP are resolved satisfactory to the taxpayer, within an average time of four and one-half days.

Goals of the Problems Resolution Program

The IRS acknowledges that taxpayers sometimes have great difficulty getting problems solved and are often ignored or shuffled among different IRS departments. The IRS' goals with the PRP are to:

- assure that taxpayers have an independent, monitored system for the resolution of problems that have not been solved through regular IRS channels

- serve as a taxpayer's advocate within the IRS to make sure that the taxpayer has a say in the IRS decision-making process, and

- identify recurring types of problems to try to improve the system.

A. Who Qualifies for Help From a PRO?

The IRS stresses that a taxpayer should contact the PRP only after attempting to fix the problem within IRS channels. Before a PRO will help, you will have to show that you tried and failed to get your IRS

problem solved normally. Be ready to provide the PRO with copies of previous IRS correspondence, notes indicating dates, times and summaries of telephone conversations.

Who initially caused the problem—you or the IRS—is immaterial, according to the Internal Revenue Manual. A PRO can't beg off by saying that you should have filed your tax return on time, paid your taxes when they were due or whatever else you did or didn't do.

1. Problems the PRP Will Pursue

The PRP won't investigate all types of difficulties you are having with the IRS. To qualify, your problem must fall into one of the situations listed below, and you must have first taken the necessary steps for the given situation.

Refunds. Before the PRP will help, you must have made at least two inquiries into the status of your refund, and at least 90 days must have passed since you filed your tax return (or amended tax return).

Example

Edith filed an amended tax return claiming a refund on July 15, 1992. On October 1, 1992, she called the Service Center and was told to expect the refund in three weeks. When she still had no refund on November 1, 1992, she called again. This time the clerk told her that he didn't know where her refund was. Edith qualifies for PRP assistance.

Inquiries. Before the PRP will help you with an IRS inquiry, you must have posed your question or requested help at least twice. In addition, at least 45 days must have passed since you made your first inquiry. Finally, either you must have not received an acknowledgment, or a final response, or you have not received a response by the date promised.

Example

Gary wrote to the IRS requesting a copy of his tax account on February 13, 1993. He received an acknowledgment indicating he would have a copy by April 7, 1993. When that date passed and he still didn't have a copy of his account, he called the IRS. The clerk told him she had no information. Gary qualifies for PRP assistance.

Notices. Before the PRP will help you with an IRS notice, you must have responded at least twice by requesting that the IRS take action. You must not have received any meaningful response from the IRS.

Example

Ooma received two tax bills a month apart. She responded to each notice with a letter stating she had paid the amount in question and enclosed copies of canceled checks as proof. When Ooma received a third bill, she qualified for PRP assistance.

Emergencies and other problems. Even if your problem doesn't fall into one of the above three categories, you still may qualify for PRP help—as long as you believe the IRS mistreated you, particularly in a collection matter.

Example 1

Peter was informed by his bank that the IRS issued an Intent to Levy Notice for his bank account. Peter never received any other notice from the IRS indicating that he owed money. Peter qualifies for PRP help.

Example 2

A Revenue Officer (tax collector) showed up at Betty's job. He asked questions about her tax debt in front of her boss and a few customers. Betty was embarrassed and afraid of losing her job. She asked the collector to leave, but he refused. Her complaint to the collector's supervisor went unanswered. Betty is afraid more visits may cause her to lose her job. Betty can call a PRO.

Example 3

The IRS filed a tax lien against Sam's property. Sam paid off the debt, but the Collection Division hasn't filed a Satisfaction of Lien. Sam is trying to buy a car, but the dealer won't arrange financing because of the lien in his credit file. Sam needs immediate help and can call a PRO for fast action.

Example 4

The IRS filed an erroneous tax lien against Janice, who had paid her tax debt. The Collection Division is dragging its feet on filing a Certificate of Release stating that the filing was in error. The lien is affecting Janice's ability to get credit. Janice qualifies for help from the PRP.

2. Problems the PRP Won't Pursue

As mentioned above, the PRP won't investigate all problems you're having with the IRS. If your matter falls into one of the following, a PRO won't help you:

- You haven't followed an IRS established administrative procedure (such as requesting an appeals hearing) to try to resolve the matter.

- The IRS *has* responded to your question or request, but you don't agree with the answer. (Although this is the IRS' official position, it is a somewhat gray area, and contacting the PRP is often worth a try. For example, if you've requested an installment agreement and the IRS rejected your proposal and is about to take your house, do call the PRP.)

- Your problem does not directly involve your tax liability. For example, the PRP won't take your complaints about IRS personnel or about documents you were denied in your Freedom of Information Act request for an auditor's file.

- Your problem is not really an IRS matter. If you don't like a particular tax law, for instance, write your Congressional Representative, not the PRP.

- Your case is in the Criminal Investigation Division of the IRS.

- The IRS has classified you as a tax protester or you have raised a similar issue, such as claiming the tax laws are unconstitutional.

- Your position is that you cannot or will not pay your tax bill. (This does not apply if you are willing to make arrangements to pay but the Collection Division has turned down your offer.)

B. Contacting a Problems Resolution Officer

As mentioned at the beginning of the chapter, PROs are found at Service Centers and IRS District Offices. (A complete list of addresses, and phone and fax numbers is in the Appendix.) If your situation is an emergency (for example, your house is scheduled to be sold tomorrow), call, fax or visit the nearest IRS District Office and ask to speak to a Problems Resolution Officer.

You can also request PRP help by calling 800-829-1040 and asking for Problems Resolution Program assistance. Or you can write and describe the problem. (A sample letter is below.) Mail or fax your letter to your local IRS District Office PRO.

If you call first, follow up with a letter concisely reiterating your problem. And because the IRS loves documentation, whether you write first or write as a follow up, include with your letter:

- a copy of your tax return (if relevant)

- copies of IRS notices and prior correspondence to and from the IRS (very important)

- clear, legible copies of canceled checks—both front and back—if you made payments that were not credited to your account, and

- a daytime telephone number and hours when you can be reached.

If you have given the PRP enough to start with, your case will be assigned to a specific Problems Resolution Officer. She will immediately begin working on your problem or assign it to a staff member.

Below is a sample letter requesting PRO assistance:

Sample PRO Letter

```
Internal Revenue Service
Problems Resolution Officer
P.O. Box 1302 (Stop 1005)
Denver, CO 80201

November 18, 1993


Re: Benedict Cooper—SSN 555-55-5555

Dear Sir or Madam:

I am applying for assistance to
straighten out a problem that I have
been unable to resolve with the IRS
Service Center.

Enclosed is a copy of a tax notice
dated September 1, 1993 in the amount
of $892.40. I paid this on July 15,
1993 when I sent in my tax return.
Enclosed is a copy of my canceled
check, front and back, which shows that
the IRS received the money.

I wrote the IRS on September 5, 1993
and sent a copy of this check. On
October 5, 1993 I received another
notice (copy enclosed) again requesting
payment. On October 10, 1993 I sent
another letter and copy of the check.
On November 15, 1993 I received a third
notice for the same amount instead of a
response to my two prior letters.

I can be reached during the day at my
work (303) 555-1800 from 9 am to 5 pm.
My address is 47 Bear Circle,
Littleton, CO 80001.

Sincerely,
Benedict Cooper
Benedict Cooper

Enclosures: Copies of IRS notices and
            my two responses
```

C. Taxpayer Assistance Order in Hardship Cases

The Taxpayers' Bill of Rights (see Chapter 15) created an IRS Ombudsman. This is the person you go to when the IRS is about to end the world as you know it. As you would expect, the Ombudsman is in Washington, but has delegated his power to quickly intervene on behalf of taxpayers to local IRS District Offices, including the one nearest you.

The Ombudsman works through the local Problems Resolution Officers. They can order the IRS to cease from any action that causes a "significant hardship" by issuing a Taxpayer Assistance Order (TAO). Or, more likely, they will intervene and try to work out a solution to your problem without actually issuing a formal TAO.

Taxpayers most often request a TAO in the following situations:

- The IRS has seized, or has threatened to seize your bank account or car. You need to pay rent or your family will be thrown out on the street, and you need that car to get to work.

- Your paycheck was garnished by the IRS leaving you less than $500 per month to live on. You are willing to enter into a reasonable payment plan with the IRS, but unless you can get the wage garnishment stopped you will be out on the street.

1. What Constitutes a Significant Hardship to the IRS?

Whether or not a PRO will give you emergency assistance depends on her view of the seriousness of your hardship. The IRS Problems Resolution Program Handbook liberally advises PROs as follows:

> *Generally, when deciding the presence of a significant hardship, accept any application unless there is a clear reason not to do so. Any doubt should be resolved in the taxpayer's favor.*

In my experience, most PROs take this obligation seriously and really try to help.

Nevertheless, PROs are not doormats. In order for the PRO to act, you must show more than that

the IRS has seized or is about to seize your property— in other words, an IRS seizure, is not, in and of itself, a significant hardship. The IRS's seizure or other drastic action must interfere with one or more of the following:

- your ability to obtain or keep shelter, food and clothing for you and your family
- your need for transportation to work
- your employment
- your ability to get medical care for you or family
- your education
- your credit rating, or
- your ability to meet a business payroll or stay out of bankruptcy (the IRS is less likely to help a business than an individual, however).

PROs are further directed to weigh evidence of your being "overwhelmed by the enormity of the tax situation." They are sensitive to your emotional state, whether it is tears or talk of doing yourself harm (never intimate doing anyone at the IRS any harm). Far be it from me to suggest that you have a nervous breakdown in front of a PRO, but...

PROs are instructed *not* to hold against you:[1]

- the degree you were at fault in causing the hardship
- your past history of IRS difficulties
- the type of tax that you owe—income, payroll, or whatever, and
- the PRO's opinions and values—for instance, if part of your problem stems from a charitable donation you made to the Church of Snake Worshippers, the PRO can't consider her distaste for snakes in deciding whether to help you.

---

[1] Internal Revenue Manual 1279 (10) (70).

2. Getting Hardship Relief—Calling the IRS' 911 Line

To ask for hardship relief from the Ombudsman, you must request a Taxpayer Assistance Order. You can do this orally by calling your local IRS District PRP (the telephone numbers are in the Appendix) or 1-800-829-1040.

A better way to request a Taxpayer Assistance Order is by using IRS Form 911, Application for Taxpayer Assistance Order. A blank copy is in the appendix and a completed sample is below. Once you've filled in the form, send it to the IRS at either the local PRP office or your IRS Service Center (both addresses are in the Appendix). I usually FAX the Form 911—the PRP fax numbers are also in the

Appendix. It is not necessary to hire a Tax Pro to request a Taxpayer Assistance Order.

In most cases, you will hear by telephone from the PRP within five days. Someone from the PRP will let you know if your problem has been solved, or why it hasn't been.

Nationwide, the IRS claims that it helps about half of all taxpayers who apply for Taxpayer Assistance Orders. In fewer than 1% of those cases, however, does the PRP formally issue an order requiring the IRS to stop certain action. In the rest of the successful cases, relief is granted informally.

 Submit a 911 form to the IRS PRP any time you feel that the IRS is ignoring you or treating you unfairly. It is easy to do and you have absolutely nothing to lose.

News flash. As we go to press (January 1994), Congress is considering revising the Taxpayers' Bill of Rights. Senator Pryor of Arkansas leads the way. The bill (called T2) contains provisions strengthening the Problem Resolution Program and giving the Ombudsman more independence and authority to help taxpayers. Hopefully, by the time you read this the new Taxpayer's Bill of Rights will be enacted into law. (See Chapter 15 for more details on T2).

Form **911** (Rev. April 1991)	Department of the Treasury – Internal Revenue Service **Application for Taxpayer Assistance Order (ATAO) to Relieve Hardship**

Note: Filing this application may result in extending the statutory period of limitations. (See instructions.)

Section I.   **Taxpayer Information**

1. Name(s) as shown on tax return Harry Hambone Loretta Hambone	2. SSN/EIN 555-55-5555	3. Spouse's SSN 222-22-2222
	4. Tax form 1040	5. Tax period ended 1991
6. Current address (Number and street, apt. no., rural route) 1234 Haviture Way	7. City, town, or post office, state, and ZIP code Burgertown, MI 99999	
8. Person to contact Harry or Loretta Hambone	9. Telephone number (555)555-4444	10. Best time to call Anytime

11. Description of problem (If more space is needed, attach additional sheets.)

The IRS is taking most of my pay and has taken all money out of our checking account. We called Mr. Jones whose name was on the IRS notice and he said that there was nothing he could do about it.

12. Description of significant hardship and relief requested (If more space is needed, attach additional sheets.)

We do not have money to pay our rent and the landlord says he will kick us out in 3 days if we don't pay. We have 3 children and Loretta is 8 months pregnant.

I need all of my paycheck to take care of our bills. We could pay the IRS something monthly on the bill if they would let us.

13. Signature of taxpayer or Corporate Officer (See instructions.)	14. Date	15. Signature of spouse shown in block 1	16. Date

Section II.   **Representative Information**   (If applicable)

17. Name of authorized representative	18. Firm name
19. Street address or P.O. Box	20. City, town or post office, state and ZIP code
21. Telephone number	22. Best time to call	23. Centralized Authorization File (CAF) number
24. Signature	25. Date

Section III.   (For Internal Revenue Service only)

26. Name of initiating employee	27. ☐ IRS identified ☐ Taxpayer request	28. Telephone	29. Function	30. Office	31. Date

Form **911** (Rev. 4-91)

APPLICATION FOR TAXPAYER ASSISTANCE ORDER TO RELIEVE HARDSHIP (FORM 911)

FAMILY, FRIENDS, HEIRS AND THE IRS

9

The tax laws contain numerous rules affecting folks related by blood or marriage, and people who own property together whether or not they are legally related. In addition, a taxpayer's responsibilities don't end with his death—his heirs will have to carry on with the taxman. Maybe the old saying should be changed to "nothing is certain except death and MORE taxes."

A. It's a Family Affair

If you are married, divorced or a parent, be sure to familiarize yourself with special rules for dealing with the IRS.

1. Filing Tax Returns—Joint or Separate?

Married couples always have the option of filing a joint tax return or filing separate tax returns. And, if only one spouse has income, the other doesn't have an obligation to file a return. The only qualification for filing jointly is that the couple be legally married as of December 31 of the tax year. Occasionally, it pays, taxwise, for married couples to file separate returns. If in doubt, calculate your tax liability both ways each year.

Another less obvious reason some married couples file separate tax returns is to relieve each other of financial responsibility if the IRS should later audit one of them, or if one or the other is unable to pay a tax bill. Both spouses are liable for the taxes owed on a joint return. But, only the spouse in whose name a separate return is filed is liable for his or her income taxes.

Example 1

Leon and Margaret are married and always file their tax returns jointly. Leon owns a dry cleaning business for which they reported losses on their tax return. Leon and Margaret were audited, and the IRS discovered that Leon's business actually made a profit, as Leon had lied about his business income. They couldn't pay the resulting audit bill and the IRS filed a Notice of Federal Tax Lien, damaging both Leon's

and Margaret's credit rating. The IRS may collect on it from any jointly or separately owned property of either spouse.

Example 2

Now assume that Leon and Margaret file separate tax returns. Leon filed the phony tax return, but Margaret's return showed only her wages and a few non-suspicious deductions. Both were audited. Margaret's audit resulted in "no change." Leon was slapped with the same $22,000 bill. When Leon was unable to pay, the IRS filed a Notice of Federal Tax Lien, damaging only Leon's credit rating and subjecting only Leon's assets to IRS collection if he doesn't pay.

A. THE INNOCENT SPOUSE RULE

There is one exception to the law making both currently married (or former) spouses responsible for an IRS debt. It's called the *innocent spouse rule*.[1] Under this provision of the law, a spouse (or more commonly, an ex-spouse) may be relieved of liability, which typically results from an IRS audit, if:

- the tax bill is for unreported income or overstated deductions of at least 25% of the total income originally reported

  OR

- there is a "substantial understatement of tax attributable to grossly erroneous items of (only) one spouse"

  AND

- the couple filed a joint return

- the spouse claiming to be innocent did not know about the unreported income or overstated deduction, and had no reason to know about it, and did not benefit from it (this last one disqualifies most innocent spouses)

  AND

- holding the spouse responsible would be unfair.

---

[1] Internal Revenue Code § 6013(e).

The innocent spouse rule is strictly applied. Neither the IRS nor the courts readily accept pleas of "innocence" under this law. For example, the Tax Court recently denied a wife's claim of innocence, although she had not known of her husband's cheating. The Court reasoned that she *should have known* that the income reported on her joint return was way too low to support her family's lifestyle. The unfortunate conclusion is that only if the husband had squirreled the non-taxed lucre away and clothed his wife in rags would she have won her case.

Usually, innocent spouse claims are made by divorced taxpayers. People who are still married, however, can use the innocent spouse rule to hold property beyond the IRS' reach.

Example

Francisco and Imelda filed a joint return, were audited and were found to have substantially underreported Francisco's income. Francisco had skimmed about $60,000 from his delicatessen. Imelda convinced the IRS that she was an innocent spouse—she knew nothing about the income, had no reason to know about it (she was in the hospital recovering from surgery when Francisco did their taxes), did not benefit from it (Francisco blew the money gambling) —and that it would be unfair to hold her liable. Francisco changed his ways, agreed to a payment plan with the IRS and the marriage survived. Imelda went back to work and from her savings bought a home in her name alone, which was safe from the IRS.

B. CLAIMING INNOCENT SPOUSE PROTECTION

TIP   Don't be shy about bringing up the innocent spouse rule if you think it might apply. You can and should cry "innocent spouse" at all IRS stages of the proceeding—with the auditor, appeals officer, Tax Court or collector.

The IRS hasn't created a form to submit request for relief based on the innocent spouse rule. Instead, ask for relief, orally and in writing, every chance you get. If the IRS will not act on your requests then you may try filing Form 656 requesting an Offer in Compromise, based on the doubt as to your liability for the tax debt. (See Chapter 6, Section E.) You do not have to offer any payment using Form 656 in an "innocent spouse" case.

The IRS must consider your oral and written explanations as well as statements of others, including the "guilty" spouse. Whenever possible, supply documentary evidence. In Imelda's case, she gave the IRS hospital records showing where she was when the return was filed and photographs of their modest apartment and old car, showing that they were not living high off the hog.

2. Divorce and the IRS

Alimony (sometimes called maintenance or spousal support) is a frequent audit issue. It is tax deductible to the payer and taxable as income to the recipient, if ordered by a court or in a *written* agreement of both parties. If you are paying alimony under an informal oral agreement, you cannot deduct those payments on your tax return. If you are receiving alimony based on an oral agreement, you do not have to report those payments as income.

In addition, if you report alimony as income, you can deduct the portion of your attorneys' fees paid to secure or collect that money. Furthermore, all fees paid to any professional—attorneys, accountants and financial planners—for advice on tax consequences of a divorce are deductible if you itemize your deductions on your tax return.

 Often couples going through divorce allocate their responsibility to pay the IRS taxes currently owed or "any taxes assessed in the future" in a marital settlement agreement. The IRS, however, is *not* bound by such an agreement or court order and will go after both parties. If the (former) spouse who is not obligated under the agreement winds up footing the tax bill, she has the legal right to seek reimbursement from her (former) mate. The IRS will not agree to split a joint tax debt. Instead, it will collect against the spouse who is the easier target.

AVOIDING LIABILITY FOR YOUR SPOUSE'S DISHONESTY WITH THE IRS[2]

The "innocent spouse" rule isn't the only way to avoid liability for your spouse's underreporting or overdeducting to the IRS. The rules differ, depending on what state you lived in when you filed your return. These rules—including the innocent spouse rule—are briefly described below.

Community Property States (Arizona, California, Idaho, Louisiana, Nevada, New Mexico, Texas, Washington and Wisconsin)

Innocent Spouse Rule:

- you and your spouse did not file a joint income tax return

- you did not know and did not have reason to know of the unreported income (this means you had no knowledge of the amount of the income *and* you had no knowledge of the existence of the item of income itself)

- the income belongs solely to your spouse

- it would be unfair to include the unreported income in your income, and

- you did not receive any benefit from the unreported income.

Abandoned Spouse Rule:

- you and your spouse were married at some time during the calendar year

- you lived separate and apart during the entire calendar year

- you did not file a joint return, and

- you did not receive any portion of your spouse's income.

Denying Benefit of Community Property Law Rule:

If your spouse acts as if he or she is solely entitled to a portion of community income and does not tell you about that income by the time your tax return is due, your spouse will be solely responsible for reporting the income. This is because even when spouses file separate returns, each must report one half of the combined community income.

Non-Community Property States (the rest)

Innocent Spouse Rule:

- there is a substantial understatement of tax from income and deductions of the other spouse

- you did not know and did not have reason to know of the dishonesty—this claim presents a problem because a spouse is required to read a joint return before signing it

- it would be unfair to hold you liable, and

- you did not receive any benefit from the unreported income.

All States

Forgery Rule:

If you had no income and believed that you were not obligated to file a return, you will not be assumed to have authorized your spouse to sign your name on a joint return and may be able to claim that your spouse forged your name to a joint return.

On the other hand, if you have your own income and do not file separately, the IRS will assume you intended to file jointly and you cannot claim that your spouse forged your name to a joint return.

Duress Rule:

- you must have been unable to resist the demands of your spouse to sign the return, and

- you would not have signed the return if the pressure was not applied.

---

[2]This chart is taken from *Divorce and Money: How to Make the Best Financial Decisions During Divorce,* by Violet Woodhouse, Victoria Felton-Collins, with M.C. Blakeman (Nolo Press).

3. Parenting and the IRS

The IRS seems to pop up in all areas of our lives, including parenting. Be sure you know the rules on paying child support and claiming the dependency deduction.

A. CHILD SUPPORT—IS IT DEDUCTIBLE?

Unlike alimony, child support is neither deductible for the paying parent, nor reportable as income for the recipient parent. If you pay or receive "family support" (alimony and child support combined as one payment) you can deduct (or need to report as income) only the portion that represents alimony.

B. DIVORCED AND UNMARRIED PARENTS (OR MARRIED PARENTS FILING SEPARATELY)— WHO GETS THE DEPENDENCY EXEMPTION?

Children can qualify as tax exemptions, as we all know. Married couples filing a joint return simply list their children's names, ages and Social Security numbers, and then enter the number of exemptions on their tax return. Divorced parents, unmarried parents and married parents who file separately (this includes separated but not yet divorced parents), however, cannot both claim the same children as tax exemptions. The IRS may audit both returns if it discovers this error on one parent's return.

In the absence of a written agreement, the general IRS rule is that the parent who has the children for the longest part of the year is entitled to the exemption. This usually means the mother because she most often gets primary physical custody.

But if the father furnishes over 50% of the child's support, he is entitled to the exemption. He must file with his tax return IRS Form 8332, Release of Claim to Exemption for Child of Divorced or Separated Parents, signed by the mother. (A copy is in the Appendix.) If the father claims the exemption without filing this form, he may have to prove that he furnished over 50% of the support for the kids if the IRS questions his return.

C. CHILD SUPPORT COLLECTING BY THE IRS

One of the most powerful child support collection methods available is an interception of the owing parent's federal income tax refund. In 1991, over $500 million was collected by the IRS out of tax refunds to cover delinquent child support. And, this figure was a 12% increase over 1990. The average amount of refund grabbed was $600.

If you owe more than $150 and the other parent complains or receives welfare, the local District Attorney can call the IRS. Before your refund is taken, you should (although I've never seen the IRS follow this procedure) receive a written "intercept notice" which will tell you what's going on and give you the chance to request a hearing. But the claims you can make at a hearing are limited. Judges only want to hear that the back support has been paid or that the notice requests more than you owe.[3] Only in rare cases will a judge listen to a hard-luck story and a claim of a desperate need for the funds. To most judges, adult hard-luck stories are not as heart-breaking as kids not being supported.

If you are now married (to someone other than the custodial parent to whom you owe support), your spouse should attend the hearing and file a claim for her share of the refund. The IRS cannot send her portion to your child's other parent to satisfy a child support debt of yours, even in community property states. (The community property states are Arizona, California, Idaho, Louisiana, Nevada, New Mexico, Texas, Washington and Wisconsin.)

If all or a part of your refund is intercepted wrongly—for example, you were never told of your right to schedule a hearing, the IRS took too much, or your spouse's share was not withheld—you can request a reimbursement. You do this by filing an amended tax return (Form 1040X, Amended U.S. Individual Income Tax Return). If you're requesting the refund because your spouse's share was not withheld, you must also complete Form 8379, Injured Spouse Allocation. Copies of both forms are in the Appendix.

---

[3]A custodial parent may not be told when the hearing will be or may decide not to attend. If the intercept notice incorrectly states an amount you owe, and is based on information given by the custodial parent, you need to ask her to attend, or ask the court to order her to attend if she won't on her own.

States (with income taxes) also intercept tax refunds to satisfy child support debts. In Nebraska, for example, court clerks report all child support arrears to the state for an interception of the tax refund. As with federal intercepts, you should be sent a notice and given the chance to schedule a hearing. Your spouse may have the right to file a claim to have her share withheld from what is sent to your child's other parent.

B. Owning Property Jointly

Many people—friends, parents and children, siblings, lovers and married people who file their taxes separately—own property together. There are several tax dangers of co-ownership, however.

- If the joint property is held for investment, the IRS may challenge the way the co-owners allocated their tax liability—meaning how they reported property income or losses, and the gain or loss on the sale of the property.

Example

Marcus bought a warehouse which he rents to a moving company. He put title to the property in his name and his daughter Anita's name. Anita attended college in another state and was only vaguely aware that her father had put her name on the deed. After a severe winter, Marcus needed to do substantial repairs and renovations to the building, and the rents that year did not cover the expenses. Consequently, Marcus took the entire loss on his tax return for the year. He was audited, and the IRS ruled that as co-owner, he could deduct only one-half of the loss. Anita was entitled to deduct the other half of the loss. Anita had no income, however, and the loss was of no tax benefit to her.

- If one joint owner owes the IRS, the entire property may become an IRS seizure target. For instance, the IRS can easily grab a joint bank account you hold with your mother, brother or lover to satisfy their tax debt or yours.

Example

Let's stick with Marcus and Anita. Several years after Anita graduates from college, she opens a business. The business folds and she's left owing the IRS $34,000. The IRS issues a seizure notice, indicating that it plans to take the warehouse because of Anita's one-half ownership. Before the seizure actually happens, Marcus calls the IRS collector (Revenue Officer) and then a Problems Resolution Officer to object to the seizure. He follows up in writing. If Marcus presents evidence showing that he is the true owner—he paid the deposit and all the mortgage payments—the IRS may hold off from seizing. (See Chapter 7 for more information on seizures, and Chapter 8 for information on contacting a Problems Resolution Officer.)

- At the death of a joint owner, the IRS may allocate ownership in such a way to maximize the taxes it receives—meaning a heavier tax debt on the estate than might have been intended. (See Section C.3, below for an example of this problem.)

TIP None of the IRS assumptions in the three scenarios, above, are impossible to over- come. There is much legal precedent allowing joint owners to:

- allocate income, losses and deductions unequally

- keep their share of joint property away from the IRS, and

- prove that true property ownership is not necessarily what is stated on a deed or other title document.

But to convince an auditor, appeals officer or Tax Court judge, you will have to provide testimony and other evidence showing that the way title is held does not reflect the property's true ownership. (See Chapter 3, Sections E and G.) If this is your situation, see a Tax Pro—preferably a tax lawyer.

C. Death and Taxes

This is not a book about estate planning to minimize the taxes owed at death. There is a lot of good information on the subject, including *Plan Your Estate*, by Denis Clifford (Nolo Press). You can also get free information on death-related taxes from the IRS. Call 800-829-3676 and ask for Publication 448, Federal Estate and Gift Taxes.

Nevertheless, there are death-related IRS issues you should be aware of. Unhappily, IRS problems don't always stop at death—at least for the survivors. Past taxes can be collected from your estate. And, audits begun before your death (or even after) must be defended by your executor. She is legally responsible for seeing that all income or estate taxes are paid before your heirs get their shares.

If you are an heir, executor or administrator and are concerned about taxes owed on the estate of someone who has recently died, call the IRS and ask for Publication 559, Tax Information for Survivors, Executors and Administrators.

1. Filing a Federal Estate Tax Return

If the gross value of your estate (all property you leave at death) exceeds $600,000, your executor must file a federal estate tax return (Form 706). Anything over $600,000 is taxed—except if it is left to your spouse.

If the net worth of your estate is less than $600,000, your survivors will have no liability for federal taxes—assuming you haven't made any gifts of more than $10,000 to one recipient (except your spouse) in a single year during your lifetime. This means that you can't avoid the estate tax by making large gifts (over $10,000 per person per year) during your lifetime.

Example

Doug's estate consists of a money market account of $100,000 and two houses. One house has a market value of $400,000 with $300,000 still owing on the mortgage. The market value of the other house is $200,000; the mortgage balance is $100,000.

Gross Estate	Net Estate
$100,000 (money market)	$100,000 (money market)
400,000 (first house)	100,000 (house's equity)
+ 200,000 (second house)	+ 100,000 (house's equity)
$700,000 (Gross Estate)	$300,000 (Net Estate)

Because Doug's gross estate exceeds $600,000, his executor will have to file a federal estate tax return. The estate won't owe any federal taxes, however, because the net value is less than $600,000. It may owe state death taxes, however, depending on the state Doug lived in.

If Doug had owned the two houses free and clear, his estate would have owed federal estate taxes on $100,000—the amount by which his estate exceeded his $600,000 exemption.

2. IRS Audits of Estate Tax Returns

Estate tax returns have a much higher audit probability than income tax returns—at least 25% of all returns are selected. During an estate tax audit, the deceased taxpayer's last two income tax returns may be reviewed, if not formally audited, as well. The IRS reserves its best auditors, usually lawyers, for estate tax audits. The implication is that you should hire an experienced Tax Pro to prepare an estate tax return.

Internal Revenue Manual 4350 tells IRS auditors to look out for certain "red flags" on estate tax returns such as:

- Debts or other claims against the estate by heirs (other than what they would otherwise inherit). This type of claim reduces a gross estate that would otherwise be taxable. For example, the estate tax return filed by Jr. shows a $50,000 promissory note from Sam (the deceased parent) to Jr. An IRS auditor will want details on why Sam owed Jr. money to make sure this is not just a ruse to avoid the estate tax.

- The use of any "discount" on an asset's value below its fair market value. This is a strategy often used by Tax Pros to value family corporation stock at less than its full worth. This technique can work if it meets specific tax rules.

- Missing schedules or documentation that would normally accompany an estate tax return is always suspect.

Valuing assets. The most common issue in estate tax audits is the value of assets in the estate. It is easy to value bank accounts and common stocks and bonds. But, real estate, close corporation stock, art, antiques and other personal property can present valuation issues for the IRS to probe into.

Some states with death taxes have court-appointed appraisers make valuations of property. The IRS, however, does not appraise estate property —at least not in the first instance. The IRS on an audit of an estate tax return can, and frequently does, challenge valuations listed—sometimes even if they were made by a court appointed appraiser. The ultimate responsibility for proving valuations rests with the executor of the estate. He should always get bona fide appraisals of all items of property in the estate and list these values on the IRS Form 706 estate tax return.

If you are the executor of an estate with gross assets that may be worth at least $600,000, consult a good probate or tax lawyer. (See Chapter 13 for information on finding a lawyer). The danger is that you can be held *personally* liable to the IRS as well as the heirs if you understate

or don't pay all estate taxes due—including those that may be assessed on a subsequent audit.

Example

Randolph, a kindly executor, filed a federal estate return for his deceased old friend, Gregory. He valued various estate assets according to what Gregory had told him these items were worth shortly before Gregory had died.

Randolph then distributed the estate's assets to Gregory's two sons who promptly blew their inheritances. The IRS audited the estate tax return two years later and found the estate assets were undervalued by over $200,000. The estate was hit with a tax bill of $100,000. "But, all of the estate assets are gone," Randolph said. "Too bad," said the IRS. Legally, Randolph, as executor of the estate, was liable for these taxes.

If Randolph had gotten bona fide appraisals on all assets he would have made sure the valuation of the assets was defensible against IRS attack.

An executor may stave off an IRS estate tax audit by attaching copies of appraisals and other documents supporting valuations to the federal estate tax return. This type of evidence is the *first* thing the IRS looks for in deciding whether or not to audit an estate tax return.

3. Joint Ownership and Death

You cannot escape federal estate taxes through joint ownership of property, unless your co-owner is your spouse. As mentioned in Section B, above, if a joint owner of property dies, the danger exists that the IRS may reallocate the ownership shares in a way to maximize the taxes owed.

This issue is a concern only for *non-spouse* co-owners who hold their property as joint tenants—a form of ownership that allows the survivor(s) to automatically inherit the deceased person's share without going through probate.

Example

Hilda (mother) and Gertie (daughter) jointly own an apartment building with a market value of $900,000 and no outstanding mortgage. Hilda bought the building many years ago as an investment, with the proceeds of a life insurance policy she received when her husband died. When Gertie reached adulthood, Hilda added her to the deed so that Gertie would inherit the building without going through probate.

After Hilda died, Gertie filed a federal estate tax return listing the building's value at $450,000, thinking that only her mother's one-half ownership portion was taxable. The IRS audited the return, reallocated the entire $900,000 to Hilda's estate. This produced a tax bill on the $300,000 excess value over Hilda's $600,000 estate tax exemption. Gertie had to take out a mortgage on the apartment building to pay the estate tax bill.

Unfortunately, the IRS was correct. Because Gertie never contributed money to the acquisition of the building, it was never hers for tax purposes.

Fraud and Tax Crimes: Do You Really Have to Worry?

10

It is a crime to cheat on your taxes. In 1990, however, only 2,472 Americans were convicted of tax crimes—.0022% of all taxpayers. This number is astonishingly small, taking into account that the IRS estimates that 17% of us cheat in some way or another. And, the number of convictions for tax crimes has decreased over the past decade.

The point is that the statistical likelihood of your being convicted of a tax crime is almost nil. Nevertheless, if you are in the unlucky minority of people criminally investigated by the IRS, you need more than this book. Hire the best tax and/or criminal lawyer you can find.

According to the IRS, 75% of the cheating is done by individuals—mostly middle income earners. Most of the rest of the cheating is done by corporations. Service industry workers, from handypeople to doctors, are the worst offenders. For example, the IRS claims that waiters and waitresses underreport their tips by an average of 84%.

A. How People Cheat on Their Taxes

Most cheating is from deliberate (actual or willful), not just negligent, underreporting of income. A 1990 government study found the bulk of the under-reporting of income was done by self-employed restaurateurs, clothing store owners and—you'll no doubt be shocked—car dealers. Telemarketers and salespeople came in next, followed by doctors, lawyers (heavens!), accountants (heavens, again!) and hairdressers.

Self-employed taxpayers overdeducting business-related expenses—most commonly auto repairs and expenses—came in a far distant second on the cheating hit parade. Surprisingly, the IRS has concluded that only 6.8% of deductions are overstated or just plain phony.

B. If You Are Caught Cheating

If you are caught cheating, the auditor can assess you with civil fine penalties or refer your case for criminal investigation.

1. The Auditor Suspects You of Fraud

Auditors are trained to look for tax fraud—a willful act done with the intent to cheat the IRS—that dark area beyond honest mistakes. Using a false Social Security number, keeping two sets of financial books or claiming a blind spouse as a dependent when you are single, are all examples of fraud. While auditors are trained to look for fraud, however, they rarely suspect it. They know the tax law is complex and expect to find a few errors in every tax return. They will give you the benefit of the doubt most of the time.

Fraud or Negligence?

If you made a careless mistake on your tax return, you might get a 20% penalty tacked on to your tax bill. While not good, this sure beats the cost of tax fraud—a 75% civil penalty. You also could face criminal prosecution. The line between negligence and fraud is not always clear, however, even to the IRS and the courts.

While auditors aren't detectives, they are trained to spot common types of wrongdoing, called "badges of fraud." Examples include a business with two sets of books or without any records at all, freshly made false receipts and checks altered to increase deductions. (Altered checks are easy to spot by comparing written numbers with computer coding on the check or bank statements.)

The Internal Revenue Manual directs auditors suspecting fraud to contact the IRS Criminal Investigation Division (CID). (See Section C, below.) In reality, auditors make very few fraud referrals—no matter what they find. Not only do auditors give taxpayers the benefit of the doubt, but making a fraud referral is too much paperwork. If auditors find a couple of obviously phony receipts, they usually will quietly disallow them and move on. Fraud referrals, however, are more often made in "special project" audits. These are targeted audits of particular industries and professions, such as contractors or doctors.

You will not be informed by the auditor if she has made a fraud referral. One indication, however, may be an audit stopping midstream for no apparent reason. But never assume a fraud referral was made just because you don't hear from the auditor. Because fraud referrals are rare, the auditor is probably just behind in her work.

Even if the auditor does not refer suspected fraud to the CID, the auditor may probe into fraud during your audit. If she finds it, she can impose civil fraud penalties against you. According to the IRS, the greatest amount of tax fraud is from understated income. The second most common type is overstated or phony deductions and exemptions. It is typified by tax returns claiming exemptions for dependents who have long since left home, died or were never born. Fraud is also seen in the exaggeration of deductions, such as adding a zero to $200 making it $2,000, or by claiming a casualty loss for a non-existent accident.

A. INDIRECT METHODS OF PROVING FRAUD

Direct proof of fraud by the IRS usually consists of finding overstated or phony deductions and exemptions. The same type of proof is not usually available for income reporting. To show fraudulent income underreporting, the IRS usually must rely on "indirect" methods.

Specific items. If you cashed a check received in your business and pocketed the money without entering it in your books, this check is deemed a "specific item" and can be viewed as evidence of fraudulent intent. If the auditor suspects fraud, she may talk to your business' customers to compare checking account deposits and actual payments received.

The IRS usually wants more than just one specific item to make a fraud case—unless the item was for many thousands of dollars. You could always argue that one or two items were negligently left out of your income reporting, but a number of omitted items shows a pattern of fraud.

Bank deposits. This is the IRS' favorite method to prove unreported income because it is so easy. The auditor simply adds up all deposits in your bank accounts. If the total exceeds your reported income, you may be suspected of fraud.

Of course, there are many non-taxable sources of bank deposits—loans, gifts, inheritances, sales of assets and tax exempt income (such as municipal bond interest)—to name a few. Also, transfers from one bank account to another appear to be multiple deposits under this method. Point this out to the auditor. And sometimes deposits in your accounts may really belong to other family members and friends who do not have their own accounts.

Expenditures. To calculate your living expenses, the auditor totals up your canceled checks and adds known or estimated expenses you paid by cash. If the total is greater than your reported income, the auditor will suspect fraud. Auditors can use statistical reference books showing costs of various necessities in your community—the minimum costs of food and shelter, for example. You must then explain where you got the money to pay your bills. You could be living off savings from prior years, selling assets or receiving loans or gifts. If the IRS tries to confirm your expenses, the auditor will ask you to complete IRS Form 4822, Statement of Annual Living Expenses. *Don't—it can only hurt you, not help. You have no legal obligation to fill it out.*

Net worth. The auditor adds up all of your assets and deducts all of your liabilities for the start and end of the tax year under audit. If there was an increase in your net worth—what you own minus what you owe—without an increase in income from the previous tax year, you may be suspected of fraud.

Again, there may be many valid explanations as to how your net worth can increase besides unreported income. You may have received non-taxable gifts or inheritances. Or your assets may have appreciated in value.

 As explained under the expenditures method above, the auditor may ask you to fill out IRS Form 4822 stating your living expenses for the year in question. Again, don't. Respond that you didn't keep track of every penny you spent for the year and don't want to guess. Or accept the form, tell the auditor you will consider it and then throw it away. The IRS cannot punish you for refusing to give this information. If an auditor is intent on proving fraud, he will do it with or without your cooperation.

B. PENALTIES FOR TAX FRAUD

You will probably never face *criminal* fraud penalties. At least 98% of the time, the IRS penalizes fraud only by *civil* penalties—fines of 75% added to the amount of tax due from fraud. For example, if the additional tax due from fraud is $10,000, the penalty is $7,500, for a total of $17,500. Interest will also be added on to both the tax and the fraud penalty, starting on the date the return was due or filed, whichever is later.

C. DEFENDING AGAINST ALLEGED TAX FRAUD

The three defenses most often raised by lawyers to fight tax fraud allegations are "cash hoard," "non-taxable income" and "honest mistake." Don't expect the IRS to accept any of these defenses at face value. A skilled attorney is better able to persuade and carry your defense to the IRS than you are. Combating tax fraud, like brain surgery, is not a do-it-yourself project.

Cash hoard. This defense can be raised whenever the IRS uses either the bank deposits, expenditures or net worth method of proving fraud. There is no law (not yet anyway) against having cash in any amount—buried in your back yard or safe deposit box. The IRS' only legitimate concerns with your cash holdings are whether or not it was taxable

income, and if you reported it and paid tax on it. The IRS is suspicious of people who hold large amounts of cash rather than investing it or putting it in an interest bearing account.

Non-taxable source. The receipt of money is not always taxable income, as discussed above. You may innocently acquire wealth by gift, loans, inheritances and other ways which aren't taxable. This defense can be coupled with the cash hoard defense.

Honest mistake. If you make an error on your tax return, it is not fraud. For example, you didn't report profit from a sale of investment real estate because you believed you had two years to reinvest the proceeds without tax consequences. In reality, the law only allows you 180 days. Because intent to cheat the IRS is required for fraud, your mistaken belief is a valid defense to a tax fraud charge—but you must convince a judge or jury that it really was a mistake.

 Don't lie. No matter how bad things get, don't lie. Lying to an auditor who suspects tax fraud can only make matters worse. The right against self-incrimination is guaranteed by the Fifth Amendment to the U.S. Constitution. You have the right to remain silent before the IRS whenever there is a possibility you may be charged with a crime. You do not, however, have the right to lie. Lying to an auditor can result in a felony conviction with up to three years in prison and a $100,000 fine.

2. The Auditor Refers for Criminal Investigation

If the IRS believes you've cheated on your taxes, it has several options:

Ignore the problem. If the amount is small, an IRS auditor may overlook it. This happens if an auditor just wants the file closed and off her desk—and has found other significant adjustments. She may leave it at that and never refer your file to the IRS' Criminal Investigation Division (CID). (CIDs are discussed just below.)

Impose civil penalties. IRS employees generally do not ignore cheating. Instead, most will add civil (as opposed to criminal) penalties on to your tax bill, especially if you have cheated but your case is too small to send to the CID.

For example, an auditor can add a 20% penalty to your bill if she finds that your tax error was "accuracy related." If she concludes you owe an additional $1,500 of taxes, the penalty would bring the bill to $1,800.

By contrast, if the auditor finds that your omission or overdeduction was "fraudulent," she could add a 75% penalty, bringing your $1,500 tax bill to $2,625. And, interest will be added to both the penalty and the taxes until they are paid in full. The IRS imposes civil penalties routinely—about 25 million times per year. (The IRS can impose criminal penalties only as a result of criminal conviction. See Section D.4, below.)

Begin a criminal investigation. If the IRS suspects that you have substantially cheated the IRS, the IRS Criminal Investigation Division (CID) can investigate. The CID gets cases from one of four sources:

- Referrals from other IRS divisions, most often from auditors who discovered unreported income during an examination.
- Tips from law enforcement agencies—the IRS isn't concerned with the non-tax crime itself, often a drug-related offense, but whether or not the illegal income was reported.

Example

When Morgan was arrested for suspected drug trafficking, $150,000 in cash was in his car's trunk. After his arrest, the police notified the CID. The CID looked at Morgan's tax return, where he reported only $35,000 of income. The CID immediately began a formal investigation.

- Tips from citizens—ex-spouses or disgruntled employees and business associates often report people to the IRS. Here, however, the CID follows up on only the best documented tips, because it has found that many are not provable and are motivated by spite.
- IRS undercover or sting operations—in some instances, CID employees pose as buyers of businesses to find "off the books" income. Unwary sellers who brag about second sets of books and how much cash the business takes in get nailed. Other undercover operations investigate gross discrepancies in reported income and a taxpayer's lifestyle. This is how the U.S. government finally got Al Capone!

Example

Roy owned a pawn shop and was featured in a newspaper article on successful businesspeople. Roy posed for the paper in front of his waterfront home and Rolls Royce. Several months later, Roy was audited. The IRS wanted to know how someone lived so well while reporting only $20,000 a year income. The audit turned into a CID investigation. Two CID agents pored over six years of Roy's financial records, business and personal. Eighteen months later Roy was indicted for tax evasion.

At the conclusion of the criminal tax investigation, the CID has two options—drop it forever or recommend that the Justice Department prosecute the taxpayer for a tax crime. The IRS, which is part of the Treasury Department, cannot directly prosecute anyone. If the investigation is terminated, it doesn't mean you've gotten off completely. Your case will be sent (back) to an auditor who will probably impose civil penalties.

You will be pleased to know that in the majority of investigations, the CID does *not* recommend prosecution. The Justice Department will prosecute only a select few cases. Therefore, the CID won't waste its time referring, and in some cases even seriously investigating, a case unless it feels it has a sure—or pretty sure—winner.

If the CID does recommend prosecuting and the Justice Department agrees and you are convicted, you can be imprisoned or given probation, fined, or possibly both. And these fines can add up. For example, if you're convicted of failing to file a tax return for three separate years, you can be sent to prison for up to a year and fined $25,000 for each year you didn't file. You will also have a permanent criminal record.

And after a criminal conviction, an auditor will further slap civil penalties on your underpayment of taxes. This is all perfectly legal and does not constitute "double jeopardy"—a criminal law concept that prohibits you from being tried, convicted or sentenced more than once for the same crime.

If you are prosecuted but found not guilty, you will nonetheless probably be audited.

C. IRS Criminal Investigations

The Criminal Investigation Division (CID) is the IRS police force. Most criminal investigators are called Special Agents, who work out of local IRS District Offices. Special Agents don't wear uniforms, but they do carry badges and have guns. Make no mistake—they are detectives highly trained by the IRS. If anyone identifies himself as an IRS Special Agent, you or someone you know is under investigation for a tax crime. Most Special Agents travel in pairs, for their protection and to corroborate oral evidence gathered during an investigation.

The CID is divided into General and Special Enforcement sections. Special Enforcement investigates organized crime, drugs and unions. General Enforcement investigates ordinary taxpayers and everything else.

Will You Know If You're Being Investigated?

Unless and until you are formally charged, you may not know that you're being investigated by the CID. The IRS does not have to tell you, but often does. Of course, a friend, an employee, your accountant, your tax preparer, your lawyer or anyone else contacted by the IRS during the investigation might tell you. The IRS cannot legally swear these people to secrecy.

You might be able to find out indirectly if you are under investigation. When a criminal investigation begins, IRS personnel must complete and file Form 4135, Criminal Control Notice. This data is entered into your Master File in the IRS computer. Your tax account is frozen, meaning that no refunds can be made or payments credited to your account.

To find out if Form 4135 has been filed, send a token tax payment to the IRS. If a freeze is in effect, you should be notified that your payment is being held in a "suspense" account. And you should also request a printout of your account by calling 800-829-1040 or visiting your local District Office. The printout should note a Form 4135 filing or show that the payment was not credited to your account if a CID investigation is underway. If it does, start to worry.

Alert! The IRS may never send your requested printout if it has a criminal investigation "freeze code" in the computer. If you call on the phone to find out, IRS employees are told to lie to you if you ask whether or not a Form 4135 has been filed.

1. How Special Agents Conduct Investigations

Remember, very few taxpayers are criminally investigated. Only if the IRS has good suspicions of wrongdoing does it send out its elite police—Special Agents—to look into the matter. The investigation has two parts—first is an interview with the taxpayer's friends, business associates, professional advisors and anyone else who the IRS feels has information. Only later will the Special Agents usually contact the targeted taxpayer himself.

A. CONTACTING EVERYONE AROUND THE TAXPAYER

CID investigations are unbelievably thorough, often taking a year or more. The IRS spends more time investigating a criminal tax case than other police departments devote to murder cases. This intense preparation is why so few people are charged with federal tax crimes—the CID recommends prosecution to the Justice Department only when it is certain or nearly certain of a conviction.

The CID spares no expense, regardless of the amount of the taxes due. If you are under investigation, the Special Agent may talk to your friends, neighbors, co-workers, employees, business associates, bankers, insurance agents and even travel agents. Your spouse may also be contacted without your knowledge—so be ready for this. Your mail may be under surveillance, in cooperation with the Postal Service, but this is uncommon. The IRS can't open mail, but follows leads from return addresses on envelopes. In extreme cases, the IRS may get copies of bills from phone companies, follow taxpayers or get a court order authorizing a phone tap.

Special Agents are adept at intimidating businesspeople and bankers into giving information about taxpayers under investigation. Don't expect even your most trusted advisors to protect you if the IRS comes calling. Even your accountant can be compelled by the IRS to give evidence against you.

Attorney-Client Privilege

The only person who can't be forced to speak about you is your lawyer. Lawyers and clients have a special relationship that is given protection under the law—called the "attorney-client privilege." It means that your lawyer cannot disclose to the IRS anything you tell her, even if you admit to founding a religion which operates on the basic premise "pay no taxes." If an accountant is employed by your attorney to help her render legal advice, the accountant's work also falls under the attorney-client privilege and cannot be disclosed to the IRS. But the accountant's work must have been provided for a purpose other than preparing a tax return to be protected by the privilege.

CID investigations work in the reverse order of regular detective probes. Columbo, Magnum or Miss Marple start with a dead body—and then figure out whodunnit. Step 1 is the crime; step 2 is finding the culprit. This is the standard solving-the-mystery approach.

In contrast, IRS investigations begin with an allegation from a source, usually an auditor or informant, that a tax crime *may* have been committed. Then Special Agents work at building a case against the taxpayer. Step 1 is the suspect; step 2 is finding the crime. Special Agents are good at their work, too; they are among the best trained of all government employees and have almost unlimited resources behind them.

When IRS Special Agents Contact Your Associates and Friends

If you're contacted by Special Agents about another person, don't assume you're safe. In fact, don't answer their questions if there is any possibility you could be connected to the taxpayer under probe. And read "connected to" broadly. If you worked as a bookkeeper in a dress shop for several years and the owner is under investigation for underreporting income, you may not yet be the subject of an investigation, but there's a chance you will be. Keep quiet. Say you want to speak to a lawyer.

If there is no possible tie in, however, the law does not allow you to protect others by withholding information or lying. You may, however, legally tell someone else that the IRS was asking about them.

If someone tells you that she has been contacted in an IRS criminal investigation of you and asks you what to say, don't give her any suggestions. Never ask anyone to lie to the IRS for you. You both could get into big trouble. Don't call the IRS and ask what's going on, either. Instead, call a tax or criminal lawyer fast.

B. WHAT TO DO IF THE CID CONTACTS YOU

If the CID is building a case against you, you may be the last person interviewed. By the time the Special Agents get to you, they may have looked at thousands of records and spoken to 20 potential witnesses—your banker, ex-spouse, accountant, former employees or others with knowledge of your financial affairs. If, after going this far, the CID still wants to talk to you, more than likely your case is about to be recommended to the Justice Department for prosecution. The *only* purpose in questioning you at this stage is to get a confession or other damaging admission—the icing on the IRS' cake.

If you're contacted by the CID and are the target of an investigation, a Special Agent must tell you so immediately. He is also required to read to you the "Miranda" rights—the right to remain silent, the

right to an attorney and the warning that anything you say can and will be used against you. Believe him and keep your mouth shut. Answer only the question, "Are you August Fondue?"

It is highly unlikely that you'll be arrested on the spot or even asked to go to the IRS office. Simply state that you want to contact an attorney and that someone will get back to them. Don't call an attorney while the Special Agents are present, unless they threaten you with immediate arrest, or something similar, if you don't cooperate. Wait until they leave, you have calmed down and you can speak freely. If you don't know a criminal-tax attorney to call, see Chapter 13.

How about trying to talk the Special Agents out of pursuing their case against you? Forget it—it's a bad idea. It makes no difference to them if your mother is sick, you have money problems or your marriage is falling apart. Not only won't the Special Agents care, but mentioning your problems only strengthens the IRS' position; giving an excuse often shows that you knew what you did was wrong. Similarly, don't lie. Lying is as serious a crime as tax evasion.

 Keep your mouth shut—take this advice seriously. If you give the Special Agents any room, they'll probably ask you just about anything. They may start with "soft" background questions, but will rapidly progress to tough ones designed to trap you. And many CID questions won't be genuine—that is, the Special Agents already know the answers and are asking only to see if you will lie.

The kinds of questions typically asked by Special Agents include:

Have you reported all of your income?

Where are your bank accounts, safe deposit boxes?

Can you tell us about the cars, boats, planes and real estate that you own?

Do you gamble?

What is the procedure for reporting sales in your business?

Do you keep a lot of cash on hand?

Who are your business associates?

Have you traveled out of the country recently?

Have you or any of your businesses been audited?

Faced with a barrage of questions like these, from trained Agents who show up unannounced, most taxpayers completely fall apart. They either blurt out a confession or a lie within five minutes of when the Special Agent arrived. This gives the Justice Department the rope to hang them with.

2. IRS Considerations in Deciding Whether or Not to Recommend Prosecution

One of the IRS' chief considerations in deciding whether or not to recommend prosecution is how strong a case it thinks it has. If you were caught red-handed or confessed, you can be sure of a recommendation. But remember—the government has to prove your guilt "beyond a reasonable doubt." If you keep your mouth closed, a good criminal-tax lawyer may be able to mount a decent defense. As a general rule, if you have even a little evidence in your favor, the IRS may decline to recommend prosecution, and only impose civil penalties (fines) instead.

Of equal importance to the strength of the case to the IRS is its publicity value—locally or nationwide. A prominent doctor or movie star is a juicy plum for the IRS, but you may not be. The agency firmly believes that front-page publicity makes other tax cheaters think twice. The CID also analyzes personality traits of the taxpayer, including age, physical and mental health, previous criminal record. How would a jury react to the person? Leona "only the little people pay taxes" Helmsley was no doubt selected for prosecution because the IRS guessed she'd be an unsympathetic figure. The judge and jury (and most Americans) obviously agreed.

Finally, the CID looks at the amount you allegedly cheated the government out of. The larger your indiscretion, the more likely the Special Agents

will recommend prosecution. The average amount of taxes owed in criminal cases is over $70,000.

The bad news: When the CID recommends prosecution, and the Justice Department accepts the case, the chances of conviction are better than 90%. And, most people convicted go to prison.

The good news: The government is quite concerned with maintaining this high rate of conviction. For everyone prosecuted, dozens of others who have been investigated are not.

3. Crimes You Can Be Charged With

If the CID concludes its investigation and decides to recommend prosecution, it will turn its evidence over to the Justice Department. An Assistant United States Attorney decides which crimes to charge you with. There are numerous federal tax crimes, but individual taxpayers are usually charged with one (or more) of three: tax evasion, filing a false return or not filing a tax return.

Tax evasion. Tax evasion is defined as "intentional conduct to defeat the income tax laws." Any sort of tax scheme to cheat the government can fall into this broad category. Tax evasion is a felony. The maximum prison sentence is five years; the maximum fine is $100,000.[1]

Filing a false return. Filing a false return is what it sounds like—you must have filed a tax return which contained a "material misstatement," such as describing your line of work as bricklaying when you are a bookie. More taxpayers are charged with filing a false return than with tax evasion because in a filing-a-false-return case, the government does not have to prove an intent to evade the income tax laws—only an intent to file a false return. Filing a false return is a felony that comes with a maximum prison sentence of three years and a maximum fine of $100,000.[2]

Failure to file a tax return. This is the least serious tax crime you are likely to be charged with. It's defined as intentionally failing to file a return when you were obligated to do so. (Not everyone must file tax returns. For example, only those people earning above a specified amount must file. The minimum changes from year to year.) Not filing a tax return is a misdemeanor. The maximum prison sentence is one year in jail for each year not filed. The maximum fine is $25,000 fine for each year not filed. The maximum number of years you can be criminally punished for not filing is six years.

D. If You Are Prosecuted

Once the Justice Department receives a taxpayer file recommended for criminal prosecution, an Assistant U.S. Attorney reviews it. If he feels that the IRS has a strong case against the taxpayer for a felony such as tax evasion, he will prepare an indictment to take before a federal grand jury, which usually goes along with the request for prosecution. (You can be criminally charged for a tax misdemeanor—such as not filing a tax return—without grand jury indictment.)

If you are charged, you will either be arrested or ordered to report before a federal judge or magistrate (a person like a judge) to enter a plea of guilty or not guilty. You might be required to post bail to stay out of prison before your trial, but more likely you will be released without having to post bail.

If you ever find yourself in this position and don't have a criminal or tax lawyer, get one immediately. Don't delay, as the government has already completed its investigation. Your lawyer will need time to catch up—learn the government's case—and prepare your defense. And although you may think you're up a creek without a paddle, the government's case may be legally defective or your attorney may recognize defenses to the charges.

1. Should You Plead Not Guilty?

Unless you have made a "plea bargain" with the government before your first court appearance, you should initially plead "not guilty." Remember: The IRS recommends for prosecution only those cases in which conviction seems a near certainty. The Justice Department weeds even further. Therefore, it's not surprising that over two-thirds of all defendants eventually plead guilty without going to trial.

Most of these are plea bargains, meaning the taxpayer agrees to plead guilty if the Justice Department agrees to reduce or drop some charges, or both. For example, if a taxpayer is charged with three years of tax evasion, the government may drop two years of charges in exchange for a guilty plea of one year of tax evasion. Sometimes the government will also agree to a light sentence, or at least not recommend a heavy one to the judge. The ultimate sentence will depend on a probation report and federal laws governing sentences.

2. What the Government Must Prove in a Tax Case

If you don't plead guilty, you will eventually have a trial. At the trial, the Justice Department and the IRS, working together, must prove you are guilty of the crimes charged. Essentially, the government must show you acted intentionally and that you are guilty "beyond a reasonable doubt."

---

[1] Internal Revenue Code § 7201.

[2] Internal Revenue Code § 7206 (1).

Intent. The primary element of any tax crime is intent. In criminal law, this intent is called "*willfulness*." If the government can't prove you acted intentionally, you can't be convicted. Put another way, you can't be convicted of a tax crime if you only made a mistake, even if it was a big mistake. For example, if you didn't file a tax return because you honestly believed that 65-year-olds didn't have to file any longer, you did not act intentionally.

Before you senior citizens get carried away with this example, bear in mind that to succeed, you will have to convince a jury that your mistaken belief was honest. Given that most people remember watching their parents or grandparents fill out returns—and many people, in fact, completed those returns for their elderly relatives—you will have a hard time convincing your 12 peers that your omission was an honest mistake. More believable is a recent immigrant who did not report his income from investments made back home, which he wrongly thought was tax exempt.

Beyond a reasonable doubt. All crimes must be proven "beyond a reasonable doubt." If a juror has any degree of doubt that the taxpayer did what he was accused of or acted intentionally, the government's case will fail. For instance, without additional evidence showing an intent to cheat the IRS, a juror may not believe "beyond a reasonable doubt" that the immigrant who omitted his foreign investment income was filing a false tax return. The reasonable doubt standard is why the Justice Department prosecutes only airtight cases.

3.   Your Chance of Being Convicted of a Tax Crime

Not everyone charged with a tax crime is found guilty—although the Justice Department has a 90% conviction rate. But there is hope. For example, keep in mind the story of Dr. Rudy Mays.

Dr. Mays worked at an inner city clinic. Over 80% of his income was from Medicare, with the rest paid mostly in cash. He was indicted for income tax invasion when the IRS found that he had reported $240,000 in total income in a year in which his Medicare income alone was $280,000.

Dr. Mays was offered a plea bargain—if he'd plead guilty, the charge would be reduced and he'd receive probation, not a prison term. But this plea bargain meant that Dr. Mays' medical license would be revoked, ending his career. He rejected the offer and went to trial.

Dr. Mays testified that he was a man of medicine, but a poor businessman. He relied on his bookkeeper and accountant; he signed whatever they put in front of him. The prosecuting attorney scoffed at this "defense" by telling the jury that everyone bears the responsibility for the accuracy of their tax returns. The jury sympathized with the good Doctor and found him not guilty.

P.S. Immediately after the trial, the IRS began an audit. Dr. Mays had to pay thousands of dollars in taxes, interest and fraud penalties, but at least he stayed out of jail and kept his medical license.

In a U.S. Supreme Court, the conviction of Mr. Cheek, an airline pilot found guilty of tax evasion, was reversed.[3] Mr. Cheek's defense was that he had formed a belief, based on materials provided by a tax protester group, that certain income tax laws did not apply to him. The trial judge told the jury not to consider this as a defense to tax evasion. The Supreme Court, however, held that his mistaken belief was a valid defense, and ordered Mr. Cheek to be retried. The question in the new trial was whether Mr. Cheek's belief was a good faith misunderstanding of the tax laws or was a criminal intent to evade paying taxes.

Mr. Cheek wasn't as lucky his second time around in court as he was his first. In January of 1992, Mr. Cheek was convicted by a new jury of deliberately evading paying taxes, filing a false refund claim and failing to file seven years of tax returns. The judge sentenced him to one year and one day in prison and fined him $62,000.[4]

---

[3]*United States v. Cheek*, 111 S.Ct. 604 (1991).

[4]*Wall Street Journal*, March 25, 1992.

4. If You Are Convicted of a Tax Crime

If you are convicted of a tax crime after a trial, you will likely have to serve some time in prison. Several factors enumerated in the Federal Sentencing Guide-lines determine how severe the sentence will be.

If, however, you reach a plea bargain, chances are better that you will be fined and/or placed on probation, or sent to a half-way house, rather than sent to jail. Added to the fine may be the costs incurred by the government in prosecuting you.

In general, public figures are most likely to go to jail. Back in the '30s, President Hoover ordered that our income tax evasion law be used to put away the most notorious man of his day, Al Capone. This is the only charge ever made to stick on Scarface, who found his way to Alcatraz.

Today, instead of landing on the Rock, tax convicts are usually sent to a "Club Fed" minimum security facility filled with bankers, lawyers, politicians and Wall Street sharpies. The average length of time served for a tax crime is a little less than two years. If this sounds like a breeze, think twice. Tax alumni of the federal prison system all agree that it was a humiliating and crushing experience. And licensed professionals—lawyers, doctors, stockbrokers and CPAs—lose their professional licenses after conviction.

Phillip S. Fry, author of *Pay No Income Tax Without Going to Jail*, was apparently unclear on the concept. In 1986, he pleaded guilty to tax fraud and, you guessed it, went to jail. Other tax criminals with whom you are probably familiar and their prison terms include:

- Pete Rose—five months
- Chuck Berry—four months
- Aldo Gucci—one year
- Sun Myung Moon—18 months
- Leona Helmsley—four years.

One of my favorite stars of yesteryear, Sophia Loren, served 17 days in jail in her native Italy for tax evasion. (It appears that big stars get off lighter in Italy than in the U.S. So if you're thinking of evading taxes, maybe you want to brush up on your Italian and find a job in Venice, Florence or Rome.)

SMALL BUSINESSES: WHEN IRS TROUBLE COMES 11

If you are in business for yourself, or you work for someone who is, know that the IRS is watching.[1] The three major concerns of the IRS in this area are:

- Are workers wrongly classified as "independent contractors" when they are legally employees?

- Is the business making payroll tax deposits?

- Are cash transactions—especially large cash transactions—made to the business being reported to the IRS?

A. Self-Employed—You're a Prime Audit Target

Because the IRS claims that most tax cheats are in the ranks of the self-employed, it is not surprising that this group is more closely scrutinized than are wage earners. If the IRS chooses to come after you by way of an audit—or worse, a criminal investigation—be aware that the agency can easily get your bank and other financial records. If you've been foolish enough to deposit unreported income in your accounts, the IRS will find it.

If audited, the IRS will most likely investigate the following issues:

- Did you report all of your sales or receipts?

- Did you write off your personal living expenses as business expenses?

- Does your lifestyle exceed the amount of self-employment income reported?

- Did you write off automobile expenses for travel which was not business-related?

- Did you claim large business entertainment expenses?

If you are self-employed and audited, be sure to read Chapter 3 and concentrate on Section C.2.

---

[1]This chapter provides an overview of the most common small business tax issues. For further information, see *The Small Business Tax Survival Handbook*, by Frederick W. Daily (Nolo Press), available late 1994.

B. Employees or Independent Contractors?

If your business is improperly treating workers as self-employed—that is, as independent contractors—you may find yourself in trouble if the IRS audits. The IRS has the power to change the classification of any worker, with expensive consequences for the employer.

By calling workers "independent contractors," business owners avoid reporting requirements and withholding taxes and FICA from their workers' paychecks. And, these businesses avoid the expense of matching FICA contributions and unemployment tax. The tax savings to a business and reduced paperwork can be significant—unless you get caught. Then you can be taxed and penalized up to 35% of the amount of the pay given to the wrongly classified worker, plus interest.

In any event, a business must keep track of the total amounts paid to true independent contractors. At the end of each calendar year, you are required to file Form 1099, Statement for Recipients, for each independent contractor you paid over $600. You must also send a copy of Form 1099 to the contractor herself.

Many employers fail to file Form 1099s or give them to their independent contractors. If the IRS finds that you failed to issue a Form 1099, your audit penalty can be almost twice what it would be for just wrongly classifying employees alone as independent contractors.[2]

 Misclassification of independent contractors is an IRS priority. In the 1990s, the IRS has targeted for audit businesses suspected of wrongly classifying workers. To date, targets have included building contractors, medical professionals, graphic designers and neighborhood beauty shops.

If you are caught, the IRS can assess an employer not only the payroll taxes that should have been collected and paid, but also any of the employee's

---

[2]Internal Revenue Code § 3509.

unpaid income taxes. As the penalties and interest mount, businesses can receive post-audit bills totaling 50% of the wages paid. For example, if you paid Millie Ways $20,000 and called her an independent contractor, the IRS might hit you with a $10,000 total bill for misclassification when you are audited several years later.

1. How to Classify a Worker

To determine who qualifies as an independent contractor, the IRS suggests that you review Form SS-8, Determination of Employee Work Status for Purposes of Federal Employment Taxes and Income Tax Withholding. (A copy is in the Appendix.) Here is a summary of the factors that the IRS looks at:

FACTORS TENDING TO SHOW THE WORKER IS AN EMPLOYEE

- You require—or can require—the worker to comply with your instructions about when, where and how to work.
- You train the worker to perform services in a particular manner.
- You integrate the worker's services into your business operations.
- You require the worker to render services personally; the worker can't hire others to do some of the work.
- You hire, supervise and pay assistants for the worker.
- Your business has a continuing relationship with the worker or work is performed at frequently recurring intervals.
- You establish set hours of work.
- You require the worker to devote the majority of the work week to your business.
- You have the worker do the work on your premises.
- You require the worker to do the work in a sequence that you set.

- You require the worker to submit regular oral or written reports.
- You pay the worker by the hour, week or month, unless these are installment payments of a lump sum agreed to for a job.
- You pay the worker's business or traveling expenses.
- You furnish significant tools, equipment and materials.
- You have the right to discharge the worker at will and the worker has the right to quit at will.

FACTORS TENDING TO SHOW THE WORKER IS AN INDEPENDENT CONTRACTOR

- The worker hires, supervises and pays her assistants.
- The worker is free to work when and for whom she chooses.
- The worker does the work at her own office or shop.
- The worker is paid by the job or receives a straight commission.
- The worker invests in facilities used in performing services, such as renting an office.
- The worker can realize a profit or suffer a loss from her services, such as a worker who is responsible for paying salaries to her own employees.
- The worker performs services for several businesses at one time—although sometimes a worker can be an employee of several businesses.
- The worker makes her services available to the general public.
- The worker can't be fired so long as she meets the contract specifications.

2. People Who Are Automatically Employees

In most situations, the status of a worker is determined by the so-called common law factors. There are, however, certain workers who fall into special categories, and for whom the usual IRS criteria don't apply. For example, the federal tax laws say that certain workers are *automatically employees*. These include:

- officers of corporations who provide service to the corporation

- food and laundry drivers

- full-time salespeople who sell goods for resale

- full-time life insurance agents working mainly for one company, and

- at-home workers who are supplied with material and given specifications for work to be performed.

3. Exempt Employees and Business Owners

Federal laws also provide that licensed real estate agents and door-to-door salespeople are generally treated as "non-employees" or "exempt employees," (but may be treated as employees for the purpose of liability and workers' compensation).

If you are a sole proprietor or partner in your own business, you're neither an employee nor an independent contractor. You're responsible for paying your own income tax and Social Security self-employment tax. If you're a shareholder in a corporation but provide services to the corporation, you're generally an employee.

Additional State Rules

The IRS list of factors is similar to the standards followed in most states for state taxes and unemployment rules, but there can be some differences. For example, in California, a person working for a licensed contractor who performs services requiring certain state licenses is classified as an employee unless the worker has a valid contractor's license. If you plan to hire independent contractors, check with the employment office in your state to see if there are special rules in effect.

---

4. How the Independent Contractor Rules Are Applied

To better understand how the IRS tests are applied, let's look at two workers—one an employee and the other an independent contractor—who provide the same type services but fall into different legal categories.

Example 1—Employee

Wendy Wordsmith teaches advertising part-time at a community college. In addition, she does work for ABC Enterprises writing the company's newspaper ads, catalogs and consumer information leaflets. Wendy works every Wednesday and Friday at the company's offices. She receives a fixed salary each week for her two days of work. Wendy reports to the owner of the company and receives direct supervision and instructions from the owner. The company furnishes a desk and also the supplies that she needs to do her job. Wendy writes advertising exclusively for ABC Enterprises; she's not allowed to do this kind of writing for anyone else. Wendy is an employee of the company.

Example 2—Independent Contractor

XYZ Distributors, a similar-sized company, has similar needs for advertising on an occasional basis. But when XYZ needs a newspaper ad or catalog produced, it calls upon Frank Freelance to do the work. Frank works out of his home and occasionally farms out some of his overflow work to some other writers whom he pays directly. Frank owns his own computer and word processing software, and pays for his own expenses of doing business. Each time he completes a job for XYZ, he sends the company an invoice. Frank writes ads for several different companies. He clearly is an independent contractor and not an employee.

Part-time Workers—Beware!

John operates a small desktop publishing shop specializing in writing and designing brochures, flyers and other promotional materials for small businesses. At the start, John does most of the work himself, turning any overload over to others with similar skills. John collects from the customer and pays these people as independent contractors. So far, so good.

But as John's business grows, he arranges for part-time help on a fairly regular basis. Sue, Ted and Ellen regularly handle the overflow, working in John's offices under his broad supervision an average of about two days per week each. The rest of the time they work for themselves. John continues to treat them as independent contractors. By law, he shouldn't. If he continues along this line, he's tempting fate—and the IRS. John is exercising significant control over these workers and using their services in-house on a regular basis. Under the IRS guidelines, he should be treating them as part-time employees.

5. How Business Owners Can Protect Themselves

Here are some suggestions that will help you to prove a worker was properly classified as an independent contractor if you are audited.

- Enter into a written contract with the independent contractor. Spell out the responsibilities of each party and how payment is to be determined for each job. The contract should allow the independent contractor to hire his or her own assistants.

- Require the independent contractor to furnish all or most of the tools, equipment and material needed to complete the job.

- Have the independent contractor do all or most of the work at his or her own place—not at your business premises.

- Make it clear that the independent contractor is free to offer services to other businesses and not just your company.

- Pay for work by the job rather than by the hour, week or month. Have the independent contractor submit invoices for each job before you make payment.

- Specifically state in your contract that the contractor will carry his or her own business license and insurance, including workers' compensation coverage.

- Require the worker to furnish proof to you that she is reporting what you pay her on her tax return.

TIP The IRS invites businesses or workers to submit Form SS-8, for an IRS analysis of whether or not a particular worker qualifies as an independent contractor. I don't suggest that anyone alert the IRS to their situation. Better yet, consult a Tax Pro who can advise you how to stay out of the danger zone.[3]

C. Payroll Taxes—IRS Dynamite

If you are a business owner with employees, each payroll period you must withhold the following from each employee's paycheck:

- federal (and maybe state) income tax, and

- FICA contributions, which includes both Social Security and Medicare.

The amount of federal income tax withheld from each employee's earnings depends upon how the employee completed his wage withholding form (W-4). The FICA contribution is a percentage of the employee's gross earnings, which you must match.

An employer must pay the IRS by depositing the withheld taxes with a bank qualified as a depository for federal taxes. You must use a federal tax report

---

[3]For additional information on independent contractors, we heartily recommend *The Legal Guide for Starting and Running a Small Business*, By Fred S. Steingold (Nolo Press).

form with your payment. Many states have similar tax provisions.

Although the money is withheld each pay period, your requirement as an employer is to deposit payroll taxes either monthly or quarterly. In addition, you must file the following forms with the IRS:

- Form 941, Employer's Quarterly Federal Tax Return. This form must be filed every three months as long as your business has employees. On it, you report the amount of your employees' federal income tax and FICA withheld for the previous quarter.

- Form 940, Employer's Annual Federal Unemployment Tax Return (FUTA). This form must be filed once a year. On it, you report your total quarterly deposits for unemployment taxes and FICA based on your employees' gross pay. These FUTA taxes are paid by the business and are not withheld from its employees' paychecks.

According to the IRS, the *majority* of businesses are delinquent in filing or paying employment taxes at one time or another. This is a tremendous concern to the IRS, which considers payroll taxes the most serious of all tax debts. The theory of the law is that the employer acts as a collector for the government, holding its workers' taxes "in trust" until paid over to the IRS. Consequently, the IRS views operating a business while owing payroll taxes as illegally borrowing money from the U.S. Treasury.

Like all other income-related taxes, paying payroll taxes is based on the principle of self-assessment. If you don't file Form 941s, or you file them and don't deposit the taxes due, the IRS will assess you the taxes owed when it catches up with you.

 IRS collectors are extremely tough to deal with if you owe payroll taxes. Review Chapter 6 for how to deal with IRS collections. Keep in mind that Revenue Officers can seize assets and force you out of business if you owe back payroll taxes.

D. The Dreaded Trust Fund Recovery Penalty

Given our recent recession, here's a familiar scenario: Your business is struggling. You pay the rent and your employees' wages, but not the payroll taxes. You know things will turn around next month, however, when the big order comes in. And Christmas is just around the corner; you are sure you'll pull out of the slump and be able to pay Uncle Sam in full.

Six months go by. The economy has worsened. Orders stopped coming in and holiday sales were terrible. Your suppliers have sued you and your landlord is threatening to evict. You haven't filed payroll tax forms or deposited payroll taxes for the last four quarters. You shut down and sell your assets to pay off the creditors—although you don't pay the IRS the payroll taxes you owe. You manage to avoid bankruptcy by the skin of your nose.

If you did this, woe unto you. You probably should have paid the IRS first, and then if need be, filed for bankruptcy to handle the rest of your debts. This is because the IRS is the creditor to be most feared.

When payroll taxes haven't been paid, the IRS legally can review a company's books, speak to various employees and then hold its owners, managers, bookkeepers and even some clerks—personally responsible for the payroll taxes due. The IRS transfers the business payroll tax obligation to individuals—penalizing them for the business' failure to make the payroll tax deposits. This is known as the Trust Fund Recovery Penalty.

Because the penalty is equal to the amount of the taxes owed, it's also called the "100% Payroll Penalty."[4] And although in most instances the Trust Fund Recovery Penalty is transferred to employees of a defunct business, the IRS can—and will—impose the liability on people working for an ongoing business which is seriously delinquent in paying payroll taxes.

---

[4]Internal Revenue Code § 6672. It used to be called the "100% penalty." In 1993, it became the Trust Fund Recovery Penalty.

The relevant section of the Internal Revenue Code § 6672 states:

Any person required to collect, truthfully account for, and pay over any tax imposed by this title who willfully fails to collect such tax, or truthfully account for and pay over such tax, or willfully attempts in any manner to evade or defeat any such tax or the payment thereof, shall, in addition to other penalties provided by law, be liable for a penalty equal to the total amount of the tax evaded, or not collected, or not accounted for and paid over.

The IRS makes over 50,000 Trust Fund Recovery Penalty assessments each year, averaging about $21,000 per business—and $21,000 per responsible person.

Note that the IRS has only three years to *assess* the Trust Fund Recovery Penalty against responsible people after the tax was originally assessed against the business. Once the Trust Fund Recovery Penalty is assessed against the responsible people, the IRS has ten years to *collect* it from them.

How Businesses Can Minimize Payroll Tax Trouble

To minimize your IRS problems, always make federal payroll tax deposits when they are due. Never borrow from your employees' tax funds. Even if you eventually make the payment to the IRS, the late payment penalties and interest can be substantial. Pay Uncle Sam first, not last. If you can't pay, then maybe you shouldn't be in business.

One good way to see that payroll taxes get paid on time is to use a bonded payroll tax service to both file and make all payroll tax deposits. Many banks, as well as companies like ADP and Safeguard offer this service at reasonable prices. If they goof up and don't get a payment in on time, they will pay the late payment penalty.

If your business is able to make only a partial payment of payroll taxes, write on the lower left-hand portion of the check that the "payment is designated to trust fund portion" of the tax. Also, enclose a letter stating that you designate the payment to the trust fund portion.

The trust fund portion is the employee's income tax and FICA contributions. The rest—the employer's FICA contribution—can be paid last, if necessary, because the Trust Fund Recovery Penalty does not apply to that portion. This allows a business to reduce the amount that the IRS might otherwise assess against responsible persons.

1. How the IRS Determines the Responsible People

On average, the IRS finds 1.6 "responsible persons" for each defunct business owing payroll taxes. There is no limit, however, and it's not uncommon for six or more people to be declared equally responsible. And all are "jointly and severally" liable for the entire amount, meaning that the penalty is not divided or apportioned among the group—each person owes *all* of it to Uncle Sam.

Example

Skyrocket Enterprises went out of business owing $60,000 in payroll taxes. The IRS finds Zoe, Emily and Robb responsible for the money owed. Each is liable for the whole $60,000 and the IRS will go after the easiest target. The IRS can't collect more than $60,000 total, however. If Zoe pays, Emily and Robb are off the hook. If this happens, Zoe may be able to sue Emily and Robb in state court and get back $40,000, if she can collect from them.

The Trust Fund Recovery Penalty is one of the scariest parts of the entire tax code. The Penalty can be assessed against low-level or innocent employees who never dreamed it could happen. IRS investigations of businesses owing payroll taxes are carried on by specially trained Revenue Officers. They begin by putting together a list of people who had authority over paying the bills of the business. The primary considerations are:

- who made (or makes) the financial decisions in the business?

- who signed (or signs) the checks?

- who had (or has) the power to pay or direct payment of bills?

- who had (or has) the duty of tax reporting?

To get this information, the Revenue Officer may interview everyone associated with the business whose name comes up when she asks the above four questions. Also, the IRS can get bank and corporate records to obtain the names of people on bank signature cards and to show who actually signed checks and who were the corporate officials.

Once the IRS has a list of potentially responsible people, the Revenue Officer narrows it down. Anyone whom the Revenue Officer believes acted "willfully" in preventing the IRS from receiving the payroll taxes stays on the list—all others go. Unfortunately, willful does not mean that you intentionally tried to beat the government out of payroll taxes. It means only that you knew about the taxes and ignored paying them. Under this test, the IRS has found $100-per-week bookkeepers liable for enormous sums of money. The reasoning is that if the bookkeeper paid other bills, she could have paid the IRS. That's "willful" to the IRS.

Despite IRS policy to the contrary, Revenue Officers often stretch the facts in finding responsible persons. Most vulnerable are people with check-signing authority and with corporate titles.

Check-signing authority. Revenue Officers love to rely on this factor—it's easy. They assume that anyone who had or has the authority to sign checks is guilty. But IRS regulations state that the Trust Fund Recovery Penalty should not be imposed based on check-signing authority alone.[5] And, courts have held that an employee with no financial interest in the business, but who signed checks under the explicit directions of a boss, should not be held responsible.

Corporate titles. Running a close second to check-signing authority is the IRS assumption that anyone with a corporate title—President, Secretary or Treasurer—is a responsible person. IRS policy, however, states that this presumption should be made only if the corporate officers do not cooperate in the IRS' investigation of the delinquent payroll taxes.[6] In many small corporations, corporate titles bear little relationship to who really runs the business.

Frequently, the situation is that you are truly "responsible" for the Trust Fund Recovery Penalty but not for all the tax periods that are owed. You aren't liable for the Trust Fund Recovery Penalty for payroll taxes owed before you came onto the scene or after you departed.

---

[5]Internal Revenue Manual 5632.1(3).

[6]IRS Policy Statement P-5-60.

IRS Interviews of Potentially "Responsible People"

In interviewing each potentially responsible person, Revenue Officers ask the questions on IRS Form 4180, Report of Interview with Individual Relative to 100-Percent Penalty Recommendation, now called Report of Interview Held With Persons Relative to Recommendation of Trust Fund Recovery Penalty Assessments. (A copy is in the Appendix.) If you are ever called for IRS questioning about a defunct business with which you were associated, study the form ahead of time so that you won't be caught off guard. You should also review the form with a Tax Attorney before meeting the IRS. Some Revenue Officers accept a filled-in Form 4180 in lieu of an interview, but most want to see you in person.

If the IRS asks to talk to you about payroll taxes, you can bring a representative with you—a tax lawyer, CPA or enrolled agent. (See Chapter 13.) And you should, especially if you were the book-keeper, check writer or had financial responsibilities in the business.

2. Appealing a Trust Fund Recovery Penalty

If you are found to be a responsible person by a Revenue Officer, you will be sent a notice and a tax bill. Don't be unduly surprised if this happens. Revenue Officers tend to find as many people "responsible" as is remotely possible. But their decisions can be protested to the Appeals Division, where many Trust Fund Recovery Penalty responsible person findings are reversed by Appeals Officers. If you don't think you really were responsible, then you should definitely appeal.

The procedure is similar to an appeal of an audit.[7] A sample protest (appeal) letter follows.

---

[7]You can also go to court to contest the Trust Fund Recovery Penalty assessment if your appeal is denied. See Section D.3, below.

Sample Letter to Appeal Trust Fund Recovery Penalty

September 20, 1994

District Director
Internal Revenue Service
P.O. Box 408
Church Street Station
New York, NY 10008

Protest of Trust Fund Recovery Penalty
Sandy Swinger
SSN: 555-55-5555

Dear Sir or Madam:

By this writing, I am filing my protest of the proposed assessment of a Trust Fund Recovery Penalty. I request a hearing. I have enclosed copies of IRS Letter 1153 (DO) and Form 2751 dated September 10, 1994.

I deny that I was a "responsible person" and/or was "willful" in not paying over employment taxes for Crazy Calhoun's Incorporated under the meaning of Internal Revenue Code Section 6672.

I never had any authority to make any tax payments to the IRS or to order another person to do so while I was employed by Crazy Calhoun's. I never had a financial stake in the business, other than as a salaried employee. I was never an officer or director of the corporation. I was only the manager of the bar operation and subject to the direction of the president, Tom Ranoff.

Under penalties of perjury, I declare that I have examined the statement of facts presented in this protest and to the best of my knowledge and belief, they are true, correct and complete.

Sincerely,

Sandy Swinger

Sandy Swinger

Copy to Manuel Indiana, Revenue Officer

Enclosed: IRS Letter 1153 (DO) and
           Form 2751

In addition, appealing a proposed Trust Fund Recovery Penalty assessment will buy time—even if you're clearly responsible. An IRS collector can't come knocking at your door. And, interest does not run during the time an appeal is being considered. For example, if you are eventually found responsible for $50,000 in unpaid payroll taxes and your appeal process takes a year, you'll avoid about $3,500 in interest. Once the appeal is over and the tax is assessed, however, interest starts to run again.

SANDY AND CRAZY CALHOUN'S—A CASE HISTORY

Crazy Calhoun's was a popular singles spot owned by three partners. At the height of its glory, the least competent of the partners, Tom, bought out the other two partners. Tom lived in the fast lane and preferred play to work. He let his employees run the business. His neglect and expensive tastes caused the business to fall behind in its bills—including federal payroll taxes.

Sandy was a longtime employee of Crazy Calhoun's. She worked her way up from cocktail waitress to bar manager. Because C.O.D. liquor deliveries during Tom's frequent absences needed to be paid, Sandy was authorized to sign checks. She was uneasy about it, but went along because she knew if the bar didn't have any booze, she'd be out of a job.

One day, a Revenue Officer showed up asking for Tom, who was out. The Officer said he was padlocking the doors if he didn't get immediate payment of at least $2,000 for back payroll taxes. Sandy replied that she had authority to write checks for liquor deliveries only, unless Tom specified more. Several times in the past, Tom had phoned the bookkeeper saying that Sandy could sign payroll checks. Sandy asked her fellow workers what to do. They all agreed Tom would want her to write the check to the IRS, so she did.

Several months later Crazy Calhoun's was padlocked by the same Revenue Officer. By then, Tom had disappeared. Suppliers had stopped making deliveries for nonpayment; most employees had quit. Sandy got a new job. Eventually, Tom showed up in jail in Hawaii.

Sandy is found "responsible"

About two years later, a new IRS Revenue Officer paid a surprise visit to Sandy at home. Unlike the first guy, this man was very nice. He said he was investigating Crazy Calhoun's and needed to ask a few questions. He went through an interview and asked Sandy to sign a statement, thanked her and left.

Two months later Sandy found in her mailbox an IRS notice of "Proposed Assessment of Trust Fund Recovery Penalty." The nice man had found Sandy liable for $128,000 in payroll taxes of Crazy Calhoun's. She was hysterical. At 28 years old, Sandy owned a five-year-old Chevy, some old furniture and a cat. She earned $350 a week as a waitress and was supposed to pay an IRS bill on which interest and penalties were running at over $1,500 per month.

Sandy appeals

Sandy hired an attorney for her appeals hearing. The attorney felt that Sandy had a fair chance of winning an appeal. The most difficult thing to overcome would be the statement—Form 4180—that she had signed. The Form is designed to virtually guarantee anyone interviewed will be found liable.

Her attorney sought out other former Crazy Calhoun employees, who backed Sandy's story that she never had authority to pay business taxes. The former manager, Jack, was living 2,500 miles away. Jack was sympathetic and said Sandy was telling the truth. He was afraid to put this in writing for fear the IRS would come after him.

Lois, the former bookkeeper, had prepared checks for the business but never signed them. She was not being pursued by the IRS. She gave a statement that Sandy could sign checks only to pay for liquor C.O.D.s and that Tom had sole authority to pay all other bills. Sandy's lawyer submitted a statement from Lois.

At the hearing, Sandy's lawyer presented a statement from Lois and her own statement summarizing the attorney's conversation with Jack. Also, Sandy stated she had paid the IRS only once, under the duress of the Revenue Officer. At the end of the hearing, the Appeals Officer stated that the case was closed. About 60 days later, Sandy received his report—she was not held to be responsible for the taxes.

3. If You Lose Your Trust Fund Recovery Penalty Appeal

Many Trust Fund Recovery Penalty cases don't have endings as happy as Sandy's. If you really were a responsible person—that is, you knew about, had the authority to pay and should have paid the payroll taxes—there may be no way to avoid the penalty. Nevertheless, if you find yourself in this awful predicament, keep reading to find your options:

Go to court. You have the right to challenge a Trust Fund Recovery Penalty in court. Unlike contesting the outcome of an audit, however, you cannot sue in Tax Court. Instead, you must file your lawsuit in either the U.S. District Court nearest to you or the U.S. Court of Claims in Washington, DC.

To sue in a District Court or the Court of Claims, you must first pay a portion of the taxes claimed due and then file a lawsuit seeking a refund. The minimum amount you must pay is equal to the unpaid payroll taxes due for one employee for one quarter of any pay period. This means that if you are found liable for a large amount—say $50,000—under the Trust Fund Recovery Penalty, you only need to pay the taxes for a minor employee—perhaps only $100—to contest the whole $50,000.

As a practical matter, you will need an attorney to sue in either a District Court or the Court of Claims. (See Chapter 5, Section D.) Going to either of these courts is an expensive proposition. Expect to pay a minimum of $10,000 in legal costs.

File for Chapter 13 bankruptcy. A Trust Fund Recovery Penalty can't be out-and-out canceled (discharged) in a Chapter 7 bankruptcy. You can include the penalty, however, in a Chapter 13 bankruptcy repayment plan. Most bankruptcy judges will expect your plan to provide for repayment of all of the Trust Fund Recovery Penalty. Some bankruptcy judges, however, will allow a debtor to pay only a portion of it, and then wipe out the balance when the Chapter 13 is completed. See Chapter 6, Section F, for a description of the two types of bankruptcy. To try to get the Trust Fund Recovery Penalty partially wiped out in Chapter 13, you may need the help of a good bankruptcy lawyer.

Pay. If you throw in the towel, you should deal with the Trust Fund Recovery Penalty as you would with any other kind of tax bill. See Chapter 6 to find out your options. Your best bets are to try to set up an installment agreement (Chapter 6, Section D.6) or better yet, try to reduce your liability through an Offer in Compromise (Chapter 6, Section E).

Request a non-assessment. A little known Tax Code provision allows people found responsible for Trust Fund Recovery Penalties to request a non-assessment.[8] I have had this request granted on occasion when my client was broke and the IRS did not believe it would ever collect the penalty.

E. Cash Transactions Over $10,000

The IRS, as part of a government campaign against the underground economy in general, and drug-related money laundering in particular, requires that cash and "cash equivalent" business transactions over $10,000 be reported to the IRS. These reports are called CTRs or Currency Transaction Reports. Some state tax agencies have similar laws.

Cash equivalents include traveler's checks, money orders and bank drafts. Personal checks are exempt from the reporting requirement, presumably

---

[8]Internal Revenue Code § 6672; Internal Revenue Manual 5542.3.

because banks keep copies of personal checks, thereby creating a paper trail.

All businesses (including banks) that receive cash or cash equivalents must report each customer's name and each transaction over $10,000 on IRS Form 8300. (For a detailed pamphlet explaining this law, see IRS Publication 1544, Reporting Cash Payments of Over $10,000.)

Form 8300 identifies people who unload non-taxed money by purchasing luxury goods—such as cars, yachts and jewels, or taking trips. But anytime you receive over $10,000 in cash or cash equivalents in one business transaction, you must complete Form 8300. And when you deposit that money into your bank—or if your total cash receipts for a day exceed $10,000—your bank will report you to the IRS unless you are specifically exempt from this law—and few people are exempt.

You can't avoid this law by separating one $10,000 transaction into several smaller ones. If multiple transactions from the same source exceed $10,000, you must file Form 8300. Similarly, if you make three cash deposits of $4,000 at different times

over a few days, your bank is obligated to report them as one transaction.

If you don't file a CTR when you should have and the IRS finds out, you can be fined, audited. You can also get in trouble criminally—CTR violations are investigated by the the IRS Criminal Investigation Division. (See Chapter 10.)

In short, it can cause you more problems than if you had reported the cash in the first place. The reason is that at present, the IRS doesn't have the staff to check out more than a small percentage of Form 8300 filers. I doubt if they ever will.

Few businesspeople get in trouble for failing to report cash transactions over $10,000. But if your business deals in cash—for example, you own a bar, restaurant, laundromat or grocery store—be aware that the IRS will no doubt suspect you of skimming cash off your receipts. The audit potential of cash businesses is much higher than average. Overcoming IRS assumptions of underreporting income isn't impossible, but if you're audited, you'll have an uphill battle. You will need clear inventory and financial records. (See Chapter 3, Section E, on how to prepare for an IRS audit.)

Penalties and Interest 12

IRS-imposed penalties and interest charges are discussed throughout the book. I cover them here in a separate chapter because these fines are often expensive and cause so many headaches to so many taxpayers. For example, I once saw a $7,000 tax bill with $15,000 added in interest and penalties. Information on taxes and penalties, from the IRS' perspective, is in Notice 746, Information About Your Notice, Penalty and Interest. (A copy is in the Appendix.)

Some questions I frequently get:

Is it possible to get the IRS to drop a penalty?

What can I do about the interest on my audit bill?

How many different ways can the IRS penalize me?

Can I negotiate a penalty down?

Does the IRS ever have to pay me interest?

A. Penalties Added to Tax Bills

When the IRS hits you with a tax bill, it usually adds penalties and interest. These are two distinct and different charges. (Interest is covered in Section B, below.) Penalties are added by IRS computers or by IRS personnel. Penalties are authorized whenever you file or pay your taxes late, or have been found to owe additional taxes or have failed to file or complete a tax form.

Although penalties were originally meant to punish errant taxpayers (that's why they are called penalties), they are now considered an official source of revenue in our national budget. Reflecting this, in the past decade the IRS increased the total dollar amount of penalties imposed on taxpayers by 1,000%. In a recent year, 25 million penalties were assessed for over $6,000,000,000. (Yes, that's six *billion* dollars.) In short, penalties have become a tax—on a tax.

Take heart—you may be able to beat the IRS at the penalty game. The IRS can remove a penalty if you can show that your failure to comply with the tax law was due to "reasonable cause." (See Section D, below.)

1. Post-1990 Penalties

The federal tax penalty structure changed effective January 1, 1990. (Penalties on taxes due before 1990 are still based on the old rules outlined in Section A.2, below.) Many of the 150 or so old penalties were consolidated into two new categories—called accuracy and fraud penalties.

Accuracy penalties. The IRS can add a 20% penalty to your tax bill (not including any interest) if IRS personnel find that you have understated your income tax liability on a tax return.

Fraud penalties. If the IRS concludes after an audit that you did not report income on your tax return due to fraud, it can add a fraud penalty. This penalty is 75% of the amount you underreported.

Or, if the IRS finds that you fraudulently failed to file a return, it can slap you with a penalty (15% for every month you didn't file for up to five months) based on the taxes owed. This second penalty is rarely imposed. The IRS usually just hits you with a late filing penalty, instead of a fraud penalty. (See Section A.3, below.)

2. Pre-1990 Penalties

For taxes and returns due before 1990, the most common penalties are *negligence* and *fraud*.

Negligence penalties. If the IRS concludes that you underpaid out of negligence in complying with the tax laws, the agency can add a penalty of 5% of the tax due to your bill. This 5% penalty is also added to the accumulated interest. And, the IRS can impose this penalty in addition to other penalties on your bill.

Fraud penalties. The penalty is 75%, the same as the current rate. It's calculated differently, but for this discussion, the difference is not important.

3. Pre- and Post-1990 Penalties

When the IRS revamped the penalty structure, it kept its most commonly imposed penalties—late filing and late payment. It also retained penalties against negligent return preparers, on tax protesters and on employers who fail to make payroll tax deposits on time. (See Chapter 11, Sections C and D, for more information on the payroll penalties.)

Failure to pay taxes penalty. The IRS can add to your bill a penalty of $1/2$% to 1% per month of the amount you failed to pay. The amount starts at $1/2$%. Once the IRS issues a Notice of Intent to Levy (see Chapter 7), the agency can raise the penalty to 1%. Generally, the penalty starts on April 16, the day after your income tax return was due if you are in individual taxpayer.

Late filing of a return penalty. If you filed your return late, the IRS can impose a penalty of 5% per month of the taxes due, not to exceed 25% total. In other words, you "max out" on the penalty if, after five months (September 16—five months and one day after April 15), you still haven't filed your return and paid the taxes due on the return. If you file late but don't owe any taxes there is no penalty.

Combined penalty. If you both file late and fail to pay your taxes, the IRS can impose a combined penalty, which is a little bit less than the individual penalties for each. It is 5% of the unpaid tax for each month (or part of the month) your return is late. The 5% consists of a $4^1/2$% late filing penalty and a $1/2$% failure to pay penalty. When you reach $22^1/2$% (five months) for filing late, the penalty rate on the late filing portion of the combined penalty freezes. The failure-to-pay portion of the combined penalty continues to accrue at $1/2$% per month until it reaches its maximum of 25%. Thus, the maximum combined penalty is $47^1/2$%.

Late filing penalties and late payment penalties (or the combined penalty) can be "stacked"—imposed in addition to other penalties such as accuracy (post-1990), negligence (pre-1990) or fraud penalties.

B. Interest on Tax Bills

The second unwelcome addition to every overdue tax bill is IRS-charged interest. If you do not pay your taxes on time, you are considered to be borrowing money from Uncle Sam. Congress does not like to lend money interest-free (except to various dictators and deadbeat foreign countries), so it requires the IRS to charge interest on these "loans."

The interest rate is also set by Congress.[1] The rate is adjusted every quarter and compounded daily —this means that interest is being charged on interest. For older tax bills, interest calculations cannot be easily verified unless you have a computer with software emulating the IRS' program and changing the rate every three months. At the time of this writing (January 1995), the interest rate on tax bills is 8% per year.

C. Understanding Penalty and Interest Notices

When you receive a tax notice stating that you owe money to the IRS, it usually includes a penalty and

---

[1]The formula used to compute the interest rate is complex. Essentially, it's three percentage points above the average market yield on short-term federal debt obligations.

interest charge. If you don't understand how the IRS computed the penalties and interest—I'd be surprised if you did—you should request a PINEX (Penalty and Interest Notice Explanation) from the IRS. Call the taxpayer assistance number (800-829-1040) or write your Service Center or ask your local District Office collection division to mail you a PINEX. Expect to wait 30 to 60 days for it to arrive.

A PINEX is a multi-paged computer printout which is fairly easy (as IRS communications go) to understand and includes:

- a listing of your tax account showing all tax penalty and interest computations

- dates, interest rates, penalties assessed and any credits (payments or refunds)

- principal sums (taxes) on which interest and penalties were charged

- explanations of which particular penalties were applied to your bill, and

- summary of your account with balance due, including up-to-date penalty and interest amounts.

TIP Be sure to check the PINEX to see that you agree with the amount of the taxes owed, and that you have been given credits for all payments you made. The IRS is often wrong.

D. Reducing or Eliminating Penalties and Interest

The IRS can eliminate or reduce a penalty if you show then a "reasonable cause" for doing so. The term the IRS uses for an elimination or reduction of a penalty is "abatement." About one-third of IRS-imposed penalties are later canceled. Interest, however, is rarely abated. By law, interest can be canceled only if it was erroneously applied. Additionally, if you qualify for an Offer in Compromise, the IRS may reduce the interest you owe. (See Chapter 6, Section E.) This is the method by which most interest charges are abated—"reasonable cause"—does not work to reduce interest charges.

Abatements can be granted at any IRS level—Service Center, Automated Collection System or personnel at District Offices.

1. "Reasonable Cause" for a Penalty Abatement

The key to having a penalty removed is to show the IRS reasonable cause for your failure to observe the tax law. What constitutes "reasonable cause" is a fuzzy area of the law. Often, a good excuse is whatever the IRS officer decides it is. The IRS does, however, offer some guidance on reasonable cause in the Internal Revenue Manual:[2]

Any sound reason advanced by a taxpayer as the cause for delay in filing a return, making deposits... or paying tax when due will be carefully analyzed.... Examples of...reasonable cause:

1. *Death or serious illness of the taxpayer or... immediate family. In the case of a corporation, estate, [or] trust...death or serious illness must have been of an individual having sole authority to execute the return or make the deposit or payment.*

2. *Unavoidable absence of the taxpayer....*

3. *Destruction by fire or other casualty of the taxpayer's place of business or records.*

4. *Taxpayer was unable to determine amount of deposit of tax due for reasons beyond taxpayer's control....*

5. *Taxpayer's ability to make deposits or payments has been materially impaired by civil disturbances.*

6. *Lack of funds is an acceptable reasonable cause for failure to pay any tax or make a deposit... only when a taxpayer can demonstrate the lack of funds occurred despite the exercise of ordinary business care and prudence.*

7. *Other explanations may be acceptable.... Acceptable explanations of delinquency are not limited....Any reason...established that the*

---

[2]IRS Policy Statement P-2-7.

taxpayer exercised ordinary business care and prudence but was nevertheless unable to comply within the prescribed time will be accepted as reasonable cause.

Practical suggestions. If possible, you will want to rely on one of the first six items in requesting a penalty abatement for reasonable cause. Specifically, you will want to assert that you acted with "ordinary business care and prudence" but still couldn't file or pay your taxes on time.

If none of the first six reasons fit your situation, try to come within the catch-all, category 7. "Other" explanations that might work include:

- Reliance on a Tax Pro who steered you wrong. For example, if your accountant or bookkeeper caused the tax problem by giving you bum advice or filing the wrong form, say so. (Bear in mind that the IRS might counter that because you picked the Tax Pro, you are responsible for his action.)

- The IRS wouldn't help you earlier. If you called, wrote or visited the IRS and got the wrong information or no response when you tried to clear things up, make the point. Be sure to provide copies of letters you sent, the names of all IRS personnel you spoke with, and the dates and summaries of your conversations.

- Someone else caused your problem. For example, if your employer submitted an incorrect 1099 or W-2 form, be sure to tell it to the IRS.

- If your penalty is the result of a late payment, you can plead that you would have suffered an "undue hardship" if you had paid on time. Be warned that this is a tough sell to the IRS. You will need to show that had you paid your taxes on time, you would not have been able to put food on the table. The IRS is often sympathetic if the hardship is medical-related, including alcohol or drug abuse. Again, you'll need documentation, such as letters from doctors explaining your condition.

TIP If it's true, stress your clean past IRS record. Emphasize that you've never before requested an abatement, had a penalty assessed against you or have been behind in paying your taxes.

2. How to Request a Penalty Abatement

Because most penalties are imposed by IRS Service Centers, you should start the abatement process there. As soon as you receive a tax notice that includes penalties, write back and ask for an abatement. If you send a letter, use a format like the sample, below. Alternatively, use IRS Form 843, Claim for Refund and Request for Abatement. (A copy is in the Appendix.) Attach a copy of the IRS notice sent to you.

Also enclose copies (keep the originals) of substantiating documents—such as a doctor's statement, fire department report, insurance claim or death certificate of a family member. Without supporting paper, your abatement request may not get serious consideration. You might also enclose payment for the underlying tax, and designate on your check that the payment is for the tax portion only. If nothing else, paying the tax stops the accrual of interest on that balance. Send the letter with enclosures to the address in the notice, and use the IRS enclosed self-addressed envelope, if one was sent.

TIP Make several copies of any letter you send to the IRS. Service Centers are notorious for ignoring or losing taxpayer correspondence. So, be prepared to send the additional copies whenever you get a notice containing penalties before you get a reply to your initial abatement request.

Sample Letter Requesting Abatement of Penalties

```
To: Adjustments/Correspondence Branch
IRS Service Center
P.O. Box 9941
Ogden, UT 84409

Re: Request for Penalty Abatement

From: Sanford Majors
43 Valley Road
Salt Lake City, UT 84000

SSN: 55-555-5555

November 3, 1994

To Whom It May Concern:

I am requesting an abatement of penalties
asserted in the IRS notice enclosed dated
5/5/94 in the amount of $2,312.10.

The reason I [select one]: filed late, paid
late, didn't report some income was that
[fill in your reason, such as]:
```

- I was suffering from a nervous breakdown
- My wife had just passed away
- My house burned down on April 14 with all of my tax records
- I was a hostage in Lebanon
- **any other excuse**

```
Enclosed is a [describe your documents, such as]:
```

- Letter from Dr. Freud explaining my condition which prevented me from filing my tax return on time
- Death certificate confirming my wife's passing
- Report from the fire department
- Letter from the U.S. State Department confirming my status as a hostage
- **any other documentation**

```
I have also enclosed payment that covers
the amount of the underlying taxes I owe.
[Optional, but a good idea if you can
afford to make the payment.]

Please abate these penalties for
"reasonable cause." I can be reached at
801-555-3444 during daytime hours.

Thank you,

Sanford Majors
Sanford Majors

Enclosed: IRS Tax Notice; Doctor's
letter,death certificate, fire report,
letter from State Department [or whatever]
```

3. If Your Abatement Request Is Rejected

If the IRS officially rejects your request, you will get a written notice denying abatement. You then have *four options* besides accepting your fate:

1. Appeal. You can file a protest—a letter requesting an appeal. See the sample letter, below.

Sample Letter Appealing Denial of Abatement of Penalties

```
IRS Service Center
P.O. Box 9941
Ogden, UT 84409

Re: Appeal of Penalty Abatement

Sanford Majors
43 Valley Road
Salt Lake City, UT 84000

SSN: 55-555-5555

January 15, 1995

To Whom it May Concern:

I wish to appeal the denial of my penalty
abatement request, which I received on
January 10, 1995. A copy of the denial is
attached.

The grounds for my appeal is that I had a
reasonable cause for [state type of
penalty]: filing late, paying late, not
reporting some income because [state
reasons]:
```

- I was in a coma
- My tax preparer had just died
- **any other excuse**

```
I can prove my condition with [state type
of proof]:
```

- Letter from Dr. Stein proving my condition
- Death certificate confirming my tax preparer's death
- **any other documentation**

```
Thank you,

Sanford Majors
Sanford Majors

Enclosed: IRS Tax Notice; Dr. Stein's
letter; death certificate [or whatever]
```

Send your appeal letter to the Service Center, not the District Office. Unlike an appeal of an audit, the IRS does not grant you an appeal hearing after an abatement request is rejected. The appeal is handled by mail or telephone by the "penalty unit" at your IRS Service Center.

2. Request a transfer of your file. Write the Service Center requesting that your file be transferred to your local IRS District Office. You can now raise the penalty abatement with a Revenue Officer face-to-face. This gives you a second opportunity to convince the IRS that your penalty should be removed.

3. Pay and claim a refund. One way to get the IRS collector off your back is to pay the penalty and then file for a refund. Your refund request will have to be submitted to your Service Center on Form 843, Claim for Refund and Request for Abatement. (It's in the Appendix with instructions.) You can either attach a letter of explanation similar to the one you tried in your original abatement request, or give your reasonable cause explanation on Form 843—assuming you didn't submit your first abatement request on Form 843. If your Form 843 Claim is refused, you can sue in a U. S. District Court or the Court of Claims (see Chapter 5, Section D). Rarely, however, are tax penalties large enough to justify the costs of going to court.

4. Make an Offer in Compromise. An Offer in Compromise is a formal procedure for contesting or negotiating any IRS bill, including a penalty. (See Chapter 6, Section E.) To be successful, you must file Form 656, Offer in Compromise, at any collection level of the IRS. You will need to show doubt about your *liability* for the penalty. This is yet another opportunity to present your "reasonable cause" argument as to why you should not be liable for the penalty. An Offer in Compromise is always a long shot, but is worth a try.

4. Abating Interest—It's Very Difficult

As mentioned in Section B, above, Congress makes it very hard to get interest removed from a tax bill. Of course, if a tax or penalty is canceled for any reason, interest on it should be wiped out as well. Usually the IRS computer does this automatically,

but check your bill to make sure. Other than removing interest on a tax or penalty cut from your bill, the tax code authorizes the abatement of interest in only the following circumstances:

1. The IRS was wrong in charging interest—meaning that either you paid the tax when it was due or didn't owe any taxes on which interest could be charged. If this happens to you, write to the Service Center, explain what is wrong and ask for an interest abatement. If that doesn't work, call the Problems Resolution Officer at your local District IRS office. (See Chapter 8.) You also can sue in U.S. District Court or Court of Claims to recover interest already paid, but this is too costly to be a practical alternative.

2. The IRS wrongfully sent you a refund, wants its money back and is charging you interest all the way back to the time you received the check. This is not so unusual. Tax refund checks sometimes come out of the blue. Many taxpayers find themselves having to repay such a windfall.[3] You are entitled to an interest abatement as long as *your actions* did not cause the refund. Once the IRS asks for its money back, it can, however, charge you interest from that date until you repay it.

3. The interest resulted from delays of the IRS in performing "ministerial acts." This happens frequently. This covers things such as IRS delays in sending a tax bill after you agree to an audit Examination Report. (See Chapter 3, Section H.) You are entitled to an abatement of all but the first 30 days of the delay.[4] For example, if, following an audit, a bill with interest arrives 90 days after you sign the Examination Report, you can have the last 60 days of interest abated.

Unfortunately, the exception for ministerial acts does not cover interest that mounts while you challenge a bill or the IRS is performing an audit, or while you appeal or go to Tax Court. This interest cannot be abated.

[3]Internal Revenue Code § 6404.

[4]Revenue Procedure 87-42; IRS Regulation 301.6404-2T.

TIP   Interest may be abated as part of an Offer in Compromise. (See Chapter 6, Section E.) This is your best chance of getting out from under an interest bill—if you qualify.

5.   How to Request an Interest Abatement

To request an interest abatement for reason 1, 2 or 3, follow the form letter in Section D.2, above. Instead of alleging reasonable cause (the ground for a penalty abatement) use the language in items 1, 2 or 3, such as "The IRS wrongfully sent me a refund and is charging interest. I should not have to pay interest because my actions did not cause the refund to be sent." Although interest is abated only rarely, it never hurts to ask and costs only 29¢.

E. Designating Your Tax Payments

You can tell the IRS that the payment you make is to be applied to your tax account. If you don't, the IRS allocates it first to taxes, then to interest and last to penalties, starting with the *oldest* tax period for which you owe. For example, you owe $10,000 in taxes, penalties and interest for several of the past eight years. You make a $1,500 payment. You would want to specify that it is to be applied to the most recent year, and/or to interest first. Why would you do this, you might just ask? Read on.

There are several reasons to designate payments. If the interest on a tax bill is for a *business* tax debt,

designating a payment to interest might give you a deductible expense on this year's tax return.

A second possible reason is that once taxes are assessed, the IRS has ten years to collect these taxes, penalties and interest. If part of your tax bill is for a year for which the ten-year limit is about to expire, then designate your payments toward your most recent tax debts. For example, suppose in 1995 you want to make a payment to your tax debt, which is for 1985 and 1988. Designate the payment to the 1988 tax year, because the 1985 tax debt will probably expire on April 16, 1996 (assuming you filed your 1985 tax return by April 15, 1986).

How to designate a payment. When you make any tax payment by check or money order, write in the lower left-hand corner your Social Security number and the tax year(s) you are paying. Also, enclose a letter with the payment clearly stating that you want the payment applied to the tax year(s) noted on your check or money order. Still the IRS may misapply the funds, usually to the oldest tax period. (If you're concerned that the IRS might misapply the funds, you can request an account statement. See Chapter 1, Section A.)

If your payments are not allocated as you requested, send photocopies of your designation letter and the checks or money orders to show the IRS that payments were not applied according to your instructions. If you can supply proof of your designation of payment, the IRS will correct its records. If the IRS refuses or ignores your request, complain to the Problems Resolution Officer. (See Chapter 8.)

HELP BEYOND THE BOOK: TAX PROFESSIONALS AND TAX INFORMATION

13

This book gives you strategies for coping with most tax problems—audits, bills (collections) and Tax Court. But this may not be enough. If you need more help, try any of these:

- *Tax Professionals (Tax Pros)*. An Enrolled Agent, Certified Public Accountant or tax attorney can provide tax information, guidance or representation before the IRS.
- *IRS*. The IRS has free tax publications, telephone pre-recorded and live information, and taxpayer service representatives at many offices.
- *Library*. You can research tax questions in larger public libraries and law libraries in your community.

A. Finding and Using a Tax Pro

We believe you can successfully take on the IRS alone most of the time. But if you feel over your head or want professional reassurance, consider speaking with or hiring a Tax Pro.

Under the Taxpayers' Bill of Rights (Chapter 15 contains the complete text), you have the right to have a representative handle any IRS matter for you. This means you never have to face the IRS if you don't want to. You also have the right to consult a Tax Pro during the process whenever you are taking on the IRS by yourself.

In general, you can safely go it alone in the two most common, but serious, IRS situations:

- you are being audited and your records are in order, you can substantiate everything on your return and you have nothing to hide, or
- the IRS is seeking to collect an overdue tax bill of $10,000 or less and you can pay it off within 36 months.

But before making any decision on proceeding alone or working with a Tax Pro, weigh the pros and cons of each.

GOING IT ALONE

PRO: You save professional fees.

CON: It takes a lot of time.

You may find it very stressful.

You may say or do the wrong thing.

CONSULTING A TAX PRO BEFORE FACING THE IRS ON YOUR OWN

PRO: You get the information you need and gain confidence.

It's cheaper than hiring a Tax Pro to represent you.

CON: Most Tax Pros charge for a consultation.

HIRING A TAX PRO TO REPRESENT YOU BEFORE THE IRS

PRO: The IRS respects knowledgeable Tax Pros.

You don't have to face the IRS.

Tax Pros know tax issues.

CON: Tax Pros are expensive if they are good.

You understand your tax records best.

You lose some control over your case, and you risk hiring someone who is inexperienced or incompetent.

1. How Tax Pros Can Help

Myth: The IRS will think I am guilty of something if I hire a Tax Pro or will get mad at me for not facing them myself.

Fact: Most auditors and collectors prefer dealing with experienced Tax Pros. It makes their job easier. Good Tax Pros know what the IRS wants and don't waste IRS personnel time.

If you face an audit, collection of a tax bill or a Tax Court hearing—and you've decided to at least consult a Tax Pro—here are the ways an experienced Tax Pro can help:

Consultation and advice. A Tax Pro can analyze your situation and advise you on the best plan of action. Rarely is there only one way to handle an IRS matter. She should describe your alternatives so you can make an informed choice. Of course, a Tax Pro might give you a sales pitch for her services, so weigh what she tells you against what you have learned by reading this book and your own judgment. If the Tax Pro is advising you to pursue a course of action you believe is excessively expensive, dishonest or completely futile (or worse, all three), find another Tax Pro. There are good ones and bad ones, like any profession.

Negotiation. Tax Pros often possess negotiating skills. And, an experienced Tax Pro should know what kinds of deals can and can't be made with the IRS.

Representation. Experienced Tax Pros know IRS procedures and how to maneuver around the IRS bureaucracy. Tax Pros can neutralize the intimidation factor the IRS knows it holds over you. And, if you have something to hide, a Tax Pro usually can keep the lid on it better than you can.

2. Types of Tax Pros

For an audit, collection or an appeals hearing, you can choose among Enrolled Agents, tax attorneys and Certified Public Accountants. A fourth category —tax return preparers with no professional certifications—can help you around April 15, but legally they cannot represent you before the IRS. (See Section C, below.)

Enrolled Agent (EA). An EA is usually a full-time tax advisor and tax preparer who is permitted to practice before the IRS in all matters. Most EAs cannot represent you in Tax Court, however. They earn the designation "Enrolled Agent" by either passing a difficult IRS exam or having at least five years of experience working for the IRS. They also must participate in continuing education programs to retain their EA designations.

There are approximately 24,000 EAs in the U.S., 6,000 of whom are members of the National Association of Enrolled Agents. EAs are the least expensive of all Tax Pros. For a cost-effective approach to handling a tax problem, consider an EA.

Tax Attorney. Tax attorneys are lawyers who do various types of tax-related work including complex tax and estate planning, IRS dispute resolution and sometimes tax return preparation. To assure competence, look for a tax attorney with either a special

tax law degree (LL.M.-Tax) or a certification as a tax law specialist from a State Bar Association. If more than $10,000 is at stake, the IRS is accusing you of committing fraud or you're headed to Tax Court, call a tax attorney.

Certified Public Accountant (CPA). CPAs are licensed and regulated in all states. They do sophisticated accounting and business audit work, and prepare tax returns. To become a CPA, an accountant must have a college degree and work experience with a CPA firm, and must pass a series of rigorous examinations. Some CPAs have a great deal of IRS experience, but many do little IRS work. Of those that do, many are as good as tax attorneys and charge about the same or even a little less. Some CPAs, however, are not as aggressive as tax lawyers when facing IRS personnel.

3. How to Choose a Tax Pro

There are several ways to find a good Tax Pro. Asking the IRS is not one of them.

Personal referrals. This is frequently the best source. Ask friends, relatives and acquaintances whose judgment you trust for the names of Tax Pros who helped them. If the Tax Pros you call can't help you, ask them for a referral. Be careful, however, when selecting a Tax Pro this way. That a professional did well once doesn't guarantee she'll do so in your case.

Your tax preparer or accountant. Your tax return preparer or accountant might have a good recommendation of a Tax Pro who can help you deal with an IRS problem.

Prepaid legal plans. Prepaid legal plans offer some basic services for a low monthly fee and often offer discounted fees for additional work. Participating attorneys get clients who are attracted by the low cost, and then sell the more expensive services. Few lawyers in prepaid legal plans have tax experience, however. Tax attorneys rarely participate because of relatively low fees paid by the plans.

Audit assistance or preparer guarantees. Some tax preparers offer "audit assistance" free with their return preparation service. One chain says they will "go with you" to the IRS to explain how a return was prepared. This service may fall short of actual representation. And, there is no guarantee the person going with you knows anything about your case or the tax law. Not all tax preparers are created equal—not by a long shot.

Advertising. Various directories (including the phone book) and newspapers carry lists of Tax Pros. Look under "Accountants," "Tax Return Preparers" and "Attorneys-Tax." Some Tax Pros offer a first consultation by phone or in their office at no charge. Bear in mind, however, that anyone heavily advertising may be new to the game.

Professional associations and referral panels. Most local bar associations will give out the names of tax attorneys who practice in your area. But bar associations don't meaningfully screen the attorneys listed; those who are listed may not be experienced or competent. To find an EA in your area, call the National Association of Enrolled Agents at 800-424-4339 or 301-984-6232. To find a CPA, try calling a local or state CPA society.

4. What to Look for in a Tax Pro

Once you have the name of a Tax Pro, call and ask to speak with him directly. If he is too busy to talk to you—and your call isn't transferred to another tax specialist—assume the office is too busy to handle your case and call the next person on your list.

When you speak to a Tax Pro, try to develop a rapport. Mention how you got his name, especially if it was a personal referral. Then get to the point—tell him your tax problem. If he doesn't handle your type of case, ask for the names of some professionals who do.

Here are some other suggestions for making a good match:

- Don't be in a hurry to hire the first Tax Pro you speak to. Your decision is important and rarely is there only one person for the job. Talk to a few. Choose the one you communicate with best—do you understand her questions and answers?

- Question the Tax Pro carefully about her IRS experience. No matter how well she knows the tax code, prior IRS dealings is key. Previous IRS employment is not always a plus; it may have forever impressed the IRS point of view on her. Also, be skeptical if she hasn't been in practice at least five years.

- Does the Tax Pro seem to be aggressive or timid in discussing your case? If she seems awed by the IRS, find someone else.

- Does the Tax Pro give you a feeling of confidence? Ask her the likely outcome of your case. While no one can predict the future, her answer should create trust. Look for an honest response, not necessarily a rosy picture.

⟪TIP⟫ If you lose faith in your Tax Pro, find another one fast. But don't dismiss the first one until you get a second opinion on what she is doing. And don't fire a Tax Pro simply because nothing is happening. Frequently, inaction is because the IRS is dragging its feet. Remember—delay often works to your advantage in dealing with the IRS.

5. Tax Pros' Fees

Be sure to get an understanding about the Tax Pro's fees at your first meeting. Does she charge by the hour or does she quote a flat (fixed) fee? Most professionals charge $25 to $250 per hour, depending on where you live, the type of case and the type of Tax Pro. To some extent, you can control costs. Tax Pros can be either hired as consultants, meaning you handle your own case and ask for advice as needed, or hired to represent you start to finish. In other words, going to a Tax Pro need not be an all or nothing affair.

Although uncertainty about costs leaves most folks uncomfortable, many good Tax Pros shy away from quoting flat fees. When they do, it's usually for straightforward matters. But even if the Tax Pro won't give you a firm estimate, she should be able to "ballpark" a range of hours necessary for your case. For example, I usually figure 5–15 hours of my time for full representation in an office audit or a collection matter. For appeals and field audits, I put in 10–40 hours.

Most Tax Pros require a fee and cost retainer paid in advance, often equal to the minimum time estimated as needed on the case. For example, on a typical audit or collection case, I require a $1,500 retainer.

Tips on Controlling a Tax Pro's Fees

- If you like the Tax Pro but not her fee, ask if she can do it for less. If she isn't very busy, she may be flexible on fee and payment arrangements. Small tax firms or solo practitioners are more likely than professionals in large offices to negotiate their fee.

- Ask for a written fee agreement and monthly billings with itemized statements of time and services rendered. This will keep the Tax Pro honest and keep the large bill "fee shock" down. In many states, attorneys are required to give you a written fee agreement before starting work.

- If you disagree with a bill you receive, call your Tax Pro. If the firm is interested in retaining your business, it should listen to your concerns, adjust the bill or work toward satisfying you. If the Tax Pro won't budge, call your state or local CPA society or your state's bar association. Many groups have panels that help professionals and clients mediate fee disputes.

B. Tax Pros and Audits

If you're being pursued by a tax collector or you're headed to Tax Court, the information in Section A, above, and in Chapters 5 and 6, should guide you in your decision about using a Tax Pro. Audits, however, require special attention—spending a small percentage of your potential IRS exposure for professional help can be a wise investment for the peace of mind and confidence that good advice brings. Before reading this information, however, read Section A, above and Chapter 3.

If you consult a Tax Pro, bring your IRS audit notice, tax return and documents on which the return was prepared to the first meeting. If you face an *office* (as opposed to a field) audit, go over the audit letter checklist with the Tax Pro—explain why you reported your income as you did or took the deductions that the IRS is now questioning. Ask the Tax Pro what documentation will help you prove your position.

If you face a *field* audit, your audit won't be limited to any pre-prepared list of items to be examined. This makes a field audit more difficult than an office audit. Show the Tax Pro your return and ask which items you would expect the IRS to question. Specifically ask the Tax Pro if he sees any legal problem areas and how to deal with them. You might ask the Tax Pro to photocopy some supporting tax law authority or to prepare a memorandum of law pertaining to your case to show the auditor.

In either type of audit, ask the Tax Pro for suggestions on how best to explain and present your documents to the auditor. You may want the Tax Pro's assistance in making summaries or spreadsheets showing your business or investment transactions. The more clearly you present information, the less time you will spend with the auditor. Auditors appreciate and, more importantly, reward well-prepared taxpayers.

If your Tax Pro was the preparer of the tax return, ask her to explain all figures and schedules to you. If she has workpapers or notes used to prepare your return, ask for copies and interpretations, if needed. You won't necessarily show them to the auditor—they may be just for your reference.

1. The Right Type of Tax Pro

Enrolled Agents can represent you before the IRS in audits. If you face complex legal issues or the IRS accuses you of fraud, hire a tax attorney or CPA. In some cases you may need both.

Your tax return preparer can accompany you to the audit. She can't go in your place unless she is an attorney, CPA or Enrolled Agent. She can explain how your return was prepared. Sometimes this is all you need, but many audit issues are not so simple. Finally, your relatives or business employees can represent you at an audit if you give them permission on IRS Form 2848. (Call 800-829-3676 to get this form.) I don't recommend it, however, I don't see any harm in bringing them along for support.

2. Tax Pro Analysis After an Audit

If you handled your own audit and it did not turn out well, you might want to ask a Tax Pro why. A Tax Pro can analyze the Examination Report, tax return and documents you produced at the audit. He will also want to know what you said and what the auditor said about items that are disputed. The Tax Pro is evaluating the strengths and weaknesses of your legal position.

If the Tax Pro believes you are at least in a legal gray area, he will examine the quality of the documents and the credibility of your explanations. In an hour or so, he should be able to decide whether you have a leg on which to stand. If you do, he can tell you if you should try again with the auditor or her manager, or if you would benefit from a formal appeal. (See Chapter 4.)

C. Hiring a Tax Return Preparer

Whether or not you have IRS problems may depend on the accuracy of your tax return and who prepares it. The Commissioner of the IRS has said that the "tax system has become so complex…something must be done to make it less burdensome." Until this happens, consider having a Tax Pro prepare your returns unless your income situation is very simple.

You might also lessen your chance of being audited by having a professional preparation. Many IRS insiders have said that IRS "classifiers" (see Chapter 3, Section B.1) are more likely to pick self-prepared returns for audit than those signed by a reputable Tax Pro.

Most Enrolled Agents, tax attorneys and CPAs prepare tax returns. Others call themselves "tax preparers," but are not admitted to practice before the IRS and cannot represent you there. Fees for preparing individual income tax returns range from $20 to $750 (and up), depending on the complexity of your return and the type of tax preparer.

Whether you hire a tax preparer or do it yourself, you alone are responsible for the accuracy of the tax forms. So, check out the qualifications of the preparer you hire. Neither the IRS nor most states license tax preparers. Almost anyone can call himself a tax return preparer.

I recommend staying away from nationwide chain tax preparers. Their fees may be low, but their work product is inconsistent. These "McTax" outfits depend on inexperienced seasonal employees earning as little as $5 an hour. Emphasis is on quantity not quality, and workers earn bonuses for turning out a lot of returns. You may never meet the actual preparer of your return. And even if you do, chances are she won't be around after April 15 if you—or the IRS—have questions about your return.

For most people, Enrolled Agents are the best bet to prepare a tax return. Their prices are higher than chains, but lower than CPAs and tax attorneys. If you know you want a tax preparer for many years down the road, start looking long before the tax season starts and go back to that preparer every year.

 Tax Preparers to Avoid. Never hire a tax preparer who bases his fee on a percentage of the refund you will receive, guarantees refunds in all cases or will not sign your tax return as the preparer. If the IRS catches a sleazy preparer, it casts out its audit net to bring in the preparer's clients.

D. Researching Tax Questions

Although most tax matters require no research, some do. Your auditor may go beyond whether or not you can prove your deductions. Instead, the question may be whether or not the deductions are *legally allowable*. For example, your home office expenses may be disallowed not because you didn't prove them, but because the auditor says that you don't qualify for a home office deduction. So, you must know what are the legal requirements to qualify for a home office.

There are many good sources to augment the information in this book.

1. Free IRS Information

The IRS offers free publications, and telephone and face-to-face help. To meet with someone from the IRS in person, call your nearest local IRS office. There, you can talk to a Taxpayer Service Representative.

A. IRS PUBLICATIONS

The IRS publishes a series of taxpayer pamphlets nicknamed "pubs," numbered from 1 to 1000. They contain basic tax information on all kinds of issues—from the IRS' point of view, of course. For example, Publication 334, Tax Guide for Small Businesses, covers a variety of rules from how to claim depreciation of a business vehicle to how to report losses on the sale of assets.

These pubs are free at most IRS offices or by calling 800-829-3676 (FORM). Start with Publication 910, Guide to Free Tax Services, and use it to request the tax information you need. (The list of Free Tax Publications, excerpted from Publication 910, is in the Appendix.) Order as many pubs as you need—they're free. It usually takes several weeks to get them by mail.

B. IRS TELEPHONE INFORMATION

The IRS offers a Taxpayer Assistance toll-free line at 800-829-1040. This service is staffed with live people, and is for questions on tax preparation and tax notice questions.

The IRS also has a toll-free pre-recorded tax information line, Tele-Tax, at 800-829-4477. The Appendix has a list of the topic numbers and subjects that correspond to the pre-recorded messages. (This list is from Publication 910.)

The best I can say about these two telephone services is that they are free. They will give you only the official IRS position, which is conservative and not necessarily helpful—and many times the answers are misleading or outright wrong. Start, but don't stop here, with your tax law research.

2. Private Tax Guides

Numerous privately published tax guides can answer your tax questions.

A. POPULAR GUIDEBOOKS

You probably have seen the books that come out each winter, including *The Arthur Young Tax Guide* (Ballantine Books), J.K. Lasser's *Your Income Tax* (Prentice Hall), *The Arthur Andersen Tax Guide* (Perigle Books) and *Consumer Reports Tax Guide* (Consumer Reports Books).

These guides cover the legal grounds for income reporting and deduction taking. They are easier to read than IRS publications and have better examples of how the tax law works. I favor *The Arthur Young*

Tax Guide because it's the most complete, although it is not always the easiest to understand. These guides are inexpensive—$10 to $20—and found in most libraries as well.

If you are preparing for an audit, find a tax book covering the year your audited return was prepared. This isn't always possible—stores carry the most recent books. Libraries, however, may have prior editions. If you can't find a book for the exact year, a newer one should be okay, as the tax law affecting most audit issues usually does not change much from year to year.

B. TAX PRO DESKBOOKS AND GUIDES

Accountants and attorneys use more sophisticated tax deskbooks. The three top professional guides are *Master Tax Guide* (Commerce-Clearing House), *Master Federal Tax Manual* (Research Institute of America) and the *Federal Tax Guide* (Prentice-Hall). They are all about 600 pages of fine print. Don't let this scare you, as you may need to read only a few pages. These deskbooks summarize the law on the most common tax law problems. They are available in libraries, especially law libraries, and sell in bookstores for about $25.

Many IRS personnel prefer the *Master Tax Guide* (Commerce-Clearing House). If you have a choice of which of the three to consult, you may want to use that one.

3. Other Research Materials— Using the Library

The original source materials for the tax law are the Internal Revenue Code and Congressional Committee Reports. IRS Regulations and federal court decisions interpret the law further and provide illustrations of how it is applied to a set of facts. These books are found in federal building libraries, large public libraries and law libraries. Most are technical in the extreme and are only recommended as a cure for insomnia. The guidebooks listed in Section D.2, above, are an attempt to make sense out of this mass of legalese, and are your better bets.

Nevertheless, if you want to take a look at some of this material, you can start by finding your nearest law library. Call your local court clerk, a nearby college or a lawyer and ask where the nearest law library open to the public is located. (Many private law libraries limit their patrons to lawyers, judges and law students.)

Once you get to the library, look in the card catalogue or computer database of the library's volumes for the following material:

- Internal Revenue Code
- IRS Regulations
- U.S. Tax Court (and other federal court) opinions, and
- Books by research companies and legal scholars explaining the tax law (such as this book and the various tax guides mentioned earlier in the chapter).

You will have serious difficulty if you just try to dive into the material. Preferably, you will have the number or name of an Internal Revenue Code section, an IRS Regulation or a case that you want to read.

Once armed with the call numbers of the tax materials and the citation or topic you want to research, you have two choices: try to find the material—and then the citation or topic—yourself or throw yourself on the mercy of the library staff. The second choice is the far superior one. Tell the librarian that you need tax law information. Ask that you be pointed toward the materials. If the librarian has the time, she might even show you how to use the books. But be warned that few librarians (actually, few human beings) have any familiarity with tax law, so don't expect too much.

Further Reading and Reference List for Dealing with IRS Problems

- *IRS Practice & Policy* (Tax Management Inc.). This is an expensive but very up to date, monthly supplemented looseleaf service. It contains the Internal Revenue Manual. ($595 per year)

- *IRS Practice & Procedure*, by Michael I. Saltzman (Warren, Gorham & Lamont). This book is by the number one authority on the subject. I consider this to be the bible on IRS procedure. ($115)

- *Representing the Audited Taxpayer Before the IRS, Representation Before the Collection Division of the IRS,* and *Representation Before the Appeals Division of the IRS* (Callaghan & Co.). All three are looseleaf and supplemented annually. They are written clearly by experienced people in the field. I especially recommend the collection book, the best of its kind. ($59.95 each)

- *When You Can't Pay Your Taxes,* Robert S. Schreibman (Dow-Jones Irwin). This book comes in two versions—a low-priced simplified paper-back and a hardbound professional version. The paperback is a bargain. ($16.95, $75 hardbound)

- *How to Defend Yourself Against the IRS,* Sandor Frankel and Robert S. Fink (Simon & Schuster). The portion that deals with civil and criminal fraud is very good. The book was originally published in 1985 and may be difficult to find or out of print. ($16.95)

- *Peyron Tax Accountants Communique* (monthly newsletter). (800) 821-4965. This can keep you up to date on new IRS policies and tax cases. ($44 per year)

WHEN YOU OWE STATE INCOME TAXES

14

All states except Alaska, Florida, Nevada, New Hampshire, South Dakota, Texas, Washington and Wyoming impose a state income tax. Usually the filing requirements, penalties and collection techniques mirror those of the IRS. For more specific information, write or call your state taxing authority. (See Appendix for list of state agencies.) If you are lucky enough to live in a state without an income tax, you can safely skip this chapter.

A. The IRS and State Taxing Authorities

States with income taxes have computer systems interlinked with the IRS. Only Nevada does not share its residents' income information with the IRS. Because of our federal government's generosity with taxpayer information—especially audit and collection notices—most states rely on IRS data instead of creating their own systems.

But that doesn't mean states are lax in pursuing delinquent taxpayers. Most state taxing authorities act quickly when they receive IRS information. In fact, many states act on IRS-supplied information before the IRS does. By the time the IRS comes to collect, you may have set up a state installment plan or lost your property to a state tax collector, leaving little for the IRS. Why the IRS gives this information to the states before it acts on it is a mystery.

Audit adjustments. Because of the computer linkage, if you are audited by the IRS your state automatically finds out. If the IRS makes adjustments, the state can change your state tax bill without conducting a separate audit. If you contest an IRS audit in Tax Court, you may need to notify your state's income tax department to prevent a premature state tax assessment. Send the state agency a copy of your Tax Court Petition. (See Chapter 5). Request that no further action be taken until your case has been decided.

States seldom audit individual taxpayers. They prefer to let the IRS audit you and then tag on a bill. States are more likely to audit businesses or individuals with very high income. If you are audited by your state taxing authority, most of the general principles of this book will apply.

Most state tax assessments can be appealed as with IRS audits. If your appeal of a proposed state assessment is rejected—even an assessment following a state audit—you cannot contest the tax bill in most state courts before paying as you can with the IRS. Instead, you must pay the taxes and go to court to get the money back.

Collections. If the IRS pursues you as a non-filer, so probably will your state. If the IRS sends you any other kind of tax adjustment billing, expect one from your state as well. Most states automatically dun taxpayers based on IRS bills. So, if the IRS makes a mistake in the bill, the state will too.

B. Does Your State Have a Taxpayers' Bill of Rights?

Some states have enacted their versions of the federal Taxpayers' Bill of Rights. To find out if your state has, and to obtain a copy, call or write your state taxing authority. (Addresses and phone numbers are listed in the Appendix.) Many of the state bills include grievance procedures. The California Bill, for example, gives taxpayers the right to have an administrative hearing to protest an improper seizure of property.

Also, ask if your state has an ombudsman or taxpayer advocate to assist people who need help with state tax problems. State taxpayer advocates act much the same as IRS Problem Resolution Officers. For example, they sometimes can get wage levies released or property returned, if convinced that the seizure threatens the taxpayer's health or welfare.

If your state has an ombudsman or advocate whom you want to contact, first try by phone. If that fails, write or show up at the advocate's office. If you write, include your home and work telephone numbers in your letter and the best times to reach you.

C. Time Limits to Assess and Collect State Income Taxes

Once you file a federal return, the IRS generally has three years to *assess* additional taxes against you—usually by way of an audit. (In some situations, the IRS has six years. See Chapters 3 and 6.) State time limitations vary from one to five years and are in the chart, below.

Once additional taxes are assessed the IRS has ten years to *collect* them. Again, state limitations differ tremendously and are in the chart, below.

Beware—in many states, the period to collect the tax is renewable, that is, is not limited by the period indicated in the chart. In California, for example, the ten-year period can be renewed twice for a total of 30 years. That information is not in the table. (If your state is not on the list, it is because it does not have a state income tax.)

D. State Tax Collection Departments

Like the IRS, each state usually has a computerized collection system. It sends out a series of notices asking the taxpayer to pay in full or make arrangements for paying. If you don't respond, the state will begin involuntary collection—just like the IRS—by filing liens and seizing your property. (See Chapter 7.) States act quickly at grabbing taxpayers' property, often much faster than the IRS. And some states hire private collection agencies, usually to go after taxpayers who have moved out of state.

If you disagree with the state's assessment notice, your state probably has an appeals process. In many states, the process is similar to the IRS'. If your state doesn't have a specific form to file a protest and request an appeals hearing, follow the sample protest letter in Chapter 4, Section B.

In some states, you may be offered an informal conference before going to a formal appeal hearing. If you lose an appeal, you must pay the tax and then either file a claim for a refund or sue for a refund in regular state court. In some states, you will have to do both. A few states let taxpayers go to court without first paying a tax bill, similar to going to U.S. Tax Court.

Many state tax agencies don't run as smoothly as the IRS. That's pretty scary, huh? Letters are lost and calls not returned. Most state taxing authorities are supposed to respond to requests within a certain number of days. If the agency denies receiving your letter or won't return calls, however, what can you do?

If possible, avoid lost mail and unreturned phone calls by dealing with the state taxing authority in person. Always get the name and direct telephone number of any employee you talk to. This fixes some responsibility and may keep him from vanishing when you call back. If you reach any agreement over the phone or in person, immediately back it up with a confirming letter. Later, if another "civil servant" tries to deny that an agreement was reached, ask to speak to a supervisor or the state taxpayer advocate.

E. Settling Your Bill

Most state income tax collectors operate similarly to IRS collectors—that is, they will allow you to pay in installments, they can seize assets, they may settle tax bills for less than the full amount owed and they can suspend collection if you show hardship.

TIME LIMITS TO ASSESS AND COLLECT TAXES

State	Number of years to assess	Number of years to collect
Alabama	3	6
Arizona	4	6
Arkansas	3	10
California	4	10
Colorado	1	6
Connecticut	3	No specified period
Delaware	3	6
District of Columbia	3	3
Georgia	3	No specified period
Hawaii	3	No specified period
Idaho	3	6
Illinois	3	5
Indiana	3	No specified period
Iowa	3	No specified period
Kansas	3	1
Kentucky	4	5
Louisiana	3	3
Maine	3	No specified period
Maryland	3	4
Massachusetts	3	No specified period
Michigan	4	No specified period
Minnesota	3.5	5
Mississippi	3	No specified period
Missouri	3	5
Montana	5	No limit
Nebraska	3	Five years after lien filed
New Jersey	3	No specified period
New Mexico	3	10
New York	3	6
North Carolina	3	No limit
North Dakota	3	No specified period
Ohio	4	No specified period
Oklahoma	3	No specified period
Oregon	3	No specified period
Pennsylvania	3	No specified period
Rhode Island	3	No specified period
South Carolina	3	10
Tennessee	5	6
Utah	3	No specified period
Vermont	3	6
Virginia	3	20
West Virginia	3	5
Wisconsin	4	No specified period

1.   Getting a Payment Plan

Most tax collectors will grant installment agreements if they don't believe you can make a full payment. In a few states, to get an installment plan, you must prove that you would be deprived of the necessities of life if your assets or wages were seized. As with the IRS, you may be able to get a time payment agreement with the state by requesting it over the phone or in writing. Your best chance may be to visit the state tax office in person. You may have to make an appointment or go to the office and wait in line.

You will be required to make a financial disclosure. As with the IRS financial disclosure form, most state forms require you to list your assets, bank accounts and employer's name and address.

Many states use an abbreviated version of the IRS Forms 433. (See Chapter 6, Section D.) State forms usually don't have enough room for listing all expenses. Therefore, before meeting with a state tax collector, thoroughly review Chapter 6, fill out IRS Form 433-A (and 433-B if you own a businesses). Gather together your proof of expenses (such as credit card bills and rent receipts). Expect an argument if you list expenses the collector does not think are necessary. For example, you may get a hard time for listing charitable contributions, cigarette expenses or entertainment.

Also, provide a copy of your most recent pay stub. If your pay varies due to bonuses or overtime, take the lowest recent stub. If you are self-employed, take in your last tax return—unless your income has dropped since then. Prepare a financial statement projecting your income and expenses for the next 12 months.

States don't usually have enough people on staff to stringently verify the information in a financial statement. State tax offices tend to accept any documentation that appears to be genuine. This doesn't mean, however, that you should be less than truthful. Let your conscience be your guide.

State tax collectors often begin with the attitude of "take it or leave it." They demand payment plan commitments on the spot, without much negotiating. And often they reject requests for agreements to last more than 12 months. Push for longer if you need it. Most can give you more time to pay, regard-less of what they tell you. Even if you get an installment agreement, the state taxing authority may file a tax lien in your county, just like the IRS. (See Section E.2, below.)

Coordinating Installment Plans With the IRS and Your State Tax Department

If you owe federal and state income taxes at the same time, coordinate your payment plan negotiations. Let each taxing agency know you owe the other. Make your federal and state financial disclosure forms match. Propose payment plans at the same time with payments in proportion to your total tax debt.

Example

Hamlet owes Minnesota $3,000 for state income taxes and the IRS $12,000. Although it's a strain, he scrapes together $500 a month to pay his back taxes. He offers $100 to the state and $400 to the IRS. When questioned about his allocation, Hamlet says, "What could be more fair? I owe the IRS four times as much as I owe Minnesota. I should pay in that proportion."

If you owe the state far less than you owe the IRS, another option is to pay off the state before dealing with the IRS. Negotiating is simpler when your monster has one head, not two. Also, states seize wages and property more quickly than does the IRS. Finally, if you borrow money to pay off the state, you can list this debt on your IRS financial disclosure form.

---

2.   Enforced Collection—Seizing Assets

As mentioned earlier, states sometimes act quicker than the IRS in seizing property when you don't pay your tax bill. State laws vary as to the maximum amount of wages that the state can take. In California, for example, the state taxing authority cannot take more than 25% of your net pay. Keeping your bank account from tax collectors—state or federal—should be a major concern. (See Chapter 6, Section D.5, on protecting your bank accounts after making a financial disclosure.)

After you have made your financial disclosures, the state agency will have a list of your assets, such as your bank accounts, car and home. Most state taxing authorities have the power to seize houses, but policy may dictate against it. Even if the state does take your house, you may be entitled to a portion of the equity in it, called the "homestead exemption."

Homestead exemptions *do not* protect you from the IRS. But in some states, if the state taxing authority takes a house to pay a state tax debt, the agency must pay the homeowner the amount of his homestead exemption. To find out the law in your state, you'll need to check with an attorney or do some legal research. (See Chapter 13.)

3. Bankruptcy

State tax bills can be handled in a federal bankruptcy action. If the state taxing authority is about to take your property, filing for bankruptcy could give you the reprieve you need. Collection activities must stop. Older state tax debts may even be canceled (discharged) in a Chapter 7 bankruptcy. And, if your state tax debts don't qualify for a complete discharge, you can force a payment plan in a Chapter 13 bankruptcy on the state tax department. (See Chapter 6, Section F.)

4. Compromising a State Tax Assessment

If you're on the verge of desperation, you may be able to settle an IRS tax bill through the Offer in Compromise procedure. (See Chapter 6, Section E.) Many states, too, will seriously consider an offer to settle a tax bill for less than what is owed. Call the state tax agency and ask how to make an offer to settle you tax bill. If you are told it can't be done, speak to the clerk's supervisor. Keep talking to supervisors until you are satisfied you have received the final word.

5. Suspending Collection

If you can convince the state tax collector that paying the bill now would be a hardship, you may be able to get the agency to suspend collection activities. You will first have to make a financial disclosure, in person, in writing or perhaps on the phone. (See Section E.1, above.) The state will likely balk, so be persistent with your request.

F. When All Else Fails, Try Your Political Connections

If the state tax agency is treating you unfairly, use whatever political connections you can muster. Someone in your broad circle of friends, relatives, acquaintances or professional associations may know a state representative, assemblyperson or senator. State tax agencies tend to be more sensitive to political pressures than is the IRS. It's certainly worth a try as a last resort.

TAXPAYERS' BILL OF RIGHTS 15

Senator David Pryor of Arkansas, author of the 1988 Taxpayers' Bill of Rights, promised that it would "stem the abuse of taxpayers by the IRS and provide redress when abuse does occur. It marks a victory for the little taxpayer. It levels the playing field." The result is IRS Publication 1, Your Rights as a Taxpayer, reprinted at the end of this chapter. It is the most readable document ever published by the IRS.

While Senator Pryor is the best friend a taxpayer has in Washington, the Taxpayers' Bill of Rights is only a modest start in the right direction. While the IRS must now publish in plain English a pamphlet explaining taxpayer rights, other key provisions of the bill were gutted after the IRS put pressure on Congress. Most disappointing, the bill didn't produce major changes in the way the IRS does business. Nevertheless, if you're audited or sent an adjustment (billing) notice, familiarize yourself with the Taxpayers' Bill of Rights.

TAXPAYERS' BILL OF RIGHTS' KEY FEATURES

- Publication 1, Your Rights as a Taxpayer, must be mailed to you with your first IRS notice concerning delinquent taxes. The IRS is not required to send it with an audit notice, but often does. Publication 1 spells out for the first time a taxpayer's rights during any IRS non-criminal interview, including examinations (audits), appeals and collections.

- The Taxpayers' Bill of Rights created a few new taxpayer rights, including the right to:

  ✓ Propose an installment payment plan if you can't pay your entire tax bill. While you can't force the IRS to let you pay in installments, the agency must fairly consider your request. (See Chapter 6, Section D.6.)

  ✓ Tape record most IRS meetings, such as audits, appeals and collection interviews. In general, this is not a good idea—it would probably make an IRS agent guarded and hard to deal with. I've never done it and I don't know anyone who has. You don't have a right to record telephone calls or to videotape a meeting with the IRS, however.

  ✓ Not meet with the IRS personally if you have a qualified representative. She must be a lawyer, Certified Public Accountant or Enrolled Agent. (See Chapter 13.)

  ✓ Stop an audit or other meeting so that you can contact a Tax Pro for advice. (See Chapter 3, Section G.3.)

  ✓ Not be forced to meet with the IRS at an inconvenient time or place. Congress expressed concern about IRS auditors forcing small businesses owners to close down during an audit. The audit must be held elsewhere, but the IRS can visit the business to verify inventory and other items relating to a tax return. (See Chapter 3, Sections C.1 and C.2.)

  ✓ Get penalties removed if you rely on incorrect written advice from the IRS (not including information that appears in IRS publications). This "right" is of almost no value—written advice is nearly impossible to get from the IRS.

Also in the Taxpayers' Bill of Rights:

- The IRS created the position of Ombudsman. This taxpayer advocate can issue a Taxpayer Assistance Order (TAO) if a proposed IRS action, such as a seizure of property, will cause a "significant hardship." This is the best feature of the Taxpayers' Bill of Rights. The ombudsman works through the Problems Resolution Program at IRS District Offices and Service Centers. (See Chapter 8.) You can also appeal to the ombudsman if the IRS erroneously filed a tax lien.

- IRS production quotas are forbidden. IRS auditors and collectors cannot be rated or promoted based on how much taxes they assess or collect. Unofficially, however, IRS personnel (collectors and auditors) are judged by how many files they close—and sometimes, they are monitored as to how much revenue they generate.

- You must be given a written Notice of Intent to Levy before the IRS seizes your property. You then have 30 days to contest the legality of the seizure. In practice, this provides little help because if you owe and haven't paid the taxes, you have no legal ground to contest. This provision does give you time to negotiate with the IRS to stop the seizure, however. (See Chapter 7, Section F.)

- The Taxpayers' Bill of Rights increased the list and amounts of property and wages that are exempt from IRS seizure. They are still very small amounts of money. (See Chapter 7, Section D.) The bill also prohibits the seizure of your principal residence without a District Director or an assistant personally approving. Revenue Officer "Rambo" can no longer decide to take your home on his own.

- You can sue the IRS if its collectors intentionally disregard the law. Theoretically, you can get up to $100,000 plus your legal costs. This provision has such stringent conditions, however, that few people will ever be able to use it. And, if you lose your case, the IRS can get damages against you!

 Almost annually, the U.S. Congress considers a stronger Taxpayers' Bill of Rights II (T2), usually introduced into their respective houses by Senator David Pryor and Representative J.J. Pickle. Key features of T2 would:

- Make the IRS Ombudsman and Problems Resolution Officers (PROs) independent of the IRS. (I love this one best of all.)

- Create an administrative appeal procedure, called the "Taxpayer Rights Review," outside the IRS. The government employees who would staff the office would be called "Super PROs." Super PROs would have specific review authority in the following matters:

  ✓ recovery of-out-of pocket costs by taxpayers in fighting the IRS

  ✓ release of erroneous, premature or incorrectly filed liens

  ✓ recovery of civil damages for certain unauthorized collection actions

  ✓ abatement of interest for unreasonable IRS delay

  ✓ recovery of damages due to failure to release liens

  ✓ review of installment agreement disputes, and

  ✓ granting of Taxpayer Assistance Orders that require the IRS to take certain actions.

- Eliminate the need to show "significant" hardship to qualify for a Taxpayer Assistance Order. Under the T2, any degree of hardship would be sufficient.

- Require the IRS to automatically grant installment agreements to taxpayers with clean payment records (for the prior three years) and who owe less than $10,000. (This was partially adopted as policy by the IRS in 1993.)

- Require the IRS to give taxpayers 30-day notice before terminating an installment agreement. (The IRS adopted this as policy in 1993, but with a ten-day notice.)

- Prevent the IRS from imposing a "failure to pay" penalty while an installment agreement is in effect. (Currently, the penalty adds $1/2$% per month to a tax bill.)

- Require the IRS to pay tax refund recipients the same rate of interest the IRS charges on late payments. (The IRS now pays one percentage point less.)

- Require the IRS to send duplicate tax bill notices to spouses who do not file joint returns.

- Require the IRS, on request by a spouse, to disclose its collection efforts against the other spouse regarding a jointly owed bill.

- Require the IRS to notify credit reporting agencies after removing a Notice of Federal Tax Lien.

- Raise the exemption level for levies on personal property from $1,100 to $1,500. (I think $5,000 to $10,000 would be about right if the government really wants to be fair.)

- Allow IRS personnel to accept an Offer in Compromise without getting approval of IRS lawyers. (This was adopted as policy by the IRS in 1993.)

- Guarantee taxpayers an appeals hearing and the right to go to Tax Court before the IRS assesses the Trust Fund Recovery Penalty on any "responsible person." (Presently, the IRS doesn't have to grant an appeals hearing but it often does. And, the law does not allow you to go to Tax Court to contest a Trust Fund Recovery Penalty.)

- Bar the IRS from assessing the Trust Fund Recovery Penalty on any person (except significant owners or people who decide not to deposit payroll taxes) who notifies the IRS of the business' failure to pay within 30 days of the taxes' due date.

- Bar the IRS from assessing the Trust Fund Recovery Penalty on unpaid, volunteer members of any board of trustees or directors of a tax exempt organization that fails to pay its payroll taxes. (The IRS adopted this as policy in 1993.)

- Allow taxpayers to rely on any written IRS guidance (including press releases, information releases or revenue rulings) without penalty if the IRS later takes a position inconsistent with the written information.

Your Rights

AS A TAXPAYER

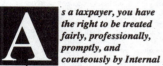

As a taxpayer, you have the right to be treated fairly, professionally, promptly, and courteously by Internal Revenue Service employees. Our goal at the IRS is to protect your rights so that you will have the highest confidence in the integrity, efficiency, and fairness of our tax system. To ensure that you always receive such treatment, you should know about the many rights you have at each step of the tax process.

Department of the Treasury
Internal Revenue Service
Publication 1 (Rev. 10-90)

Cat. No. 64731W

Free Information and Help in Preparing Returns

You have the right to information and help in complying with the tax laws. In addition to the basic instructions we provide with the tax forms, we make available a great deal of other information.

Taxpayer publications. We publish over 100 free taxpayer information publications on various subjects. One of these, Publication 910, *Guide to Free Tax Services*, is a catalog of the free services and publications we offer. You can order all publications and any tax forms or instructions you need by calling us toll-free at 1-800-TAX-FORM (829-3676).

Other assistance. We provide walk-in tax help at many IRS offices and recorded telephone information on many topics through our *Tele-Tax* system. The telephone numbers for *Tele-Tax*, and the topics covered, are in certain tax forms' instructions and publications. Many of our materials are available in Braille (at regional libraries for the handicapped) and in Spanish. We provide help for the hearing-impaired via special telephone equipment.

We have informational videotapes that you can borrow. In addition, you may want to attend our education programs for specific groups of taxpayers, such as farmers and those with small businesses.

In cooperation with local volunteers, we offer free help in preparing tax returns for low-income and elderly taxpayers through the Volunteer Income Tax Assistance (VITA) and Tax Counseling for the Elderly (TCE) Programs. You can get information on these programs by calling the toll-free telephone number for your area.

Copies of tax returns. If you need a copy of your tax return for an earlier year, you can get one by filling out Form 4506, *Request for Copy of Tax Form*, and paying a small fee. However, you often only need certain information, such as the amount of your reported income, the number of your exemptions, and the tax shown on the return. You can get this information free if you write or visit an IRS office or call the toll-free number for your area.

Privacy and Confidentiality

You have the right to have your personal and financial information kept confidential. People who prepare your return or represent you *must* keep your information confidential.

You also have the right to know why we are asking you for information, exactly how we will use any information you give, and what might happen if you do not give the information.

Information sharing. Under the law, we can share your tax information with State tax agencies and, under strict legal guidelines, the Department of Justice and other federal agencies. We can also share it with certain foreign governments under tax treaty provisions.

Courtesy and Consideration

You are always entitled to courteous and considerate treatment from IRS employees. If you ever feel that you are not being treated with fairness, courtesy, and consideration by an IRS employee, you should tell the employee's supervisor.

Protection of Your Rights

The employees of the Internal Revenue Service will explain and protect your rights as a taxpayer at all times. If you feel that this is not the case, you should discuss the problem with the employee's supervisor.

Complaints

If for any reason you have a complaint about the IRS, you may write to the District Director or Service Center Director for your area. We will give you the name and address if you call our toll-free phone number listed later.

Representation and Recordings

Throughout your dealings with us, you can represent yourself, or, generally with proper written authorization, have someone represent you in your absence. During an interview, you can have someone accompany you.

If you want to consult an attorney, a certified public accountant, an enrolled agent, or any other person permitted to represent a taxpayer during an interview for examining a tax return or collecting tax, we will stop and reschedule the interview. We cannot suspend the interview if you are there because of an administrative summons.

You can generally make an audio recording of an interview with an IRS Collection or Examination officer. Your request to record the interview should be made in writing, and must be received 10 days before the interview. You must bring your own recording equipment. We also can record an interview. If we do so, we will notify you 10 days before the meeting and you can get a copy of the recording at your expense.

Payment of Only the Required Tax

You have the right to plan your business and personal finances so that you will pay the least tax that is due under the law. You are liable only for the correct amount of tax. Our purpose is to apply the law consistently and fairly to all taxpayers.

If Your Return is Questioned

We accept most taxpayers' returns as filed. If we inquire about your return or select it for examination, it does not suggest that you are dishonest. The inquiry or examination may or may not result in more tax. We may close your case without change. Or, you may receive a refund.

Examination and inquiries by mail. We handle many examinations and inquiries entirely by mail. We will send you a letter with either a request for more information

or a reason why we believe a change needs to be made to your return. If you give us the requested information or provide an explanation, we may or may not agree with you and we will explain the reasons for any changes. You should not hesitate to write to us about anything you do not understand. If you cannot resolve any questions through the mail, you can request a personal interview. You can appeal through the IRS and the courts. You will find instructions with each inquiry or in Publication 1383, *Correspondence Process.*

Examination by interview. If we notify you that we will conduct your examination through a personal interview, or you request such an interview, you have the right to ask that the examination take place at a reasonable time and place that is convenient for both you and the IRS. If the time or place we suggest is not convenient, the examiner will try to work out something more suitable. However, the IRS makes the final determination of how, when, and where the examination will take place. You will receive an explanation of your rights and of the examination process either before or at the interview.

If you do not agree with the examiner's report, you may meet with the examiner's supervisor to discuss your case further.

Repeat examinations. We try to avoid repeat examinations of the same items, but this sometimes happens. If we examined your tax return for the same items in either of the 2 previous years and proposed no change to your tax liability, please contact us as soon as possible so we can see if we should discontinue the repeat examination.

Explanation of changes. If we propose any changes to your return, we will explain the reasons for the changes. It is

important that you understand these reasons. You should not hesitate to ask about anything that is unclear to you.

Interest. You must pay interest on additional tax that you owe. The interest is generally figured from the due date of the return. But if our error caused a delay in your case, and this was grossly unfair, we may reduce the interest. Only delays caused by procedural or mechanical acts not involving the exercise of judgment or discretion qualify. If you think we caused such a delay, please discuss it with the examiner and file a claim for refund.

Business taxpayers. If you are in an individual business, the rights covered in this publication generally apply to you. If you are a member of a partnership or a shareholder in a small business corporation, special rules may apply to the examination of your partnership or corporation items. The examination of partnership items is discussed in Publication 556, *Examination of Returns, Appeal Rights, and Claims for Refund.* The rights covered in this publication generally apply to exempt organizations and sponsors of employee plans.

An Appeal of the Examination Findings

If you don't agree with the examiner's findings, you have the right to appeal them. During the examination process, you will be given information about your appeal rights. Publication 5, *Appeal Rights and Preparation of Protests for Unagreed Cases,* explains your appeal rights in detail and tells you exactly what to do if you want to appeal.

Appeals Office. You can appeal the findings of an examination within the IRS through our Appeals Office. Most

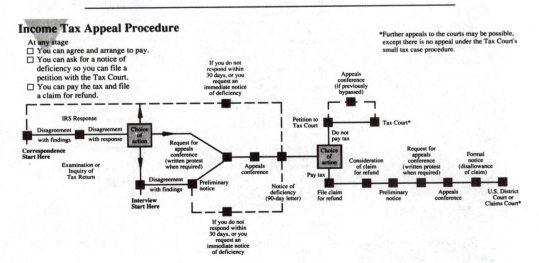

Income Tax Appeal Procedure

At any stage
☐ You can agree and arrange to pay.
☐ You can ask for a notice of deficiency so you can file a petition with the Tax Court.
☐ You can pay the tax and file a claim for refund.

*Further appeals to the courts may be possible, except there is no appeal under the Tax Court's small tax case procedure.

differences can be settled through this appeals system without expensive and time-consuming court trials. If the matter cannot be settled to your satisfaction in Appeals, you can take your case to court.

Appeals to the courts. Depending on whether you first pay the disputed tax, you can take your case to the U.S. Tax Court, the U.S. Claims Court, or your U.S. District Court. These courts are entirely independent of the IRS. As always, you can represent yourself or have someone admitted to practice before the court represent you.

If you disagree about whether you owe additional tax, you generally have the right to take your case to the U.S. Tax Court if you have not yet paid the tax. Ordinarily, you have 90 days from the time we mail you a formal notice (called a "notice of deficiency") telling you that you owe additional tax, to file a petition with the U.S. Tax Court. You can request simplified small tax case procedures if your case is $10,000 or less for any period or year. A case settled under these procedures cannot be appealed.

If you have already paid the disputed tax in full, you may file a claim for refund. If we disallow the claim, you can appeal the findings through our Appeals Office. If you do not accept their decision or we have not acted on your claim within 6 months, then you may take your case to the U.S. Claims Court or your U.S. District Court.

Recovering litigation expenses. If the court agrees with you on most issues in your case, and finds that our position was largely unjustified, you may be able to recover some of your administrative and litigation costs. To do this, you must have used all the administrative remedies available to you within the IRS. This includes going through our Appeals system and giving us all the information necessary to resolve the case.

Publication 556, *Examination of Returns, Appeal Rights, and Claims for Refund,* will help you more fully understand your appeal rights.

Fair Collection of Tax

Whenever you owe tax, we will send you a bill describing the tax and stating the amounts you owe in tax, interest, and penalties. Be sure to check any bill you receive to make sure it is correct. You have the right to have your bill adjusted if it is incorrect, so you should let us know about an incorrect bill right away.

If we tell you that you owe tax because of a math or clerical error on your return, you have the right to ask us to send you a formal notice (a "notice of deficiency") so that you can dispute the tax, as discussed earlier. You do not have to pay the additional tax at the same time that you ask us for the formal notice, if you ask for it within 60 days of the time we tell you of the error.

If the tax is correct, we will give you a specific period of time to pay the bill in full. If you pay the bill within the time allowed, we will not have to take any further action.

We may request that you attend an interview for the collection of tax. You will receive an explanation of your rights and of the collection process either before or at the interview.

Your rights are further protected because we are not allowed to use tax enforcement results to evaluate our employees.

Payment arrangements. You should make every effort to pay your bill in full. If you can't, you should pay as much as you can and contact us right away. We may ask you for a complete financial statement to determine how you can pay the amount due. Based on your financial condition, you may qualify for an installment agreement. We can arrange for these payments to be made through payroll deduction. We will give you copies of all agreements you make with us.

If we approve a payment agreement, the agreement will stay in effect only if:

You give correct and complete financial information,

You pay each installment on time,

You satisfy other tax liabilities on time,

You provide current financial information when asked, and

We determine that collecting the tax is not at risk.

Following a review of your current finances, we may change your payment agreement. We will notify you 30 days before any change to your payment agreement and tell you why we are making the change.

We will not take any enforcement action (such as recording a tax lien or levying on or seizing property), until after we have tried to contact you and given you the chance to voluntarily pay any tax due. Therefore, it is very important for you to respond right away to our attempts to contact you (by mail, telephone, or personal visit). If you do not respond, we may have no choice but to begin enforcement action.

Release of liens. If we have to place a lien on your property (to secure the amount of tax due), we must release the lien no later than 30 days after finding that you have paid the entire tax and certain charges, the assessment has become legally unenforceable, or we have accepted a bond to cover the tax and certain charges.

Recovery of damages. If we knowingly or negligently fail to release a lien under the circumstances described above, and you suffer economic damages because of our failure, you can recover your actual economic damages and certain costs.

If we recklessly or intentionally fail to follow the laws and regulations

for the collection of tax, you can recover actual economic damages and certain costs.

In each of the two situations above, damages and costs will be allowed within the following limits. You must exhaust all administrative remedies available to you. The damages will be reduced by the amount which you could have reasonably prevented. You must bring suit within 2 years of the action.

Incorrect lien. You have the right to appeal our filing of a Notice of Federal Tax Lien if you believe we filed the lien in error. If we agree, we will issue a certificate of release, including a statement that we filed the lien in error.

A lien is incorrect if:

You paid the entire amount due before we filed the lien,

The time to collect the tax expired before we filed the lien,

We made a procedural error in a deficiency assessment, or

We assessed a tax in violation of the automatic stay provisions in a bankruptcy case.

Levy. We will generally give you 30 days notice before we levy on any property. The notice may be given to you in person, mailed to you, or left at your home or workplace. On the day you attend a collection interview because of a summons, we cannot levy your property unless the collection of tax is in jeopardy.

Property that is exempt from levy. If we must seize your property, you have the legal right to keep:

Necessary clothing and schoolbooks,

A limited amount of personal belongings, furniture, and business or professional books and tools,

Unemployment and job training benefits, workers' compensation, welfare, certain disability payments, and certain pension benefits,

The income you need to pay court-ordered child support,

Mail,

An amount of weekly income equal to your standard deduction and allowable personal exemptions, divided by 52, and

Your main home, unless collection of tax is in jeopardy or the district director (or assistant) approves the levy in writing.

If your bank account is levied after June 30, 1989, the bank will hold your account up to the amount of the levy for 21 days. This gives you time to settle any disputes concerning ownership of the funds in the account.

We generally must release a levy issued after June 30, 1989, if:

You pay the tax, penalty, and interest for which the levy was made,

The IRS determines the release will help collect the tax,

You have an approved installment agreement for the tax on the levy,

The IRS determines the levy is creating an economic hardship, or

The fair market value of the property exceeds the amount of the levy and release would not hinder the collection of tax.

If at any time during the collection process you do not agree with the collection officer, you can discuss your case with his or her supervisor.

If we seize your property, you have the right to request that it be sold within 60 days after your request. You can request a time period greater than 60 days. We will comply with your request unless it is not in the best interest of the government.

Access to your private premises. A court order is not generally needed for a collection officer to seize your property. However, you don't have to allow the employee access to your private premises, such as your home or the non-public areas of your business, if the employee does not have court authorization to be there.

Withheld taxes. If we believe that you were responsible for seeing that a corporation paid us income and social security taxes withheld from its employees, and the taxes were not paid, we may look to you to pay an amount based on the unpaid taxes. If you feel that you don't owe this, you have the right to discuss the case with the collection officer's supervisor. You may also request an appeals hearing within 30 days of our proposed assessment of employment taxes. You generally have the same IRS appeal rights as other taxpayers. Because the U.S. Tax Court has no jurisdiction in this situation, you must pay at least part of the withheld taxes and file a claim for refund in order to take the matter to the U.S. District Court or U.S. Claims Court.

The amount of tax withheld from your wages is determined by the W-4, *Employees Withholding Allowance Certficate*, you give your employer. If your certificate is incorrect, the IRS may instruct your employer to increase the amount. We may also assess a penalty. You have the right to appeal the decision. Or, you can file a claim for refund and go to the U.S. Claims Court or U.S. District Court.

Publications 586A, *The Collection Process (Income Tax Accounts)*, and 594, *The Collection Process (Employment Tax Accounts)*, will help you understand your rights during the collection process.

The Collection Process

To stop the process at any stage, you should pay the tax in full. If you cannot pay the tax in full, contact us right away to discuss possible ways to pay the tax.

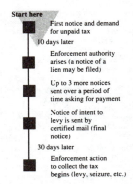

Start here

First notice and demand for unpaid tax

10 days later

Enforcement authority arises (a notice of a lien may be filed)

Up to 3 more notices sent over a period of time asking for payment

Notice of intent to levy is sent by certified mail (final notice)

30 days later

Enforcement action to collect the tax begins (levy, seizure, etc.)

Refund of Overpaid Tax

Once you have paid all your tax, you have the right to file a claim for a refund if you think the tax is incorrect. Generally, you have 3 years from the date you filed the return or 2 years from the date you paid the tax (whichever is later) to file a claim. If we examine your claim for any reason, you have the same rights that you would have during an examination of your return.

Interest on refunds. You will receive interest on any income tax refund delayed more than 45 days after the **later** of either the date you filed your return or the date your return was due.

Checking on your refund. Normally, you will receive your refund about 6 weeks after you file your return. If you have not received your refund within 8 weeks after mailing your return, you may check on it by calling the toll-free Tele-Tax number in the tax forms' instructions.

If we reduce your refund because you owe a debt to another Federal agency or because you owe child support, we must notify you of this action. However, if you have a question about the debt that caused the reduction, you should contact the other agency.

Cancellation of Penalties

You have the right to ask that certain penalties (but not interest) be cancelled (abated) if you can show reasonable cause for the failure that led to the penalty (or can show that you exercised due diligence, if that is the applicable standard for that penalty).

If you relied on wrong advice you received from IRS employees on the toll-free telephone system, we will cancel certain penalties that may result. But you have to show that your reliance on the advice was reasonable.

If you relied on incorrect written advice from the IRS in response to a written request you made after January 1,

1989, we will cancel any penalties that may result. You must show that you gave sufficient and correct information and filed your return after you received the advice.

Special Help to Resolve Your Problems

We have a Problem Resolution Program for taxpayers who have been unable to resolve their problems with the IRS. If you have a tax problem that you cannot clear up through normal channels, write to the Problem Resolution Office in the district or Service Center with which you have the problem. You may also reach the Problem Resolution Office by calling the IRS taxpayer assistance number for your area. If you are hearing-impaired with TV/Telephone (TTY) access, you may call 1-800-829-4059.

If your tax problem causes (or will cause) you to suffer a significant hardship, additional assistance is available. A significant hardship may occur if you cannot maintain necessities such as food, clothing, shelter, transportation, and medical treatment.

There are two ways you can apply for relief. You can submit Form 911, *Application for Taxpayer Assistance Order to Relieve Hardship*, which you can order by calling 1-800-TAX-FORM (829-3676). You can choose instead to call 1-800-829-1040, to request relief from your hardship. The Taxpayer Ombudsman, Problem Resolution Officer, or other official will then review your case and may issue a Taxpayer Assistance Order (TAO), to suspend IRS action.

Taxpayer Assistance Numbers

You should use the telephone number shown in the white pages of your local telephone directory under U.S. Government, Internal Revenue Service, Federal Tax Assistance. If there is not a specific number listed, call toll-free 1-800-829-1040.

You can also find these phone numbers in the instructions for Form 1040. You may also use these numbers to reach the Problem Resolution Office. Ask for the Problem Resolution Office when you call.

U.S. taxpayers abroad may write for information to:

Internal Revenue Service
Attn: IN:C:TPS
950 L'Enfant Plaza South, S.W.
Washington, D.C. 20024

You can also contact your nearest U.S. Embassy for information about what services and forms are available in your location.

✿U.S. GOVERNMENT PRINTING OFFICE: 1991-286-335

The 25 Most Asked Questions

16

1. How long should I keep my tax papers?

At least three years, but six years is better. In general, the IRS has up to three years after you file your tax return to complete an audit of you. Thus, you should keep records substantiating deductions and other tax benefits a minimum of three years. For example, if you filed on April 15, 1992 for 1991, keep those records until at least April 16, 1995.

To be safe, you may want to keep your records for six years. The IRS can audit you without a time limit if the IRS feels you filed a fraudulent return, or for up to six years after you filed a return if the IRS feels you underreported your income by 25% or more. You never know what the IRS will do.

You should keep records showing purchase costs of real estate, stocks and other investments for at least three years after you sell the assets. This is because you must be able to show your tax gain or loss. If you have rolled-over gains from your sales of residences, keep records of every purchase and sale made, for your lifetime.

2. How long should I worry if I haven't filed tax returns?

Six years, and maybe longer. The government has six years from the date the non-filed return was due to criminally charge you with failing to file a tax return. There is no time limit, however, for auditing you, collecting taxes and assessing civil penalties for not filing. If you didn't file for 1958 you still have an obligation, if you owed taxes for that year. It is not until you actually do file a return that the audit time limit (three years) and collection time limit (ten years) starts to run.

As a practical matter, don't worry about the taxes owed on a non-filed return due more than six years ago if you haven't heard from the IRS. The IRS usually doesn't go after non-filers after six years—unless your liability for the taxes is clear and you owe a large amount of taxes. And the IRS may even have purged its computer files or have lost its records. In the mid-1980s, the

IRS revamped its computer system; some pre-1985 tax records disappeared in the shuffle.

3. How many people cheat on their taxes?

In a recent Yankelovich poll, one out of five Americans admitted to cheating the IRS on their tax returns. The IRS says that 18% of us don't comply with the tax laws on a regular basis. If you throw in people who cheat by not filing tax returns, the number is closer to one in four. Undoubtedly the figure would be higher if wage earners did not have taxes withheld by their employers and the self-employed did not have their earnings reported to the IRS on 1099 forms.

Arguably, cheating by self-employed people approaches 100%. It may just be a question of degree—did you ever mail a personal letter with a business-bought stamp?

4. If I can't pay my taxes, should I file my return anyway?

Yes. Filing saves you from being criminally charged (unlikely) or hit with a fine (highly likely) for failing to file a tax return. Interest also runs, and will continue to build up until you pay. Of course, filing without paying will bring the IRS collector into your life, but the collector is easier to deal with if he doesn't have to hunt you down for non-filing. The sooner you start dealing with the problem, the better.

5. Can I get an extension to pay my taxes without paying penalties and interest?

Probably not. Although you can get extensions to file your tax return, you still must pay your taxes by April 15 or the IRS can impose a penalty. Only if you plead "undue hardship" on IRS Form 1127 might the IRS grant you up to six months extra to pay your taxes. And the IRS may require that you post a security, such as a bond or mortgage before giving you the extension, which is impractical for most people. Few payment extensions are granted. Even then, only penalties, not interest, stop accruing.

6. My state had an amnesty period for non-filers. Can I ever hope the IRS will have one?

Maybe—it is being seriously discussed in Congress. The IRS has always opposed tax amnesty legislation—which lets non-filers come forward without being criminally prosecuted or civilly fined—and such bills have all died in Congress to date. The IRS' reasoning is that after the amnesty period expires, significant numbers of people won't file, expecting the IRS to have another amnesty program. Based on the success of the states trying amnesty programs, I think the IRS is wrong.

7. Who has access to my IRS file?

The federal Privacy Act of 1976 makes tax files "confidential" and not public records. The law has many exceptions, however, and furthermore security is lax. Over 200 types of IRS files are routinely shared with other federal and state agencies. Most leakage of information is the result of sloppy state agencies who are granted access to IRS files. Furthermore, computer hackers have broken into government databases. While violation of the Privacy Act is a crime, rarely is any one prosecuted under it.

8. Is it true that the IRS pays rewards for turning in tax cheaters?

Yes, but you're not going to get rich and you won't get paid unless and until the IRS collects from the cheater. The IRS pays about 8% of the first $100,000 it collects and 1% of the balance. Of course, any reward you recover is taxable income. Identities of informers are kept secret, but tax cheats usually know who reported them—mostly ex-spouses or disgruntled business associates.

In a recent year, the IRS paid out a total of only $1.5 million for tips, on $72 million collected. The IRS places no priority on investigating tips and then looks for ways to avoid paying rewards. And, most of the time, you will

never know what action is taken on your tip. If you want to try it, use IRS Form 211. (P.S. Rumor has it that turning someone into the IRS can result in the informant being investigated!)

9. Should I notify the IRS when I move?

Yes, unless you think you can hide from a tax bill. (Some people seem to be able to, but they have to be constantly on the move. I don't recommend living your life like this.) Submit your change of address on IRS Form 8822. (One is in the Appendix.) A Post Office change of address form is not acceptable to the IRS. Notifying the IRS assures that you will get collection and audit notices, which have strict time limits for answering and appealing.

10. What should I do if I don't get a refund due me?

If you filed your tax return at least eight weeks ago, call the IRS tax refund hotline at 800-829-4477, Monday-Friday, 7:00 am to 11:30 pm. If that doesn't work, call the taxpayer assistance office at 800-829-1040. If you still don't get a refund, call the Problems Resolution Program at your local District Office or Service Center. If you filed your return on or before April 15 and don't receive your refund until after May 31, the IRS must pay you interest.

If you don't get a refund, don't assume the IRS messed up. Instead, the refund may have been intercepted to pay other state or federal taxes you owe; a defaulted student, SBA or other federal government loan; delinquent child support; or a public benefit, such as Social Security, overpayment.

11. What should I do if I encounter a dishonest IRS employee?

Report her. Dishonest employees are a rarity at the IRS. They are among the cleanest in the federal government. If you find one, however, call the Chief Inspector of the IRS at 800-366-4484 or write him at P.O. Box 589, Benjamin

Franklin Station, Washington, DC 20044-0589. You can make your complaint anonymously, if you wish.

12. Can the IRS charge me interest if I was incorrectly sent a refund and the IRS now wants it back?

It depends. The Internal Revenue Manual states that "taxpayers should not be held liable for interest on…erroneous refunds if the IRS was clearly at fault…and the taxpayer is cooperative in repaying." If you caused the refund and can't afford to repay it, however, the IRS can charge interest from the time it requested the repayment.

13. How legitimate are the seminars and books by "tax experts" claiming you don't have to pay income taxes?

Not at all. Some of these people are very convincing. But if they had any legitimacy, I'd be first in line to stop paying taxes. Constitutional arguments against the tax laws are routinely struck down by U.S. federal courts. One of the latest scams involves multiple family trusts, limited partnerships and transfers of money to offshore banks. These schemes can confuse and slow down the IRS, but they are bogus, period. Would a federal judge—whom you will appear before if you are prosecuted for tax evasion and whose salary comes from the federal government—ever likely uphold one of these schemes? Get serious.

14. Do auditors use computers? If so, does it make it harder to beat an audit?

Yes—they are used. No—it doesn't make it harder to beat an audit. During the 1980s, IRS Revenue Agents (IRS personnel who conduct audits at taxpayers' homes or offices) were issued Zenith portable computers. The cost was in excess of $200 million—plus training and software development. Many of the 18,000 computers now gather dust, not data. Few auditors really learned how to use them. The rest complained that the computers and printers were too heavy to lug around.

In 1993, the IRS started issuing new lightweight computers to try again. Time will tell if the experiment will work the second time around.

15. What are my chances of getting through an audit without owing additional taxes?

Not good and getting worse. Less than 20% of audit victims make a clean getaway. The IRS audits fewer taxpayers than ten years ago, but the size of the adjustments made in audits has greatly increased. The IRS, thanks to its sophisticated computer selection process, is more likely than ever to audit returns in which adjustments are almost a certainty. If you're audited, you probably won't beat it completely, so focus on limiting the damage from an audit.

16. I am being audited and the deadline for filing this year's return is fast approaching. Should I file?

Not if you can help it. The danger in filing is that the new return is fair game for the auditor, and she may get permission from her manager to expand the audit to include that return.

Instead of filing, get IRS Form 4868 and send it to the IRS by April 15 to obtain an automatic extension to file until August 15. If the audit is still going on in August, request a second extension on IRS Form 2688. You must file it by August 15. If the second extension is granted, you will have until October 15 to file your return.

If the audit is still alive on October 15, don't file until it is completed. As long as you have paid all the taxes due and have no fraudulent intent, you won't incur any penalties or interest for not meeting the deadline. If you owe additional money, send in your payment with a letter stating that the payment is to be applied to the current tax year. The auditor can't make you file your return; if she asks you about it simply say "I am not yet ready to file."

17. I am being audited and haven't heard from the auditor for months. What can I do to get the audit over with?

Don't do anything. IRS auditors are instructed to close audits within 28 months of the date you filed your tax return (or the date it was due, April 15, whichever is later). For example, if you filed your 1990 return on April 15, 1991, the IRS wants the audit completed by August 15, 1993. Legally the IRS has eight more months (until April 14, 1994) but auditors are instructed to complete the audit with at least eight months to spare to allow time for the IRS to process appeals.

If you haven't heard from the auditor, it could mean a number of things. The auditor may have been transferred or terminated. Or your file may be sitting in a pile awaiting processing somewhere in the IRS. When your file resurfaces, a new auditor is under a deadline to close it, which can work in your favor. And, in the best of all worlds, the time limit for completing the audit may expire while your file is in IRS never-never land. So leave the sleeping dog alone.

18. The auditor (or collector) is impossible to get along with. What can I do?

First, try to put yourself into the shoes of that person. Most IRS employees are 9-to-5 types just trying to do a job and get through the day. Their pay is often too low to support a family in most areas that have high costs of living. They deal with hostile and untruthful citizens all day long.

Understandably, IRS morale is low. Would you like this kind of job?

And even if an agent doesn't like you for some reason, she doesn't get paid bonuses for giving you a hard time. If you've exchanged harsh words through an audit or collection interview, instead of escalating the war, clear the air. For instance, say "I'm sorry we can't get along. But let's try to get through this and get it over with, okay?"

If that doesn't work, ask to see the manager. Chances are the manager will try to smooth things over and may even take over the file herself.

19. I have always deducted a certain expense. During a recent audit, the deduction was denied and now I know I was wrong all those other years. Should I say anything?

Let your conscience be your guide. If your audit is still going on, the auditor can make adjustments in other "open" years—periods for which the three-year time limit to complete the audit (from the date you filed your return) hasn't yet expired. This is usually the year before and the year after the audited year. The auditor may ask you to give her copies of your tax returns for those years. You're not legally obligated to. If you don't, she may request them from the Service Center. But this is a lot of paperwork and often she just lets it pass. You don't have to worry about being audited on returns due and filed more than three years ago—unless your deduction is deemed fraudulent.

If you feel guilty, give the auditor copies of your tax returns for the "open" years and accept the disallowances. Or file amended tax returns and pay the additional taxes you owe.

20. Do I have to let the IRS into my home?

No. No IRS employee may enter your home without an express invitation from you or another rightful occupant. The only exception is if the IRS has a court order, which I've never seen. A field (as opposed to office) auditor may ask to come in to verify your home office deduction during an audit, but you don't have to let him in. Of course, if you don't, he'll no doubt disallow the deduction.

21. Can the IRS take my house for a tax bill?

Yes, but the Taxpayers' Bill of Rights discourages the IRS from seizing residences. Furthermore, IRS collectors cannot decide on their own to seize your home. Only a local District Director or his assistant can make this decision. The Director's job is politically sensitive. Your Congressional representative or Senator can bring some pressure to stop a seizure. And you can request a Taxpayer Assistance Order from an IRS Problems Resolution Officer.

The IRS doesn't like publicity about taxpayers losing their homes, but the IRS will take a home as a last resort to collect a tax bill. Usually this means that you have totally failed to communicate or cooperate with the IRS Collections Division. And if the IRS takes your house, any state homestead law, which would entitle you to keep all or some of the equity in your house from creditors won't help you.

22. I recently got married. Am I responsible for my spouse's past taxes?

No, but your property might be at risk of IRS seizure for your spouse's tax bill—if you aren't careful. In general, property owned by one spouse before marriage remains that spouse's property during marriage. Property acquired during marriage, however, is generally considered the joint property of the spouses, although married couples can own property separately in most states. It's when couples own property together that IRS problems can arise. The IRS can go after jointly owned assets to cover the tax debt of just one spouse.

Be particularly aware of these specific problem areas:

- Gifts. If one spouse (without a tax debt) gives the other spouse (with the tax debt) an interest in property, the IRS can grab it. For example, a wife deeds her separate property house to her husband and herself as joint tenants. The IRS can seize the house for the husband's debt, although the IRS would have to pay the wife for her half of the house once the house is sold.

- Commingled property. If spouses deposit their funds into a joint account and use that account to pay joint expenses, the IRS will deem the funds "commingled." This means that the IRS can take the entire account to satisfy the pre-marital debt of one spouse.

  If the couple uses their commingled funds to purchase real estate, and the IRS seizes that property to pay the pre-marital tax debt, the IRS must give the non-debtor spouse one-half of the sales proceeds.

- Wages. The IRS, quite unfairly, can take the wages of one spouse to pay for the pre-marital tax debt of the other spouse. Some couples have divorced just to stop the IRS from taking the wife's wages for taxes owed by the husband prior to marriage. They continued to live together after the divorce, but the wife's earnings are no longer within the IRS' grasp.

23. How likely am I to get in trouble for tax fraud?

Not very. Fewer than 2% of all taxpayers are ever investigated for tax fraud. And even if you're investigated, the likelihood of being civilly fined for, or criminally charged with, tax fraud is under 20%. The average amount of taxes owed by a taxpayer when the IRS files criminal fraud charges is over $70,000. To some extent, whether you are ever criminally charged depends on your line of work. Most of those prosecuted for tax fraud work in organized crime or are public figures.

24. Can I ever sue the IRS?

Yes, but it is difficult to win and you probably won't get much if you do. For instance, one provision of the law allows you to sue the IRS for wrongfully placing liens or levying property, but you can't recover more than $1,000. Very few lawyers would take a case to federal court if the top prize is only $1,000, and you will get overwhelmed if you tried to represent yourself in federal court. (Note: The proposed Taxpayers' Bill of Rights II—see Chapter 15—expands taxpayers rights to sue the IRS and may make it easier in the future.)

25. Can I recover my accountant's and lawyer's fees for fighting the IRS?

It's possible, but difficult. The law provides that if you win, you can get fees and costs awarded up to $25,000. Attorney's fees are seldom awarded, and when they are, it's at a rate of $75 per hour (far lower than what most tax lawyers actually charge). And, to win, you must "substantially prevail" in court, the IRS must have taken an "unreasonable position" and you must have exhausted all procedural remedies within the IRS before going to court.

Fees paid in an IRS administrative proceeding (such as an appeals hearing) can be recovered only if you prove that the IRS brought an "unreasonable claim." So far, few taxpayers have ever recovered against the IRS and it's unlikely that more than a handful ever will under the present laws.

GLOSSARY OF TAX TERMS

Note: *These terms are defined as they are used in this book. They may have different meanings in other contexts.*

Abatement   The IRS' partial or complete cancellation of taxes, penalties or interest owed by a taxpayer.

ACS   See **Automated Collection System.**

Adjustment   Change to your income tax liability as you reported in your tax return by an IRS auditor or Service Center.

Amended Tax Return   A tax return filed within three years to make one or more changes to a previously filed tax return. Taxpayers usually file amended tax returns to claim a refund. Amended individual income tax returns must be filed on IRS Form 1040X. (A copy is in the Appendix.)

Appeal   The IRS administrative process for taxpayers to contest decisions, such as an audit, within the IRS. Most, but not all, administrative decisions can be appealed within the IRS.

Assess   The IRS process of recording a tax liability in the account of a taxpayer.

Asset   Any property you own that has a monetary value.

Audit   An IRS review of the correctness of a tax return. The IRS official term for an audit is "examination." See also **Field Audit, Office Audit.**

Auditor   An IRS Examination Division employee who reviews the correctness of a tax return. See also **Revenue Agent, Tax Auditor.**

Automated Collection System   A computerized collection process in which IRS collectors contact delinquent taxpayers by telephone and mail. Often abbreviated as ACS.

Bankruptcy   Federal law—separate from the Internal Revenue Code—which, in limited circumstances, can be used by taxpayers to eliminate their tax debts (Chapter 7 bankruptcy). In other instances, taxpayers can use bankruptcy to pay off their tax debts in monthly installments (Chapter 13 bankruptcy).

Basis (Tax Basis)   Usually refers to the cost of an asset, which may be adjusted for tax reporting purposes downward by depreciation or upward by improvements.

Certified Public Accountant (CPA)   CPAs are the most highly skilled of those in the accounting profession. They do sophisticated accounting and business audit work, and prepare tax returns. To earn the professional designation of CPA, an accountant must have a college degree and work experience with a CPA firm, and must pass a series of rigorous examinations. CPAs are regulated by state law and are allowed to practice before the IRS.

Claim for Refund   Taxpayers who feel that they have overpaid their taxes may file a claim to the IRS for a refund. The IRS provides Form 843 for claims. (A copy is in the Appendix.) An amended tax return (Form 1040x) is also treated as a claim for a refund. In general, taxpayers who pay the taxes assessed against them by the IRS can also later file a claim for a refund. If the claim is denied, the taxpayer can sue for a refund (called a "refund suit") in a federal District Court or the U.S. Court of Claims. See also **Amended Tax Return.**

Code   See **Internal Revenue Code.**

Cohan Rule   The rule that emerged from a federal court decision (*Commissioner of Internal Revenue v. George M. Cohan*) which allows taxpayers to use approximations in an audit when they don't have documentation of an actual expense.

Collection Division   The branch of the IRS which is staffed by tax collectors at the IRS Service Center, Automated Collection System or District Office.

Commissioner of Internal Revenue   The head of the entire IRS organization.

Correspondence Audit   An IRS examination conducted by mail.

Criminal Investigation Division (CID)   The branch of the IRS that investigates taxpayers to determine whether or not they have committed tax crimes. See also **Fraud.**

Death   The other certainty.

Deduction   An expense which the Internal Revenue Code allows taxpayers to subtract from their income to reduce the amount on which they owe taxes.

Delinquent Return   A tax return not filed by the legal due date or by the dates allowed through the IRS extension periods.

Dependent   See **Exemption.**

Depreciation   A tax deduction allowed for the wear-and-tear on an income-producing business or asset, such as a business automobile or rental real estate.

Disallowance   An IRS finding at audit that you weren't entitled to a tax benefit claimed on your tax return, usually a deduction or loss. See also **Adjustment.**

Discriminant Function   An IRS computer program which measures every tax return filed for its audit

potential. The Discriminant Function assigns each tax return a DIF score; the higher the DIF score, the higher the audit possibility.

District Offices   Local IRS offices out of which auditors, collectors, taxpayer service representatives, criminal investigators and Problems Resolution Officers work.

Documentation   Any tangible proof which substantiates an item on your tax return, usually an expense claimed as a deduction. Documentation is ordinarily something in writing.

Enrolled Agent (EA)   An EA is a tax advisor and tax preparer permitted to practice before the IRS. An EA earns his designation by either passing a difficult IRS exam testing his tax knowledge or having at least five years of employment by the IRS. EAs also must participate in annual continuing education programs to retain their designations.

Examination   Official IRS terminology for an audit. See **Audit.**

Exemption   Exemption has two meanings in the tax context. First, exemption refers to the dollar amount that all taxpayers may subtract from their income on their tax returns corresponding to the number of people they support as dependents (including themselves). Second, exemption refers to the limited list of property that the IRS cannot take if it levies on your property to satisfy your tax debt.

Extension   Income tax returns are normally due to the IRS by April 15. An extension to file gives a taxpayer extra time to file a return *but not to pay the taxes owed*. A taxpayer can obtain an automatic extension until August 15 to file by filing a form with the IRS. A taxpayer can request a second extension until October 15 by filing another form with the IRS. The second extension is discretionary with the IRS. A taxpayer can also request an extension to pay taxes, but such a request is rarely granted.

Failure to File Tax Return   The most frequently charged tax crime. It is legally defined as intentionally failing to file a return when you were obligated to do so. It is a misdemeanor punishable by up to one year in jail and/or a fine of $25,000 for each year not filed.

Fair Market Value   The price a buyer and seller of property would agree upon as fair, when neither is under any compulsion to buy or sell.

Field Audit   An examination that takes place outside the IRS offices—at your business, home or tax representative's office. See also **Audit, Revenue Agent.**

Fifth Amendment   A well-known right guaranteed by the U.S. Constitution that protects people from being forced by the government to incriminate themselves. You can assert your Fifth Amendment right against the IRS by refusing to answer questions or provide documents.

Filing   The act of giving in person or placing in the mail a tax return or other IRS document.

Fraud   Conduct meant to deceive the IRS or cheat in the assessment or payment of any tax liability. Fraud can be either civil (a penalty of 75% of the taxes owed) or criminal (tax evasion, a felony with a maximum prison sentence of five years and a maximum monetary fine of $100,000, or filing a false return, a felony with a maximum prison sentence of three years and a maximum monetary fine of $100,000).

Fraud Referral   A transfer to the IRS Criminal Investigation Division from another department when IRS personnel suspect a taxpayer of tax fraud. See also **Criminal Investigation Division.**

Freedom of Information Act   A federal law giving people the right to see U.S. government documents, including their IRS files.

Gift   Transfer of property without any financial payment in return. A true gift is not taxable to the recipient but may cause tax consequences for the giver, depending on the size of the gift.

Gross Income   Income from all sources which taxpayers must report on their income tax returns. Not all money received is income for tax purposes, however. See also **Taxable Income.**

Group Manager   The immediate superior of an auditor or tax collector at an IRS District Office.

Income   All monies and other things of value you receive, except items specifically exempted by the tax code. For example, a gift or inheritance is not considered income. See also **Gross Income, Taxable Income.**

Independent Contractor   A self-employed worker. Income taxes and Social Security contributions are not withheld or made by the business for whom the services are performed. Each year, businesses that hire independent contractors must file a Form 1099 with the IRS for each independent contractor paid more than $600 for the preceeding year.

Information Return   A report filed with the IRS showing monies paid by or to a taxpayer. The most common information returns are Form W-2 (wages) and Form 1099 (independent contractors and other income, such as interest paid by a bank, stock dividends or royalties).

Installment Agreement (IA)   An IRS monthly payment plan for past taxes.

Internal Revenue Code (IRC)   The tax laws of the U.S. as enacted by Congress. Also called the "tax code" or "code."

Internal Revenue Manual (IRM)   A collection of handbooks which set forth the internal operating guidelines for IRS personnel. Most, but not all, of the manual is now public information.

Internal Revenue Regulations   See **Regulations.**

Internal Revenue Service (IRS)   The tax law administration branch of the U.S. Treasury Department.

Jeopardy Assessment   An expedited procedure by which the IRS determines your tax liability without first notifying you. A jeopardy assessment is rare and usually limited to when the IRS believes you are about to flee the country or hide assets.

Joint Tax Return   An income tax return filed by a married couple.

Levy   An IRS seizure of your property or wages to satisfy a delinquent tax debt.

Lien   See **Tax Lien.**

Limitation on Assessment and Collection   See **Statute of Limitations.**

Market Value   See **Fair Market Value.**

Negligence   Whenever you have carelessly disregarded the tax law in preparing a tax return, the IRS can deem your conduct negligent and impose a penalty (fine) against you. Also called an Accuracy Related Penalty.

Non-Filer   A person or entity who does not file a tax return even though required by law to do so.

Notice of Deficiency   See **90-Day Letter.**

Notice of Tax Lien   See **Tax Lien.**

Offer in Compromise   A formal written proposal to the IRS to settle your tax account balance for less than the amount the IRS says you owe. An Offer in Compromise must be submitted on IRS Form 656. (A copy is in the Appendix.)

Office Audit   An IRS examination of your tax return by a tax auditor at a local IRS office. See also **Audit, Field Audit, Tax Auditor.**

Ombudsman   The head IRS troubleshooter who acts for taxpayers with problems not solved through normal IRS channels. The ombudsman works through the Problems Resolution Officers in IRS District Offices and Service Centers. See also **Problems Resolution Officer, Problems Resolution Program.**

Payroll Taxes   Federal income tax and FICA contributions—which includes both Social Security and Medicare—a business must deposit regularly and report quarterly to the IRS for each employee. These are also called Trust Fund Taxes. See also **Trust Fund Recovery Penalty.**

Penalties   Civil fines imposed on taxpayers who disobey tax laws.

Personal Property   Any item of property that is not real estate—such as cash, stocks, cars and the shirt on your back.

Petition   A written form filed with the U.S. Tax Court to contest a proposed IRS tax assessment. See also **Tax Court.**

Power of Attorney   A form you sign appointing a tax representative to deal with the IRS on your behalf.

Problems Resolution Officer (PRO)   An IRS troubleshooter who acts for taxpayers with problems not solved through normal IRS channels. Problems Resolution Officers (PROs) work in District Offices and Service Centers. See also **Ombudsman, Problems Resolution Program.**

Problems Resolution Program   An IRS section to assist taxpayers with problems not solved to their satisfaction in normal IRS channels. The program is administered by Problems Resolution Officers. See also **Ombudsman, Problems Resolution Officer.**

Property   See **Personal Property, Real Property.**

Protest   A written or oral request to appeal a decision within the IRS. See also **Appeal.**

Real Property   Real estate, consisting of land and structures attached to it.

Reconsideration   A discretionary IRS procedure which lets you reopen a closed audit or other tax assessment previously made.

Records   A collection of tangible proof, usually in writing, which shows income, expenses and financial transactions. Records are one form of documentation.

Refund Suit   See **Claim for Refund.**

Regular Tax Case   A Tax Court case in which a taxpayer contests $10,000 or more per tax year. This is a complex proceeding, in which formal rules of procedure and evidence apply. See also **Petition, Small Tax Case, Tax Court.**

Regulations   IRS written interpretations of selected Internal Revenue Code provisions. See also **Internal Revenue Code, Revenue Procedures, Revenue Rulings.**

Representative   See **Tax Representative, Tax Professional.**

Return   See **Tax Return.**

Revenue Agent   An IRS employee who conducts a field, as opposed to office, audit. See also **Audit, Field Audit, Office Audit.**

Revenue Officer   A tax collector who works out of an IRS District Office.

Revenue Procedures   IRS interpretations of selected Internal Revenue Code provisions which specify the procedures taxpayers must follow to comply with certain sections of the tax code. See also **Internal Revenue Code, Regulations, Revenue Rulings.**

Revenue Rulings   IRS interpretations of selected Internal Revenue Code provisions as applied to specific factual circumstances. See also **Internal Revenue Code, Regulations, Revenue Procedures.**

Seizure   See **Levy.**

Self-Employed   Anyone who works for herself, not receiving wages from an employer. See also **Independent Contractor.**

Service Centers   Ten regional IRS facilities where tax returns are filed and processed. Most IRS notices come from Service Centers.

Small Tax Case   A Tax Court case in which a taxpayer contests less than $10,000 per tax year. This is a simple, small claims court type proceeding, in which formal rules of procedure and evidence don't apply. See also **Petition, Regular Tax Case, Tax Court.**

Special Agent   An IRS officer who investigates suspected tax crimes. See also **Criminal Investigation Division (CID).**

Statute of Limitations   Differing time limits imposed by Congress on the IRS for assessing and collecting taxes, on the Justice Department for charging taxpayers with tax crimes and on taxpayers who claim refunds.

Summons   A legal order issued by the IRS compelling a taxpayer or other person or entity (such as a taxpayer's employer or bank) to appear or provide financial information to the IRS.

Tax Attorney   A lawyer who does various types of tax-related work including tax and estate planning, IRS dispute resolution and tax return preparation. To assure tax knowledge, a tax attorney should have either a special tax law degree (LL.M.-Tax) or a certification as a tax law specialist from a state bar association.

Tax Auditor   An IRS employee who conducts an office, as opposed to field, audit. See also **Audit, Field Audit, Office Audit.**

Tax Code   See **Internal Revenue Code.**

Tax Court   The only U.S. federal court where a taxpayer can contest an IRS tax assessment without first paying the taxes claimed due by the IRS. See also **Petition, Regular Tax Case, Small Tax Case.**

Tax Fraud   See **Fraud.**

Tax Law   The Internal Revenue Code, written by Congress, and the decisions of all federal courts which interpret it. See also **Internal Revenue Code.**

Tax Lien   Whenever you owe money to the IRS and don't pay after the IRS has demanded payment, the IRS has a claim against your property. This is called a tax lien, which arises automatically by "operation of law." The IRS has the right to inform the public that you are subject to a tax lien. This is done by recording a Notice of Federal Tax Lien at the county recorder's office or with your Secretary of State's office. A tax lien allows the IRS to seize (levy on) your property to satisfy your tax debt. See also **Levy.**

Tax Preparer   A person who fills in your tax return forms for a fee.

Tax Professional   Anyone working privately in the tax field, such as an accountant or tax lawyer. I call them Tax Pros. See also **Certified Public Accountant, Enrolled Agent, Tax Representative, Tax Attorney, Tax Preparer.**

Tax Representative   A type of tax professional legally qualified to represent you before the IRS. See also **Certified Public Accountant, Enrolled Agent, Tax Attorney.**

Tax Return   A form that nearly all individuals, partnerships and corporations are required to file each year with the IRS stating income, exemptions, credits and deductions.

Taxable Income   The amount of income on which you must pay taxes each year. It's determined on your tax return by subtracting deductions and exemptions from your gross income. See also **Deductions, Exemptions, Gross Income.**

Taxpayer Account   An IRS computer record containing your taxpaying history. You tax account includes all tax assessments, penalties and interest, and credits for payments for each tax year.

Taxpayer Assistance Order (TAO)   An order that a Problems Resolution Officer can issue to override an action taken by another division of the IRS. See also **Ombudsman, Problems Resolution Officer, Problems Resolution Program.**

Taxpayer Compliance Measurement Program (TCMP) A process where the IRS national computer randomly selects a group of individual taxpayers every three years for an intensive audit. Data obtained from TCMP audits is used by IRS computers to determine which tax returns will be selected for future audits.

Taxpayer Identification Number (TIN)   An IRS assigned number used for computer tracking of tax accounts. For individuals, it is their Social Security number (SSN). For other entities, such as corporations and trusts, it is a separate 13-digit number called the employer identification number (EIN).

Taxpayers' Bill of Rights   A 1988 federal law imposing standards and limits on the IRS, and establishing your rights in dealing with the agency.

Tele-Tax   IRS pre-recorded tax topics information, available by telephone. (A list of topics is in the Appendix.)

Third Party   Any person or entity other than the IRS or you, who has knowledge of your finances, such as your bank, stockbroker or employer.

Trust Fund Recovery Penalty   A tax law giving the IRS the power to assess unpaid payroll taxes against "responsible" individuals involved in a business owing the taxes. See also **Payroll Taxes.**

Trust Fund Taxes   See **Payroll Taxes.**

Unreported Income   Any income you were required to report on your income tax return, but didn't.

Waiver   Voluntarily giving up a legal right, such as the right to have the IRS collection period on a delinquent tax debt expire. Often, the IRS requires waivers in exchange for granting installment agreements.

Willful   Intentional conduct which violates the tax laws and can subject the wrongdoer to criminal prosecution.

Workpapers   Notes made by accountants and IRS auditors which explain items or adjustments made on a tax return. See also **Adjustment, Disallowance.**

100% Payroll Penalty   See **Trust Fund Recovery Penalty.**

30-Day Letter   IRS written notice following an audit giving you 30 days to protest the audit by requesting an IRS appeals hearing.

90-Day Letter   The letter the IRS must send if it seeks to impose additional taxes—usually after an audit—which you don't agree to. The letter gives you 90 days to file a Petition in U.S. Tax Court to protest the proposed assessment of taxes. If you don't file a Petition, the tax assessment becomes final. Also called a "Notice of Deficiency." See **Tax Court, Petition.**

Appendix

Addresses and Phone Numbers of State Income Tax Taxing Authorities

Form 433-A   Collection Information Statement for Individuals

Form 433-B   Collection Information Statement for Businesses

Form 433-D   Installment Agreement

Form 433-F   Collection Information Statement

Form 656   Offer in Compromise

Form 843   Claim for Refund and Request for Abatement

Form 911   Application for Taxpayer Assistance Order (ATAO)

Form 1040X   Amended U.S. Individual Income Tax Return

Form 1127   Application for Extension of Time for Payment of Tax

Form 1902-B   Report of Individual Income Tax Examination Changes

Form 4180   Report of Interview with Individual Relative to 100-Percent Penalty Recommendation

Form 4506   Request for Copy of Tax Form

Form 4700   Examination Workpapers and Supplement

Form 8332   Release of Claim to Exemption for Child of Divorced or Separated Parents

Form 8379   Injured Spouse Claim and Allocations

Form 8822   Change of Address

Form SS-8   Determination of Employee Work Status for Purposes of Federal Employment Taxes and Income Tax Withholding

Notice 746   Information About Your Notice, Penalty and Interest

Publication 5   Appeal Rights and Preparation of Protests for Unagreed Cases

Publication 17   Your Federal Income Tax (page 252, The Examination and Appeals Process)

Publication 594   Understanding The Collection Process

Publication 910   Guide to Free Tax Services (pages 1–11, 25–28)

Publication 1320   Operation Link (pages 7–12, Addresses of Problems Resolution Offices)

Publication 1383   The Correspondence Process (Income Tax Accounts)

Publication 1494   Table for Figuring Amount Exempt from Levy on Wages, Salary and Other Income

United States Tax Court Petition

United States Tax Court Designation of Place of Trial

Election of Small Tax Case Procedure and Preparation of Petitions

ADDRESSES AND PHONE NUMBERS OF STATE INCOME TAX TAXING AUTHORITIES

STATE	PHONE NUMBER	ADDRESS
Alabama	(205) 242-1000	Department of Revenue, Income Tax Division, P.O. Box 2401, Montgomery, AL 36140-0001
Arizona	(602) 255-3381	Department of Revenue, Taxpayers' Assistance, 1600 West Monroe, Phoenix, AZ 85007
Arkansas	(501) 682-7250	State Income Tax, P.O. Box 3628, Little Rock, AR 72203
California	(800) 852-5711	Franchise Tax Board, P.O. Box 942840, Sacramento, CA 94240-0040
Colorado	(303) 534-1209	Department of Revenue, Income Tax Account Services, 1375 Sherman, Denver, CO 80261
Connecticut	(203) 566-8520 (800) 321-7829	Department of Revenue Services, 92 Farmington Ave., Hartford, CT 06105, Attn: Taxpayer Services
Delaware	(302) 739-5251	Department of Revenue, 820 North French St., Wilmington, DE 19899
District of Columbia	(202) 727-6027	Department of Finance and Revenue, Taxpayer Services, 441 4th Street NW, Suite 550, Washington, DC 20001
Georgia	(404) 656-4071	Department of Revenue, 2082 East Exchange Pl., Suite 120, Tucker, GA 30084
Hawaii	(808) 587-4242 (800) 222-3229	Oahu District Office, P.O. Box 259, Honolulu, HI 96809
Idaho	(208) 334-7660	State Tax Commission, P.O. Box 36, Boise, ID 83722
Illinois	(217) 782-3336 (800) 732-8866	Department of Revenue, Springfield, IL 62719-0001
Indiana	(317) 232-2240	Department of Revenue, 100 North Senate, Room N105, Indianapolis, IN 46204
Iowa	(515) 281-3114 (800) 367-3388	Department of Revenue and Finance, Taxpayer Service, P.O. Box 10457, Hoover State Office Building, Des Moines, IA 50319
Kansas	(913) 296-3051	Department of Revenue, P.O. Box 12001, Topeka, KS 66612-2001
Kentucky	(502) 564-4580	Revenue Cabinet, P.O. Box 1190, Station 56, Frankfort, KY 40602
Louisiana	(504) 925-7537	Department of Revenue and Taxation, P.O. Box 201, Baton Rouge, LA 70821
Maine	(207) 287-3695 (800) 773-7895	Bureau of Taxation, Income Tax Section, State Office Building, Station 24, Augusta, ME 04333-0024
Maryland	(410) 974-3117 (800) 638-2937	Income Tax Division, Annapolis, MD 21411
Massachusetts	(617) 727-4545 (800) 392-6089	Department of Revenue, Taxpayers Assistance Bureau, 100 Cambridge St., Room 200, Boston, MA 02204
Michigan	(517) 373-3200 (800) 487-7000	Department of Treasury, Treasury Building, 430 West Allegan St., Lansing, MI 48933

STATE	PHONE NUMBER	ADDRESS
Minnesota	(612) 296-3781	Department of Revenue, Taxpayer Technical Support, Mail Station 4453, St. Paul, MN 55146-4453
Mississippi	(601) 359-1141	State Tax Commission, P.O. Box 960, Jackson, MS 39215
Missouri	(314) 751-4550	Department of Revenue, P.O. Box 2200, Jefferson City, MO 65105
Montana	(406) 444-2981	Department of Revenue, Sam Mitchell Building, P.O. Box 5805, Helena, MT 59604-5805
Nebraska	(402) 471-2971 (800) 742-7474	State Income Tax, Nebraska State Office Building, P.O. Box 94818, Lincoln, NE 68509
New Jersey	(609) 588-3800 (800) 323-4400	Division of Taxation, CN 269, Trenton, NJ 08646-0269
New Mexico	(505) 827-0700	Taxation and Revenue Department, P.O. Box 630, Santa Fe, NM 87504-0630
New York	(518) 438-8581 (800) 225-5829	State Tax Department, W.A. Harriman Campus, Albany, NY 12227
North Carolina	(919) 733-3991 (800) 222-9965	Department of Revenues, Individual Income Tax Division, P.O. Box 25000, Raleigh, NC 27640
North Dakota	(701) 224-2770 (800) 638-2901	Office of State Tax Commissioner, Individual Income Tax, State Capitol, 600 East Boulevard Ave., Bismarck, ND 58505-0599
Ohio	(614) 846-6712 (800) 282-1780	Department of Taxation, P.O. Box 476, Columbus, OH 43270-0001
Oklahoma	(405) 521-3125 (800) 522-8165	Tax Commission, Income Tax Division, 2501 North Lincoln Blvd., Oklahoma City, OK 73194
Oregon	(503) 378-4988 (800) 356-4222	Department of Revenue, 955 Center St., NE, Salem, OR 97310 (Toll-free number used January through April)
Pennsylvania	(717) 787-8333	Department of Revenue, Bureau of Individual Taxes, Harrisburg, PA 17128-0605
Rhode Island	(401) 277-2905	Division of Taxation, 1 Capitol Hill, Providence, RI 02908
South Carolina	(803) 737-5000	Tax Commission, P.O. Box 125, Columbia, SC 29214
Tennessee	(615) 741-2594 (800) 342-1003	Income Tax, Andrew Jackson Building, 3rd Floor, 500 Deaderick St., Nashville, TN 37242
Utah	(801) 530-4848 (800) 862-4335	State Tax Commission, 160 East Third Street South, Salt Lake City, UT 84134
Vermont	(802) 828-2865	Department of Taxes, Pavilion Office Building, 109 State St., Montpelier, VT 05609-1401
Virginia	(804) 367-8031	Department of Taxation, P.O. Box 1115, Richmond, VA 23208
West Virginia	(304) 348-3333 (800) 642-9016	Taxpayer Services Division, P.O. Box 3784, Charleston, WV 25337-3784
Wisconsin	(608) 266-2772	Department of Revenue, Audit Bureau, P.O. Box 8906, 4638 University Ave., Madison, WI 53708

Form **433-A**
(Rev. January 1994)

Collection Information Statement for Individuals

NOTE: Complete all blocks, except shaded areas, Write "N/A" *(not applicable)* in those blocks that do not apply.

1. Taxpayer(s) name(s) and address	2. Home phone number ( )	3. Marital status
County _____	4.a. Taxpayer's social security number	b. Spouse's social security number

Section I.   Employment Information

5. Taxpayer's employer or business *(name and address)*	a. How long employed	b. Business phone number ( )	c. Occupation
	d. Number of exemptions claimed on Form W-4	e. Paydays	f. *(Check appropriate box)* ☐ Wage earner ☐ Partner ☐ Sole proprietor

6. Spouse's employer or business *(name and address)*	a. How long employed	b. Business phone number ( )	c. Occupation
	d. Number of exemptions claimed on Form W-4	e. Paydays	f. *(Check appropriate box)* ☐ Wage earner ☐ Partner ☐ Sole proprietor

Section II.   Personal Information

7. Name, address and telephone number of next of kin or other reference	8. Other names or aliases	9. Previous address(es)

10. Age and relationship of dependents living in your household *(exclude yourself and spouse)*

11. Date of Birth ▶	a. Taxpayer	b. Spouse	12. Latest filed income tax return *(tax year)*	a. Number of exemptions claimed	b. Adjusted Gross Income

Section III.   General Financial Information

13. Bank accounts *(include savings & loans, credit unions, IRA and retirement plans, certificates of deposit, etc.)*

Name of Institution	Address	Type of Account	Account No.	Balance
		Total *(Enter in Item 21)*		

Form **433-A** (Rev. 1-94)

14. Charge cards and lines of credit from banks, credit unions, and savings and loans

Type of Account or Card	Name and Address of Financial Institution	Monthly Payment	Credit Limit	Amount Owed	Credit Available
Totals *(Enter in Item 27)* ▶					

15. Safe deposit boxes rented or accessed *(List all locations, box numbers, and contents)*

16. **Real Property** *(Brief description and type of ownership)*	**Physical Address**
a.	
	County _____
b.	
	County _____
c.	
	County _____

17. **Life Insurance** *(Name of Company)*	Policy Number	Type	Face Amount	Available Loan Value
Total *(Enter in Item 23)* ▶				

18. Securities *(stocks, bonds, mutual funds, money market funds, government securities, etc.):*

Kind	Quantity of Denomination	Current Value	Where Located	Owner of Record

19. Other information relating to your financial condition. If you check the yes box, please give dates and explain on page 4, Additional Information
Comments:

a. Court proceedings ☐ Yes ☐ No	b. Bankruptcies ☐ Yes ☐ No
c. Repossessions ☐ Yes ☐ No	d. Recent transfer of assets for less than full value ☐ Yes ☐ No
e. Anticipated increase in income ☐ Yes ☐ No	f. Participant or beneficiary to trust, estate, profit sharing, etc. ☐ Yes ☐ No

Asset and Liability Analysis

Description	Current Market Value	Liabilities Balance Due	Equity in Asset	Amount of Monthly Payment	Name and Address of Lien/Note Holder/Obligee	Date Pledged	Date of Final Payment
0. Cash							
1. Bank accounts (from Item 13)							
2. Securities (from Item 18)							
3. Cash or loan value or Insur.							
4. Vehicles (model, year, license, tag#)							
a.							
b.							
c.							
5. Real property (From Section III, item 16) a.							
b.							
c.							
6. Other assets							
a.							
b.							
c.							
d.							
e.							
7. Bank revolving credit (from Item 14)							
8. Other Liabilities (Including judgments, notes, and other charge accounts) a.							
b.							
c.							
d.							
e.							
f.							
g.							
9. Federal taxes owed							
0. Totals			$	$			

Internal Revenue Service Use Only Below This Line

Financial Verification/Analysis

Item	Date Information or Encumbrance Verified	Date Property Inspected	Estimated Forced Sale Equity
Personal Residence			
Other Real Property			
Vehicles			
Other Personal Property			
State Employment (Husband and Wife)			
Income Tax Return			
Wage Statements (Husband and Wife)			
Sources of Income/Credit (D&B Report)			
Expenses			
Other Assets/Liabilities			

Section V.   Monthly Income and Expense Analysis

Income			Necessary Living Expenses	
Source	**Gross**	**Net**		
31. Wages/Salaries *(Taxpayer)*	$	$	42. Rent *(Do not show mortgage listed in item 25)*	$
32. Wages/Salaries *(Spouse)*			43. Groceries (no. of people _____)	
33. Interest - Dividends			44. Allowable installment payments *(IRS use only)*	
34. Net business income *(from Form 433-B)*			45. Utilities (Gas $ _____ Water $ _____	
35. Rental Income			Electric $ _____ Phone $_____)	
36. Pension *(Taxpayer)*			46. Transportation	
37. Pension *(Spouse)*			47. Insurance (Life $_____ Health $ _____	
38. Child Support			Home $ _____ Car $ _____)	
39. Alimony			48. Medical *(Expenses not covered in item 47)*	
40. Other			49. Estimated tax payments	
			50. Court ordered payments	
			51. Other expenses *(specify)*	
41. **Total Income**	$	$	52. **Total Expenses** *(IRS use only)*	$
			53. Net difference *(income less (IRS necessary living expenses) use only)*	$

Certification   **Under penalties of perjury, I declare that to the best of my knowledge and belief this statement of assets, liabilities, and other information is true, correct, and complete.**

54. Your signature	55. Spouse's signature *(if joint return was filed)*	56. Date

Additional information or comments:

Internal Revenue Service Use Only Below This Line

Explain any difference between Item 53 and the installment agreement payment amount:

Name of originator and IDRS assignment number:	Date

Form **433-B**
(Rev. June 1991)

Department of the Treasury — Internal Revenue Service

Collection Information Statement for Businesses

(If you need additional space, please attach a separate sheet)

NOTE: Complete all blocks, except shaded areas. Write "N/A" *(not applicable)* **in those blocks that do not apply.**

1. Name and address of business	2. Business phone number ( )

County_____

3. *(Check appropriate box)*

☐ Sole proprietor ☐ Other *(specify)*
☐ Partnership _____
☐ Corporation _____

4. Name and title of person being interviewed	5. Employer Identification Number	6. Type of business

7. Information about owner, partners, officers, major shareholder, etc.

Name and Title	Effective Date	Home Address	Phone Number	Social Security Number	Total Shares or Interest

Section I. General Financial Information

8. Latest filed income tax return ▶	Form	Tax Year ended	Net income before taxes

9. Bank accounts *(List all types of accounts including payroll and general, savings, certificates of deposit, etc.)*

Name of Institution	Address	Type of Account	Account Number	Balance
	Total *(Enter in Item 17)*	▶		

10. Bank credit available *(Lines of credit, etc.)*

Name of Institution	Address	Credit Limit	Amount Owed	Credit Available	Monthly Payments
Totals *(Enter in Items 24 or 25 as appropriate)*	▶				

11. Location, box number, and contents of all safe deposit boxes rented or accessed

Form 433-B (Rev. 6-91)

12. Real property

Brief Description and Type of Ownership	Physical Address
a.	County _____
b.	County _____
c.	County _____
d.	County _____

13. Life insurance policies owned with business as beneficiary

Name Insured	Company	Policy Number	Type	Face Amount	Available Loan Value
		Total *(Enter in Item 19)*	▶		

14a. Additional information regarding financial condition *(Court proceedings, bankruptcies filed or anticipated, transfers of assets for less than full value, changes in market conditions, etc.; include information regarding company participation in trusts, estates, profit-sharing plans, etc.)*

b. If you know of any person or organization that borrowed or otherwise provided funds to pay net payrolls:	a. Who borrowed funds?
	b. Who supplied funds?

15. Accounts/Notes receivable *(Include current contract jobs, loans to stockholders, officers, partners, etc.)*

Name	Address	Amount Due	Date Due	Status
		$		
	Total *(Enter in Item 18)* ▶	$		

Section II.

Asset and Liability Analysis

Description (a)		Cur. Mkt. Value (b)	Liabilities Bal. Due (c)	Equity in Asset (d)	Amt. of Mo. Pymt. (e)	Name and Address of Lien/Note Holder/Obligee (f)	Date Pledged (g)	Date of Final Pymt. (h)
16. Cash on hand								
17. Bank accounts								
18. Accounts/Notes receivable								
19. Life insurance loan value								
20. Real property (from Item 12)	a.							
	b.							
	c.							
	d.							
21. Vehicles (Model, year, and license)	a.							
	b.							
	c.							
22. Machinery and equipment (Specify)	a.							
	b.							
	c.							
23. Merchandise inventory (Specify)	a.							
	b.							
24. Other assets (Specify)	a.							
	b.							
25. Other liabilities (Including notes and judgments)	a.							
	b.							
	c.							
	d.							
	e.							
	f.							
	g.							
	h.							
26. Federal taxes owed								
27. Total								

Form 433-B (Rev. 6-91)

Section III. Income and Expense Analysis

The following information applies to income and expenses during the period _____ to _____

Accounting method used

Income

28. Gross receipts from sales, services, etc.	$
29. Gross rental income	
30. Interest	
31. Dividends	
32. Other income (Specify)	
33. Total Income ▶	$

Expenses

34. Materials purchased	$
35. Net wages and salaries Number of Employees _____	
36. Rent	
37. Allowable installment payments (IRS use only)	
38. Supplies	
39. Utilities/Telephone	
40. Gasoline/Oil	
41. Repairs and maintenance	
42. Insurance	
43. Current taxes	
44. Other (Specify)	
45. Total Expenses (IRS use only) ▶	$
46. Net difference (IRS use only) ▶	$

Certification

Under penalties of perjury, I declare that to the best of my knowledge and belief this statement of assets, liabilities, and other information is true, correct, and complete.

47. Signature	48. Date

Internal Revenue Service Use Only Below This Line

Financial Verification/Analysis

Item	Date Information or Encumbrance Verified	Date Property Inspected	Estimated Forced Sale Equity
Sources of Income/Credit (D&B Report)			
Expenses			
Real Property			
Vehicles			
Machinery and Equipment			
Merchandise			
Accounts/Notes Receivable			
Corporate Information, if Applicable			
U.C.C. : Senior/Junior Lienholder			
Other Assets/Liabilities:			

Explain any difference between Item 46 (or P&L) and the installment agreement payment amount:

Name of Originator and IDRS assignment number	Date

Form **433-D**
(Rev. April 1994)

Installment Agreement

check box if pre-assessed modules included ☐

Name and address of taxpayer(s)	Social security or employer identification number
	(primary) *(secondary)*
	Telephone number *(home)* *(business)*
	Kinds of taxes *(form numbers)* Tax periods
	Amount owed as of _____ Earliest CSED $

Employer *(name and address)*	Financial institutions *(names and addresses)*	For assistance: Call 1-800-829-1040 or write: _____ Service Ctr. _____ City, State and Zip Code

I/We agree that the federal taxes shown above, PLUS ALL PENALTIES AND INTEREST PROVIDED BY LAW, will be paid as follows:

$ _____ will be paid on _____ and $ _____ will be paid no later than the _____ of each month thereafter until the total liability is paid in full. I/we also agree that the above installment payment will be increased or decreased as follows:

Date of increase *(or decrease)*	/ /	/ /
Amount of increase *(or decrease)*	$	
New installment amount	$	

AGREEMENT LOCATOR NUMBER: ___ ___ ___ ___
(circle)

0   No future action is required

5   Financial review date: ___ ___ / ___ ___
              m m   y   y

6   SCCB — Monitor ES compliance:
    Amount per quarter $ _____
    (If amount(s)/quarters will vary, provide details.)

Conditions of this agreement:

We must receive each payment by the date shown above; if you have a problem, contact us immediately.
This agreement is based on your current financial condition. We may change or cancel it if our information shows that your ability to pay has changed significantly.
We may cancel this agreement if you don't give us updated financial information when we ask for it.
While this agreement is in effect, you must file all federal tax returns and pay any taxes you owe on time.
We will apply your federal or state tax refunds (if any) to the amount you owe until it is fully paid. (This includes the Alaska Permanent Fund dividend for Alaska residents.)

Additional Conditions: (To be filled in by IRS)

- If you don't meet the conditions of this agreement, we will cancel it, and may collect the entire amount you owe by levy on your income, bank accounts or other assets, or by seizing your property.
- We may cancel this agreement at any time if we find that collection of the tax is in jeopardy.
- We will apply all payments on this agreement in the best interest of the United States.
- The IRS Collection Division must accept this agreement, and it may require managerial approval. If it is not accepted or approved, we will notify you.
- **A NOTICE OF FEDERAL TAX LIEN** *(check one)*
  - ☐ **HAS ALREADY BEEN FILED**
  - ☐ **WILL BE FILED IMMEDIATELY**
  - ☐ **WILL BE FILED WHEN TAX IS ASSESSED**
  - ☐ **MAY BE FILED IF THIS AGREEMENT DEFAULTS**

Your signature	Title *(if corporate officer or partner)*	Date	Originator's name, title and IDRS assignment number *(or district)*:
Spouse's signature *(if a joint liability)*		Date	
Agreement examined or approved by *(signature, title, function)*		Date	Originator Code:

YOU MAY HAVE YOUR INSTALLMENT AGREEMENT PAYMENT DEDUCTED FROM YOUR CHECKING ACCOUNT EACH MONTH (DIRECT DEBIT); IF YOU CHOOSE THIS OPTION, FOLLOW THE DIRECTIONS ON THE BACK OF YOUR COPY OF THIS FORM.

If you agree to Direct Debit, initial here:

_____

and attach a blank voided check.

- I (we) authorize the IRS and the depository (bank) identified on the attached voided check to deduct payments (debit) from my (our) checking account or correct errors on the account. This authorization remains in effect until I (or either of us) notify IRS in writing to stop or until the liability covered by this agreement is satisfied.
- I (we) understand that if the depository is unable to honor IRS's request for payment due to insufficient funds in my (our) account on the payment due date I (we) will be charged a penalty of $15 or two percent of the payment request, whichever is greater. If the payment request is for less than $15, the penalty is the amount of the request.

CAT. NO. 16644M   **Part 2 — Taxpayer's Copy**   Form **433-D** (Rev. 4–94)

INSTRUCTIONS TO TAXPAYER

If not already completed by an IRS employee, in the space provided, enter:

> your name and current address;
>
> your social security number and/or your employer identification number (whichever applies to your tax liability);
>
> the complete name and address of your employer(s) and your bank(s);
>
> your home and work/business telephone number(s);
>
> the amount you are able to pay now as a partial payment;
>
> the amount you are able to pay each month (or the amount determined by IRS personnel; and
>
> the date you prefer to make this payment (this must be the same day for each month, from the 1st to the 28th). We must receive your payment by this date. If you elect the direct debit option, this is the day you want your account debited.

If you choose to have your monthly payment automatically deducted from your checking account (direct debit), put your initials in the space provided in the bottom left corner, give the bank copy to your bank and attach a blank, voided check to the IRS copy of this form.

On the same day each month, your checking account will automatically be debited for the amount of your monthly payment. Be sure to update your checkbook each month. IRS won't send you a reminder notice about this.

When you have finished, sign and date the Installment Agreement and return it to either the office where you received it or mail it to your service center.

If you have any questions regarding the direct debit process or the completion of this form, please call the toll-free number on the front of this form.

Note: When making an installment, please be sure to:

1. Write your social security or employer identification number on each payment.

2. Make check or money order payable to "Internal Revenue Service."

3. Make each payment in an amount at least equal to that specified in this agreement.

4. Don't double one payment and skip the next without contacting us first.

5. Enclose with each payment a copy of the reminder notice (if you received one), in the envelope provided.

6. Mail your payment on time to the proper IRS office, even if you didn't receive a reminder notice. (Note: we must receive it by the due date.)

7. Contact us immediately if you can't meet the terms of this agreement.

This agreement will not affect your liability (if any) for backup withholding under Public Law 98-67, the Interest and Dividend Tax Compliance Act of 1983.

Form **433-F** (Rev. April 1994)	**Department of the Treasury - Internal Revenue Service** **Collection Information Statement** *(If you need additional space, please attach a separate sheet with your name(s) and Social Security number(s).)*

Your name(s) and address *(Including county)*	Phone numbers *(circle best daytime number)* Home: Your work: Your spouse's work:
	Social Security numbers Yours: Your Spouse's
Your employer or business *(name and address)*	Your spouse's employer or business *(name and address)*

Real estate *(Home and other Real Estate)*

County/Description	Value	Balance Owed	Equity	Monthly Payment

Other assets *(Cars, Boats, RV's, etc.)*

County/Description	Value	Balance Owed	Equity	Monthly Payment

Bank accounts *(include Savings & Loans, Credit Unions, Certificates of Deposit, Individual Retirement Accounts, Lines of Credit, etc.)*

Name of Institution	Address	Type of account	Balance

Monthly Income

Your net pay	$
Your spouse's net pay	
Social Security or Pensions	
Profit from your business	
Other income *(source):*	
Total income	$

Monthly Expenses

Rent	$
Groceries	
Utilities *(Electricity, Heating, Gas, Water, Phone)*	
Transportation *(gas, bus fares)*	
Medical *(doctors, & medicine not paid by insurance)*	
Insurance *(Auto, Health, Life, Homeowners/Rental)*	
Estimated Tax Payment (1040ES)	
Other *(explain)*	
Credit Cards	
Loan Payments *(not listed above)*	

Additional Information *(expected changes to income, health, etc.)*

Under penalties of perjury, I declare that to the best of my knowledge and belief this statement of assets, liabilities, and other information is true, correct, and complete.

Your signature	Spouse's signature	Date

Departamento del Tesoro — Servicio de Impuestos Internos (IRS)

Declaración de Información Sobre Colección
(Collection Information Statement)

Si ud. necesita espacio adicional, favor de juntar una hoja separada con su(s) nombre(s) y número(s) de seguro social.

Su(s) nombre(s) y dirección (incluyendo el distrito o condado)	Números telefónicos (circule el mejor número telefónico donde se le puede encontrar durante el día)
	Hogar:
	Su trabajo:
	El trabajo de su cónyuge:
	Números de seguro social
	El suyo _____ El de su cónyuge _____
Su empleador o negocio (nombre y dirección)	El empleador o negocio de su cónyuge (nombre y dirección)

Propriedad inmueble (hogar u otras propriedades inmuebles)

Distrito (Condado)/Descripción	Valor	Cantidad adeudada	Equidad	Pago mensual

Otros bienes (carros, botes, vehículos de recreación, etc.)

Distrito (Condado)/Descripción	Valor	Cantidad adeudada	Equidad	Pago mensual

Cuentas bancarias (incluyendo instituciones de ahorros y préstamos, certificados de depósito, cuentas de pensiones individuales (IRA), líneas de crédito, etc.)

Nombre de la institución	Dirección	Clase de cuenta	Balance

Ingresos mensuales

Su pago neto	$
El pago neto de su cónyuge	
Pagos de seguro social o de pensiones	
Ganancias de su negocio	
Otros ingresos (origen):	
Ingreso total	$

Gastos mensuales

Renta	$
Utilidades (electricidad, calefacción, gas, agua, teléfono)	
Transportación (gasolina, precio de autobus)	
Gastos médicos (doctores, & medicinas no pagadas por el seguro)	
Seguro (de auto, salud, vida, residencia/alquiler)	
Pagos de impuestos estimados (1040ES)	
Otros gastos (explique)	
Tarjetas de crédito	
Pagos de préstamo (no listados arriba)	

Información adicional (cambios anticipados a los ingresos, la salud, etc.)

Bajo penalidad de perjurio, yo declaro que a mi mejor conocimiento y creencia esta declaración de bienes, deudas u otra información es verdadera, correcta y completa.

Su firma	La firma de su cónyuge	Fecha

Form **656**
(Rev. Sept. 1993)

Department of the Treasury—Internal Revenue Service
Offer in Compromise

▶ **See Instructions Page 5**

(1) Name and Address of Taxpayers

For Official Use Only	
Offer is *(Check applicable box)* ☐ Cash *(Paid in full)* ☐ Deferred payment	Serial Number *(Cashier's stamp)*

(2) Social Security Number

(3) Employer Identification Number

Alpha CSED Ind. _____

To: Commissioner of Internal Revenue Service

Amount Paid
$

(4) I/we (includes all types of taxpayers) **submit this offer to compromise the tax liabilities plus any interest, penalties, additions to tax, and additional amounts required by law (tax liability)** for the tax type and period checked below: (Please mark "X" for the correct description and fill-in the correct tax period(s), adding additional periods if needed.)

☐ Income tax for the year(s) 19_____ , 19_____ , 19_____ , and 19_____

☐ Trust fund recovery penalty (formerly called the 100-percent penalty) as a responsible person of _____
_____(enter business name) for failure to pay withholding and Federal Insurance Contributions Act taxes (Social Security taxes) for the period(s) ended _____ /_____ /_____ , _____
/_____ /_____ , _____ /_____ /_____ , _____ /_____ /_____ (for example - 06/30/92)

☐ Withholding and Federal Insurance Contributions Act taxes (Social Security taxes) for the period(s) ended _____ /_____
/_____ , _____ /_____ /_____ , _____ /_____ /_____ , _____ /_____ /_____ (for example - 06/30/92)

☐ Federal Unemployment Tax Act taxes for the year(s) 19_____ , 19_____ , 19_____ , and 19_____

☐ Other (Be specific.) _____

(5) I/we offer to pay $ _____ .

If you aren't making full payment with your offer, describe below when you will make full payment (for example – within ten (10) days from the date the offer is accepted): See the instructions for Item 5.

_____

_____

_____

As required by section 6621 of the Internal Revenue Code, the Internal Revenue Service (IRS) will add interest to the offered amount from the date IRS accepts the offer until the date you completely pay the amount offered. IRS compounds interest daily, as required by section 6622 of the Internal Revenue Code.

(6) I/we submit this offer for the reason(s) checked below:

☐ Doubt as to collectibility ("I can't pay.") You must include a completed financial statement (Form 433-A and/or Form 433-B).

☐ Doubt as to liability ("I don't believe I owe this tax.") You must include a detailed explanation of the reason(s) why you believe you don't owe the tax.

IMPORTANT: SEE REVERSE FOR TERMS AND CONDITIONS

I accept waiver of the statutory period of limitations for the Internal Revenue Service.	Under penalties of perjury, I declare that I have examined this offer, including accompanying schedules and statements, and to the best of my knowledge and belief, it is true, correct and complete.	
Signature of authorized Internal Revenue Service Official	(8a) Signature of Taxpayer-proponent	Date
Title	Date	(8b) Signature of Taxpayer-proponent	Date

Dispose of prior issues.

Part 1 IRS Copy

Cat. No. 16728N

Form **656** (Rev. 9-93)

(7) By submitting this offer, **I/we understand and agree to the following terms and conditions:**

(a) I/we voluntarily submit all payments made on this offer.

(b) IRS will apply payments made under the terms of this offer in the best interests of the government.

(c) If IRS rejects the offer or I/we withdraw the offer, IRS will return any amount paid with the offer. If I/we agree in writing, IRS will apply the amount paid with the offer to the amount owed. If I/we agree to apply the payment, the date the offer is rejected or withdrawn will be considered the date of payment. I/we understand that IRS will not pay interest on any amount I/we submit with the offer.

(d) I/we will comply with all provisions of the Internal Revenue Code relating to filing my/our returns and paying my/our required taxes for five (5) years from the date IRS accepts the offer.

(e) I/we waive and agree to the suspension of any statutory periods of limitation (time limits provided for by law) for IRS assessment and collection of the tax liability for the tax periods checked in item (4).

(f) IRS will keep all payments and credits made, received, or applied to the amount being compromised before this offer was submitted. IRS will also keep any payments made under the terms of an installment agreement while this offer is pending.

(g) IRS will keep any refund, including interest, due to me/us because of overpayment of any tax or other liability, for tax periods extending through the calendar year that IRS accepts the offer. This condition doesn't apply if the offer is based only on doubt as to liability.

(h) I/we will return to IRS any refund identified in (g) received after submitting this offer. This condition doesn't apply if the offer is based only on doubt as to liability.

(i) The total amount IRS can collect under this offer can't be more than the full amount of the tax liability.

(j) I//we understand that I/we remain responsible for the full amount of the tax liability unless and until IRS accepts the offer in writing and I/we have met all the terms and conditions of the offer. IRS won't remove the original amount of the tax liability from its records until I/we have met all the terms and conditions of the offer.

(k) I/we understand that the tax I/we offer to compromise is and will remain a tax liability until I/we meet all the terms and conditions of this offer. If I/we file bankruptcy before the terms and conditions of this offer are completed, any claim the IRS files in the bankruptcy proceeding will be a tax claim.

(l) Once IRS accepts the offer in writing, I/we have no right to contest, in court or otherwise, the amount of the tax liability.

(m) The offer is pending starting with the date an authorized IRS official signs this form and accepts my/our waiver of the statutory periods of limitation. The offer remains pending until an authorized IRS official accepts, rejects, or withdraws the offer in writing. If I/we appeal the IRS decision on the offer, IRS will continue to treat the offer as pending until the Appeals Office accepts or rejects the offer in writing. If I/we don't file a protest within 30 days of the date IRS notifies me/us of the right to protest the decision, I/we waive the right to a hearing before the Appeals Office about this offer in compromise.

(n) The waiver and suspension of any statutory periods of limitation for assessment and collection of the amount of the tax liability described in item (4), continues to apply:

(i) while the offer is pending (see (m) above),

(ii) during the time I/we haven't paid all of the amount offered,

(iii) during the time I/we haven't completed all terms and conditions of the offer, and

(iv) for one additional year beyond the time periods identified in (i), (ii), and (iii) above.

(o) If I/we fail to meet any of the terms and conditions of the offer, the offer is in default, and IRS may:

(i) immediately file suit to collect the entire unpaid balance of the offer;

(ii) immediately file suit to collect an amount equal to the original amount of the tax liability as liquidated damages, minus any payments already received under the terms of this offer;

(iii) disregard the amount of the offer and apply all amounts already paid under the offer against the original amount of tax liability;

(iv) file suit or levy to collect the original amount of the tax liability, without further notice of any kind.

IRS will continue to add interest, as required by section 6621 of the Internal Revenue Code, on the amount IRS determines is due after default. IRS will add interest from the date the offer is defaulted until I/we completely satisfy the amount owed. IRS compounds interest daily, as required by section 6622 of the Internal Revenue Code.

INSTRUCTIONS

Background

Section 7122 of the Internal Revenue Code allows delegated Internal Revenue Service (IRS) officials to compromise a tax liability before we refer it to the Department of Justice. The term "tax liability" is the total amount a taxpayer owes, including taxes, penalties, interest, additions to tax, and additional amounts required by law.

Reasons for Compromise

We (IRS) can compromise the amount owed for the following reasons:

(1) Doubt as to collectibility, i.e., doubt that we can collect the full amount owed
("I can't pay") and/or

(2) Doubt as to liability, i.e., doubt as to whether you owe the amount (I don't believe I owe this tax").

We can't legally accept a compromise based on doubt as to collectibility when there is no doubt that we can collect the full amount owed. We also can't legally accept a compromise based on doubt as to liability when the amount owed has already been decided in court.

If you submit an offer based on doubt as to liability, you must include a written statement describing in detail why you don't believe you owe the liability.

IRS Policy

We will accept an offer in compromise when it is unlikely that we can collect the full amount owed and the amount you offered reasonably reflects collection potential. An offer in compromise is an alternative to declaring a case currently not collectible or to a long-term installment agreement. Our goal is to collect what we can at the earliest possible time with the least cost to the government.

In delinquent tax cases where an offer in compromise appears to be a workable solution, an IRS employee will discuss the compromise alternative with you and help prepare the required forms if necessary. You are responsible for making the first specific proposal for compromise.

Our offer in compromise process will be successful only if you make an adequate compromise proposal consistent with your ability to pay and we make prompt and reasonable decisions. Taxpayers are expected to provide reasonable documentation to verify their ability to pay. The goal is a compromise which is in the best interest of both the taxpayer and IRS. Acceptance of an adequate offer also creates a fresh start for the taxpayer regarding future filing and payment requirements.

How to Figure An Acceptable Offer

An acceptable offer must include all amounts available from the following sources: (You may use the spaces provided to figure the minimum amount you must offer.)

(1) The **liquidating value of your assets** (value if you are forced to sell) minus debts against specific assets that have priority over IRS.

Liquidating value of assets	$ _____
Minus: Debts with priority	$ _____
Value of available assets	$ _____

NOTE: The following examples are debts which you should NOT subtract because IRS has priority over them:

— amounts you owe on credit cards;

— loans you secured without pledging assets as security;

— any amount you borrowed after we recorded a Notice of Federal Tax Lien.

(2) The **amount we could collect from your present and future income**. Generally, the collectible amount is your income minus necessary living expenses. We usually consider what we can collect over five years. Figure the amount as follows:
Average monthly income minus necessary expenses
x 60 months = value of income
$ _____

(3) The **amount collectible from third parties**. We may be able to collect part or all of the amount you owe from third parties through the trust fund recovery penalty or transferee liabilities (assets you transferred below market value or transferred assets you still use). Show any amount that we might collect from such sources.
$ _____

(4) **Assets or income that are available to you but may not be available to IRS** for direct collection action, e.g., property outside the United States. Show any amount you have access to.
$ _____

(5) **Minimum offer** (total items (1) through (4))
$ _____

If your offer is less than the minimum offer amount from item (5), we can't process your offer. If the minimum offer total is more than the amount owed, IRS can't process your offer. You must pay the full amount owed. We will return this form to you.

Offer Investigation

IRS will investigate your offer to determine if the offered amount is the maximum you can pay. This means that we may ask for information to verify your financial statement (Form 433-A or 433-B). We may ask you to increase the amount of your offer or to change the terms of payment, or we may find that we can't accept your offer.

Questions IRS Will Consider

The IRS goal is a compromise that is in the best interest of both the government and the taxpayer. It is your responsibility to show us why it would be in the government's best interest to accept your proposal. When we consider your offer we must ask the following questions:

(1) Could we collect the entire amount owed through liquidation of your assets or through an installment agreement based on your present and future income? If the answer is "yes," we can't accept your offer.

(2) Could we collect more from your assets and future income than you offered? If the answer is "yes", you must offer a larger amount or we will reject your offer.

(3) Would we be better off waiting until a future date because the evidence shows that collection in the future would result in more money than you now offer? If the answer is "yes", you must offer a larger amount or we will reject your offer.

(4) Would the taxpaying public believe that acceptance of your offer was a reasonable action? If the answer is "no", we will reject your offer.

The fact that you currently have no assets or income doesn't mean that IRS should simply accept anything that you offer because that is all we can collect now. IRS won't decide that "something is better than nothing". For example, it is not usually in our best interest to accept $25 on a $1,000 liability or $1,000 on a $100,000 liability. It is usually better for us to reject a nominal amount and wait to see what collection potential arises during the remainder of our ten year collection period.

As we state in our policy, we will accept your offer only if you submit a legitimate proposal that is in the government's best interest.

Possible Additional Requirements

Generally IRS believes that you benefit if we accept your offer because you can then manage your finances without the burden of a tax liability. Therefore, we may require you to submit one of the following agreements before we accept your offer:

(1) A written agreement that requires you to pay a percentage of future earnings.

(2) A written agreement to give up certain present or potential tax benefits.

Tax Compliance

We won't accept your offer if you haven't filed all required returns. In addition, we will expect you to have paid all estimated tax payments and Federal tax deposits due as of the date you file the offer. Please note that the terms of the offer also require your future compliance (i.e., filing and paying) for five years after acceptance.

Suspending Collection

Submitting an offer doesn't automatically suspend our collection activity. If there is any indication that you filed the offer only to delay collection of the tax or that delay would interfere with our ability to collect the tax, we will continue collection efforts. **If you agreed to make installment payments before you submitted your offer, you should continue making those payments.**

How to Complete Form 656

(Item 1) Enter your full name and address. If the tax liability is owed jointly by a husband and wife and both wish to make an offer, show both names. If you owe one amount by yourself (such as employment taxes), and at the same time owe another amount jointly (such as income taxes), but only one person is submitting an offer, complete only one Form 656. If you owe one amount yourself and another amount jointly, and both joint parties submit an offer, you must complete two Forms 656, one for the separate amount and one for the joint amount.

(Item 2) Please enter a social security number for each taxpayer.

(Item 3) If you operate a business, please enter your employer identification number.

(Item 4) Please mark "X" for all liabilities you offer to compromise, listing the specific periods involved. If the type of liability is not preprinted, please specify the type of tax and periods of liability.

(Item 5) Please enter the total amount you offer. Don't include any amount you have already paid or that IRS has already collected. If you send the whole amount with your offer, make no further entry in item 5. If you aren't sending the whole amount with your offer, please describe the details of your offer, including:

(1) Any amount you deposited with this offer.

(2) Any amount you deposited for a prior offer and now want applied to this offer.

(3) The amount of any subsequent payment(s) you will make and the date you will make them.

You should pay the full amount of the offer in the shortest possible time. Under no circumstances should payment extend beyond two years. However, if we find that

you can pay in a shorter time, we will require you to pay the full amount offered in less than two years, or we will reject your offer. If you pay earlier, it will reduce the amount of interest due, since IRS charges interest from the date of acceptance until the date you pay the full amount offered.

Item 5 Examples:

(1) $30,000: $5,000 deposited with the offer and $25,000 to be paid within ninety (90) days from the date of acceptance.

(2) $103,000: To be paid within ninety (90) days from the date of acceptance.

(3) $50,000: $10,000 deposited with the offer, $20,000 to be paid within thirty (30) days from the date of acceptance, and $20,000 to be paid within sixty (60) days from the date of acceptance.

If you send a payment with your offer or at any later date, IRS will deposit it in a special fund while we consider your offer. IRS won't pay interest whether your payment is ultimately applied to an accepted offer, applied to the amount owed (if you agree), or returned to you. When IRS cashes your check, that doesn't mean your offer is accepted.

(Item 6) Please check one or both reasons.

(Item 7) It is important that you understand that when you make this offer, you are agreeing that:

(a) Any statutory period for assessment and collection of the amount owed is suspended while the offer is pending, during the time you haven't fulfilled any term or condition of the offer, and for one year after the offer is no longer pending and after the date you fulfill all terms and conditions of the offer.

(b) You won't contest, in court or otherwise, the amount owed if we accept your offer.

(c) You give up any overpayments (i.e., refunds) for all tax periods prior to and including the year IRS accepts your offer.

(d) IRS can reinstate the entire amount owed if you don't comply with all the terms and conditions of the offer, including the requirement to file returns and pay tax for five years.

(Item 8) All persons submitting the offer should sign and date Form 656.

Where to File Your Offer

You should file your offer in compromise in duplicate in the IRS district office in your area. If you have been working with a specific IRS employee on your case, you should file the offer with that employee.

Financial Statement

If you submit your offer on the basis of doubt as to collectibility, you must also submit Form 433-A, Collection Information

Statement for Individuals, or Form 433-B, Collection Information Statement for Businesses. If you are an individual and you operate a business, you must submit both forms.

You must complete all blocks on these forms. Write N/A (not applicable) in any blocks that don't affect you. Please pay particular attention to line 26, Other Assets, on Form 433-A and line 24, Other Assets, on Form 433-B. You should list pension plans, profit sharing plans, and Individual Retirement Accounts on those lines. When you send Form 433-A and/or Form 433-B, you should include documentation to verify values of assets, encumbrances, and income and expense information. When you determine the "Current Market Value" of assets on Forms 433-A and 433-B, use the "quick sale" or "liquidating value."

Returning Your Offer

We will return your offer to you for clarification if we can't process it because it contains any of the following problems:

(1) the taxpayer isn't adequately identified,

(2) the liabilities to compromise aren't identified,

(3) no amount is offered,

(4) appropriate signatures aren't present,

(5) financial statements aren't submitted,

(6) the amount offered doesn't equal the minimum offer amount required (See **How to Figure An Acceptable Offer** above). We figure that amount directly from the information you submit on Forms 433-A and 433-B.

If We Reject Your Offer

If you submit an offer based on doubt that we can collect the full amount owed and we find that you can pay more than you offered, we will reject your offer. We will also reject an offer based on doubt that you owe the liability if we still believe that you do owe it. In either case, you may have the right to protest our decision. However, you don't have the right to protest our decision if you haven't filed all required returns or if you don't provide reasonable documentation to verify the amount you can pay.

If you submit a protest, an appeals officer will consider your case. We include specific instructions about filing a protest if we decide to reject your offer.

Public Disclosure

Please note that the law requires that all accepted offers in compromise be available for review by the general public. Therefore, it is possible that the details of your personal financial affairs may become publicly known.

Form **843**

(Rev. January 1994)

Department of the Treasury
Internal Revenue Service

Claim for Refund and Request for Abatement

▶ See separate instructions.

OMB No. 1545-0024
Expires 1-31-97

Use Form 843 only if your claim involves one of the taxes shown on line 3a or a refund or abatement of interest, penalties, or additions to tax on line 4a.

Note: Do not use Form 843 if your claim is for—
- An overpayment of income taxes;
- A refund of fuel taxes; or
- An overpayment of excise taxes reported on Form 720, 730, or 2290.

Please type or print		
Name of claimant		Your social security number
Address (number, street, and room or suite no.)		Spouse's social security number
City or town, state, and ZIP code		Employer identification number
Name and address shown on return if different from above		Daytime telephone number ( )

1	Period—prepare a separate Form 843 for each tax period	2	Amount to be refunded or abated
	From , 19 , to , 19		$

3a Type of tax, penalty, or addition to tax:

☐ Employment   ☐ Estate   ☐ Gift   ☐ Excise (other than excise taxes reported on Form 720, 730, or 2290)

☐ Penalty IRC section ▶ _____

b Type of return filed (see instructions):

☐ 706   ☐ 709   ☐ 940   ☐ 941   ☐ 990-PF   ☐ 4720   ☐ Other (specify)

4a Request for abatement or refund of:

☐ Interest caused by IRS errors and delays (under Rev. Proc. 87-42—see instructions).

☐ A penalty or addition to tax as a result of erroneous advice from the IRS.

b Dates of payment ▶

5 **Explanations and additional claims.** Explain why you believe this claim should be allowed, and show computation of tax refund or abatement of interest, penalty, or addition to tax.

Signature. If you are filing Form 843 to request a refund or abatement relating to a joint return, both you and your spouse must sign the claim. Claims filed by corporations must be signed by a corporate officer authorized to sign, and the signature must be accompanied by the officer's title.

Under penalties of perjury, I declare that I have examined this claim, including accompanying schedules and statements, and, to the best of my knowledge and belief, it is true, correct, and complete.

Director's Stamp
(Date received)

Signature (Title, if applicable. Claims by corporations must be signed by an officer.)   Date

Signature   Date

For Paperwork Reduction Act Notice, see separate instructions.   Cat. No. 10180R   Form **843** (Rev. 1-94)

Form **911**
(Rev. January 1994)

Department of the Treasury – Internal Revenue Service

Application for Taxpayer Assistance Order *(ATAO)*
(Taxpayer's Application for Relief from Hardship)

If sending Form 911 with another form or letter, put Form 911 on top.

Note: If you have not tried to obtain relief from the IRS office that contacted you, use of this form may not be necessary. Use this form only after reading the instructions for When To Use This Form. Filing this application may affect the statutory period of limitations. (See instructions for line 14.)

Section I.   Taxpayer Information

1. Name*(s)* as shown on tax return	2. Your Social Security Number	4. Tax form
	3. Social Security of Spouse Shown in 1.	5. Tax period ended

6. Current mailing address (number & street). For P.O. Box, see instructions	Apt. No.	8. Employer identification number, if applicable.
7. City, town or post office, state and ZIP Code		9. Person to contact

If the above address is different from that shown on latest filed tax return and you want us to update our records with this new address, check here.........❏	10.Daytime telephone number ( )	11. Best time to call

12. Description of significant hardship *(If more space is needed, attach additional sheets.)*

A T A O

13. Description of relief requested *(If more space is needed, attach additional sheets.)*

14. Signature of taxpayer or Corporate Officer *(See instructions.)*	15. Date	16. Signature of spouse shown in block 1	17. Date

Section II.   Representative Information *(If applicable)*

18. Name of authorized representative (Must be same as on Form 2848 or 8821)	22. Firm name
19. Centralized Authorization File (CAF) number	23. Mailing address

20. Daytime telephone number ( )	21. Best time to call	

24. Representative Signature	25. Date

Section III.   (For Internal Revenue Service only)

26. Name of initiating employee	27. ❏ IRS Identified ❏ Taxpayer request	28. Telephone ( )	29. Function	30. Office	31. Date

Cat. No. 16965S

Form **911** (Rev. 1-94)

Instructions

When To Use This Form: Use this form to apply for relief from a **significant hardship** which may have already occurred or is about to occur if the IRS takes or fails to take certain actions. A significant hardship normally means not being able to provide the necessities of life for you or your family. Examples of such necessities include, but are not limited to: food, shelter, clothing, or medical care. You may use this form at any time. Instead of using this form, **however, the IRS prefers that requests for relief first be made with the IRS office that most recently contacted you.** In most cases, the relief needed can be secured directly from the appropriate IRS employee. For example, Collection employees handle requests for payment arrangements on late taxes or releases of levy on wages, salaries, or bank accounts; Taxpayer Service employees handle requests for immediate refunds of overpaid taxes; Examination employees handle requests for review of additional tax assessments when the taxpayer has had no opportunity to present proof of claimed deductions.

If an IRS office will not grant the relief requested, or will not grant the relief in time to avoid the significant hardship, you may submit this form. No enforcement action will be taken while we are reviewing your application.

Note: Do not use this application to change the amount of any tax you owe. If you disagree with the amount of tax assessed, see **Publication 1, Your Rights as a Taxpayer.**

Where To Submit This Form: Submit this application to the Internal Revenue Service, Problem Resolution Office, in the district where you live. For the address of the Problem Resolution Office in your district or for more information, call the local Taxpayer Assistance number in your local telephone directory or 1-800-829-1040.

Overseas Taxpayers: Taxpayers residing overseas should submit this application to the Internal Revenue Service., Problem Resolution Office, Assistant Commissioner (International), P.O. Box 44817, L'Enfant Plaza Station, Washington, D.C. 20026-4817.

Caution: Incomplete applications or applications submitted to the incorrect office may result in delays. If you do not hear from us within one week of submitting Form 911, please contact the Problem Resolution Office where you sent your application.

Section I. Taxpayer Information

1. Name(s) as shown on tax return. Enter your name as it appeared on the tax return for each period you are asking for help even if your name has changed since the return was submitted. If you filed a joint return, enter both names.

4. Tax form. Enter the tax form number of the form for which you are requesting assistance. For example, if you are requesting assistance for a problem involving an individual income tax return, enter "1040." If your problem involves more than one tax form, include the information in block 12.

5. Tax period ended. If you are requesting assistance on an annually filed return, enter the calendar year or the ending date of the fiscal year for that return. If the problem concerns a return filed quarterly, enter the ending date of the quarter involved. File only one Form 911 even if multiple tax periods are involved. If the problem involves more than one tax period, include the information in block 12.

6. Current mailing address (number and street). If your post office does not deliver mail to your street address and you have a P.O. box, show your box number instead of your street address.

8. Employer Identification Number. Enter the employer identification number (*EIN)* of the business, corporation, trust, etc., for the name you showed in block 1.

9. Person to contact. Enter the name of the person to contact about the problem. In the case of businesses, corporations, trusts, estates, etc., enter the name of a responsible official.

10. Daytime telephone number. Enter the daytime telephone number, including area code, of the person to contact.

12. Description of significant hardship. Describe the action(s) being taken (or not being taken) by the Internal Revenue Service that are causing you significant hardship. If you know it, include the name of the person, office, telephone number, and/or address of the last contact you had with IRS regarding this problem.

13. Description of relief requested. Be specific. If your remaining income after paying expenses is too little to meet an IRS payment, give the details. Describe the action you want the IRS to take.

14. and 16. Signature(s) If you filed a joint return it is not necessary for both you and your spouse to sign this application for your account to be reviewed. If you sign the application the IRS **may** suspend applicable statutory periods of limitations for the assessment of additional taxes and for the collection of taxes. If the taxpayer is your dependent child who cannot sign this application because of age, **or someone incapable of signing the application because of some other reason,** you may sign the taxpayer's name in the space provided followed by the words "By (your signature), parent (or guardian)." If the application is being made for other than the individual taxpayer, a person having authority to sign the return should sign this form. Enter the date Form 911 is signed.

Section II. Representative Information

Taxpayers: If you wish to have a representative act in your behalf, you must give your representative power of attorney or tax information authorization for the tax form(s) and period(s) involved. (*See Form 2848, Power of Attorney and Declaration of Representative and Instructions or Form 8821, Tax Information Authorization, for more information.*)

Representatives: If you are an authorized representative submitting this request on behalf of the taxpayer identified in Section I, complete blocks 18 through 25, attach a copy of Form 2848, Form 8821, or the power of attorney. Enter your Centralized Authorization File (*CAF)* number in block 19. The CAF number is the unique number that Internal Revenue Service assigns to a representative after a valid Form 2848 or Form 8821 is filed with an IRS office.

(For IRS Use Only)

ATAO Code	How recieved	Date of Determination	PRO signature

Form **911** (Rev. 1-94)

Form 1040X

(Rev. October 1993)

Amended U.S. Individual Income Tax Return

Department of the Treasury—Internal Revenue Service

▶ See separate instructions.

OMB No. 1545-0091
Expires 10-31-96

This return is for calendar year ▶ 19_____ , OR fiscal year ended ▶ _____ , 19_____ .

Please print or type

Your first name and initial	Last name
Your social security number	
If a joint return, spouse's first name and initial	Last name
Spouse's social security number	
Home address (number and street). If you have a P.O. box, see instructions.	Apt. no.
Telephone number (optional) ( )	
City, town or post office, state, and ZIP code. If you have a foreign address, see instructions.	For Paperwork Reduction Act Notice, see page 1 of separate instructions.

Enter name and address as shown on original return. If same as above, write "Same." If changing from separate to joint return, enter names and addresses from original returns.

A Service center where original return was filed

B Has original return been changed or audited by the IRS? ☐ Yes ☐ No
If "No," have you been notified that it will be? . . . . ☐ Yes ☐ No
If "Yes," identify the IRS office ▶

C Are you amending your return to include any item (loss, credit, deduction, other tax benefit, or income) relating to a tax shelter required to be registered? . . . . ☐ Yes ☐ No
If "Yes," you must attach **Form 8271**, Investor Reporting of Tax Shelter Registration Number.

D Filing status claimed. **Note:** *You cannot change from joint to separate returns after the due date has passed.*

On original return ▶ ☐ Single ☐ Married filing joint return ☐ Married filing separate return ☐ Head of household ☐ Qualifying widow(er)

On this return ▶ ☐ Single ☐ Married filing joint return ☐ Married filing separate return ☐ Head of household ☐ Qualifying widow(er)

Income and Deductions (see instructions)

Caution: *Be sure to complete Part II on page 2.*

			A. As originally reported or as previously adjusted (see instructions)	B. Net change— Increase or (Decrease)—explain on page 2	C. Correct amount
1	Total income	1			
2	Total adjustments (such as IRA deduction, alimony paid, etc.)	2			
3	Adjusted gross income. Subtract line 2 from line 1 . . .	3			
4	Itemized deductions or standard deduction	4			
5	Subtract line 4 from line 3	5			
6	Exemptions. If changing, fill in Parts I and II on page 2 . .	6			
7	Taxable income. Subtract line 6 from line 5	7			
8	Tax (see instructions). Method used in col. C ..!...................	8			
9	Credits (see instructions)	9			
10	Subtract line 9 from line 8. Enter the result but not less than zero .	10			
11	Other taxes (such as self-employment tax, alternative minimum tax, etc.)	11			
12	Total tax. Add lines 10 and 11	12			
13	Federal income tax withheld and excess social security, Medicare, and RRTA taxes withheld. If changing, see instructions	13			
14	Estimated tax payments	14			
15	Earned income credit	15			
16	Credits for Federal tax paid on fuels, regulated investment company, etc.	16			
17	Amount paid with Form 4868, Form 2688, or Form 2350 (application for extension of time to file) .	17		
18	Amount paid with original return plus additional tax paid after it was filed	18		
19	Total payments. Add lines 13 through 18 in column C	19		

Tax Liability (lines 8–12)

Payments (lines 13–19)

Refund or Amount You Owe

20	Overpayment, if any, as shown on original return or as previously adjusted by the IRS . . .	20	
21	Subtract line 20 from line 19 (see instructions)	21	
22	**AMOUNT YOU OWE.** If line 12, column C, is more than line 21, enter the difference and see instructions .	22	
23	**REFUND** to be received. If line 12, column C, is less than line 21, enter the difference . . .	23	

Sign Here

Keep a copy of this return for your records.

Under penalties of perjury, I declare that I have filed an original return and that I have examined this amended return, including accompanying schedules and statements, and to the best of my knowledge and belief, this amended return is true, correct, and complete. Declaration of preparer (other than taxpayer) is based on all information of which the preparer has any knowledge.

▶ _____ Your signature   Date

▶ _____ Spouse's signature. If a joint return, BOTH must sign.   Date

Paid Preparer's Use Only

Preparer's signature ▶	Date	Check if self-employed ☐	Preparer's social security no.
Firm's name (or yours if self-employed) and address ▶		E.I. No.	
		ZIP code	

Cat. No. 11360L

Form **1040X** (Rev. 10-93)

Part I Exemptions. See Form 1040 or Form 1040A instructions.	**A.** Number originally reported	**B.** Net change	**C.** Correct number
If you are not changing your exemptions, do not complete this part. **If claiming more exemptions,** complete lines 24–30 and, if applicable, line 31. **If claiming fewer exemptions,** complete lines 24–29.			

24 Yourself and spouse **24**			
Caution: *If your parents (or someone else) can claim you as a dependent (even if they chose not to), you cannot claim an exemption for yourself.*			
25 Your dependent children who lived with you **25**			
26 Your dependent children who did not live with you due to divorce or separation **26**			
27 Other dependents **27**			
28 Total number of exemptions. Add lines 24 through 27 . . . . . **28**			

29 Multiply the number of exemptions claimed on line 28 by the amount listed below for the tax year you are amending. Enter the result here and on line 6.

Tax Year	Exemption Amount	But see the instructions if the amount on line 3 is over:
1993	$2,350	$81,350
1992	2,300	78,950
1991	2,150	75,000
1990	2,050	Not applicable for tax year 1990.

29 [ ]

30 Dependents (children and other) not claimed on original return:

(a) Dependent's name (first, initial, and last name)	(b) Check if under age 1 (under age 2 if a 1990 return)	(c) If age 1 or older (age 2 or older if a 1990 return), enter dependent's social security number	(d) Dependent's relationship to you	(e) No. of months lived in your home

No. of your children on line 30 who lived with you . . ▶ [ ]

No. of your children on line 30 who **didn't** live with you due to divorce or separation (see instructions) ▶ [ ]

No. of dependents on line 30 not entered above . ▶ [ ]

31 If your child listed on line 30 didn't live with you but is claimed as your dependent under a pre-1985 agreement, check here ▶ [ ]

Part II Explanation of Changes to Income, Deductions, and Credits

Enter the line number from page 1 for each item you are changing and give the reason for each change. Attach all supporting forms and schedules for items changed. If you don't, your Form 1040X may be returned. Be sure to include your name and social security number on any attachments.

If the change pertains to a net operating loss carryback or a general business credit carryback, attach the schedule or form that shows the year in which the loss or credit occurred. See instructions. Also, check here . . . . ▶ [ ]

_____

_____

_____

_____

_____

_____

_____

_____

Part III Presidential Election Campaign Fund. Checking below will not increase your tax or reduce your refund.

If you did not previously want to have $3 (or $1 if a 1992 return) go to the fund but now want to, check here . . . . ▶ [ ] $3 for 1993   [ ] $1 for 1992

If a joint return and your spouse did not previously want to have $3 (or $1 if a 1992 return) go to the fund but now wants to, check here . . . . ▶ [ ] $3 for 1993   [ ] $1 for 1992

Department of the Treasury
Internal Revenue Service

Instructions for Form 1040X
(Revised October 1993)
Amended U.S. Individual Income Tax Return
Section references are to the Internal Revenue Code.

Paperwork Reduction Act Notice

We ask for the information on this form to carry out the Internal Revenue laws of the United States. You are required to give us the information. We need it to ensure that you are complying with these laws and to allow us to figure and collect the right amount of tax.

The time needed to complete and file this form will vary depending on individual circumstances. The estimated average time is: **Recordkeeping,** 1 hr., 12 min.; **Learning about the law or the form,** 20 min.; **Preparing the form,** 1 hr., 11 min.; and **Copying, assembling, and sending the form to the IRS,** 35 min.

If you have comments concerning the accuracy of these time estimates or suggestions for making this form more simple, we would be happy to hear from you. You can write to both the **Internal Revenue Service,** Attention: Reports Clearance Officer, PC:FP, Washington, DC 20224; and the **Office of Management and Budget,** Paperwork Reduction Project (1545-0091), Washington, DC 20503. **DO NOT** send this form to either of these offices. Instead, see **Where To File** on page 2.

General Instructions

Purpose of Form

Use Form 1040X to correct **Form 1040, Form 1040A, Form 1040EZ, Form 1040NR,** or **Form 1040PC.** If you used TeleFile to file your original return, you can call 1-800-829-1040 for details on how to complete Form 1040X. You may also use Form 1040X to make certain elections after the prescribed deadline. For details, see Rev. Proc. 92-85, 1992-2 C.B. 490.

File a separate Form 1040X for each year you are amending. If you are changing your Federal return, you may also have to change your state return. Please note that it often takes 2 to 3 months to process Form 1040X.

Filing Form 1045

You may use **Form 1045,** Application for Tentative Refund, instead of Form 1040X if:

● You are applying for a refund resulting from a net operating loss or general business credit carryback, AND

● Less than 1 year has elapsed since the end of the year in which the loss or credit arose.

For more details, see the separate instructions for Form 1045.

When To File

File Form 1040X only after you have filed your original return. Generally, Form 1040X must be filed within 3 years after the date the original return was filed, or within 2 years after the date the tax was paid, whichever is later. A return filed early is considered filed on the date it was due.

A Form 1040X based on a bad debt or worthless security must generally be filed within 7 years after the due date of the return for the tax year in which the debt or security became worthless. For more details, see section 6511.

A Form 1040X based on a net operating loss carryback or a general business credit carryback generally must be filed within 3 years after the due date of the return for the tax year of the net operating loss or unused credit.

Carryback Claims

You must attach copies of the following to Form 1040X if it is used as a carryback claim.

● Pages 1 and 2 of Form 1040 and Schedules A and D, if applicable, for the year in which the loss or credit originated. At the top of these forms, write "Attachment to Form 1040X—Copy Only—Do Not Process."

● Any Schedules K-1 you received from any partnership, S corporation, estate, or trust for the year of the loss or credit that contribute to the loss or credit carryback.

● Any form or schedule from which the carryback results such as Form 3800 or Schedule C or F.

● The forms or schedules for items refigured in the carryback year such as Form 6251, Form 3468, or Schedule A.

All information described above must be attached to your Form 1040X, if applicable, or your Form 1040X will be returned for the attachments.

Note: *If you filed a joint or separate return for some, but not all, of the years involved in figuring the loss or credit carryback, you may have to allocate your income, deductions, and credits. For details, get the publication that explains the type of carryback you are claiming. For example, get **Pub. 536,** Net Operating Losses, if you are claiming a net operating loss carryback, or **Pub. 514,** Foreign Tax Credit for Individuals, for a foreign tax credit carryback.*

Net Operating Loss

Attach a computation of your net operating loss using **Schedule A (Form 1045)** and, if applicable, your net operating loss carryover using **Schedule B (Form 1045).**

A refund based on a net operating loss should not include the refund of any self-employment tax reported on line 11 of Form 1040X. For more details, see Pub. 536.

Other Claims

Injured Spouse Claim.—Do not use Form 1040X to file an injured spouse claim. Instead, file only **Form 8379,** Injured Spouse Claim and Allocation.

Resident and Nonresident Aliens.— Use Form 1040X to amend **Form 1040NR,** U.S. Nonresident Alien Income Tax Return. Also, use Form 1040X if you filed Form 1040NR and you should have filed a Form 1040, 1040A, or 1040EZ, or vice versa. For details on resident and nonresident alien filing requirements, get **Pub. 519,** U.S. Tax Guide for Aliens.

To amend Form 1040NR or to file the correct return, you must do the following:

1. On Form 1040X, fill in your name, address, and identifying or social security number. Also, complete lines A and B, and Part II on page 2. Include in Part II an explanation for the changes or corrections made.

2. Attach the corrected return (Form 1040, Form 1040NR, etc.) to Form

1040X. Write "Amended" across the top of the corrected return.

3. If Form 1040X includes a Form 1040NR, file it with the Internal Revenue Service, Philadelphia, PA 19255, U.S.A. Otherwise, file Form 1040X with the service center for the place where you live. For the address, see **Where To File** below.

Where To File

Mail your return to the **Internal Revenue Service Center** for the place where you live. No street address is needed.

If you live in:	Use this address:
Florida, Georgia, South Carolina	Atlanta, GA 39901
New Jersey, New York (New York City and counties of Nassau, Rockland, Suffolk, and Westchester)	Holtsville, NY 00501
New York (all other counties), Connecticut, Maine, Massachusetts, New Hampshire, Rhode Island, Vermont	Andover, MA 05501
Illinois, Iowa, Minnesota, Missouri, Wisconsin	Kansas City, MO 64999
Delaware, District of Columbia, Maryland, Pennsylvania, Virginia	Philadelphia, PA 19255
Indiana, Kentucky, Michigan, Ohio, West Virginia	Cincinnati, OH 45999
Kansas, New Mexico, Oklahoma, Texas	Austin, TX 73301
Alabama, Arkansas, Louisiana, Mississippi, North Carolina, Tennessee	Memphis, TN 37501
Alaska, Arizona, California (counties of Alpine, Amador, Butte, Calaveras, Colusa, Contra Costa, Del Norte, El Dorado, Glenn, Humboldt, Lake, Lassen, Marin, Mendocino, Modoc, Napa, Nevada, Placer, Plumas, Sacramento, San Joaquin, Shasta, Sierra, Siskiyou, Solano, Sonoma, Sutter, Tehama, Trinity, Yolo, and Yuba), Colorado, Idaho, Montana, Nebraska, Nevada, North Dakota, Oregon, South Dakota, Utah, Washington, Wyoming	Ogden, UT 84201
California (all other counties), Hawaii	Fresno, CA 93888
American Samoa	Philadelphia, PA 19255
Guam: Permanent residents	Department of Revenue and Taxation Government of Guam 378 Chalan San Antonio Tamuning, GU 96911

Guam: Nonpermanent residents Puerto Rico (or if excluding income under section 933) Virgin Islands: Nonpermanent residents	Philadelphia, PA 19255
Virgin Islands: Permanent residents	V.I. Bureau of Internal Revenue Lockhart Gardens No. 1-A Charlotte Amalie St. Thomas, VI 00802
Foreign country: U.S. citizens and those filing Form 2555, Form 2555-EZ, or Form 4563	Philadelphia, PA 19255
All A.P.O. and F.P.O. addresses	Philadelphia, PA 19255

Information on Income, Deductions, etc.

If you have questions, such as what income is taxable or what expenses are deductible, the instructions for the return you are amending may help you. Be sure to use the Tax Table or Tax Rate Schedules for the right year to figure the corrected tax. The related schedules and forms may also help you. To get prior year forms, schedules, and instructions, call 1-800-TAX-FORM (1-800-829-3676).

Death of Taxpayer

If you are filing a Form 1040X for a deceased taxpayer, write **"DECEASED,"** the taxpayer's name, and the date of death across the top of Form 1040X.

If you are filing Form 1040X as a surviving spouse filing a joint return with the deceased, write "Filing as surviving spouse" in the area where you sign the return. If someone else is the personal representative, he or she must also sign.

Claiming a Refund for a Deceased Taxpayer.—If you are a surviving spouse filing a joint return with the deceased, file only Form 1040X to claim the refund. If you are a court-appointed personal representative or any other person claiming a deceased taxpayer's refund, file Form 1040X and attach **Form 1310,** Statement of Person Claiming a Refund Due a Deceased Taxpayer, and any other information required by its instructions.

For more details, get **Pub. 559,** Survivors, Executors, and Administrators.

Paid Preparers

Generally, anyone you pay to prepare your return must sign it. A preparer who is required to sign your return must sign it by hand in the space provided (signature stamps or labels cannot be used) and give you a copy of the return for your records. Someone who prepares your return for you but does not charge you should not sign your return.

Specific Instructions

Above your name, enter the calendar year or fiscal year of the return you are amending.

Name, Address, and Social Security Number

If amending a joint return, list your names and social security numbers in the same order as shown on the original return. If changing from a separate to a joint return and your spouse did not file an original return, enter your name and social security number first.

P.O. Box.—If your post office does not deliver mail to your home and you have a P.O. box, enter the box number instead of your home address.

Foreign Address.—If your address is outside the United States or its possessions or territories, enter the information on the line for "City, town or post office, state, and ZIP code" in the following order: city, province or state, postal code, and the name of the country. **Do not** abbreviate the country name.

Line D—Filing Status

If you and your spouse are changing from separate returns to a joint return, enter in column A the amounts from your return as originally filed or as previously adjusted (either by you or the IRS). Next, combine the amounts from your spouse's return as originally filed or as previously adjusted with any other changes you or your spouse are making to determine the amounts to enter in column B. If your spouse did not file an original return, include your spouse's income, deductions, credits, other taxes, etc., in determining the amounts to enter in column B. Then, read the instructions for column C on this page to figure the amounts to enter in that column. Both of you must sign Form 1040X. If there is any tax due, it must be paid in full.

Columns A–C

In **column A,** enter the amounts from your return as originally filed or as you later amended it. If your return was changed or audited by the IRS, enter the adjusted amounts.

In **column B,** enter the net increase or net decrease for each line you are changing. Show all decreases in parentheses. Explain each change in Part II on page 2 of the form and attach any related schedule or form. For example, if you are amending your return to itemize deductions, attach **Schedule A (Form 1040).** If you need more space, show the required information on an attached statement.

For **column C,** add the increase in column B to the amount in column A, or subtract the column B decrease from column A. For any item you do not change, enter the amount from column A in column C.

Example. Anna Arbor had originally reported $11,000 as her total income on her 1992 Form 1040EZ. She received an additional Form W-2 for $500 after she filed her tax return. Ms. Arbor would complete line 1 of Form 1040X as follows:

	Col. A	Col. B	Col. C
Line 1	$11,000	$500	$11,500

Ms. Arbor would also report any additional income tax withheld on line 13 in column B.

Lines 1–31

If you are changing only credits or other taxes, skip lines 1–7 and start with line 8. If changing only payments, skip lines 1–11 and start with line 12.

If you are only providing additional information and there are no changes to the amounts you originally reported, skip lines 1–31 and complete Part II and, if applicable, Part III.

Line 1

Enter income from all sources, such as wages, taxable interest, dividends, and net profit from business. On Form 1040, use line 23.

On Form 1040A, use line 14.

On Form 1040EZ for 1990–1992, use line 3. For 1993, use line 4.

If you are correcting wages or other employee compensation, attach the first copy or Copy B of all additional or corrected Forms W-2 you got after you filed your original return.

Line 2

Enter all adjustments to income, such as an IRA deduction or alimony paid. On Form 1040, use lines 24a–29. Be sure to include any write-in adjustment. For more details, see your Form 1040 instructions.

On Form 1040A, use lines 15a and 15b.

If you are changing the amount of your IRA deduction, write in Part II of Form 1040X "IRA deduction" and the amount of the increase or decrease. If you are changing a deductible IRA contribution to a nondeductible IRA contribution, also complete and attach **Form 8606,** Nondeductible IRAs.

Line 3

Changes you make to your adjusted gross income (AGI) can cause other amounts to increase or decrease. For example, increasing your AGI may decrease your miscellaneous itemized deductions or your credit for child and dependent care expenses. It may also increase the allowable deduction for charitable contributions or the amount of social security benefits that is taxable.

Also, changes to your AGI may change your **total** itemized deductions or your deduction for exemptions. You should refigure these items whenever you change your AGI.

Effect on Exemption Deduction.—Use the **Deduction for Exemptions Worksheet** in the Form 1040 instructions for the year you are amending to figure the amount to enter on Form 1040X, line 6, and if applicable, line 29, if any of the following apply:

● You are amending your 1993 return **and** your AGI in column A or C is over $162,700 ($108,450 if single; $135,600 if head of household; $81,350 if married filing separately).

● You are amending your 1992 return **and** your AGI in column A or C is over $157,900 ($105,250 if single; $131,550 if head of household; $78,950 if married filing separately).

● You are amending your 1991 return **and** your AGI in column A or C is over $150,000 ($100,000 if single; $125,000 if head of household; $75,000 if married filing separately).

Line 4

Itemized Deductions.—If you itemize deductions on **Schedule A (Form 1040),** enter on line 4 your total itemized deductions. On Schedule A for 1990, use line 27. For 1991–1993, use line 26.

Standard Deduction.—If you **do not** itemize, enter on line 4 your standard deduction. On Form 1040, use line 34.

On Form 1040A, use line 19.

On Form 1040EZ for 1990-1992, if you checked the **"Yes"** box on line 4 of that form, enter the amount from line 4 of Form 1040EZ on line 4 of Form 1040X. If you checked the **"No"** box, enter on line 4 of Form 1040X the amount listed below for the tax year you are amending.

Tax Year	Amount
1992	$3,600
1991	3,400
1990	3,250

On Form 1040EZ for 1993, if you checked the **"Yes"** box on line 5 of that form, enter on line 4 of Form 1040X the amount from line E of the worksheet on the back of Form 1040EZ. If you checked the **"No"** box, enter $3,700 ($6,200 if married filing jointly) on line 4 of Form 1040X.

Line 6

If you are changing the number of exemptions claimed, complete the applicable lines in Part I of the form to figure the amounts to enter on line 6. Otherwise, enter in columns A and C of line 6 the amount you claimed for exemptions on your original return. On Form 1040, use line 36. But if changes to your AGI affect your deduction for exemptions (see the line 3 instructions),

enter the net change in column B of line 6 and the correct amount in column C.

On Form 1040A, use line 21.

On Form 1040EZ for 1990-1992, if you checked the **"Yes"** box on line 4 of that form, enter zero on line 6 of Form 1040X. If you checked the **"No"** box, enter the amount listed below for the tax year you are amending.

Tax Year	Amount
1992	$2,300
1991	2,150
1990	2,050

On Form 1040EZ for 1993, if you checked the **"Yes"** box on line 5 of that form, enter on line 6 of Form 1040X the amount from line F of the worksheet on the back of Form 1040EZ. If you checked the **"No"** box, enter $2,350 ($4,700 if married filing jointly) on line 6 of Form 1040X.

Line 8

Enter your income tax before subtracting any credits. Show on this line the method you use in column C to figure your tax. For example, if you use the Tax Rate Schedules, write "TRS." If you use **Schedule D (Form 1040)** or, for 1993, the Schedule D Tax Worksheet, write "Sch. D."

Figure the tax on the taxable income you reported on line 7, column C. Attach the appropriate schedule or forms. Include on line 8 any additional taxes from **Form 4970,** Tax on Accumulation Distribution of Trusts, or **Form 4972,** Tax on Lump-Sum Distributions.

Line 9

Enter your total credits, such as the credit for the elderly or the disabled, credit for child and dependent care expenses, or credit for prior year minimum tax. On Form 1040 for 1990, use lines 41–45. For 1991–1993, use lines 41–44. Be sure to include any write-in credit.

On Form 1040A, use lines 24a and 24b.

Line 11

Include other taxes, such as alternative minimum tax, self-employment tax, tax on early distributions from qualified retirement plans, or advance earned income credit payments. Also, include any recapture of investment credit, low-income housing credit, or Federal mortgage subsidy. On Form 1040 for 1990, use lines 48–53. For 1991–1993, use lines 47–52. Be sure to include any write-in tax.

On Form 1040A, use line 26.

Lines 13–17

Enter on the applicable lines your payments and credits. On Form 1040 for 1990, use lines 55–61. For 1991–1993, use lines 54–59. If you are amending your 1993 Form 1040 and you filed **Form 8841,** Deferral of Additional 1993 Taxes, see the instructions for line 14.

On Form 1040A, use lines 28a–28c. Be sure to include any write-in payment.

On Form 1040EZ for 1990–1992, use line 6. For 1993, use line 7.

Line 13.—If you change these amounts, attach to the front of Form 1040X the first copy or Copy B of all additional or corrected Forms W-2 or Forms 1099-R that you got after you filed your original return. Enter in column B any additional Federal income tax withheld shown on Forms W-2 or 1099.

Line 14.—Enter the estimated tax payments you claimed on your original return. If you filed **Form 1040-C,** U.S. Departing Alien Income Tax Return, include the amount you paid as the balance due with the return.

If you are amending your 1993 Form 1040, include any deferral of additional 1993 taxes from line 58b of that form on line 14 of Form 1040X. Write "Form 8841" in the space to the left of line 14. The amount reported on your original return as deferred additional 1993 taxes cannot be changed even if your taxable income has increased or decreased.

Line 18

Enter the amount you paid from the "Amount You Owe" line on your **original** return. Also, include any additional tax that may have resulted if your original return was changed or examined. **Do not** include payments of interest or penalties.

Line 20

Enter the overpayment from your original return. On Form 1040 for 1990, use line 63. For 1991–1993, use line 61. On Form 1040A, use line 29. On Form 1040EZ for 1990–1992, use line 8. For 1993, use line 9. The overpayment amount must be considered in preparing Form 1040X since any refund you have not yet received from your original return will be refunded separately from any additional refund claimed on your Form 1040X.

If your original return was changed or audited by the IRS and as a result there was an additional overpayment of tax, also include that amount on line 20. **Do not** include any interest you received on any refund.

Lines 21 and 22

If line 21 is a negative amount, treat it as a positive amount and add it to the amount on line 12, column C. Enter the result on line 22. This is the amount you owe.

Attach your check or money order payable to the Internal Revenue Service for the full amount. Write your name, address, social security number, and daytime phone number on your payment. Also, write the year and type of return you are amending. For example, "1992 Form 1040." We will figure the interest due and send you a bill.

If you cannot pay the full amount shown on line 22, you may ask to make monthly installment payments. Get **Form 9465,** Installment Agreement Request, for more information. But if you and your spouse are changing from separate returns to joint returns, you cannot request an installment agreement.

Line 23

If you are entitled to a larger refund than you claimed on your original return, show only the additional amount due you. This will be refunded separately from the amount claimed on your original return (see the instructions for line 20). We will figure the interest and include it in your refund.

Lines 24–28

In column A, enter the number of exemptions claimed on your original return. In column B, enter any changes to exemptions claimed on your original return. Enter in column C the corrected number of exemptions you are claiming.

Line 29

You may have to use the **Deduction for Exemptions Worksheet** in the Form 1040 instructions to figure the amount to enter on line 29 if the amount in column A or C of line 3 is—

• Over $81,350 if amending your 1993 return,

• Over $78,950 if amending your 1992 return, or

• Over $75,000 if amending your 1991 return.

For details, see **Effect on Exemption Deduction** on page 3. If you don't have to use the worksheet, multiply the applicable dollar amount on line 29 by the number of exemptions on line 28.

Line 30

If you are amending your return to claim an exemption for a dependent, you may have to enter the dependent's social security number (SSN) in column (c) of line 30. For 1990, you must enter the SSN of any dependent who was age 2 or older on December 31, 1990. For tax years after 1990, you must enter the SSN of any dependent who was age 1 or older on December 31 of the year you are amending. If you do not enter the number or if the number is wrong, you may have to pay a $50 penalty. If your dependent does not have an SSN, see your 1993 Form 1040 or Form 1040A instructions for line 6c.

If you are claiming more than five additional dependents, show the information requested in columns (a) through (e) on an attached statement. When entering the total number of dependents in the boxes to the right of line 30, be sure to include these dependents.

If you are claiming a child who didn't live with you under the special rules for children of divorced or separated parents, you **must** do one of the following:

• **Check the box on line 31** if your divorce decree or written separation agreement was in effect before 1985 and it states that you can claim the child as your dependent.

• Attach **Form 8332,** Release of Claim to Exemption for Child of Divorced or Separated Parents, or similar statement. If your divorce decree or separation agreement went into effect after 1984 and it unconditionally states that you can claim the child as your dependent, you may attach a copy of the following pages from the decree or agreement instead of Form 8332:

1. Cover page (write the other parent's social security number on this page), and

2. The page that unconditionally states you can claim the child as your dependent, and

3. Signature page showing the date of the agreement.

For more details, see your 1993 Form 1040 or Form 1040A instructions for line 6c.

Part III—Presidential Election Campaign Fund

You may use Form 1040X to have $3 (or $1 if amending a 1992 return) go to the Presidential Election Campaign Fund if you (or your spouse on a joint return) did not do so on your original return. This must be done within 20½ months after the original due date for filing the return. For calendar year 1993, this period ends on December 31, 1995. For calendar year 1992, this period ends on December 31, 1994. A **"Yes"** designation cannot be changed.

Printed on recycled paper

Form **1127**
(Rev. 11-93)
Department of the Treasury
Internal Revenue Service

APPLICATION FOR EXTENSION OF TIME FOR PAYMENT OF TAX

(ATTN: *This type of payment extension is rarely granted because the legal requirements are so strict. Please read the conditions on the back carefully before continuing.*)

Taxpayer's Name (include spouse if your extension request is for a joint return)	Social Security Number or Employer Identification Number
Present Address	
City, Town or Post Office, State, and Zip Code	Spouse's Social Security Number if this is for a joint return

District Director of Internal Revenue at _____

(Enter City and State where IRS Office is located)

I request an extension from _____ , 19 _____ , to_____ , 19 _____
(Enter Due Date of Return)

to pay tax of $ _____ for the year ended _____ , 19 _____ .

This extension is necessary because *(If more space is needed, please attach a separate sheet):* _____

_____

_____

_____

_____

I can't borrow to pay the tax because: _____

_____

_____

To show the need for the extension. I am attaching: (1) a statement of my assets and liabilities at the end of last month (showing book and market values of assets and whether securities are listed or unlisted); and (2) an itemized list of money I received and spent for 3 months before the date the tax is due.

I propose to secure this liability as follows:

_____

_____

Under penalties of perjury, I declare that I have examined this application, including any accompanying schedules and statements, and to the best of my knowledge and belief it is true, correct, and complete.

_____   _____
SIGNATURE (BOTH SIGNATURES IF YOUR EXTENSION REQUEST IS FOR A JOINT RETURN)   *(DATE)*

The District Director will let you know whether the extension is approved or denied and will tell you if you need some form of security. However, the Director can't consider an application if it is filed after the due date of the return. We will send you a list of approved surety companies if you ask for it.

(The following will be filled in by the IRS.)

This application is   ☐ approved   for the following reasons:
                       ☐ denied

_____

_____

Interest _____   Date of assessment _____   Identifying no._____

Penalty _____   _____   _____
                                            (SIGNATURE)   *(DATE)*

CAT. NO. 17238O   *(over)*   Form **1127** (Rev. 11-93)

CONDITIONS UNDER WHICH EXTENSIONS FOR PAYMENTS MAY BE GRANTED UNDER SECTION 6161 OF THE INTERNAL REVENUE CODE

The District Director may approve additional time for you to pay your tax if you show that it will cause you undue hardship to pay it on the date it is due. You must file your application with the District Director on or before the date payment is due.

IMPORTANT!

IF YOU ARE ASKING TO PAY THE AMOUNT YOU OWE IN **INSTALLMENTS**, RATHER THAN DELAY FULL PAYMENT OF THE TAX FOR SIX MONTHS, **COMPLETE FORM 9465, INSTALLMENT AGREEMENT REQUEST**, AND ATTACH IT TO YOUR TAX RETURN WHEN YOU FILE. **DO NOT COMPLETE THIS FORM**.

For us to consider your request under Internal Revenue Code Section (IRC) 6161, we must receive it on or before the date the tax is due. It must include the following information:

> **-a complete statement of all your assets and liabilities at the end of last month**
> (showing book and market values and whether securities are listed or unlisted)
>
> **-an itemized list of money you received and spent for three months before you requested this extension**

1. **Undue hardship.**—This means more than inconvenience. You must show that you will have substantial financial loss if you pay your tax on the date it is due. (This loss could be caused by selling property at a sacrifice price.) You must show that you don't have enough cash, above necessary working capital, to pay the tax. In determining cash available, include anything you can convert into cash, and use current market prices. Also, show that you can't borrow to pay the tax, except under terms that will cause you severe loss and hardship.

2. **Limits.**—As a general rule, an extension to pay income or gift tax is limited to 6 months from the date payment is due. We may grant an extension for more than 6 months if you are abroad.

   An extension to pay a deficiency (an amount you owe after an examination of your return) in income or gift tax is limited to 18 months from the date payment is due and, in exceptional cases, up to another 12 months.

   We won't grant an extension to pay a deficiency caused by negligence, intentional disregard of rules and regulations, or fraud with intent to evade tax.

3. **Interest.**—We charge interest at the underpayment rate in Code section 6621(a)(2).

4. **Security.**—Security is the way you guarantee to pay the amount you owe. Security satisfactory to the District Director is required to get an extension. This assures that the risk to the government is no greater at the end of the extension than at the beginning. The kind of security, such as bond, notice of lien, mortgage, pledge, deed of trust of specific property or general assets, personal surety, or other, will depend on the circumstances in each case. Ordinarily, when you receive approval of your application, you will have to deposit with the District Director any collateral that you agreed to use for security. No collateral is required if you have no assets.

5. **Due date of payment.**—Before the extension runs out, you must pay the tax for which the extension is granted (without waiting for a bill from the District Director.)

6. **Filing requirements.**—Complete this form after you have read the above information and decided that this is the correct form to request the type of extension you need. Attach the three month income/expense listing as well as your asset and liability listing, and your documentation of **undue hardship** as described above. Send your completed application, along with the supporting documents to the District Director (Attn: Chief, Special Procedures function) where you maintain your legal residence or principal place of business. If, however, the tax will be paid to the Assistance Commissioner (International), file the application with that office. If you need an extension to pay estate tax, file Form 4768, Application for Extension of Time to File a Return and/or Pay U.S. Estate (and Generation Skipping Transfer) Taxes.

*U.S. GPO: 1993-301-643/92169

Report of Individual
Income Tax Examination Changes

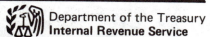 Department of the Treasury
Internal Revenue Service

Name of Taxpayer	Year	Form **1040**	Filing Status	In Reply Refer To:
Authorized Representative	Date of Report		Social Security Number	Examining District

Income and Deduction Amounts Adjusted

Explanation Number (See attached)	Item Changed	Amount Shown on Return or as Previously Adjusted	Corrected Amount of Income or Deduction	Adjustment Increase (Decrease)

A. Adjustment in income and deductions - increase (decrease) (See explanation of adjustments attached.)

B. Adjusted gross or taxable income shown on return or as previously adjusted

C. Corrected adjusted gross or taxable income

D. Corrected tax (From: ☐ Tax Table, ☐ Tax Rate Schedules, ☐ Form 8615 or ☐ Other)

E. Tax credits (general business, child and dependent care, foreign, etc.) (If adjusted, see explanation attached.)

F. Other tax (self-employment, alternative minimum, tax from recapture of Investment credit, etc.) (If adjusted, see explanation attached.)

G. Total corrected tax (line D less line E plus line F)

H. Tax shown on return or as previously adjusted

I. Adjustments to EIC/Fuels credit - increase (decrease) (If adjusted, see explanation attached.)

J. Deficiency - Increase in tax or (Overassessment - Decrease in tax) (Line G adjusted by Lines H and I)

K. Adjustments to prepayment credits - increase (decrease)

L. Balance due or (Overpayment) - Excluding interest and penalties (Line J adjusted by line K)

M. Penalties (See explanation attached) (1)

(2)

(3)

Consent to Assessment and Collection - I do not wish to exercise my appeal rights with the Internal Revenue Service or to contest in the United States Tax Court the findings in this report. Therefore, I give my consent to the immediate assessment and collection of any increase in tax and penalties, and accept any decrease in tax and penalties above, plus any interest as provided by law.

Although this report is subject to review, you may consider it as your notice that your case is closed if you are not notified of an exception to these findings within 45 days after a signed copy of the report or a signed waiver, Form 870, is received by the District Director.

Your signature _____ Date _____

Spouse's signature _____ Date _____
(IF A JOINT RETURN, BOTH MUST SIGN)

By _____ Title _____ Date _____

You may be subject to backup withholding if you under report your interest, dividend, or patronage dividend income and do not pay the required tax. The IRS may order backup withholding at 20 percent after four notices have been issued to you over a 120-day period and the tax has been assessed and remains unpaid.

The Internal Revenue Service has agreements with State tax agencies under which information about Federal Tax, including increases or decreases, is exchanged with the States. If this change affects the amount of your State income tax, you should file the required State form.

Report of Interview with Individual Relative to 100-Percent Penalty Recommendation

	Date of Interview
Notice 609 was furnished during the interview. (Check here) [ ]	Name of Interviewer

INSTRUCTIONS TO INTERVIEWER: The questions which follow are intended to be used as a guide as you conduct the interview. Other pertinent questions may be asked. You must prepare this form personally, recording the interviewee's answers. Where a question is not applicable, write "N/A." Do not leave any blocks or lines blank. Attach additional sheets if necessary.

Notice 609, Privacy Act and Paperwork Reduction Act Notice, must be given to individuals who have not received notice of their right to privacy. If furnished during the interview, check the box above. If not, explain in the case history.

IRC 6672, failure to collect and pay tax from (date) _____ to (date) _____

Section I—Background Information

1.
- a. Person interviewed (name)
- b. (address)
- c. Telephone number (home)   (work)
- d. Social Security number

2.
- a. Taxpayer (Corporation) (name)

   (address)

- b. Incorporation (date)   State where incorporated   Final wages paid (date)
- c. Has the state revoked the corporation franchise?   ☐ yes   ☐ no   If so, when?
- d. Has the corporation ever filed bankruptcy?   ☐ yes   ☐ no   If so, when?

3. Was any of the property of the corporation sold, transferred, quitclaimed, donated or otherwise disposed of, for less than fair market value, since the accrual of the tax liability?   ☐ yes   ☐ no   What happened to the corporate assets?

4.
- a. How were you associated with this corporation?
- b. Describe your duties/responsibilities.
- c. By whom were you hired?
- d. What were the dates of your employment with the corporation?

e.	Did you resign from the corporation? ☐ yes ☐ no	In writing?	☐ yes ☐ no
	When?	Is a copy of your resignation available?	☐ yes ☐ no

f.	To whom was your resignation submitted?	
g.	Did you have your name removed from the bank signature cards? ☐ yes ☐ no	When?
h.	Do you have any money invested in the corporation? ☐ yes ☐ no	Amount $

5. Have you ever been involved with another company which had tax problems? ☐ yes ☐ no

If so, explain. *(Corporate name, EIN, etc.)*

6. With what banks or financial institutions did the corporation have transactions such as checking and other accounts, loans, financing agreements, etc.? *(attach additional sheet, if necessary)*

Financial Institution	Transaction(s)	Address	Date(s)

7. Where are the financial records located?

8. Please indicate the names, dates of service and percentage of ownership for the positions indicated below.

Position	Name	Dates of Service	% Ownership
Chairman of the board			
Other Directors *(list)*			
President			
Vice President			
Secretary			
Treasurer			
Others *(shareholders, owners)*			

Section II—Ability to Direct

Please indicate whether you performed any of the duties/functions indicated below for the corporation and the timeframes during which you performed them. If another individual(s) performed these duties, please list names and applicable timeframes.

Did you...	Yes	No	Dates from	to	Did anyone else? (name)	Dates from	to
1. Hire/fire employees							
2. Manage employees							
3. Direct (authorize) payment of bills							
4. Deal with major suppliers and customers							
5. Negotiate large corporate purchases, contracts, loans							
6. Open/close corporate bank accounts							
7. Sign/countersign corporate checks							
8. Guarantee/co-sign corporate bank loans							
9. Make/authorize bank deposits							
10. Authorize payroll checks							
11. Prepare federal payroll tax returns							

Did you...	Yes	No	Dates		Did anyone else? *(name)*	Dates	
			from	to		from	to
12. Sign federal payroll tax returns							
13. Authorize payment of federal tax deposits							
14. Review federal income tax returns							
15. Determine company financial policy							

Please provide the information requested below for each individual, other than yourself, listed for the above questions. Also, please provide any additional information indicating their knowledge and/or control over the corporation's financial affairs. *(Attach additional sheets if necessary.)*

Name	Address
Phone	Social Security number

Additional information

Name	Address
Phone	Social Security number

Additional information

Name	Address
Phone	Social Security number

Additional information

Name	Address
Phone	Social Security number

Additional information

Name	Address
Phone	Social Security number

Additional information

1. When and how did you first become aware of the delinquent taxes?

2. What action did you take to see that the tax liabilities were paid?

3. Were discussions or meetings ever held by stockholders, officers or other interested parties regarding the non-payment of the taxes? ☐ yes ☐ no
   Identify who attended, the dates of the meetings, and any decisions reached.
   (Attach additional sheets, if necessary.)

4. Are minutes available from any meetings described in question 3 above? ☐ yes ☐ no

5. Who maintained or has access to the books and records of the corporation? When?
   (Please provide name, address and phone number, if possible)

6. Were financial statements ever prepared for the corporation? ☐ yes ☐ no
   If so, by whom? Who reviewed them and to whom were they submitted?
   (Please provide applicable timeframes.)

7. Did the corporation employ an outside accountant? ☐ yes ☐ no
   If so, please provide the name, address and phone number of the individual or firm.

8. Who in the corporation had the responsibility of dealing with the outside accountant?

9. Did you personally have discussions with the accountant or bookkeeper of the corporation regarding the tax liability? ☐ yes ☐ no

   If so, when?
   What was discussed?

10. Who reviewed the payroll tax returns or tax payments?

11. Who handled IRS contacts, such as IRS correspondence, phone calls from IRS, or visits by IRS personnel?

    When?
    What were the results of these contacts?

12. During the time the delinquent taxes were accruing, or at any time thereafter, were any financial obligation of the corporation paid? ☐ yes ☐ no
    If so, which ones?

13. Which individual or individuals authorized or allowed any of these obligations to be paid?

14. During the time that the delinquent taxes were accruing, or at any time thereafter, were all or a portion of the payrolls met? ☐ yes ☐ no

15. When there was not enough money to pay all the bills, what decisions were made and what actions were taken to deal with the situation?

16. Did any person or organization provide funds to pay net corporate payrolls? ☐ yes ☐ no
    If so, explain in detail.

Section IV—Special Circumstances

1. Is the corporation required to file federal excise tax returns?
   If so, are you aware of any required excise tax returns which have not been filed?
   (If either response is negative, do not complete remaining questions in Section IV.)

   ☐ yes ☐ no
   ☐ yes ☐ no

2. With respect to excise taxes, were the patrons or customers informed that the tax was included in the sales price?

   ☐ yes ☐ no

3. If the tax liability is one of the so-called "collected" taxes—transportation of persons or property and communications:

   a. Was the tax collected?

   ☐ yes ☐ no

   b. Were you aware, during the period tax accrued, that the law required collection of the tax?   ☐ yes ☐ no

Section V—Additional Comments

Is there anyone else who may have been involved or who could provide additional information regarding this matter?
☐ yes ☐ no

Please add any comments you may wish to make regarding this matter.

_____

_____

_____

_____

_____

_____

_____

_____

_____

_____

_____

_____

_____

_____

_____

I declare that I have examined the information given in this statement and, to the best of my knowledge and belief, it is true, correct and complete.

Person interviewed (*signature*)	Date
Interviewer (*signature*)	Date

Date copy given (*mailed*) to person interviewed

Form **4506**
(Rev. August 1992)
Department of the Treasury
Internal Revenue Service

Request for Copy of Tax Form

▶ **Please read Instructions before completing this form.**
▶ **Please type or print clearly.**

OMB No. 1545-0429
Expires 6-30-95

Note: Do not use this form to get tax account Information. Instead, see instructions below.

1a Your name shown on tax form	**1b** **Your social security number or employer Identification number.** (See Instructions.)
2a If a joint return, spouse's name shown on tax form	**2b** **Spouse's social security number**

3 Current name and address (including apt., room, or suite no.)

4 If copy of form is to be mailed to someone else, show the third party's name and address. (See instructions.)

5 If we cannot find a record of your tax form and you want the payment refunded to the third party, check here . . . . ▶ ☐

6 If name in third party's records differs from line 1a above, show name here. (See instructions.)

7 Check the box to show what you want:

a ☐ Copy of tax form and all attachments (including Form(s) W-2, schedules, or other forms). The charge is $4.25 for each period requested.
    Note: If these copies must be certified for court or administrative proceedings, see instructions and check here . . . . ▶ ☐

b ☐ Copy of Form(s) W-2 only. There is no charge for this. See instructions for when Form W-2 is available.

8 Tax form number (Form 1040, 1040A, 941, etc.)

9 Tax period(s) (year or period ended date). If more than four, see instructions.

10	Amount due for copy of tax form:	
a	Cost for each period	$ 14.00
b	Number of tax periods requested on line 9	0
c	Total cost. Multiply line 10a by line 10b	$ 0.00

Full payment must accompany your request. Make check or money order payable to "Internal Revenue Service."

Please Sign Here

Signature. See instructions. If other than taxpayer, attach authorization document.   Date

Telephone number of requester

Convenient time for us to call

Title (if line 1a above is a corporation, partnership, estate, or trust)

r Paperwork Reduction Act Notice, see back of form.

Form **4506** (Rev. 8-92)

Form 4700. Examination Workpapers.

Examination Workpapers

Taxpayer's name, address, SSN *(Use pre-addressed label or show changes)*	Date	Year(s)
	Examiner	Grade
	Taxpayer(s) Home Phone	Work Phone
	Reviewer	

A

Initial Interview

1. Examination technique: ☐ Correspondence
   - ☐ Undeliverable mail   ☐ No show
   - ☐ Interview with:

   _____

2. Receipt of Publication 1 ☐
3. Appeal rights and Privacy Act explained ☐
4. Continue on Form 4700-A, B or C

Representative - Power of Attorney
Name   ☐ Yes   ☐ No
                 Phone

B

Closed No Change

Issue: ☐ Letter 590   ☐ Letter 1156   ☐ Other

Examiner

C

Examination Reminders

1. Proforma Worksheets utilized where applicable
2. Alternative minimum tax
3. Inspection of prior and subsequent year return, IRM 4215
4. Probe for unreported deductions and credits
5. Scope of Examination, IRM 4253.2
6. Automatic adjustments resulting from AGI change(s)

Case Processing Reminders

1. Claim Case - Forms 2297 and 3363
2. Information Reports (IRM 4219) - Form 5346
3. FICA, Self-Employment or Tip Income Adjustments
   Forms 885-E, 885-F, and 885-T
4. Inequities, Abuses, Loopholes - Form 3558
5. Inadequate Records Notice (IRM 4271)
6. Special Handling Notice 3198

D

(Items to be considered, explored, verified)	Year	Per Return	Corrected	Adjustment	Workpapers Index

E

	Year	Per Return	Corrected	Adjustment	Workpapers Index

Form **4700** (Rev. 2-90)

Form 4700-A. Form 4700 Supplement.

Form 4700 Supplement

Taxpayer		Year(s)
Examiner		Date

		Yes	No	Comments
1. Preparer Information	A. Was return prepared for Compensation? (If Yes, complete remaining items)			
	B. Identification Penalties required?			
	C. Did preparer negotiate refund?			
	D. Did taxpayer receive a copy of return?			

2. Prior IRS Contacts or Prior Audits

☐ None ☐ Yes — Year(s)   Do Repetitive Audit Procedures apply? ☐ Yes ☐ No

Issues/Reasons: Was Amended Return(s) filed? ☐ Yes ☐ No

3. All Due Returns Filed?

	Yes	No	N/A	Comments
Individual				
Household help				
Employment				
Excise				

4. Income Probe

If reported or received none, enter (√) in block. If received but not reported, enter (X) in block and comment below.

Interest (S&L) Banks, 2nd Mortgage)	Alimony	Gifts, Inheritance
	Partnerships	Scholarship, Fellowship, Grant
Dividends	Sick Pay	Loans
Sale of assets	Child support	Social Security
Other jobs	Prizes, awards, bonuses	Welfare
Investments	Gambling/Lotteries	Unemployment compensation
Tips	Insurance	VA benefits
Commission	Estate/Trusts	Military allowance
Hobbies	State/Local Tax Refund	Foreign Bank Accounts
Rent/Royalty	Employer Reimbursement	Pensions, Annuities, Profit-Sharing
Comments should indicate nature and extent of income probe		IRA/Keogh Distributions

5. Bartering

	Yes	No
Exchange of personal services or merchandise?	Yes	No
Belong to any bartering clubs or organizations?	Yes	No

If Yes, explain fully

6. Foreign Accounts and Foreign Trusts

Is the Foreign Accounts and Foreign Trusts question appearing on the tax return answered correctly? If No, explain fully.   Yes   No   ☐ N/A

7. Exemptions

Name	Age	Relationship	Other Information

Form 4700-A (Rev. 9-84)   *(over please)*   Department of the Treasury — Internal Revenue Service

Form 4700-A. Form 4700 Supplement. (cont'd)

Complete Remaining Items After Examination

8. Solicit Payment	Payment solicited: Payment received — Include Interest Computation
	Payment solicited: Taxpayer desires to be billed

9. Prior/ Subsequent Year Return

Prior/subsequent year audit recommended?

☐ Yes — Date of AIMS Request _____ Date Information Report Submitted _____

☐ No — State reason:

10. Penalties Recommended For Taxpayer

Type	Asserted	Reason
Negligence	☐ Yes	Indicate issue(s) on which 50% interest is applicable.
	☐ No	
Delinquency	☐ Yes	
	☐ No	
Fraud	☐ Yes	Indicate issue(s) on which 50% interest is applicable.
	☐ No	
Other (State penalty)	☐ Yes	
	☐ No	

11. Preparer Conduct Penalties

Any indications of preparer negligence or fraud?	Yes	No

If Yes, explain:

12. Unagreed Case

Group Manager Involvement in Unagreed Case:

☐ Taxpayer Offered Conference with Group Manager. Date _____

Form 4700-B. Form 4700 Business Supplement.

Form 4700 Business Supplement

Taxpayer	Year
Examiner	Date

1. Brief Discription of Day-to-Day Business Operation	

2. Business History

How long in business

Number of employees	Full-Time	Part-Time

3. Accounting Method

☐ Cash | ☐ Accrual | ☐ Hybrid

Who keeps the books?

4. Cash on Hand

	Beginning of Year	End of Year
Home	$	$
Business	$	$
Elsewhere	$	$

5. Where do You Maintain Your Bank Account(s)?

Business	Account Number	Personal	Account Numt

6. Banking Practices

Were all business and personal expenses kept separately?

Were all business receipts deposited? To which account?

How are business expenses paid?

7. Safety Deposit Box

Location	Contents

8. Purchases

Any withdrawals of purchases for personal use?

9. Related Transactions

Any transactions between you and relative or related parties? If so, explain.

10. Gross Receipts

How were gross receipts calculated?

Workpaper Index _____

Form **4700-B** (Rev. 8-83)   Department of the Treasury — Internal Revenue Service

Form 4700-B. Form 4700 Business Supplement. (cont'd)

	Are inventories material? ☐ Yes ☐ No				
11. Inventories	a. Did beginning and ending balances agree with prior/subsequent returns?	Yes		No	
	b. Were there any changes in method of valuing inventories?	Yes		No	
	c. When taken:				
	How:				
	d. Include year-end purchases?	Yes		No	
	e. Any write-offs or write downs?	Yes		No	

12.	Loans, notes, mortgages payable:	AMOUNT	Per	Bus.	PAGE, EXHIBIT, SCHEDULE

13.	Capital items sold:	AMOUNT	PURCHASER	PAGE, EXHIBIT, SCHEDULE

14.	Capital items purchased:		SELLER	

Form **8332**

(Rev. March 1993)

Department of the Treasury
Internal Revenue Service

Release of Claim to Exemption
for Child of Divorced or Separated Parents

ATTACH to noncustodial parent's return each year exemption claimed.

OMB No. 1545-0915
Expires 3-31-96

Attachment
Sequence No. **51**

Name(s) of parent claiming exemption

Social security number

Part I   **Release of Claim to Exemption for Current Year**

I agree not to claim an exemption for _____

Name(s) of child (or children)

for the tax year 19_____ .

_____   _____   _____
Signature of parent releasing claim to exemption   Social security number   Date

If you choose not to claim an exemption for this child (or children) for future tax years, complete Part II.

Part II   **Release of Claim to Exemption for Future Years** *(If completed, see **Noncustodial Parent** below.)*

I agree not to claim an exemption for _____

Name(s) of child (or children)

for the tax year(s) _____ .
(Specify. See instructions.)

_____   _____   _____
Signature of parent releasing claim to exemption   Social security number   Date

---

General Instructions

Paperwork Reduction Act Notice.—We ask for the information on this form to carry out the Internal Revenue laws of the United States. You are required to give us the information. We need it to ensure that you are complying with these laws and to allow us to figure and collect the right amount of tax.

The time needed to complete and file this form will vary depending on individual circumstances. The estimated average time is: **Recordkeeping,** 7 min.; **Learning about the law or the form,** 5 min.; **Preparing the form,** 7 min.; and **Copying, assembling, and sending the form to the IRS,** 14 min.

If you have comments concerning the accuracy of these time estimates or suggestions for making this form more simple, we would be happy to hear from you. You can write to both the IRS and the Office of Management and Budget at the addresses listed in the instructions for the return with which this form is filed.

Purpose of Form.—If you are a **custodial parent,** you may use this form to release your claim to your child's exemption. To do so, complete this form and give it to the **noncustodial parent** who will claim the child's exemption. Then, the noncustodial parent must attach this form or a similar statement to his or her tax return each year the exemption is claimed.

You are the **custodial parent** if you had custody of the child for most of the year. You are the **noncustodial parent** if you had custody for a shorter period of time or did not have custody at all.

Instead of using this form, you (the custodial parent) may use a similar

statement as long as it contains the same information required by this form.

Children of Divorced or Separated Parents.—Special rules apply to determine if the support test is met for children of parents who are divorced or legally separated under a decree of divorce or separate maintenance or separated under a written separation agreement. The rules also apply to children of parents who did not live together at any time during the last 6 months of the year, even if they do not have a separation agreement.

The general rule is that the custodial parent is treated as having provided over half of the child's support if:

1. The child received over half of his or her total support for the year from both of the parents, **AND**

2. The child was in the custody of one or both of his or her parents for more than half of the year.

Note: *Public assistance payments, such as Aid to Families with Dependent Children, are not support provided by the parents.*

If both **1** and **2** above apply, and the other four dependency tests in the instructions for Form 1040 or Form 1040A are also met, the custodial parent can claim the child's exemption.

Exception. The general rule does not apply if **any** of the following applies:

• The custodial parent agrees not to claim the child's exemption by signing this form or similar statement. The noncustodial parent **must** attach this form or similar statement to his or her tax return for the tax year. See **Custodial Parent** later.

• The child is treated as having received over half of his or her total support from a

person under a multiple support agreement **(Form 2120,** Multiple Support Declaration).

• A pre-1985 divorce decree or written separation agreement states that the noncustodial parent can claim the child as a dependent. But the noncustodial parent must provide at least $600 for the child's support during the year. The noncustodial parent must also check the box on line 6d of Form 1040 or Form 1040A. This rule does not apply if the decree or agreement was changed after 1984 to say that the noncustodial parent cannot claim the child as a dependent.

Additional Information.—For more details, get **Pub. 504,** Divorced or Separated Individuals.

Specific Instructions

Custodial Parent.—You may agree to release your claim to the child's exemption for the current tax year or for future years, or both.

• Complete **Part I** if you agree to release your claim to the child's exemption for the current tax year.

• Complete **Part II** if you agree to release your claim to the child's exemption for any or all future years. If you do, write the specific future year(s) or "all future years" in the space provided in Part II.

Noncustodial Parent.—Attach Form 8332 or a similar statement to your tax return for the tax year in which you claim the child's exemption. You may claim the exemption **only** if the other four dependency tests in the Form 1040 or Form 1040A instructions are met.

Note: *If the custodial parent completed Part II, you **must** attach a copy of this form to your tax return for each future year in which you claim the exemption.*

Form **8379**

(Rev. March 1994)

Department of the Treasury
Internal Revenue Service

Injured Spouse Claim and Allocation

OMB No. 1545-1210
Expires 02-28-97

Attachment
Sequence No. **104**

Name(s) shown on return

Your social security number

Paperwork Reduction Act Notice

We ask for the information on this form to carry out the Internal Revenue laws of the United States. You are required to give us the information so that we can process your claim. We need it to ensure that you are allocating items correctly and to allow us to figure the correct amount of your claim for refund. The time needed to complete and file this form will vary depending on individual circumstances. The estimated average times are: Recordkeeping, 13 min.; Learning about the law or the form, 5 min.; Preparing the form, 58 min.; Sending the form, 31 min.

If you have comments concerning the accuracy of these time estimates or suggestions for making this form more simple, we would be happy to hear from you. You can write to both the **Internal Revenue Service,** Attention: Reports Clearance Officer, PC:FP, Washington, DC 20224; and the **Office of Management and Budget,** Paperwork Reduction Project (1545-1210), Washington, DC 20503. **Do not** send this form to either of these offices. Instead, see **How Do I File Form 8379?** below.

Are You an Injured Spouse?

You are an injured spouse if all or part of your share of the overpayment shown on your joint return was, or is expected to be, applied against your spouse's past-due child or spousal support payments or certain Federal debts such as student loans. You may file Form 8379 to claim your part of the refund if **all three** of the following apply:

1. You are not required to pay the past-due amount.

2. You received and reported income (such as wages, taxable interest, etc.) on the joint return.

3. You made and reported payments, such as Federal income tax withheld from your wages or estimated tax payments, on the joint return.

If **all three** of the above apply and you want your share of the overpayment shown on the joint return refunded to you, complete this form. The IRS will figure your part of the overpayment and send you any refund that is due. However, if you also owe past-due child support or a Federal agency debt, part or all of your share of the overpayment may be applied to that debt. Allow 6-8 weeks for the processing of this claim.

How Do I File Form 8379?

● If you have already filed the joint tax return, mail Form 8379 by itself to the same Internal Revenue Service Center where you filed the joint return. Include copies of all W-2 forms of both spouses and any Forms 1099-R showing income tax withheld.

● If you haven't filed the joint return, attach Form 8379 to your return when you file it. Write "Injured Spouse" in the upper left corner of the return.

Part I	Information About the Joint Tax Return for Which This Claim Is Filed

1 Enter the following information exactly as it is shown on the tax return for which you are filing this claim.
The spouse's name and social security number shown first on that tax return must also be shown first below.

First name, initial, and last name shown first on the return	Social security number shown first	If Injured Spouse, check here ▶ ☐
First name, initial, and last name shown second on the return	Social security number shown second	If Injured Spouse, check here ▶ ☐

If you are filing Form 8379 with your tax return, skip to line 5.

2 Enter the tax year for which you are filing this claim ▶ 19____

3 Current home address   City   State   ZIP code

4 Is the address on your joint return different from the address shown above? . . . . ☐ **Yes** ☐ **No**

5 Do you want the refund check to be payable to the injured spouse only? . . . . ☐ **Yes** ☐ **No**

6 Did you live in a community property state (Arizona, California, Idaho, Louisiana, Nevada, New Mexico, Texas, Washington, or Wisconsin) at any time during the tax year for which you are filing this claim? . . ☐ **Yes** ☐ **No**
If "Yes," which community property state(s) did you live in? _____

Note: *Overpayments involving community property states will be allocated by the IRS according to state law. Claims from California, Idaho, Louisiana, and Texas will usually result in no refund for the injured spouse.*

Go to Part II on the back.

Cat. No. 62474Q

Form **8379** (Rev. 3-94)

Part II Allocation of Items on the Joint Tax Return Between Spouses

Allocated Items	(a) Amount Shown on Joint Return	(b) Allocated to Injured Spouse	(c) Allocated to Other Spouse
7 **Income.** Allocate separate income to the spouse who earned it. Allocate joint income, such as interest earned on a joint bank account, as you determine. But be sure to allocate **all** income shown on the joint return.			
a Wages.			
b All other income. Identify the type and amount ▶			

-------------------------------			
8 **Adjustments to income.** Allocate separate adjustments, such as an IRA deduction, to the spouse to whom they belong. Allocate other adjustments as you determine . .			
9 **Standard deduction.** If you itemized your deductions, go to line 10. Otherwise, enter ½ of the amount in column **(a)** in columns **(b)** and **(c)** and go to line 11			
10 **Itemized deductions.** Allocate separate deductions, such as employee business expenses, to the spouse to whom they belong. Allocate other deductions as you determine.			
11 **Number of exemptions.** Allocate the exemptions claimed on the joint return to the spouse who would have claimed them if separate returns had been filed. Enter whole numbers only (for example, you **cannot** allocate 3 exemptions by giving 1.5 exemptions to each spouse) .			
12 **Credits.** Allocate business credits to the spouse who had the business. Allocate any child and dependent care credit claimed for a dependent to the spouse who has been allocated the dependent's exemption. **Do not** include the earned income credit; the IRS will allocate it. Allocate any other credits as you determine			
13 **Other taxes.** Allocate self-employment tax to the spouse who earned the self-employment income. Allocate any alternative minimum tax as you determine.			
14 **Federal income tax withheld.** Allocate Federal income tax withheld to each spouse as shown on Forms W-2 and 1099-R. Be sure to attach copies of these forms to your tax return, or to Form 8379 if you are filing it by itself. (Also include any excess social security, Medicare, and RRTA tax withheld on this line.)			
15 **Payments.** Allocate joint estimated tax payments as you determine, or let the IRS allocate half to each spouse. .			

Note: *The IRS will figure the amount of any refund due the injured spouse.*

Part III **Signature.** Complete this part only if you are filing Form 8379 by itself and not with your tax return.

Under penalties of perjury, I declare that I have examined this form and any accompanying schedules or statements and to the best of my knowledge and belief, they are true, correct, and complete. Declaration of preparer (other than taxpayer) is based on all information of which preparer has any knowledge.

Keep a copy of this form for your records	Injured spouse's signature		Date	Phone number (optional) ( )
Paid Preparer's Use Only	Preparer's signature ▶	Date	Check if self-employed ▶ ☐	Preparer's social security no.
	Firm's name (or yours if self-employed) and address ▶			E. I. No.
				ZIP code

36 — Missing Schedules K-1 and Schedule L (Balance Sheets)
37 — Missing Schedules K-1 and Schedule K-1 TINs
38 — Missing Schedule L (Balance Sheet) and Schedule K-1 TINs
39 — Missing Schedules K-1, Schedule K-1 TINs, and Schedule L (Balance Sheets)
45 — Missing Schedules K
46 — Missing Schedules K and Schedules K-1
47 — Missing Schedules K and Schedules L (Balance Sheets)
48 — Missing Schedules K and Schedule K-1 TINs (5 or more)
49 — Missing Schedules K, Schedules K-1, and Schedules L (Balance Sheets)
50 — Missing Schedules K, Schedules K-1, and Schedule K-1 TINs
51 — Missing Schedules K, Schedules L (Balance Sheets), and Schedule K-1 TINs
52 — Missing Schedules K, Schedules K-1, Schedules L (Balance Sheets), and Schedule K-1 TINs (5 or more)

40 Overstatement, Understatement, or Accuracy-Related Penalty — For returns due before January 1, 1990, this penalty is one or more of the following: Valuation Overstatement, Valuation Understatement, or Substantial Understatement. For returns due after December 31, 1989, the accuracy-related penalty has been added. Refer to our Examining Officer's report for an explanation of the penalty.

41 Failure to Deposit — Taxes Paid Directly to IRS — We charged a penalty because, according to our records, you paid your taxes to an unauthorized financial institution, directly to the IRS, or with your return. The penalty is 10% of each payment you didn't deposit properly.

There is a limit to the amount of tax you may pay with your return. See the list below.

Form 941 series and Form 943 —If the total accumulated taxes for your return period is less than $500, you may pay this amount with your tax return.

Form 1042 — You can pay taxes of less than $200 with your tax return.

Form 720, Form 940 — You can pay taxes of $100 or less with your tax return.

Form CT-1 — You can pay taxes of less than $100 with your tax return.

If you think we should remove or reduce this penalty, see "Removal of Penalty — Reasonable Cause." Also see Publication 15, Circular E — Employer's Tax Guide, for deposit requirements.

42 Failure To Deposit — Insufficient or Late Deposits and Taxes Paid Directly to IRS — We charged a penalty because according to our records:
— you didn't deposit the correct amounts of tax on time, and
— you made one or more of your deposits to an unauthorized financial institution, paid your tax directly to the IRS or paid the tax with your return.

We applied your deposits and payments in the date order we received them. We used your Record of Federal Tax Liability to determine where to apply your deposits. We figured the penalty on any tax not deposited, deposited late, or not deposited in the correct amounts. For additional details see **Information on Failure to Deposit Penalty,** Code 56.

43 Failure To Deposit — Taxes Paid Directly to IRS and Record of Federal Tax Liability Incomplete — We charged a penalty because you paid taxes to an unauthorized financial institution, directly to the IRS, or with your return.

Also, your Record of Federal Tax Liability was incomplete or illegible, or the liability amounts you reported didn't equal the net taxes for the tax period. Therefore,

we averaged the total tax liability and distributed it equally throughout the tax period.

We applied your deposits and payments to the averaged liabilities in the date order we received your deposits. We figured the penalty on any tax deposited in the correct amounts.

If you believe we computed the penalty incorrectly, please send us a complete breakdown of your tax liability by filling in the enclosed Form 4977 (for tax years before 1993), or Form 941, Schedule B (for tax years 1993 and later). For additional details see **Information on Failure to Deposit Penalty,** Code 56.

44 Failure To Deposit — Insufficient Late Deposits and Taxes Paid Directly to IRS and Record of Federal Tax Liability Incomplete — We charged a penalty because, according to our records:
— you didn't make your tax deposit on time or in the correct amounts,
— you made one or more of your deposits to an unauthorized financial institution, paid your tax directly to the IRS or paid the tax with your return, and
— your Record of Federal Tax Liability was incomplete or illegible, or the liability amounts you reported didn't equal the net taxes for the tax period.

We averaged your total tax liability and distributed it equally throughout the tax period. Then we applied your deposits and payments to the averaged liabilities in the date order we received your deposits. We figured the penalty on any tax not deposited, deposited late, or not deposited in the correct amounts.

If you believe we computed the penalty incorrectly, please send us a complete breakdown of your tax liability by filling in the enclosed Form 4977 (for tax years before 1993), or Form 941, Schedule B (for tax years 1993 and later). For additional details see **Information on Failure to Deposit Penalty,** Code 56.

53 Ten Percent Penalty for Internal Revenue Code (IRC) Section 444 Election — We charged a penalty because we didn't receive the full amount of the "required payment" for your IRC Section 444 election on time. The required payment is the value of the tax deferral you receive when you change your tax year under IRC Section 444.

The penalty is 10% of the part of the payment that you didn't pay on time.

If the required payment is more than $500 for any year you made an IRC Section 444 election, you must make a payment on Form 8752, Required Payment or Refund Under Section 7519, by May 15th of the following calendar year. The procedures for Reasonable Cause don't apply to this 10 percent penalty.

54 Failure to Deposit — Deposits Insufficient/Late and Incorrect Record of Federal Tax Liability — We charged a penalty because it appears that you didn't deposit the correct amounts of tax on time. Our records showed you as a semi-weekly depositor but your Form 941, Schedule B didn't have enough information on it for us to determine if you made your deposits on time or in the correct amounts.

Therefore, we averaged the liability you reported and distributed it equally. We then applied your deposits in the date order we received them. We figured the penalty on any tax not deposited, deposited late, or not deposited in the correct amounts.

For deposits due after December 31, 1989, the penalty rate is as follows:

2% — deposits made 1 to 5 days late,
5% — deposits made 6 to 15 days late,
10% — deposits made 16 or more days late.

We figured your penalty using one of the rates listed above. **When you don't pay the amount you owe within 10 days of the date of the first notice we sent you, we automatically increase the penalty rate to 15%** and include the additional penalty in your next bill.

If you believe we computed the penalty incorrectly, please complete the enclosed Form 941, Schedule B. If you think we should remove or reduce this penalty, see "Removal of Penalty — Reasonable Cause." For information on deposit requirements, see Publication 15, Circular E — Employer's Tax Guide, or Publication 51, Circular A — Agricultural Employer's Tax Guide.

55 Failure to Deposit — Incorrect Record of Federal Tax Liability and Taxes Paid Directly to IRS — We charged a penalty because your Form 941, Schedule B was incomplete and we couldn't determine if you made your deposits on time or in the correct amounts.

Therefore, we averaged the liability you reported, distributed it equally, and applied your deposits in the date order we received them. We figured the penalty on any tax not deposited, deposited late, or not deposited in the correct amounts.

Also, it appears that you paid taxes to an unauthorized financial institution, directly to the IRS, or with your tax return.

If you believe we computed the penalty incorrectly, please complete the enclosed Form 941, Schedule B. For additional details see **Information on Failure to Deposit Penalty,** Code 56.

56 Failure to Deposit — Deposits Insufficient/Late, Taxes Paid Directly to IRS, and Incorrect Record of Federal Tax Liability — We charged a penalty because, according to our records:
— you didn't make your tax deposit on time or in the correct amounts,
— you made one or more of your deposits to an unauthorized financial institution, paid your tax directly to the IRS or paid the tax with your return, and
— your Record of Federal Tax Liability was incomplete or illegible, or the liability amounts you reported didn't equal the net taxes for the tax period.

We averaged your total tax liability, distributed it equally, and applied your deposits and payments to the averaged liabilities in the date order we received them. We figured the penalty on any tax not deposited, deposited late, or not deposited in the correct amounts.

If you believe we computed the penalty incorrectly, please complete the enclosed Form 941, Schedule B. For additional details see **Information on Failure to Deposit Penalty** below.

Information on Failure to Deposit Penalty. There is a limit to the amount of tax you may pay with your return.

Form 941 series and Form 943 — If the total accumulated taxes for your return, is less than $500, you may pay this amount with your tax return.

Form 1042 — You can pay taxes of less than $200 with your tax return.

Form 720 and Form 940 — You can pay taxes of $100 or less with your tax return.

Form CT-1 — You can pay taxes of less than $100 with your tax return.

For deposits due after December 31, 1989, the penalty rate is as follows:

2% — deposits made 1 to 5 days late,
5% — deposits made 6 to 15 days late,
10% — deposits made 16 or more days late, or
10% — deposits made to an unauthorized financial institution, or payments made directly to the IRS.

We figured your penalty using one of the rates listed above. **When you don't pay the amount you owe within 10 days of the date of the first notice we sent you, we automatically increase the penalty rate to 15%** and include the additional penalty in your next bill.

If you think we should remove or reduce this penalty, see "Removal of Penalty — Reasonable Cause." Also see Publication 15, Circular E — Employer's Tax Guide, for deposit requirements.

57 Failure to Deposit — Deposits Insufficient/Late and Incorrect Record of Federal Tax Liability — We charged a penalty because, according to our records, you didn't deposit your tax using the one-day deposit rule for liabilities $100,000 or more during a deposit period.

Also, the Record of Federal Tax Liability on your return was incomplete and we couldn't determine if you made your deposits on time or in the correct amounts. Therefore, we averaged the liability you reported and distributed it equally.

Since your average amount of monthly liability was $100,000 or more, we placed the liability on the first day of your applicable semi-weekly period. We applied your deposits in the date order we received them. We figured the penalty on any tax not deposited, deposited late, or not deposited in the correct amounts.

For deposits due after December 31, 1989, the penalty rate is as follows:

2% — deposits made 1 to 5 days late,
5% — deposits made 6 to 15 days late,
10% — deposits made 16 or more days late.

We figured your penalty using one of the rates listed above. **When you don't pay the amount you owe within 10 days of the date of the first notice we sent you, we automatically increase the penalty rate to 15%** and include the additional penalty in your next bill.

If you believe we computed the penalty incorrectly, please complete the enclosed Form 941, Schedule B. If you think we should remove or reduce this penalty, see *"Removal of Penalty — Reasonable Cause."* For information on deposit requirements, see Publication 15, *Circular E — Employer's Tax Guide,* and Publication 51, *Circular A — Agricultural Employer's Tax Guide.*

58 Failure to Deposit — Deposits Insufficient/Late and Incorrect Record of Federal Tax Liability — We charged a penalty because, according to our records, you didn't deposit your tax using the one-day deposit rule for liabilities $100,000 or more during a deposit period.

Also, your Form 941 Schedule B was incomplete and we couldn't determine if you made your deposits on time or in the correct amounts. Therefore, we averaged the liability you reported and distributed it equally.

Since your average amount of liability was $100,000 or more, we placed the liability on the first day of the applicable semi-weekly period (eighth-monthly period for tax years ending on or before December 31, 1992). We applied your deposits in the date order we received them. We figured the penalty on any tax not deposited, deposited late, or not deposited in the correct amounts.

For deposits due after December 31, 1989, the penalty rate is as follows:

2% — deposits made 1 to 5 days late,
5% — deposits made 6 to 15 days late,
10% — deposits made 16 or more days late.

We figured your penalty using one of the rates listed above. **When you don't pay the amount you owe within 10 days of the date of the first notice we sent you, we automatically increase the penalty rate to 15%** and include the additional penalty in your next bill.

If you believe we computed the penalty incorrectly, please complete the enclosed Form 941, Schedule B. If you think we should remove or reduce this penalty, see *"Removal of Penalty — Reasonable Cause."* For information on deposit requirements, see Publication 15, *Circular E — Employer's Tax Guide,* and Publication 51, *Circular A - Agricultural Employer's Tax Guide.*

Interest

09 Interest — We charged interest because, according to our records, you didn't pay your tax on time. We figure interest from the due date of your return (regardless of extensions) to the date we receive your full payment or the date of this notice.

Corporate Interest — We charged additional interest of 2% because, according to our records, you didn't make your corporate tax payment within 30 days after IRS notified you of the underpayment of tax. This interest begins on the 31st day after we notify you of the underpayment on tax amounts you owe over $100,000,minus your timely payments and credits.

19 Additional Interest Charges — Please pay the amount you owe within 10 days from the date of this notice. If we don't receive your payment by then, we will continue to charge interest until you pay your tax in full.

We will also charge a penalty for paying late. The penalty is 1/2% for each month or part of a month your tax remains unpaid from the due date of your return, but may not be more than 25% of the tax you paid late. If you think we should remove or reduce this penalty, see *"; Removal of Penalty — Reasonable Cause."*

Interest Paid

Beginning with tax year 1991, you can no longer deduct interest you paid to the Internal Revenue Service as an itemized deduction on your Form 1040, Schedule A.

Interest Reduced

If we reduce interest that you previously reported as a deduction on your tax return, you must report this reduction of interest as income on your tax return for the year we reduce it.

Interest Removed-Erroneous Refund

The law requires us to remove interest up to the date we request you to repay the erroneous refund when:
— you didn't cause the erroneous refund in any way, and
— the refund doesn't exceed $50,000.

IRS may remove or reduce interest on other erroneous refunds based on the facts and circumstances involved in each case.

Netted Interest — Effective January 1, 1987, the current interest rate we pay when you overpay your tax is 1% less than the rate of interest we charge when you underpay your tax. However, if we refund an overpayment to you with interest and we have to increase your tax at a later date, we give special consideration to the interest on these accounts.

On the tax increase after the refund, we'll charge the lower refund rate of interest on the tax instead of the higher underpayment rate of interest. We'll charge the lower interest rate on the new tax (up to the amount of the refund) for the same period of time we paid interest on the overpayment.

Status of Your Account

22 Balance Less Than $1 — If the amount you owe is less than $1, you do not have to pay it.

23 Refund Less Than $1 — If your refund is less than $1, we will send it to you only if you ask for it.

24 Refund — We will refund your overpayment (plus interest when applicable), if you owe no other taxes or have no other debts the law requires us to collect.

25 This notice is not the result of an examination of your return. We notify a taxpayer when we select his/her return for examination.

Credit Adjustments

13 Withholding Credits — We've made a change to your withholding tax credits.

14 Estimated Tax Credits — We've made a change to your estimated tax credits.

15 Credits — We've made a change to your credits.

29 Erroneous Credit — We found a credit applied to your account in error. The enclosed notice shows the correct amount due.

Action Required on Balance Due Accounts

16 Payment — Please make your check or money order payable to the Internal Revenue Service. Write on your payment your social security number or employer identification number, the tax period and tax form. Mail your payment with the bottom part of your notice in the enclosed envelope or to the address on the front of your notice.

Notice About Partial Payments — Generally, we apply your payment first to tax, then to penalty, and finally to the interest you owe.

Additional Tax Concerns

Backup Withholding

If you received interest, dividends or patronage dividend income, but you didn't report the income on your tax return and you didn't pay the tax due on your tax return, you could be subject to a special income tax withholding called *Backup Withholding.* The IRS may request each payer of that income to begin withholding at a rate of 31 percent if, after we send you four notices over 120 days, a balance remains due on your account.

Federal/State Exchange Program

The Internal Revenue Service has agreements with state and certain local tax agencies to exchange information about federal tax, including increases or decreases. If this change affects the amount of your state or local income tax, you should file the required state or local form to report the change.

Form **8822**
(Rev. May 1994)
Department of the Treasury
Internal Revenue Service

Change of Address

▶ Please type or print.

▶ See instructions on back.   ▶ Do not attach this form to your return.

OMB No. 1545-1163
Expires 5-31-95

Part I — Complete This Part To Change Your Home Mailing Address

Check **ALL** boxes this change affects:

1 ☐ Individual income tax returns (Forms 1040, 1040A, 1040EZ, 1040NR, etc.)
　 ▶ If your last return was a joint return and you are now establishing a residence separate
　　 from the spouse with whom you filed that return, check here . . . . ▶ ☐

2 ☐ Employment tax returns for household employers (Forms 942, 940, and 940-EZ)
　 ▶ Enter your employer identification number here . . . . ▶ _____

3 ☐ Gift, estate, or generation-skipping transfer tax returns (Forms 706, 709, etc.)
　 ▶ For Forms 706 and 706-NA, enter the decedent's name and social security number below.

　 ▶ Name　　　　　　　　　　　　　　　　　　▶ Social security number

4a Your name (first name, initial, and last name)	4b Your social security number
5a Spouse's name (first name, initial, and last name)	5b Spouse's social security number

6 Prior name(s). See instructions.

7a Old address (no., street, city or town, state, and ZIP code). If a P.O. box or foreign address, see instructions.	Apt. no.
7b Spouse's old address, if different from line 7a (no., street, city or town, state, and ZIP code). If a P.O. box or foreign address, see instructions.	Apt. no.
8 New address (no., street, city or town, state, and ZIP code). If a P.O. box or foreign address, see instructions.	Apt. no.

Part II — Complete This Part To Change Your Business Mailing Address or Business Location

Check **ALL** boxes this change affects:

9 ☐ Employment, excise, and other business returns (Forms 720, 941, 990, 1041, 1065, 1120, etc.)
10 ☐ Employee plan returns (Forms 5500, 5500-C/R, and 5500-EZ). See instructions.
11 ☐ Business location

12a Business name	12b Employer identification number
13 Old address (no., street, city or town, state, and ZIP code). If a P.O. box or foreign address, see instructions.	Room or suite no.
14 New address (no., street, city or town, state, and ZIP code). If a P.O. box or foreign address, see instructions.	Room or suite no.
15 New business location (no., street, city or town, state, and ZIP code). If a foreign address, see instructions.	Room or suite no.

Part III — Signature

Daytime telephone number of person to contact (optional) ▶ ( )_____

Please Sign Here ▶

| Your signature | Date | If Part II completed, signature of owner, officer, or representative | Date |
| If joint return, spouse's signature | Date | Title | |

For Privacy Act and Paperwork Reduction Act Notice, see back of form.　　Cat. No. 12081V　　Form **8822** (Rev. 5-94)

Privacy Act and Paperwork Reduction Act Notice

We ask for this information to carry out the Internal Revenue laws of the United States. We may give the information to the Department of Justice and to other Federal agencies, as provided by law. We may also give it to cities, states, the District of Columbia, and U.S. commonwealths or possessions to carry out their tax laws. And we may give it to foreign governments because of tax treaties they have with the United States.

If you fail to provide the Internal Revenue Service with your current mailing address, you may not receive a notice of deficiency or a notice and demand for tax. Despite the failure to receive such notices, penalties and interest will continue to accrue on the tax deficiencies.

The time needed to complete and file this form will vary depending on individual circumstances. The estimated average time is 16 minutes.

If you have comments concerning the accuracy of this time estimate or suggestions for making this form more simple, we would be happy to hear from you. You can write to both the **Internal Revenue Service,** Attention: Reports Clearance Officer, PC:FP, Washington, DC 20224; and the **Office of Management and Budget,** Paperwork Reduction Project (1545-1163), Washington, DC 20503. **DO NOT** send this form to either of these offices. Instead, see **Where To File** on this page.

Purpose of Form

You may use Form 8822 to notify the Internal Revenue Service if you changed your home or business mailing address or your business location. Generally, complete only one Form 8822 to change your home and business addresses. If this change also affects the mailing address for your children who filed income tax returns, complete and file a separate Form 8822 for each child. If you are a representative signing for the taxpayer, attach to Form 8822 a copy of your power of attorney.

Note: *If you moved after you filed your return and you are expecting a refund, also notify the post office serving your old address. This will help forward your check to your new address.*

Prior Name(s)

If you or your spouse changed your name due to marriage, divorce, etc., complete line 6. Also, be sure to notify the **Social Security Administration** of your new name so that it has the same name in its records that you have on your tax return. This prevents delays in processing your return and issuing refunds. It also safeguards your future social security benefits.

P.O. Box

If your post office does not deliver mail to your street address and you have a P.O. box, show the box number instead of your street address.

Foreign Address

If your address is outside the United States or its possessions or territories, enter the information in the following order: number, street, city, province or state, postal code, and country. **Do not** abbreviate the country name. Be sure to include any apartment, room, or suite number in the space provided.

Employee Plan Returns

A change in the mailing address for employee plan returns must be shown on a separate Form 8822 unless the **Exception** below applies.

Exception. If the employee plan returns were filed with the same service center as your other returns (individual, business, employment, gift, estate, etc.), you do not have to use a separate Form 8822. See **Where To File** below.

Where To File

Send this form to the **Internal Revenue Service Center** shown below for your old address. But if you checked the box on line 10 (employee plan returns), send it to the address shown in the far right column.

If your old address was in:	Use this address:
Florida, Georgia, South Carolina	Atlanta, GA 39901
New Jersey, New York (New York City and counties of Nassau, Rockland, Suffolk, and Westchester)	Holtsville, NY 00501
New York (all other counties), Connecticut, Maine, Massachusetts, New Hampshire, Rhode Island, Vermont	Andover, MA 05501
Alaska, Arizona, California (counties of Alpine, Amador, Butte, Calaveras, Colusa, Contra Costa, Del Norte, El Dorado, Glenn, Humboldt, Lake, Lassen, Marin, Mendocino, Modoc, Napa, Nevada, Placer, Plumas, Sacramento, San Joaquin, Shasta, Sierra, Siskiyou, Solano, Sonoma, Sutter, Tehama, Trinity, Yolo, and Yuba), Colorado, Idaho, Montana, Nebraska, Nevada, North Dakota, Oregon, South Dakota, Utah, Washington, Wyoming	Ogden, UT 84201
California (all other counties), Hawaii	Fresno, CA 93888

Indiana, Kentucky, Michigan, Ohio, West Virginia	Cincinnati, OH 45999
Kansas, New Mexico, Oklahoma, Texas	Austin, TX 73301
Delaware, District of Columbia, Maryland, Pennsylvania, Virginia	Philadelphia, PA 19255
Alabama, Arkansas, Louisiana, Mississippi, North Carolina, Tennessee	Memphis, TN 37501
Illinois, Iowa, Minnesota, Missouri, Wisconsin	Kansas City, MO 64999
American Samoa	Philadelphia, PA 19255
Guam: Permanent residents	Department of Revenue and Taxation Government of Guam 378 Chalan San Antonio Tamuning, GU 96911
Guam: Nonpermanent residents Puerto Rico (or if excluding income under section 933) Virgin Islands: Nonpermanent residents	Philadelphia, PA 19255
Virgin Islands: Permanent residents	V. I. Bureau of Internal Revenue Lockhart Gardens No. 1-A Charlotte Amalie, St. Thomas, VI 00802
Foreign country: U.S. citizens and those filing Form 2555, Form 2555-EZ, or Form 4563	Philadelphia, PA 19255
All A.P.O. and F.P.O. addresses	Philadelphia, PA 19255

Employee Plan Returns ONLY (Form 5500 series)

If the principal office of the plan sponsor or the plan administrator was in:	Use this address:
Connecticut, Delaware, District of Columbia, Maine, Maryland, Massachusetts, New Hampshire, New Jersey, New York, Pennsylvania, Puerto Rico, Rhode Island, Vermont, Virginia	Holtsville, NY 00501
Alabama, Alaska, Arkansas, California, Florida, Georgia, Hawaii, Idaho, Louisiana, Mississippi, Nevada, North Carolina, Oregon, South Carolina, Tennessee, Washington	Atlanta, GA 39901
Arizona, Colorado, Illinois, Indiana, Iowa, Kansas, Kentucky, Michigan, Minnesota, Missouri, Montana, Nebraska, New Mexico, North Dakota, Ohio, Oklahoma, South Dakota, Texas, Utah, West Virginia, Wisconsin, Wyoming	Memphis, TN 37501
Foreign country	Holtsville, NY 00501
All Form 5500-EZ filers	Andover, MA 05501

Form **SS-8**

(Rev. July 1993)

Department of the Treasury
Internal Revenue Service

Determination of Employee Work Status
for Purposes of Federal Employment Taxes
and Income Tax Withholding

OMB No. 1545-0004
Expires 7-31-96

Paperwork Reduction Act Notice

We ask for the information on this form to carry out the Internal Revenue laws of the United States. You are required to give us this information. We need it to ensure that you are complying with these laws and to allow us to figure and collect the right amount of tax.

The time needed to complete and file this form will vary depending on individual circumstances. The estimated average time is: **recordkeeping, 34 hr., 55 min., learning about the law or the form,** 6 min. and **preparing and sending the form to IRS,** 40 min. If you have comments concerning the accuracy of these time estimates or suggestions for making this form more simple, we would be happy to hear from you. You can write to both the **Internal Revenue Service,** Attention: Reports Clearance Officer, T:FP, Washington, DC 20224; and the **Office of Management and Budget,** Paperwork Reduction Project (1545-0004), Washington, DC 20503. **DO NOT** send the tax form to either of these offices. Instead, see **General Information** for where to file.

Purpose

Employers and workers file Form SS-8 to get a determination as to whether a worker is an employee for purposes of Federal employment taxes and income tax withholding.

General Information

This form should be completed carefully. If the firm is completing the form, it should be completed for **ONE** individual who is representative of the class of workers whose status is in question. If a written determination is desired for more than one class of workers, a separate Form SS-8 should be completed for one worker from each class whose status is typical of that class. A written determination for any worker will apply to other workers of the same class if the facts are not materially different from those of the worker whose status was ruled upon.

Please return Form SS-8 to the Internal Revenue Service office that provided the form. If the Internal Revenue Service did not ask you to complete this form but you wish a determination on whether a worker is an employee, file Form SS-8 with your District Director.

*Caution: Form SS-8 is **not** a claim for refund of social security and Medicare taxes or Federal income tax withholding. Also, a determination that an individual is an employee does not necessarily reduce any current or prior tax liability. A worker must file his or her income tax return even if a determination has not been made by the due date of the return.*

Name of firm (or person) for whom the worker performed services	Name of worker
Address of firm (include street address, apt. or suite no., city, state, and ZIP code)	Address of worker (include street address, apt. or suite no., city, state, and ZIP code)

Trade name	Telephone number (include area code) ( )	Worker's social security number – –

Telephone number (include area code) ( )	Firm's taxpayer identification number –	

Check type of firm for which the work relationship is in question:
☐ **Individual** ☐ **Partnership** ☐ **Corporation** ☐ **Other** (specify) ▶

Important Information Needed to Process Your Request

This form is being completed by: ☐ Firm ☐ Worker

If this form is being completed by the worker, the IRS **must** have your permission to disclose your name to the firm.

Do you object to disclosing your name and the information on this form to the firm? . . . . ☐ **Yes** ☐ **No**

If you answer "Yes," the IRS cannot act on your request. **DO NOT complete the rest of this form unless the IRS asks for it.**

Under section 6110 of the Internal Revenue Code, the information on this form and related file documents will be open to the public if any ruling or determination is made. However, names, addresses, and taxpayer identification numbers must be removed before the information can be made public.

Is there any other information you want removed? . . . . ☐ **Yes** ☐ **No**

If you check "Yes," we cannot process your request unless you submit a copy of this form and copies of all supporting documents showing, in brackets, the information you want removed. Attach a separate statement telling which specific exemption of section 6110(c) applies to each bracketed part.

*This form is designed to cover many work activities, so some of the questions may not apply to you. **You must answer ALL items or mark them "Unknown" or "Does not apply."** If you need more space, attach another sheet.*

Total number of workers in this class. (Attach names and addresses. If more than 10 workers, attach only 10.) ▶ _____

This information is about services performed by the worker from _____ to _____
                                                 (month, day, year)   (month, day, year)

Is the worker still performing services for the firm? . . . . ☐ **Yes** ☐ **No**

If "No," what was the date of termination? ▶ _____
                                   (month, day, year)

1a Describe the firm's business ....

  b Describe the work done by the worker ....

....

2a If the work is done under a written agreement between the firm and the worker, attach a copy.

  b If the agreement is not in writing, describe the terms and conditions of the work arrangement ....

....

....

  c If the actual working arrangement differs in any way from the agreement, explain the differences and why they occur ....

....

....

3a Is the worker given training by the firm? .... ☐ **Yes** ☐ **No**

    If "Yes": What kind? ....

    How often? ....

  b Is the worker given instructions in the way the work is to be done (exclusive of actual training in 3a)? . ☐ **Yes** ☐ **No**

    If "Yes," give specific examples. ....

  c Attach samples of any written instructions or procedures.

  d Does the firm have the right to change the methods used by the worker or direct that person on how to

    do the work? .... ☐ **Yes** ☐ **No**

    Explain your answer ....

....

  e Does the operation of the firm's business require that the worker be supervised or controlled in the

    performance of the service? .... ☐ **Yes** ☐ **No**

    Explain your answer ....

....

4a The firm engages the worker:

    ☐ To perform and complete a particular job only

    ☐ To work at a job for an indefinite period of time

    ☐ Other (explain) ....

  b Is the worker required to follow a routine or a schedule established by the firm? .... ☐ **Yes** ☐ **No**

    If "Yes," what is the routine or schedule? ....

....

....

  c Does the worker report to the firm or its representative?. .... ☐ **Yes** ☐ **No**

    If "Yes": How often? ....

    For what purpose? ....

    In what manner (in person, in writing, by telephone, etc.)? ....

    Attach copies of report forms used in reporting to the firm.

  d Does the worker furnish a time record to the firm?. .... ☐ **Yes** ☐ **No**

    If "Yes," attach copies of time records.

5a State the kind and value of tools, equipment, supplies, and materials furnished by:

    The firm ....

....

    The worker ....

....

  b What expenses are incurred by the worker in the performance of services for the firm? ....

....

  c Does the firm reimburse the worker for any expenses? .... ☐ **Yes** ☐ **No**

    If "Yes," specify the reimbursed expenses ....

6a Will the worker perform the services personally? .... ☐ **Yes** ☐ **No**

  b Does the worker have helpers? . ... ☐ **Yes** ☐ **No**

    If "Yes": Who hires the helpers? ☐ Firm ☐ Worker

    If hired by the worker, is the firm's approval necessary? .... ☐ **Yes** ☐ **No**

    Who pays the helpers? ☐ Firm ☐ Worker

    Are social security and Medicare taxes and Federal income tax withheld from the helpers' wages? . . ☐ **Yes** ☐ **No**

    If "Yes": Who reports and pays these taxes? ☐ Firm ☐ Worker

    Who reports the helpers' incomes to the Internal Revenue Service? ☐ Firm ☐ Worker

    If the worker pays the helpers, does the firm repay the worker? .... ☐ **Yes** ☐ **No**

    What services do the helpers perform?

Appeal Rights and Preparation of Protests for Unagreed Cases

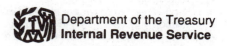

Department of the Treasury
Internal Revenue Service

Publication 5 (Rev. 11/90)
Catalog Number 46074I

If You Agree

If you agree with the examiner's findings in the enclosed examination report, please sign the agreement form and return it with our transmittal letter. By signing, you are agreeing to the amounts shown on the form.

If the agreement shows you owe additional tax you may pay it without waiting for a bill. Include interest on the additional tax and on any penalties at the applicable rate from the due date of the return to the date of payment. Figure the interest as shown in the enclosed Notice 433, Yearly interest and Certain Penalty Rates.

If you do not pay the additional tax when you sign the agreement, you will receive a bill for the additional tax. Interest is charged on the additional tax from the due date of your return to the billing date. However, you will not be billed for more than 30 days interest from the date we receive your signed agreement. No further interest or penalties will be charged if you pay the amount you owe within 10 days after the billing date.

Please make your check or money order payable to the Internal Revenue Service and include on the check or money order your social security number (individual tax) or employee identification number (business tax), the tax form number, and the tax period for which payment is being made. Do not send cash through the mail.

If the examination report shows a refund is due you, you should sign and return the agreement form promptly so the Service can send your refund sooner. You will receive interest on the refund.

If You Don't Agree

If you decide not to agree with the examiner's findings, you have the option of requesting a meeting with the examiner's supervisor to discuss the findings. If you still do not agree, we urge you to appeal your case with the Service. Most differences can be settled in these appeals without expensive and time-consuming court trials. (Appeals conferences are not available to taxpayers whose reasons for disagreement do not come within the scope of the internal revenue laws. For example, disagreement based solely on moral, religious, political, constitutional, conscientious, or similar grounds.)

The following general rules tell you how to appeal your case.

Appeals Within the IRS

You may appeal an IRS decision to a regional Appeals Office, which is independent of your local District Director or Service Center Director. The regional Appeals Office is the only level of appeal within the IRS. Appeals conferences are conducted in an informal manner.

If you want an appeals conference, write to your District Director or Service Center Director according to the instructions in our letter to you. Your director will give your request to the Appeals Office to arrange a conference at a convenient time and place. You and/or your representative should be prepared to discuss all disputed issues at the conference. Most differences are settled at this level.

Special appeals procedures, including a consolidated appeals conference, may be held for all producers in certain windfall profit tax cases. See the heading Procedures for Crude Oil Windfall Profit Tax Cases for procedures on these cases if you are appealing a windfall profit tax issue.

If an agreement is not reached at your appeals conference, or if you do not want to appeal your case to the IRS, you may, at any stage of the proceedings, take your case to court. See **Appeals to the Courts,** later.

Written Protests

When you request a conference, you may also need to file a written protest or a brief statement of disputed issues with your District Director or Service Center Director.
You do not have to file anything in writing if:
The proposed increase (including penalties) or decrease in tax, or refund, determined by the examination is not more than $2,500 for any of the tax periods involved, or

Your examination was handled by mail or in an IRS office by a tax auditor.
A brief written statement of the disputed issues is required if:
The proposed increase (including penalties) or decrease in tax, or claimed refund, determined by the examination is more than $2,500 but not more than $10,000 and

Your examination was a field examination by a revenue agent or a revenue officer.
Written protests are required:
If as a result of a field examination by a revenue agent or a revenue officer, the proposed increase (including penalties) or

decrease in tax, or claimed refund, is more than $10,000 for any tax period; or

In all employee plan and exempt organization cases; or

In all partnership and S corporation cases.
If a written protest is required, you should send it within the time limit specified in the letter you received with the examination report. Your protest should contain:

1) Your name and address,
2) A statement that you want to appeal the examination findings to the Appeals Office,
3) The date and symbols from the letter showing the proposed changes and findings you disagree with,
4) The tax periods or years involved,
5) An itemized schedule of the changes with which you disagree,
6) A statement of facts supporting your position on any issue with which you disagree, and
7) A statement stating the law or other authority on which you rely.

You must declare that the statement of facts under (6) is true under penalties of perjury. Do this by adding the following signed declaration:

"Under the penalties of perjury, I declare that I have examined the statement of facts presented in this protest and in any accompanying schedules and, to the best of my knowledge and belief, it is true, correct, and complete."

If your representative submits the protest for you, he or she may substitute a declaration stating:

1) That he or she prepared the protest and accompanying documents and
2) Whether he or she knows personally that the statement of facts in the protest and accompanying documents are true and correct.

Representation

You may represent yourself at your appeals conference, or you may be represented by an attorney, certified public accountant, or an individual enrolled to practice before the Internal Revenue Service. Your representative must be qualified to practice before the Internal Revenue Service. If your representative appears without you, he or she must file a power of attorney before receiving or inspecting confidential information. Form 2848, Power of Attorney and Declaration of Representative, or any other properly written power of attorney or authorization may be used for this purpose. You can get copies of Form 2848 from an Internal Revenue Service office.

You may also bring witnesses to support your position.

Procedures for Crude Oil Windfall Profit Tax Cases

The Statement of Procedural Rules allows the Service to provide a single consolidated appeals conference to address all oil items arising in connection with a property or lease whenever the Service determines that a consolidated procedure is necessary for effective administration of the windfall profit tax law. Generally, oil items are items taken into account in computing the windfall profit tax that can be more readily determined at the property or lease level such as:

• The tier or tiers of the crude oil;
• The quantity of crude oil in each tier;
• The adjusted base price and removal price; and
• The severance tax.

All producers having an interest in the property or lease will be permitted to participate in this conference if a written request to attend is made within 60 days of the mailing of the letter proposing the adjustment. If a written protest is required, it should also be sent within the 60-day period. If you do not agree with the adjustments but decide not to attend the conference, and the issue is appealed by the other owners, your case will be held in suspense until the final administrative determination is made.

The determination by the Appeals Office is the final administrative determination with respect to oil items arising in connection with the property or lease for the period under examination.

These procedures do not affect the producers' administrative appeal rights with respect to producer items, that is, items more readily determined at the producer level such as exemptions and independent producer status. All unagreed producers are still entitled to a separate Appeals conference to resolve producer item issues. A separate notification of appeal rights relating to producer items will generally be issued following the final administrative determination of the oil items.

See Publication 556, Examination of Returns, Appeal Rights, and Claims for Refund for additional information if you are not the producer of the oil as shown in the 60 day letter you received.

Appeals To The Courts

If you and the Service disagree after your conference or if you skipped our appeals system, you may take your case to the United States Tax Court, the United States Claims Court, or your United States District Court. (However, if you are a nonresident alien taxpayer, you cannot take your case to a United States District Court.) These courts are independent judicial bodies and have no connection with the Internal Revenue Service.

Tax Court

If your case involves a disagreement over whether you owe additional income tax, estate or gift tax, or certain excise taxes, you may go to the United States Tax Court. To do this, ask the Service to issue a formal letter, called a notice of deficiency. You have 90 days from the date this notice is mailed to you to file a petition with the Tax Court (150 days if addressed to you outside the United States). If you do not file the petition within the 90-day period (or 150 days as the case may be), the law requires that we assess and bill you for the deficiency.

If you discuss your case with the Internal Revenue Service during the 90-day period (150-day period), the discussion will not extend the period in which you may file a petition with the Tax Court.

The Court will schedule your case for trial at a location convenient to you. You may represent yourself before the Tax Court, or you may be represented by anyone permitted to practice before that Court.

NOTE: If you do not exhaust your administrative remedies, including Appeals consideration, the Court will normally request that you attempt settlement with Appeals prior to the court date.

If you dispute not more than $10,000 for any one tax year, there are simplified procedures. You can get information about these procedures and other matters relating to the Court from the Clerk of the Tax Court, 400 Second St. N.W., Washington, DC 20217.

District Court and Claims Court

You may take your case to your United States District Court or to the United States Claims Court. Certain types of cases, such as those involving manufacturers' excise taxes and employment taxes can be heard only by these courts. Generally, your District Court and the Claims Court hear tax cases only after you have paid the tax and have filed a claim for refund. You can get information about procedures for filing suit in either court by contacting the Clerk of your District Court; or the Clerk of the Claims Court. If we haven't acted on your claim within 6 months from the date you filed it, you can then file suit for refund. If we have disallowed your claim, you may request Appeals reconsideration of the disallowance, or a suit for refund must be filed no later than 2 years from the date of our disallowance. Please note that appeals reconsideration does not extend the two year period for filing suit.

Recovering Administrative and Litigation Costs

You may be able to recover your litigation and administrative costs if you are the prevailing party and if:

You exhaust all administrative remedies with the IRS, which are described in **Appeals Within the IRS** and **Written Protests.**

Your net worth is below a certain limit (see **Net worth requirements,** later), and

You provide all requested documentation and you do not otherwise unreasonably delay the administrative and court proceedings.

Prevailing party. You are the prevailing party if you meet all the following requirements:

You can show that the IRS's position in the civil proceeding was not substantially justified.

You substantially prevailed with respect to the amount in controversy, or on the most significant tax issue or set of issues in question.

You meet the net worth requirement, discussed later.

Although the court will generally decide who is the prevailing party, a final determination of liability at the administrative level is decided by the IRS. Thus, administrative costs may be received from the IRS without a taxpayer going to court.

Reasonable litigation costs generally include:

Reasonable amounts for court costs,

Expenses of expert witnesses,

The costs of studies, analyses, engineering reports, tests, or projects which the court agreed were necessary for the preparation of your case, and

Attorney fees that generally may not exceed $75 per hour.

Reasonable administrative costs generally include:

All of the costs listed under litigation costs, except court costs, and any administrative fees or similar charges made by the IRS. Administrative costs (described above) include costs incurred on or after the earlier of the date the taxpayer receives the appeals decision letter or the date of the notice of deficiency.

Net worth requirements. An individual taxpayer may be able to recover litigation and administrative costs if his or her net worth was not more than $2,000,000 when the litigation began and/or when administrative costs become recoverable. To qualify, the net worth of the owner of an unincorporated business, or a partnership, corporation, association, unit of local government, or organization cannot be more than $7,000,000 and cannot have more than 500 employees when the litigation began.

Penalty

Whenever the Tax Court determines that proceedings before it have been instituted or maintained by you primarily for delay or that your position in such proceedings is frivolous or groundless, a penalty not in excess of $25,000 shall be awarded to the United States by the Tax Court in its decision.

Publication 5 (Rev. 11-90)

*U.S. GPO:1990-517-016/22474

The Examination and Appeals Process

We examine returns for correctness of income, exemptions, credits, and deductions.

Fairness if Your Return is Examined

Most taxpayers' returns are accepted as filed. But if your return is selected for examination, it does not suggest that you are dishonest. The examination may or may not result in more tax. Your case may be closed without change. Or, you may receive a refund.

Courtesy and consideration. You are entitled to courteous and considerate treatment from IRS employees at all times. If you ever feel that you are not being treated with fairness, courtesy, and consideration by an IRS employee, you should tell the employee's supervisor. Publication 1, *Your Rights as a Taxpayer*, explains the many rights you have as a taxpayer. You can get free publications by calling our toll-free number.

Pay only the required tax. You have the right to plan your business and personal finances in such a way that you will pay the least tax that is due under the law. You are liable only for the correct amount of tax. Our purpose is to apply the law consistently and fairly to all taxpayers.

Privacy and confidentiality. You have the right to have your tax case kept confidential. Under the law, the IRS must protect the privacy of your tax information. However, if a lien or a lawsuit is filed, certain aspects of your tax case will become public record. People who prepare your return or represent you must also keep your information confidential.

You also have the right to know why we are asking you for the information, exactly how we will use it, and what might happen if you do not give it.

Examination of Returns

An examination usually begins when we notify you that your return has been selected. We will tell you which records you will need.

How returns are selected. We select returns for examination by several methods. A computer program called the Discriminant Function System (DIF) is used to select most returns. In this method, the computer uses historical data to give parts of the return a score. IRS personnel then screen the return.

Some returns are selected at random. We also select returns by examining claims for credit or refund and by matching information documents, such as Forms W–2 and 1099, with returns.

Arranging the examination. Many examinations are handled by mail. For information get the free Publication 1383, *The Correspondence Process (Income Tax Accounts)*. If we notify you that your examination is to be conducted through a personal interview, or if you request such an interview, you have the right to ask that the examination take place at a reasonable time and place that is convenient for both you and the IRS. If the time or place we suggest is not convenient, the examiner will try to work out something more suitable. However, we will make the final determination on how, when, and where an examination takes place.

Transfers to another district. Generally, your return is examined in the IRS district where you live. But if it can be examined more quickly and conveniently in another district,

such as where your books and records are located, you may ask to have the case transferred to that district.

Representation. Throughout the examination, you may represent yourself, have someone else accompany you, or, with proper written authorization, have someone represent you in your absence. If you want to consult an attorney, an enrolled agent, or any other person permitted to represent a taxpayer during an examination, we will stop and reschedule the interview. We cannot suspend the interview if you are there because of an administrative summons.

Recordings. You can generally make an audio recording of an interview with an IRS Examination officer. Your request to record the interview should be made in writing. You must notify us 10 days before the meeting and bring your own recording equipment. We also can record an interview. If we initiate the recording, we will notify you 10 days before the meeting, and you can get a copy of the recording at your expense.

Repeat examinations. We try to avoid repeat examinations of the same items, but sometimes this happens. If we examined your tax return for the same items in either of the 2 previous years and proposed no change to your tax liability, please contact us as soon as possible so that we can see if we should discontinue the examination.

Explanation of changes. If we propose any changes to your return, we will explain the reasons for the changes. It is important that you understand the reasons for any proposed change. You should not hesitate to ask about anything that is unclear to you.

Agreement with changes. If you agree with the proposed changes, you may sign an agreement form and pay any additional tax you may owe. You must pay interest on any additional tax. If you pay when you sign the agreement, the interest is generally figured from the due date of your return to the date you paid.

If you do not pay the additional tax when you sign the agreement, you will receive a bill. The interest on the additional tax is generally figured from the due date of your return to the billing date. However, you will not be billed for more than 30 days additional interest, even if the bill is delayed.

If you are due a refund, we can refund your money more quickly if you sign the agreement form. You will be paid interest on the refund.

Appealing the Examination Findings

If you do not agree with the examiner's report, you may meet with the examiner's supervisor to discuss your case further. If you still don't agree with the examiner's findings, you have the right to appeal them. The examiner will explain your appeal rights and give you a copy of Publication 5, *Appeal Rights and Preparation of Protests for Unagreed Cases*. This free publication explains your appeal rights in detail and tells you exactly what to do if you want to appeal.

Appeals Office. You can appeal the findings of an examination within the IRS through our Appeals Office. The Appeals Office is independent of your examiner and IRS District Director or Service Center Director. Most differences can be settled through this appeals system without expensive and time-consuming court

trials. If the matter cannot be settled to your satisfaction in Appeals, you can take your case to court.

Appeals to the courts. Depending on whether you first pay the disputed tax, you can take your case to the U.S. Tax Court, the U.S. Claims Court, or your U.S. District Court. These courts are entirely independent of the IRS. However, a U.S. Tax Court case is generally reviewed by our Appeals Office before it is heard by the Tax Court. As always, you can represent yourself or have someone admitted to practice before the court represent you.

If you did not yet pay the additional tax and you disagree about whether you owe it, you generally have the right to take your case to the Tax Court. Ordinarily you have 90 days from the time we mail you a formal notice (called a "notice of deficiency") telling you that you owe additional tax to file a petition with the Tax Court.

If you have already paid the disputed tax in full and filed a claim for refund (discussed later) for it that we disallowed (or on which we did not take action within 6 months), then you may take your case to the U.S. District Court or U.S. Claims Court.

Court decisions. We follow Supreme Court decisions. However, we can lose cases in other courts involving taxpayers with the same issue and still apply our interpretation of the law to your situation. You have the right to appeal our decision to do so.

Recovering litigation expenses. If the court agrees with you on most of the issues in your case, and finds the IRS's position to be largely unjustified, you may be able to recover some of your litigation expenses from us. But to do this, you must have used up all the administrative remedies available to you within the IRS, including going through our Appeals system. You may also be able to recover administrative expenses from the IRS. Free Publication 556, *Examination of Returns, Appeal Rights, and Claims for Refund*, explains your appeal rights.

Other remedies. If you believe that tax, penalty, or interest was unjustly charged, you have rights that can remedy the situation.

Claims for refund. Once you have paid your tax, you have the right to file a claim for a credit or refund if you believe the tax is too much. The procedure for filing a claim is explained in Chapter 1.

Cancellation of penalties. You have the right to ask that certain penalties (but not interest, as discussed later) be canceled (abated) if you can show reasonable cause for the failure that led to the penalty (or can show that you exercised due diligence, if that is the applicable standard for the penalty).

If you relied on wrong advice given to you by IRS employees on the toll-free telephone system, we will cancel certain penalties that may result. But you have to show that your reliance on the advice was reasonable.

Reduction of interest. If our error caused a delay in your case, and this is grossly unfair, you may be entitled to a reduction of the interest that would otherwise be due. Only delays caused by procedural or mechanical acts that do not involve exercising judgment or discretion qualify. If you think we caused such a delay, please discuss it with the examiner and file a claim.

Understanding The Collection Process

Mission

The purpose of the Internal Revenue Service is to collect the proper amount of tax revenue at the least cost; serve the public by continually improving the quality of our products and services; and perform in a manner warranting the highest degree of public confidence in our integrity, efficiency and fairness.

Existe una versión de esta publicación en español, la Publicación 594S, que puede obtener en la oficina local del Servicio de Impuestos Internos.

KEEP THIS PUBLICATION FOR A REFERENCE

Department of the Treasury
Internal Revenue Service
Publication 594 (Rev. 1-94)
Catalog Number 46596B

Introduction

This publication explains your rights and responsibilities regarding payment of Federal tax. This information applies to all taxpayers, including individuals who owe income tax and taxpayers who owe employment tax. Special rules that apply only to employers are covered in separate sections of this publication.

Although this publication discusses the legal authority that allows the Internal Revenue Service (IRS) to collect taxes, it is not intended as a precise and technical analysis of the law.

Do not ignore your tax bill. **If you owe the tax shown on a bill, you should make arrangements to pay it.** If you believe it is incorrect, contact the IRS immediately to suspend action until the mistake is corrected. See the following discussion titled "If you believe your bill is wrong," on page 3.

Important reminder about child support. By law, the IRS can collect certified child support obligations. The collection and payment of these debts, with certain exceptions, follow the same process as the collection of unpaid taxes.

Highlights

The answers to the following questions are found in this publication. After each question, you will find the appropriate heading where the topic is explained. These commonly-asked questions relate to the bill you received for your unpaid taxes.

- What if I disagree with the amount of tax that IRS says I owe?

  See "If you believe your bill is wrong," on page 3.

- Who can I call to explain my situation (why I haven't paid)?

  See "Numbers to Call for Assistance," on this page.

- What do I do if I disagree with the IRS employee?

  See "When you do not agree with decisions of IRS employees," on page 2.

- What are my rights to appeal if I disagree with an IRS decision?

  See " When you do not agree with decisions of IRS employees," "Administrative review," and "Your Appeal Rights," on pages 2, 7, and 8.

- I have tried to get the IRS to resolve my tax problems but can't.

  See "Problem Resolution Program," on page 2.

- Can I make monthly payments on my account?

  See "Making installment payments for individuals or businesses," and "Simplified installment agreements" on page 3.

- Can I settle my tax account for less than what I owe?

  See "Submitting an Offer in Compromise," on page 4.

- What if I can't pay any amount? Will you take money out of my wages?

  See "What Happens When You Take No Action to Pay," and "Levy on wages," on pages 5 and 6.

- Can I postpone paying my taxes until my financial condition improves?

  See "Delaying collection if you cannot pay," on page 3.

- I'm an employer. What happens if I cannot pay my employment taxes?

  See "What Happens When You Take No Action to Pay," and "Trust Fund Recovery Penalty Assessments for Employers," on pages 5 and 8.

- How do I make a tax deposit if I do not have tax deposit coupons for employment taxes?

  See "Paying employment taxes," on page 4.

- What happens to my tax refund if I owe taxes for prior years?

  See "If your current tax return shows a tax refund and you owe back taxes," on page 4.

- Does owing taxes have an effect on my credit?

  See "Lien," on page 5.

Numbers to Call for Assistance

If you have a question about your tax bill, you should either call the telephone number on your tax bill or the telephone number shown in the white pages of your local telephone directory under U.S. Government, Internal Revenue Service, Federal Tax Information and Assistance. If there is not a specific number listed, call toll-free **1-800-829-1040**.

Free publications and forms. To order any of our free taxpayer information publications, tax forms, or forms and instructions that are mentioned throughout this publication, call the toll-free number **1-800-TAX-FORM (1-800-829-3676)**. Or, you may write to the IRS Forms Distribution Center in your area as shown in your income tax package (for example, the Form 1040 package).

Your Rights

When dealing with the IRS, you have the right to be treated fairly, professionally, promptly, and courteously by IRS employees.

Publication 1, Your Rights As A Taxpayer. This publication explains the many rights you have at each step of the tax collection process.

Some of the topics Publication 1 covers are:

- Confidentiality of tax matters,
- Procedures for appeal,
- Canceling penalties based on showing reasonable cause,
- IRS procedures regarding seizures and your rights regarding access to your private property, and
- Payment of interest to you when refunds are sent late.

You received a copy of Publication 1 with your initial bill, which is also called a *"Notice of Tax Due and Demand for Payment."* You may also request a copy of Publication 1 from an IRS employee at or before your first in-person interview with an IRS employee.

▷ *When you do not agree with decisions of IRS employees.* If at any step of the Collection process you do not agree with the recommendation of an IRS employee, you have the right to an administrative review of the matter with the employee's manager. At your request, the employee will either arrange for you to meet with the manager or tell you the manager's name and where to contact him or her.

Who can represent you in IRS matters. You may represent yourself or you may have an attorney, certified public accountant, enrolled agent or any person enrolled to practice before the Internal Revenue Service represent you. For example you may want your tax preparer to respond to a tax bill that you believe is not correct.

To authorize another person to have access to your Federal tax information, you can use Form 2848, *Power of Attorney and Declaration of Representative*, or Form 8821, *Tax Information Authorization*, or any other properly written power of attorney or authorization. You can get copies of these forms from your local IRS office or by calling the toll-free number shown on page 1.

Sharing your tax information. Under the law, we can share your tax information with city and state tax agencies, and in some cases, the Department of Justice, other federal agencies, and persons you authorize. We can also share it with certain foreign governments under tax treaty provisions.

▷ *Transferring the location of your tax case.* You have the right to request that we transfer your tax case to another IRS office. Generally, we will transfer your case if you have a valid reason for making the request, such as a change of address.

If you move, send Form 8822, *Change of Address,* to any IRS office, so you will receive any notices sent to you. You may order this form by calling 1-800-829-3676.

Receiving receipts for payments you made to IRS. IRS must provide you with a receipt (Form 809) when you pay in cash. You have the right to ask for and receive a receipt for all payments you make. You should ask for a receipt at the time you make a payment. You also have the right to receive copies or confirmation of all contractual arrangements (such as an installment agreement) that you make with us.

Sidebar questions

▷ **1** *What do I do if I disagree with an IRS employee's decision?*

See *"When you do not agree with decisions of IRS employees."*

▷ **2** *How can I have my case transferred to another IRS office?*

See *"Transferring the location of your tax case."*

▷ **3** *How can I get help on unresolved tax problems?*

See *"Problem Resolution Program."*

▷ Problem Resolution Program (PRP)

PRP is a program designed to help taxpayers who have been unable to resolve their tax problems after repeated attempts to do so with another IRS department.

Before contacting PRP, you should first request assistance from an employee or manager in an IRS Collection office. If the problem is still not resolved, you should contact your local IRS district office and ask for PRP.

PRP provides an avenue to help resolve your problem when you believe that: 1) your account information is incorrect, 2) a significant matter or event is not being considered in your case, or 3) your rights as a taxpayer have been violated.

If you suffer a significant hardship. If you have or are about to have a significant hardship because of the collection of your tax debt, additional assistance is available. A significant hardship may occur if you cannot maintain necessities such as food, clothing, shelter, transportation, and medical treatment.

To apply for relief, you can submit Form 911, *Application For Taxpayer Assistance Order (ATAO) to Relieve Hardship,* or contact the district PRP office if the employee assigned to your case cannot or will not take action to relieve your hardship. Any IRS employee can help you apply for ATAO handling. We can help you obtain and complete the form, take the information by telephone, or you can contact the district PRP office in order to obtain and complete the form and submit it to PRP. You can also obtain Form 911 by calling 1-800-829-3676.

The Taxpayer Ombudsman or a Problem Resolution Officer will review your application and if appropriate, take steps to relieve your hardship.

When You Have Not Paid Enough Tax

If you do not pay the full amount of tax you owe, you will receive a tax bill. This bill begins the collection process. The length of the process depends on how soon you respond and pay the bill.

Understanding your tax bill. When you file your tax return with the IRS, we check it to make sure the math is accurate and to see if you have paid the correct amount of tax. If you owe tax and have not paid all of it, we will send you a bill which is called a *Notice of Tax Due and Demand for Payment.* The bill will include the tax due, plus penalties and interest that we have charged on the unpaid balance of your account from the date you should have paid your taxes.

What you can do to avoid having overdue taxes. If you owe taxes because not enough tax was withheld from your wages, you should file a new Form W-4, *Employee's Withholding Allowance Certificate*, with your employer(s) to claim a lower number of withholding allowances. If you need help computing the correct number of withholding allowances, see Publication 919, *Is My Withholding Correct?*

If you are self-employed and owe tax, you should increase your estimated tax payments. These payments are explained in Publication 505, *Tax Withholding and Estimated Tax*, and are reported on Form 1040ES, *Estimated Tax for Individuals.*

If you are an employer, see "Paying employment taxes," discussed on page 4 of this publication. For other types of taxes, see the tax instruction booklet that was mailed with your tax forms.

▶4 *If you believe your bill is wrong.* If you believe your bill is wrong, please let us know, as soon as possible, by writing to the IRS office that sent you this bill. You may also call the IRS or visit the IRS office nearest you.

To help us correct the problem, please include in your correspondence explaining the problem: 1) a copy of the bill, and 2) copies of any records, canceled checks, etc., that will help us understand what you believe is wrong.

Here is a sample format you can use for a letter:

Date

Internal Revenue Service
Address

- Your name, address, and daytime telephone number.
- Taxpayer identification number (social security number or employer identification number) as stated on bill.
- Tax form number as stated on bill.
- Tax period as stated on bill.

State your reason(s) why you believe your bill is wrong. Enclose copies of any information supporting your statement, such as copies of canceled checks or a copy of your tax return and a copy of the tax bill.

Your signature

If we find that you are correct, we will adjust your account, and if necessary, we will send you a corrected bill.

Making Arrangements to Pay Your Bill

This section explains what happens if you are unable to pay your bill in full. If you cannot pay your tax bill in full, we will analyze your ability to pay and then try to find the best way for you to pay the bill.

We will consider different methods of payment, such as paying in installments.

Note: The first part of this section applies primarily to individuals. However, many of the procedures also apply to employers. The last part of this section explains the rules that apply only to employers and payment of employment taxes.

When you pay your tax bill or send us correspondence, please do the following:

1) Include a copy of the most recent tax bill,
2) Identify the tax form number, the tax year or period, and your taxpayer identification number, as shown on your bill, in all your correspondence with us.
3) Also, write your taxpayer identification number (social security number or employer identification number, as appropriate) on your check, and
4) Enclose your payment if you owe tax.

If you can pay only part of your bill. If you cannot pay your bill in full, you should pay as much as you can and immediately write us or visit your nearest IRS office to explain your circumstances. Whenever you write, be sure to enclose a copy of your tax bill and on your letter, print your name, taxpayer identification number, and the tax form and period shown on your bill.

After we receive your letter, we will try to find the best way for you to pay your tax bill.

1) We may ask you to complete a Collection Information Statement. We use this form to review your financial condition to determine how you can pay the amount due.
2) We can ask you to sell or mortgage any assets to secure funds to pay the taxes.
3) We will ask you to secure a commercial loan if we determine that you are able to do so. A benefit of obtaining a loan is that you will avoid penalties and interest that we will continue to charge on your unpaid balance until all tax, penalties, and interest are paid.
4) We may take enforced collection action, such as issue a levy on your bank account, levy your wages, or take your other income or assets if you neglect or refuse to pay or make other arrangements to satisfy your bill in full.

▶5 *Making installment payments for individuals or businesses.* We will help you complete a *Collection Information Statement,* Form 433A or 433F for individuals, or Form 433B, for businesses. We use these forms to help us compare your monthly income with your expenses, determine if you qualify for an installment agreement, and the amount you can pay.

You can use these methods to make installment payments:

1) Personal checks, business checks, money orders, or certified funds,
2) Payroll deductions that your employer agrees to take from your salary and send to the IRS in regular payments, or
3) Electronic transfers from your bank account or other similar means.

If you have an installment agreement, you must make each payment on time. If you cannot pay on time, let us know why immediately.

Caution: While you are making installment payments, we will continue to charge your account with interest and penalties on the unpaid balance of taxes you owe plus interest on the unpaid balance of penalties and interest you owe.

Other actions that we may take include:

- Filing a Notice of Federal Tax Lien to secure the Government's interest until you make the final payment (See the section on "Liens" on pages 5-6),
- Requiring you to provide current information on your financial condition to determine any change in your ability to pay, and
- Ending the installment agreement if you do not provide financial information when requested or if you do not meet the terms of the agreement, such as paying late, missing a payment, or not filing or paying all required tax returns. If this happens, we may take enforced collection action. See "What Happens When You Take No Action To Pay," on page 5.

Note: Because your agreement is based on your financial circumstances, it could change. However, you will receive a letter 30 days in advance of any change we would make to your plan.

Simplified installment agreements. A simplified process enables many taxpayers to qualify for a streamlined installment agreement. In most cases, applying requires little paperwork and a Federal tax lien may not be required. To apply, see your tax practitioner or visit your local IRS office for details about completing Form 9465, *Installment Agreement Request.*

▶6 *Delaying collection if you cannot pay.* If we determine that you cannot pay any amount of your tax debt, we may temporarily delay collection until your financial condition improves. If we delay collection, the amount of your debt will increase because we will continue to charge a penalty for late payment and

▶4 *What if I disagree with the amount of tax that IRS says I owe?*

See "If you believe your bill is wrong."

▶5 *Can I make monthly payments on my account?*

See "Making installment payments for individuals or businesses," and "Simplified installment agreements."

▶6 *Can I postpone paying my taxes until my financial condition improves?*

See "Delaying collection if you cannot pay."

interest on your debt. During a delay, we will review your ability to pay. We may also file a Notice of Federal Tax Lien (explained on page 5) to protect the Government's interest in your assets and send you a reminder to pay.

If your current tax return shows a tax refund and you owe back taxes. If you are entitled to receive a tax refund while you still owe unpaid taxes, we will automatically apply the refund to pay the unpaid tax debt and refund the remaining balance to you.

If you are bankrupt. If you are involved in an ongoing bankruptcy proceeding, contact your local IRS office. While the bankruptcy proceeding may not eliminate your tax debt, it will temporarily stop IRS enforcement action to collect a debt related to the bankruptcy.

▶ *Submitting an Offer in Compromise.* In some accounts the amount of accruing penalties and interest is so large that the monthly payments never pay off the tax. The Offer in Compromise may be a practical way for you to resolve your outstanding tax bill. You have a legal right to submit an Offer in Compromise on your tax bill. Under certain conditions the IRS will settle unpaid accounts for less than the full amount of the balance due. This applies to all taxes (including any interest, penalty, or additional amount) arising under the Internal Revenue laws.

How to file an Offer in Compromise. You can get Form 656, *Offer in Compromise,* and Form 433A, *Collection Information Statement for Individuals*, or Form 433B, *Collection Information Statement for Business*, plus additional information regarding the filing procedure, at any IRS office. You may also call the toll-free numbers listed on page 1 for assistance or to receive tax forms or publications.

Grounds for filing an Offer in Compromise. You can submit an application for an Offer in Compromise if it is made on one or both of the following grounds:

1) Doubt as to the liability for the amount owed, or
2) Doubt as to your ability to fully pay the amount owed.

The doubt as to the amount owed in (1) above must be supported by evidence, and the compromise amount we accept depends on the degree of doubt found in your particular case. In (2) above, the amount you offer must reflect your maximum ability to pay, taking into consideration the total value of your equity in all your assets.

For example, if your equity in all assets you own is $15,000, your offer should be no less than $15,000.

If we accept your offer, we may ask you to complete a written agreement stating that you will pay the IRS a percentage of future earnings as part of the offer. You may also be asked to make a written agreement to relinquish certain present or potential tax benefits.

Note: Submission of an Offer in Compromise does not automatically stop Collection action on your account. If there is any indication that you filed the offer simply to delay collection of the tax or that the delay would interfere with collecting the tax, we will immediately continue our collection efforts.

Additional Payment Procedures for Employers

Throughout this publication, we will refer to Employer's Quarterly Federal Taxes as employment taxes. This tax is reported on Form 941, *Employer's Quarterly Tax Return. Form 940, Employer's Annual Federal Unemployment Tax Return,* is used by employers to report Federal unemployment tax.

Note: If your business receives funds from the Small Business Administration or a Small Business Investment Company, you should notify that organization about your unpaid taxes.

General information. Employment taxes are:

- The amounts you withhold from your employees for income tax and social security tax, plus
- The amount of social security tax you pay as an employer on behalf of each employee.

Although your bill includes all of the amounts above, the amounts that you have withheld from your employee's earnings are referred to as "trust fund taxes." They are called "trust fund taxes" because they are actually the employee's money which you hold in trust until you make a Federal tax deposit in that amount.

Degree of taxpayer cooperation. When we collect these unpaid taxes, we distinguish between those taxpayers who show a sincere effort to meet their tax obligations and those taxpayers who show little or no evidence of cooperation. We make this distinction because we believe that taxpayers who are making an effort to comply should be given an opportunity to resolve their bill, over a short period of time.

On the other hand, we believe that "repeater" or "chronic delinquent" trust fund cases require a swift and decisive IRS response for the following reasons:

1) The taxpayer (employer) is using "trust fund" monies as operating capital and thereby gains an unfair competitive advantage over other businesses who are complying, and
2) The taxpayer has been warned and yet continues to divert the "trust fund" monies.

Caution: The amount owed can increase dramatically if the taxpayer ignores the federal tax deposit and/or filing requirements, thus making it increasingly difficult to recover from the tax debt.

▶ *Paying employment taxes.* You should pre-pay your taxes by using Federal Tax Deposit coupons (Form 8109). If you do not have preprinted tax deposit coupons, call or visit the IRS and request a Federal Tax Deposit coupon (Form 8109-B). You should make your deposits directly to the Federal Reserve Bank in your area or to any financial institution authorized to accept Federal tax deposits.

Caution: Do not make Federal tax deposits to an IRS office. A deposit to an IRS office will not be considered as a deposit of the taxes and will subject you to a penalty. However, you may file Form 941, *Employer's Quarterly Federal Tax Return*, at an IRS office.

If any of the preprinted information on your Form 8109 is incorrect, follow the instructions in the coupon book for correcting it.

Reordering forms. You will receive a new Federal tax deposit coupon booklet automatically when you use coupon number 6 or 7 from your current book. However, if for some reason you do not receive your coupons automatically, you can call us at 1-800-829-1040 or visit your nearest IRS office and we will place the order for you.

More information on Form 8109. For more information about making federal tax deposits, you can obtain a copy of Circular E, *Employer's Tax Guide*, or Notice 109, *Information About Depositing Employment and Excise Taxes*, from any IRS office.

▶ **7** Can I settle my tax account for less than what I owe?

See "Submitting an Offer in Compromise."

▶ **8** How do I make a tax deposit if I do not have tax deposit coupons for employment taxes?

See "Paying employment taxes."

If you do not deposit taxes on time. If you do not timely pre-pay your tax using deposit coupons or if you were not required to make any deposit and/or did not include your payment when you filed your return, we will charge you interest and penalties on any unpaid balance.

We may charge you penalties for not depositing employment taxes timely up to 15% of the amount not deposited, depending upon how many days late you make the deposit.

If you do not pay withheld trust fund taxes, we may take additional collection action.

- We can require you to file and pay your taxes on a monthly rather than quarterly basis.
- We can also require you to open a special bank account and deposit the amounts required to be withheld within two banking days after you pay wages to your employees. If, after you are required to do so, you do not open a special account and make timely deposits, you may be found guilty of a misdemeanor.

▶ What Happens When You Take No Action to Pay

You will not need to read this section if you have already paid your tax or if you have made payment arrangements. Please note that before we take any of the actions explained in this section, we try to contact you and give you the opportunity to pay voluntarily.

If you do not take some action to pay your tax bill, we may take any of the following actions:

- File a Notice of Federal Tax Lien,
- Serve a Notice of Levy,
- Seize and sell your property (personal, real estate, and business property),
- Notify payers of your interest and dividend income to begin backup withholding, or
- Assess a trust fund recovery penalty, if you owe employment taxes. (See "Trust Fund Recovery Penalty Assessments for Employers," discussed on page 8).

Some of these actions are referred to as "enforced collection actions" because they are the means by which the IRS can enforce the notice and demand for tax.

▶ Lien

This section gives information to help you understand what a lien is, how it affects your credit rating, and how it is released.

Before the IRS files a Notice of Federal Tax Lien, three requirements must be met:

1) The IRS must assess the tax,
2) The IRS must send you a notice and demand for payment, and
3) You must neglect or refuse to pay the tax or otherwise resolve your tax due problems.

Once these requirements are met, a lien is created for the amount of your tax debt. This lien attaches to all your property (such as your house or car) and to all your rights to property (such as your accounts receivable).

A lien is not valid against the claims of other creditors until the IRS files a Notice of Federal Tax Lien with an appropriate official to establish priority status among these creditors. An example of this is filing a lien in the county where you own property or in the state where you conduct business.

By filing a Notice of Federal Tax Lien, the Government is providing a public notice to your creditors that the Government has a claim against all your property, including property that you acquire after the lien was filed.

Caution: Once filed, a lien may harm your credit rating.

Releasing a Lien

The IRS will issue a Release of the Notice of Federal Tax Lien:

1) Within 30 days after you satisfy the tax due (including interest and other additions to the tax) by payment or adjustment, or
2) Within 30 days after we accept a bond that you submit guaranteeing payment of the debt.

In addition, you must pay all fees charged by a state or other jurisdiction for both filing and releasing the lien. These fees will be added to the balance you owe.

Publication 1450, *Request for Release of Federal Tax Lien*, describes how to request a release of a Federal tax lien.

Automatic release of a Federal Tax Lien. A lien will release automatically if we have not refiled it before the time expires to legally collect the tax. This is usually a period of 10 years.

What you can do if IRS does not release a lien. If the IRS knowingly or negligently does not release a Notice of Federal Tax Lien when it should be released, you may sue the Federal government, but not IRS employees, for damages.

Before you file a lawsuit, you must first exhaust all administrative appeals. Also, you must file the suit within 2 years from the date when the IRS should have released the lien.

If you win a civil lawsuit, you may be awarded payment for any losses that you had because the IRS did not release the lien. You may also be paid for your share of the costs of the lawsuit. However, any costs that you could have reasonably reduced will be subtracted from that payment.

Special Release of Tax Lien — Application for a Discharge of a Federal Tax Lien against Property

Each application for a discharge of a tax lien releases the effects of the lien against one specific piece of property. If you are giving up ownership of property, such as when you sell your home, you may apply for a Certificate of Discharge.

You may receive a Certificate of Discharge if any of the following circumstances apply:

- You have other property, subject to the lien, that is worth at least two times the total of the tax you owe, plus any additions to the tax you owe and any other debts you owe on the property, such as a mortgage.
- The IRS receives the value of the government's interest in the property and you are giving up ownership.
- The IRS determines that the government's interest in the property has no value at the time you are giving up ownership.
- The property in question is being sold, and there is a dispute as to who is entitled to the sale proceeds, and the proceeds are placed in escrow while the dispute is being resolved.

▶ *I'm an employer. What happens if I cannot pay my employment taxes?*

See "What Happens When You Take No Action To Pay" (this page) and "Trust Fund Recovery Penalty Assessments for Employers" (page 8).

▶ *Does owing taxes have an effect on my credit?*

See "Lien."

11 *What effect can a levy have on my salary and bank accounts?*

See "Levy."

12 *What must happen to release a levy?*

See "Releasing a levy."

When applying for a discharge, you must send your written application in duplicate to the IRS district director where your property is located.

For assistance in requesting a discharge of a Federal Tax Lien, see Publication 783, *Instructions on How to Apply for a Certificate of Discharge of Property From the Federal Tax Lien.*

When the IRS Lien Is Secondary to Another Lien — Subordination

Subordination is made at the discretion of the IRS. It means that the IRS has allowed its lien to take a lower place than someone else's lien.

The IRS may let its lien take a lower place than a "junior lienor" (someone whose lien originally had a lower place than the IRS lien) if it receives the dollar value of the lien in the property that the junior lienor is acquiring, for example, a second mortgage.

We may also subordinate a lien if we believe that doing so would speed collection of the tax. For example, we may subordinate a lien that would allow a farmer to receive a loan to harvest a crop.

For assistance in requesting subordination of a Federal Tax Lien, see Publication 784, *How to Prepare Application for Certificate of Subordination of Federal Tax Lien.* When making this request, you should submit a written application in duplicate to the District Director in whose district your property is located.

Incorrect Lien — Your Administrative Appeal

You may appeal the filing of a Notice of Federal Tax Lien if you believe we filed the lien in error. A lien is incorrect if:

- You paid the entire amount you owed the IRS before we filed the lien,
- We assessed the tax and filed the lien when you were in bankruptcy and subject to the automatic stay during bankruptcy,
- We made a procedural error in making an assessment, or
- The time to collect the tax (called the statute of limitations) expired before we filed the lien.

Note: You may not appeal this Notice of Federal Tax Lien if you are challenging the underlying debt that generated the filing of the lien.

If we agree with your appeal, we will release the lien within 14 days after we determine that the lien was filed incorrectly. We will issue a certificate of release of an incorrect lien that includes a statement that we filed the Notice of Federal Tax Lien in error.

11 Levy

A levy is one method the IRS uses to collect tax that you have not paid voluntarily. It means we can, by legal authority, take property to satisfy a tax debt. Levies can be made on property that you hold (such as your vehicle, boat, or house) or on property that is yours, but is held by third parties (such as wages or funds on deposit at a bank).

For example, IRS may levy your wages (salary), commissions, the cash value of life insurance, licenses or franchises, securities, contracts, demand notes, accounts receivables, rental income, dividends, retirement accounts, etc.

Also, in most states that have state income taxes, the IRS can levy a state refund check and apply the state refund to a federal tax debt.

A levy is different from a lien. A lien is a claim used as security for the tax debt, while a levy is used to actually take the property to satisfy the tax debt.

Authority to levy. Generally, the IRS does not need court authorization to take levy action. However, we are required to have court authorization to enter private premises, if this is necessary, to seize property.

Generally, before IRS takes levy action, three legal requirements must be met:

1) The IRS must assess the tax and send you a "Notice and Demand" for payment,
2) You must neglect or refuse to pay the tax, and
3) The IRS must send you a Final Notice of Intent to Levy at least 30 days in advance of the levy.

We may give you this notice in person, leave it at your dwelling or usual place of business, or send it by certified or registered mail to your last known address. The bill that usually accompanies this publication is such a notice.

Caution: If we conclude that collection of your tax is threatened, we may take immediate collection action before all three requirements have been met. For example, if a taxpayer is planning to quickly leave the country, we may believe that collection is threatened or in jeopardy.

If we make a decision that collection of your tax is threatened or in jeopardy, you may seek IRS managerial or court review, or both. These procedures are explained in the letter you will receive when the demand for payment is made.

Levy on wages. If the IRS levies your salary or wages, the levy will end when one of the following occurs:

- The levy is released,
- You pay your tax debt, or
- The time expires for legally collecting the tax.

If we levy your salary or wages, contact the specific person or call the telephone number listed on the Notice of Levy for assistance.

Levy on your bank account. If the IRS levies your bank account, your bank is required to hold funds you have on deposit, up to the amount you owe, for 21 days. This period allows you time to resolve any problems about the levy or make other arrangements to pay. The bank is then required to send the money, plus interest if it applies, to the IRS.

To discuss your account, you should contact the IRS by calling the person whose name is shown on the Notice of Levy.

12 *Releasing a levy.* We must release your levy if any of the following occur:

- You pay the tax, penalty, and interest that you owe.
- The time for collection (statute of limitations) expires before the levy is served.
- You provide documentation for the IRS to determine that releasing the levy will help collect the tax.
- You have, or entered into, an approved, current installment agreement for the tax on the levy. (However, if you and the IRS have agreed that a current levy will continue while installment payments are made, we will not release it.)
- The IRS determines that the levy is creating an economic hardship.
- The fair market value of the property exceeds the levy and releasing part of the seized property would not hinder the collection of tax.

Property that cannot be levied. Certain types of property are exempt from seizure (levy) by Federal law.

They include all of the following items:

- Wearing apparel and school books. (However, expensive items of wearing apparel, such as furs, are luxuries and are not exempt from levy).
- Fuel, provisions, furniture, and personal effects for a head of household, that total up to $1,650.
- Books and tools you use in your trade, business, or profession, that total up to $1,100.
- Unemployment benefits.
- Undelivered mail.
- Certain annuity and pension benefits.
- Certain service-connected disability payments.
- Workmen's compensation.
- Salary, wages, or other income that have been included in a judgment for court-ordered child support payments.
- Certain public assistance payments.
- Assistance under the Job Training Partnership Act.
- Deposits to the special Treasury fund made by members of the armed forces and Public Health Service employees who are on permanent duty assigned outside the United States or its possessions.
- A minimum weekly exemption for wages, salary, and other income based on the standard deduction plus the number of allowable personal exemptions divided by 52. In the case of no response to the certification of exemptions, the exempt amount will be computed as if you were married filing separately with one exemption.

Publication 1494, *Table for Figuring Amount Exempt from Levy on Wages, Salary and Other Income* (Forms 668-W and 668-W(c)), can be used to determine the amount of earned income exempt from levy.

How to file a claim for reimbursement when IRS made a mistake in levying your account or misplaced your check. You may be entitled to be reimbursed for fees your bank charged you because IRS made a mistake when we levied your account.

To receive this reimbursement, you must file a claim with the IRS within one year after the bank charged you with the fee. To file your claim, use Form 8546, *Claim for Reimbursement of Bank Charges Incurred Due to Erroneous Service Levy or Misplaced Payment Check.*

You can get this form by calling the toll-free number shown on page 1 of this publication.

13 Seizures and Sales

If you do not pay (or make arrangements to resolve) your tax debt, we may seize and sell any type of real or personal property that you own or have an interest in (including residential and business property) to satisfy your tax bill. Seizure of a primary residence requires the approval from an IRS district director or assistant district director except if the collection of the tax is in jeopardy.

If we seize or levy your property, you should contact the IRS employee who made the seizure or levy for assistance.

When property cannot be seized or levied. We may not seize any of your property when the estimated cost to seize and sell the property is more than the fair market value of the property to be seized. In addition, we may not seize or levy your property on the day you attend a collection interview because of a summons.

However, we can seize or levy your property on this date if collection of the tax is in jeopardy. You may contact the IRS employee who made the seizure or levy if you have any questions.

Administrative review. You have the right to an administrative review of our seizure action when we have taken your personal property that you need to maintain your business. See "When you do not agree with decisions of IRS employees," on page 2 for information about how to apply for this review.

Notice of proposed sale. After we seize your property, we must give public notice of a pending sale. Public notice usually appears in a newspaper that is published or circulated in the county where the sale will be held. We will personally deliver the original notice of sale to you or send it to you by certified mail. After we give notice, we must wait at least 10 days before conducting the sale.

However, if the property is perishable and must be sold immediately, we are not required to wait 10 days before holding the sale.

Minimum bid. Before the sale, we will compute a "minimum bid price." This is the lowest amount that we will accept for the sale of the property to protect your interest in that property. We will tell you the minimum bid price we set, which is usually 80% or more of the forced sale value of the property, after any liens are subtracted.

If you disagree with this minimum bid price, you can appeal it by requesting that the price be recomputed by either an IRS valuation engineer or a private appraiser who can assist the IRS engineer. If you still disagree with the revised appraisal, you may obtain a second appraisal.

14 *Release of property.* Before the date of sale, we may release the property that we seized from you if you:

1) Pay us the amount of the Government's interest in the property,
2) Enter into an escrow arrangement,
3) Furnish an acceptable bond, or
4) Make an acceptable agreement for payment of the tax.

Your right to "buy back" the property. You have the right to "buy back" your personal property at any time before the sale. To do this, you must pay the tax due, including interest and penalties, and pay the expenses of seizure.

For real estate, you (or anyone with an interest in the property) may redeem it at any time within 180 days after the sale by paying the purchaser the amount paid for the property plus interest at 20% annually.

Sale procedures. You may request that we sell the seized property within 60 days. For information on how to make this request, you should contact the IRS employee who made the seizure. We will grant your request unless it is in the Government's best interest to retain the property. We will inform you in writing of our decision whether or not we are able to grant your request.

After the sale, we use the proceeds first to pay the expenses of the levy and sale. We then use any remaining amount to pay the tax bill.

If the sale proceeds are less than the total of the tax bill and the expenses of levy and sale, you will still have to pay the remaining unpaid tax.

If the sale proceeds are more than the total of the tax bill and the expenses of the levy and sale, we will notify you about the surplus money and provide you with instructions about how to request a refund. However, if a person, such as a mortgagee or other lienholder, submits a claim superior to yours, we will pay that claim before we refund any remaining funds to you based on your request.

13 *What types of property can the IRS seize?*

See "Seizures and Sales."

14 *How can I obtain a release of the seized property?*

See "Release of property."

Backup Withholding

You are legally required to report your interest, dividend, or patronage dividend income on your individual income tax return. You must report the correct amounts, and these amounts must match the amounts that the payers report to IRS. You are also required to provide your correct taxpayer identification number to all payers of interest and dividends.

15▶ *My business is closed. Can I be held responsible for unpaid "trust fund" taxes?*

See "Who is a responsible person for trust fund tax."

Usually, there is no withholding of tax on interest and dividend payments. However, if you do not report this interest and dividend income or provide the correct taxpayer identification number as required, you may be subject to backup withholding. This occurs when we notify all those who pay you interest or dividends to begin withholding income tax on these payments. You may also be subject to backup withholding if you do not provide your correct taxpayer identification number.

How to prevent backup withholding from starting. Before we notify your payers to withhold, we will send you at least four notices over a period of at least 120 days to give you a chance to correct the underreporting and pay any additional tax to avoid backup withholding.

Stopping backup withholding. Once backup withholding begins, we will stop it when:

1) The income is properly reported,
2) The income tax is paid in full,
3) You furnish the correct taxpayer identification number, and
4) The IRS notifies the payer to stop withholding.

Generally, we will notify payers to stop withholding at the end of the year if we receive full payment of the tax by October 15. If we receive full payment after October 15, they will continue withholding through the following year.

While you are subject to backup withholding, you must certify to any new payers that you are subject to backup withholding. If you falsely certify that you are not subject to backup withholding, you will be liable for a penalty of $1,000 or imprisonment for up to one year, or both. For additional information, see Publication 1506, *Under-reporter Backup Withholding* and Publications 1281 and 1679 also contain information about backup withholding and taxpayer identification numbers.

Trust Fund Recovery Penalty Assessments for Employers

To encourage prompt payment of withheld income and employment taxes, including social security and railroad retirement taxes or collected excise taxes, Congress passed a law that provides for the trust fund recovery penalty. This penalty is used as a tool for collection of unpaid employment taxes. The penalty also applies to those excise taxes which are commonly referred to as "collected" excise taxes.

If you are a "responsible person," we can apply this penalty against you immediately after you do not pay trust fund taxes in response to a notice and demand for payment. Also, we can apply this penalty regardless of whether you are out of business or without assets.

Caution: Once we assert the penalty, we can take collection action against your individual assets, such as filing a Federal tax lien if you are the responsible person(s).

Figuring the penalty amount. The amount of the penalty is equal to the unpaid trust fund tax. The penalty is computed based on two amounts which constitute trust fund tax:

1) The unpaid income taxes withheld, plus
2) The employee's portion of the FICA taxes withheld.

For collected taxes, the penalty is based on the unpaid amount of collected excise taxes.

Who Is Subject to the Penalty

We may impose the penalty against any person who is responsible for collecting or paying withheld income and employment taxes or for paying collected excise taxes AND who willfully fails to collect or pay them. Therefore, the two key elements that support this penalty assessment are *responsibility* and *willfulness*.

15▶ *Who is a responsible person for trust fund tax.* A responsible person is one who has the duty to perform and the power to direct the collecting, accounting, and paying of trust fund taxes. Therefore, responsibility involves status, duty, and authority.

This person may be:

• An officer or an employee of a corporation,
• A member or employee of a partnership,
• A corporate director or shareholder,
• A member of a board of trustees of a nonprofit organization, or
• Another person with sufficient authority and control over funds to direct their disbursement.

In some situations the responsible person may be a person who is not directly affiliated with the delinquent business. For example, the penalty may be assessed against an official or employee of a bank or other financial institution who has the authority to direct the financial affairs of the business and:

• Furnishes funds to a business and directs how the funds are to be distributed, or
• Directs the business not to pay the taxes.

Proof of willfulness. By willful, we mean conduct that is intentional, deliberate, voluntary, and knowing — as opposed to accidental conduct. You are considered to have a willful attitude if you have free will or choice and yet either intentionally disregard the law or are plainly indifferent to legal requirements.

For willfulness to exist, the responsible person must:

1) Have known about the unpaid taxes, and
2) Have used the funds to keep the business going or allowed available funds to be paid to other creditors.

Willfulness does not imply that you had acted for personal gain. For example, the courts ruled in one case that the actions of a corporate officer, in permitting withheld taxes to be used for operating expenses of the business (whether at the officer's direction or with his tacit approval) is sufficient evidence of willfullness that the trust fund recovery penalty can be charged to that officer.

In addition, if an employer meets payrolls, we can infer that sufficient funds were available to pay the tax, regardless of whether the funds were actually set aside or otherwise specifically identified for tax purposes.

Your Appeal Rights

The appeal process is outlined clearly in Publication 1, *Your Rights As A Taxpayer*. If we recommend that you pay the trust fund recovery penalty amount, you can attempt to resolve the matter informally through a discussion with the group manager of the IRS employee in your district. If you disagree with the decision of the group manager, you may request a conference before the Regional Director of Appeals.

☆ U.S. GOVERNMENT PRINTING OFFICE: 1994 365-111

FREE
Tax Services

The Internal Revenue Service (IRS) provides **FREE** tax information and services to help you throughout the year. This publication describes many of them. It gives helpful information about filing your return and answers some of the most commonly asked questions.

IRS **FREE** services include toll-free telephone service, tax information publications, tax assistance and educational programs, and audiovisual instructional materials that are available for loan to individuals and groups.

Most tax questions can be answered by reading the tax forms and instructions. If you need more information, you can turn to the **FREE** tax services the IRS offers. You may call IRS toll-free or visit your local IRS office with questions about your tax account or tax rules, or for general information about IRS procedures and services.

TELEPHONE SERVICE

Toll-free telephone assistance is available in all 50 states, the District of Columbia, Puerto Rico and the U.S. Virgin Islands. Using the toll-free telephone system, you can get answers to your tax questions and pay only local charges, if any. There is no long distance charge for your call.

During periods of peak demand for telephone assistance, you may get a busy signal. Demand may be lower early in the morning or later in the week, so you may want to call at those times.

For information on using the toll-free telephone services and for the number listed for your area, turn to the section on Toll-Free Telephone Numbers.

Tele-Tax

Tele-Tax is the IRS toll-free telephone service that provides both recorded tax information and automated refund information.

Recorded Tax Information. You can listen to tax information on about 140 topics such as filing requirements, dependents, itemized deductions, tax credits and free services available.

FREE Tax Services

Automated Refund Information. If you filed your tax return and you have not received your refund, you can check on its status by using the Tele-Tax automated refund system.

Telephone Service for People with Hearing Impairments

Toll-free telephone tax assistance is available for deaf and hearing-impaired taxpayers with access to TDD (telecommunication device for the deaf) equipment. The hours of operation are:

> January 1 through April 4
> 8:00 a.m. to 6:30 p.m.
> Eastern Standard Time

> April 5 through April 15
> 9:00 a.m. to 7:30 p.m.
> Eastern Daylight Time

> April 16 through October 31
> 9:00 a.m. to 5:30 p.m.
> Eastern Daylight Time

> November 1 through December 31
> 8:00 a.m. to 4:30 p.m.
> Eastern Standard Time

Residents of all states, including Alaska, Hawaii, Puerto Rico, and the U.S. Virgin Islands, can call 1-800-829-4059.

INFORMATION FOR PEOPLE WITH VISUAL IMPAIRMENTS

Braille tax materials are available at Regional Libraries for the Visually Impaired in conjunction with National Library Services, the Library of Congress. Currently, these materials are limited to copies of Publication 17, *Your Federal Income Tax;* Publication 334, *Tax Guide for Small Business; Forms 1040, 1040A,* and *1040EZ,* and related instructions; and the *Tax Tables.*

WALK-IN SERVICE

Assistors at most IRS offices throughout the country can help you prepare your own individual federal tax return.

If you want assistance with your tax return, you should bring the package of tax forms and instructions you received in the mail and all *Forms W-2* and *Forms 1099* showing interest or other income. Bring any other information (such as a copy of last year's return) that the assistors can use to help you.

The IRS will not prepare your tax return for you at these locations, but assistors will provide line-by-line self-help tax return assistance with you individually or in a group setting. If you have a handicap that prevents you from preparing your return through the self-help method, an assistor will prepare it for you. At most IRS offices you can also get tax forms, publications and help with questions about IRS notices or bills.

INTERNATIONAL SERVICE

If you are a taxpayer who lives outside the United States, the IRS has full-time permanent staff at 13 U.S. Embassies and Consulates around the world. These offices maintain a supply of tax forms and publications. The staff can help you with account problems and answer your questions about notices and bills.

From January 1 through June 15 each year, taxpayer service representatives travel to many cities worldwide to assist taxpayers outside the U.S. In 1993, they will visit approximately 173 foreign cities.

You may call your nearest U.S. Embassy, Consulate or IRS office listed here to find out when and where assistance will be available. These IRS telephone numbers include the country or city codes required if you are outside the local dialing area. The Nassau and Ottawa numbers include the U.S. area codes.

Bonn, Germany	{49} (228) 339-2119
Caracas, Venezuela	{58} (2) 285-4641
London, England	{44} (71) 408-8076 or 408-8077
Mexico City, Mexico	{52} (5) 211-0042 ext. 3557 or 3559
Nassau, Bahamas	(809) 322-1181
Ottawa, Canada	(613) 238-5335
Paris, France	{33} (1) 4296-1202
Riyadh, Saudi Arabia	{966} (1) 488-3800 ext. 210
Rome, Italy	{39} (6) 4674-2560
São Paulo, Brazil	{55} (11) 881-6511 ext. 287
Singapore	{65} 338-0251 ext. 247
Sydney, Australia	{61} (2) 261-9275
Tokyo, Japan	{81} (3) 3224-5466

You can also write to the Assistant Commissioner (International), 950 L'Enfant Plaza SW, IN:C:TPS, Washington DC 20024, USA, for answers to your technical or tax account questions.

TAXPAYER EDUCATION AND ASSISTANCE PROGRAMS

The IRS has programs designed to help you understand your rights and obligations under our nation's tax system. Volunteers trained by the IRS are an important part of all these programs. For times and locations of available services in your community, or to volunteer, call the IRS office in your area and ask for the Taxpayer Education Coordinator or the Public Affairs Officer.

FREE Tax Services

Educational Programs

COMMUNITY OUTREACH TAX EDUCATION

Groups of taxpayers with common tax concerns, such as retirees, farmers, small business owners and employees, can get free tax help from IRS employees or trained volunteers at convenient community locations. The assistance may be provided during the day, in the evening, or on weekends.

Community Outreach Tax Education offers two kinds of assistance. One kind provides line-by-line self-help income tax return preparation for taxpayers who want to prepare their own returns. The other provides tax seminars discussing various tax topics. Outreach sessions may be co-sponsored by community organizations and other government agencies.

SMALL BUSINESS TAX EDUCATION PROGRAM

Small business owners and other self-employed individuals can learn about business taxes through a unique partnership between the IRS and local organizations. Through workshops or in-depth tax courses, instructors provide training on starting a business, record-keeping, preparing business tax returns, self-employment tax issues and employment taxes.

The cost for this program varies. Some courses are offered free as a community service. Courses offered through an educational facility may include costs for materials in addition to tuition. Still others charge a nominal fee to offset administrative costs of sponsoring organizations.

UNDERSTANDING TAXES FOR HIGH SCHOOLS

This is an introductory tax course taught in high schools, junior high schools, and basic adult education classes nationwide. Working students find immediate

practical value in the section of the course that teaches them how to fill out their tax returns. Students also learn about the history, politics and economics of taxation and about taxpayer rights and responsibilities.

Teachers are provided with free instructional materials, including a videotape and computer software. In many areas, teachers may be able to enroll in workshops to help them prepare for course instruction.

TAXES IN U.S. HISTORY

This program contains instructional materials developed to complement eighth or ninth grade U.S. history courses. Designed for concurrent use by three teachers, the free kit includes three student video programs, a teacher's guide, and instructional posters that will help students understand the roles that taxes have played in three eras of our nation's history.

A video for teachers shows how to effectively use the kit in the classroom. The materials help teachers explain the function and nature of taxes to students at an age when many will be filing a federal income tax return for the first time.

PRACTITIONER EDUCATION

Practitioner Education provides training to people who prepare tax returns for a fee. As part of this program, Practitioner Institutes are held in every state in cooperation with colleges, state bureaus of revenue, and professional associations. Tax professionals can learn about recent tax law changes at these Practitioner Institutes, which will enhance the professional quality of the services they provide.

Assistance Programs

VOLUNTEER INCOME TAX ASSISTANCE

Volunteer Income Tax Assistance (VITA) provides free help to people

who cannot afford professional tax assistance. After completing IRS training, VITA volunteers help prepare basic tax returns for taxpayers with special needs, including persons with disabilities, the elderly, and non-English speaking taxpayers. VITA sites are usually located at libraries, community colleges, schools, shopping malls, and other convenient locations in the community.

TAX COUNSELING FOR THE ELDERLY

Tax Counseling for the Elderly (TCE) provides free tax help to people aged 60 or older, especially those who are disabled or who have special needs. Volunteers who provide tax counseling are often retired individuals associated with non-profit organizations that receive grants from the IRS. The grants help pay out-of-pocket expenses for the volunteers to travel to homes, retirement homes, or special TCE sites. Sites are conveniently located in neighborhood centers, libraries, churches and other places in the community.

STUDENT TAX CLINICS

Student Tax Clinics are sponsored by law and graduate accounting schools. They are staffed by student volunteers who provide free tax assistance to taxpayers who would not normally obtain counsel when faced with a tax audit or examination. Students who have received special permission from the IRS may represent taxpayers before the IRS during examination and appeals proceedings.

BANK, POST OFFICE AND LIBRARY PROGRAM

The IRS supplies free tax preparation materials to many banks, post offices, libraries, and reference areas in technical schools, military bases, prisons, community colleges and other locations. Participating libraries have tax forms available for copying, reference sets of

IRS publications and audiovisual materials on preparing *Forms 1040EZ, 1040A, 1040,* and *Schedules A* and *B.* Banks, post offices and other sites stock *Forms 1040EZ, 1040A* and *1040,* and the instructions and related schedules.

MEDIA INFORMATION MATERIALS

The IRS provides a variety of print and audiovisual tax information materials to the news media for use in informing the public about current tax issues and assistance. Much of this information is not limited to news media use only. Organizations, colleges, libraries or other community service groups can contact their local IRS Public Affairs Officer or Taxpayer Education Coordinator to find out how to get these materials.

Printed Media

Newspapers and other print media across the country receive written tax information materials for their readers. IRS Public Affairs Officers send news releases, question-and-answer columns, and other items about taxes to their local media. Topics range from farming to electronic tax filing.

One popular item the IRS produces is the *Tax Supplement.* It contains articles and graphics in a clipsheet format ready for paste up and printing. Newspapers can use it as a special tax section or publish articles from it as a regular series at tax time.

These materials can also be used in other printed media such as organizational newsletters and school newspapers.

Audiovisual Media

Special audiovisual programming includes radio and TV shows where viewers can phone in their tax

questions. For example, the IRS produces tax clinics for broadcast on public television stations. The clinics highlight the various tax forms and schedules, address changes in the tax law, give helpful filing hints and provide information on where to get free assistance.

IRS-produced films and videotapes are available for loan to interested groups or organizations without charge. To order, call the Taxpayer Education Coordinator or Public Affairs Officer at your local IRS office.

"Hey, We're Being Audited!"

This sensible and light-hearted film portrays the life of an average American family, the Walters, after being called in for an IRS tax audit. They represent the normal actions and reactions of taxpayers and how they prepare for the examination. The IRS examiner and her trainee are also highlighted as their roles depict the IRS side of the process. Information on the audit and appeals process and taxpayers' rights are explained throughout the film. (28 ½ mins.; ½″ VHS and ¾″ videocassettes.)

"A Sensible Approach for the Future of Your Business" and "You've Got To Do This"

These two films aimed at practitioners and taxpayers offer comprehensive information on electronic filing of tax returns.

For practitioners, "A Sensible Approach for the Future of Your Business" explains what electronic filing is, how to register with the IRS to offer electronic filing, and how it will benefit their business. (12:21 mins.; ½″ VHS and ¾″ videocassettes.)

For taxpayers, "You've Got To Do This" explains how electronic filing works and how they may get quick refunds. It encourages people to file

electronically. (6:48 mins.; ½″ VHS and ¾″ videocassettes.)

"Form 8300: Why You Should File"

This video is designed to inform businesses about their reporting requirements to the IRS for "cash" transactions over $10,000. It deals with commonly asked questions about *Form 8300* and covers the results of noncompliance. Businesses affected by these transaction reporting requirements include car dealers, jewelers, travel agents, art dealers and hotel agents. (14:15 mins.; ½″ VHS and ¾″ videocassettes.)

"A Video Guide To Taxes-1992"

People looking for a quick update of tax law changes and general tax information for individual tax returns can find it in the instructional videocassette. It is targeted at first-time filers and those who prepare their own returns. The videocassette is in both English and Spanish and is also available on audiocassette. (28 mins.; ½″ VHS videocassette.)

"¿Por Qué Nosotros, Los García?"

This Spanish-language film explains taxpayers' examination and appeal rights. (28 mins.; 16mm film and ¾″ videocassette.)

"¿Por Qué Los Impuestos?"

Realizing that there is a lack of knowledge about the U.S. tax system in the Hispanic community, the editor of a Spanish weekly newspaper assigns an eager, new reporter to the story. The reporter uncovers the history of taxation, how taxes are used, the rights and responsibilities of taxpayers, and the different kinds of IRS assistance available. The film is especially suitable for social studies and history courses at adult education and community centers. (10 mins.; 16mm film, ½″ VHS and ¾″ videocassettes.)

FREE TAX PUBLICATIONS

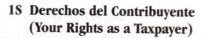

The Internal Revenue Service provides many free publications to help you when filling out your tax return. Most people find the publications listed on this page to be all they need to better understand the tax rules for individuals, small businesses, farming, fishing, and recent tax changes.

You may want to order one of these publications first, and then if you need more detailed information on any topic, order the specific publication about it. The publication title is usually enough to describe the contents, but where the title may not be enough, there is a brief description. Forms and schedules related to the contents of each publication are shown after each listing.

These publications and forms can be ordered by calling IRS toll-free at 1-800-829-3676.

1 Your Rights as a Taxpayer

To ensure that you always receive fair treatment in tax matters, you should know what your rights are. This publication explains your rights at each step in the tax process.

1S Derechos del Contribuyente (Your Rights as a Taxpayer)

Spanish version of Publication 1.

3 Tax Information for Military Personnel (Including Reservists Called to Active Duty)

This publication gives information about the special tax situations of active members of the Armed Forces. It includes information on items that are includible in and excludable from gross income, alien status, dependency exemptions, sale of residence, itemized deductions, tax liability, and filing returns.

Forms 1040, 1040A, 1040EZ, 1040NR, 1040X, 1310, 2106, 2688, 2848, 3903, 3903F, 4868 and *W-2.*

4 Student's Guide to Federal Income Tax

This publication explains the federal tax laws that are of particular interest to high school and college students. It describes the student's responsibilities to file and pay taxes, how to file, and how to get help.

Forms 1040EZ, W-2 and *W-4.*

17 Your Federal Income Tax

This publication can help you prepare your individual tax return. It takes you step by step through each part of the return. It explains the tax laws in a way

that will help you better understand your taxes so that you pay only as much as you owe and no more.

The tax table, tax rate schedules, and earned income credit tables are included in this publication.

Forms 1040, 1040A, 1040EZ, Schedules A, B, D, E, EIC, R, SE, Forms W-2, 2106, 2119, 2441, 3903.

225 Farmer's Tax Guide

This publication explains the federal tax laws that apply to farming. It discusses the kind of farm income you must report and the different deductions you can take.

Form 1040, Schedules A, D, F, SE and *Forms 4136, 4562, 4684, 4797, 6251.*

334 Tax Guide for Small Business

This publication explains some federal tax laws that apply to businesses. It explains the tax responsibilities of the four major forms of business organizations—sole proprietorship, partnership, corporation, and S corporation.

Schedule C (Form 1040), Schedule K-1 (Forms 1065 and 1120S), Forms 1065, 1120, 1120-A, 1120S, 4562.

595 Tax Guide for Commercial Fishermen

This publication explains the federal tax laws as they apply to the fishing industry. It is intended for sole proprietors who use *Schedule C (Form 1040)* to report profit or loss from fishing. It does not cover corporations or partnerships.

Schedule C (Form 1040), Forms 1099-MISC, 4562, 4797.

The following publications supplement the general ones previously listed. They provide a few more details on specific topics and are shown in numerical order.

15 Circular E, Employer's Tax Guide
Forms 940, 941, and 941E.

51 Circular A, Agricultural Employer's Tax Guide
Form 943.

54 Tax Guide for U.S. Citizens and Resident Aliens Abroad
This publication discusses the tax situations of U.S. citizens and resident aliens who live and work abroad. In particular, it explains the rules for excluding income and excluding or deducting certain housing costs.
Forms 2555, 2555EZ, 1116, and 1040, Schedule SE (Form 1040).

80 Circular SS, Federal Tax Guide for Employers in the Virgin Islands, Guam, American Samoa, and the Commonwealth of the Northern Mariana Islands
Forms 940, 941SS and 943.

179 Circular PR, Guía Contributiva Federal Para Patronos Puertorriqueños (Federal Tax Guide for Employers in Puerto Rico)
Forms W-3PR, 940PR, 941PR, 942PR, and 943PR.

349 Federal Highway Use Tax on Heavy Vehicles
This publication explains which trucks, truck-tractors, and buses are subject to the federal highway use tax on heavy motor vehicles, and how to figure and pay any tax due on the taxable vehicle.
Form 2290.

378 Fuel Tax Credits and Refunds
This publication explains the credit or refund allowable for the federal excise taxes paid on certain fuels, and the income tax credit available for alcohol used as a fuel.
Forms 843, 4136 and 6478.

448 Federal Estate and Gift Taxes
Forms 706 and 709.

463 Travel, Entertainment, and Gift Expenses
Some business-related travel, entertainment and gift expenses may be deductible.
Form 2106.

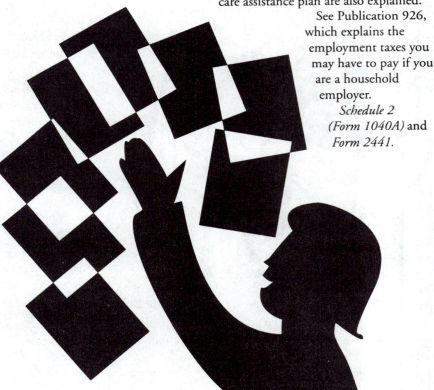

501 Exemptions, Standard Deduction, and Filing Information
Forms 2120 and 8332.

502 Medical and Dental Expenses
Explains which medical and dental expenses are deductible, how to deduct them and how to treat insurance reimbursements you may receive for medical care.
Schedule A (Form 1040).

503 Child and Dependent Care Expenses
You may be able to take a credit if you pay someone to care for your dependent who is under age 13, your disabled dependent, or your disabled spouse. For purposes of the credit, "disabled" refers to a person physically or mentally not capable of self-care.

Tax rules covering benefits paid under an employer-provided dependent care assistance plan are also explained.

See Publication 926, which explains the employment taxes you may have to pay if you are a household employer.
Schedule 2 (Form 1040A) and Form 2441.

504 Divorced or Separated Individuals

Form 8332.

505 Tax Withholding and Estimated Tax

Forms W-4, W-4P, W-4S, 1040-ES, 2210, and *2210F.*

508 Educational Expenses

Some work-related educational expenses may be deductible.

Form 2106 and *Schedule A (Form 1040).*

509 Tax Calendars for 1993

510 Excise Taxes for 1993

This publication covers in detail the various federal excise taxes reported on *Form 720.* These include environmental taxes; facilities and service taxes on communications and air transportation; fuel taxes; manufacturers' taxes; vaccines; tax on heavy trucks, trailers, and tractors; luxury taxes; and tax on ship passengers. It briefly describes other excise taxes and which forms to use in reporting and paying the taxes.

Forms 11-C, 637, 720, 730, 6197, 6627, 8743, and *8807.*

513 Tax Information for Visitors to the United States

Briefly reviews the general requirements of U.S. income tax rules for foreign visitors who may have to file a U.S. income tax return during their visit. Most visitors who come to the United States are not allowed to work in this country. Check with the Immigration and Naturalization Service before taking a job.

Forms 1040C, 1040NR, 2063, and *1040-ES (NR).*

514 Foreign Tax Credit for Individuals

If you paid foreign income tax, you may be able to take a foreign tax credit or deduction to avoid double taxation. This publication explains which foreign taxes qualify and how to figure your credit or deduction.

Form 1116.

515 Withholding of Tax on Nonresident Aliens and Foreign Corporations

This publication provides information for withholding agents who are required to withhold and report tax on payments to nonresident aliens and foreign corporations. Included are three tables listing U.S. tax treaties and some of the treaty provisions that provide for reduction of or exemption from withholding for certain types of income.

Forms 1042 and *1042S, 1001, 4224, 8233, 1078, 8288, 8288-A, 8288-B, 8804, 8805,* and *W-8, 8813,* and *8709.*

516 Tax Information for U.S. Government Civilian Employees Stationed Abroad

517 Social Security for Members of the Clergy and Religious Workers

This publication discusses social security coverage and the self-employment tax for the clergy.

Forms 2106, 1040, 4029 and *4361, Schedule SE (Form 1040)* and *Schedule C (Form 1040).*

519 U.S. Tax Guide for Aliens

This comprehensive publication gives guidelines on how to determine your U.S. tax status and figure your U.S. tax.

Forms 1040, 1040C, 1040NR, 2063, and *Schedule A (Form 1040).*

520 Scholarships and Fellowships

This publication explains the tax rules that apply to U.S. citizens and resident aliens who study, teach, or conduct research in the United States or abroad under scholarships and fellowship grants.

Forms 1040A and *1040EZ.*

521 Moving Expenses

Explains whether or not certain expenses of moving are deductible. For example, if you changed job locations last year or started a new job, you may be able to deduct your moving expenses. You also may be able to deduct expenses of moving to the United States if you retire while living and working overseas or if you are a survivor or dependent of a person who died while living and working overseas.

Forms 3903, 3903F, and *4782.*

523 Selling Your Home

Explains how to treat any gain or loss from selling your main home.

Form 2119.

524 Credit for the Elderly or the Disabled

You may be able to claim this credit if you are 65 or older, or if you are retired on disability and were permanently and totally disabled when you retired.

Schedule R (Form 1040) and *Schedule 3 (Form 1040A).*

525 Taxable and Nontaxable Income

526 Charitable Contributions

Schedule A (Form 1040) and *Form 8283.*

527 Residential Rental Property

Explains rental income and expenses and how to report them on your return. It also discusses the sale of rental property and other special rules that apply to rental activity.

Schedule E (Form 1040), and *Forms 4562* and *4797.*

529 Miscellaneous Deductions

This publication discusses expenses you may be able to take as miscellaneous deductions on *Schedule A (Form 1040)*, such as business employee expenses and expenses of producing income. It does not discuss other itemized deductions, such as the ones for charitable contributions, moving expenses, interest, taxes, or medical and dental expenses.

Schedule A (Form 1040), Form 2106.

530 Tax Information for First-Time Homeowners

531 Reporting Income from Tips

Explains how tip income is taxed as well as the rules for keeping records and reporting tips to your employers. It focuses on employees of food and beverage establishments, but recordkeeping rules and other information may also apply to other workers who receive tips, such as hairdressers, cab drivers and casino dealers.

Forms 4070 and *4070A.*

533 Self-Employment Tax

Payment of self-employment tax is explained. This is a social security and Medicare tax for people who work for themselves.

Schedule SE (Form 1040).

534 Depreciation

Form 4562.

535 Business Expenses

536 Net Operating Losses

Form 1045, Schedules A and *B.*

537 Installment Sales

Some sales arrangements provide for part or all of the selling price to be paid in a later year. These are installment sales. If you finance the buyer's purchase of your property instead of having the buyer get a loan or mortgage from a bank (or other lender), you probably have an installment sale.

Form 6252.

538 Accounting Periods and Methods

Forms 1128 and *3115.*

541 Tax Information on Partnerships

Form 1065, Schedules K and *K-1 (Form 1065).*

542 Tax Information on Corporations

Forms 1120 and *1120-A.*

544 Sales and Other Dispositions of Assets

This publication explains how to figure gain and loss on various transactions, such as trading or selling an asset used in a trade or business, and it explains the tax results of different types of gains and losses.

Schedule D (Form 1040), Forms 4797 and *8824.*

547 Nonbusiness Disasters, Casualties, and Thefts

This publication explains when you can deduct a disaster, casualty, or theft loss occurring from events such as hurricanes, earthquakes, tornadoes, fires, floods, vandalism, loss of deposits in a

bankrupt or insolvent financial institution, and car accidents. It also explains how to treat the reimbursement you receive from insurance or other sources.

Form 4684.

550 Investment Income and Expenses

Forms 1099-INT, 1099-DIV, 4952, 6781, and *8815,* and *Schedules B* and *D (Form 1040).*

551 Basis of Assets

This publication explains how to determine the basis of property, which is usually its cost.

552 Recordkeeping for Individuals

553 Highlights of 1992 Tax Changes

554 Tax Information for Older Americans

Schedules B, D, and *R (Form 1040),* and *Forms 1040, 1040A,* and *2119.*

555 Federal Tax Information on Community Property

This publication may help married taxpayers who reside in a community property state—Arizona, California, Idaho, Louisiana, Nevada, New Mexico, Texas, Washington or Wisconsin. If you file a separate tax return, you should understand how community property laws affect the way you figure your tax before completing your federal income tax return.

556 Examination of Returns, Appeal Rights, and Claims for Refund

Forms 1040X and *1120X.*

556S Revisión de las Declaraciones de Impuesto, Derecho de Apelación y Reclamaciones de Reembolsos (Examination of Returns, Appeal Rights, and Claims for Refund)

(Spanish version of Publication 556.) *Forms 1040X* and *1120X.*

557 Tax-Exempt Status for Your Organization

Discusses the rules and procedures that apply to organizations seeking and retaining exemption from federal income tax under section 501(a) of the Internal Revenue Code of 1986.

Forms 990, 990EZ, 990PF, 1023, and 1024.

559 Survivors, Executors, and Administrators

This publication can help you report and pay the proper federal income tax if you are responsible for settling a decedent's estate. It answers many questions that a spouse or other survivor faces when a person dies.

Forms 1040, 1041, and 4810.

560 Retirement Plans for the Self-Employed

Plans discussed include Simplified Employee Pensions (SEPs) and Keogh (H.R. 10) plans.

Forms 5305-SEP and *5500EZ.*

561 Determining the Value of Donated Property

Form 8283.

564 Mutual Fund Distributions

This publication discusses the tax treatment of distributions paid or allocated to an individual shareholder of a mutual fund.

Form 1040, Schedules B and *D (Form 1040),* and *Form 1099-DIV.*

570 Tax Guide for Individuals with Income from U.S. Possessions

This publication is for individuals with income from American Samoa, Guam, the Commonwealth of the Northern Mariana Islands, Puerto Rico, and the U.S. Virgin Islands.

Forms 4563, 5074, and *8689.*

571 Tax-Sheltered Annuity Programs for Employees of Public Schools and Certain Tax-Exempt Organizations

This publication explains the rules concerning employers qualified to buy tax-sheltered annuities, eligible employees who may participate in the program, and the amounts that may be excluded from income.

Form 5330.

575 Pension and Annuity Income (Including Simplified General Rule)

Explains how to report this income and discusses the special tax treatment for lump-sum distributions from pension, stock bonus, or profit-sharing plans.

Forms 1040, 1040A, 1099-R and *4972.*

578 Tax Information for Private Foundations and Foundation Managers

Form 990-F.

579S Cómo Preparar la Declaración de Impuesto Federal (How to Prepare the Federal Income Tax Return)

Forms 1040, 1040A, and *1040EZ.*

583 Taxpayers Starting a Business

Schedule C (Form 1040), and *Form 4562.*

584 Nonbusiness Disaster, Casualty, and Theft Loss Workbook

587 Business Use of Your Home

Schedule C (Form 1040), Forms 4562 and *8829.*

589 Tax Information on S Corporations

Form 1120S and *Schedule K-1 (Form 1120S).*

590 Individual Retirement Arrangements (IRAs)

The tax rules for IRAs are explained as well as the penalties for not following them. An IRA is a personal savings plan that offers you tax advantages to set aside money for your retirement.

Forms 1040, 1040A, 5329 and *8606.*

593 Tax Highlights for U.S. Citizens and Residents Going Abroad

A brief review of various U.S. tax provisions that apply to U.S. citizens or resident aliens who live or work abroad and expect to receive income from foreign sources.

594 Understanding the Collection Process

This publication explains your rights and duties as a taxpayer who owes federal taxes. It also explains how the IRS fulfills its legal obligation to collect these taxes.

594S Comprendiendo el Proceso de Cobro (Understanding the Collection Process)

(Spanish version of Publication 594.)

596 Earned Income Credit

If you work and have a child living with you, you may qualify for the earned income credit. This publication discusses who may receive the credit, how to figure and claim the credit and how to receive advance payments of the credit.

Forms W-5, 1040, 1040A, and Schedule EIC.

596SP Crédito por Ingreso del Trabajo (Earned Income Credit)

(Spanish version of Publication 596.)

597 Information on the United States-Canada Income Tax Treaty

This publication reproduces the text of the U.S.-Canada income tax treaty and explains the provisions that often apply to U.S. citizens or residents who have Canadian source income. It also discusses certain tax problems that may be encountered by Canadian residents who temporarily work in the United States.

598 Tax on Unrelated Business Income of Exempt Organizations

This publication explains the tax provisions that apply to most tax-exempt organizations that regularly operate a trade or business that is not substantially related to its exempt purpose. Generally, a tax-exempt organization with gross income of $1,000 or more from an unrelated trade or business must file a return and pay any taxes due.

Form 990-T.

686 Certification for Reduced Tax Rates in Tax Treaty Countries

This publication explains how U.S. citizens, residents, and domestic corporations may certify to a foreign country that they are entitled to tax treaty benefits.

721 Tax Guide to U.S. Civil Service Retirement Benefits

Forms 1040 and 1040A.

850 English-Spanish Glossary of Words and Phrases Used in Publications Issued by the Internal Revenue Service

901 U.S. Tax Treaties

This publication discusses the reduced tax rates and exemptions from U.S. taxes provided under U.S. tax treaties with foreign countries. It is intended for residents of those countries who receive income from U.S. sources.

Form 1040NR.

904 Interrelated Computations for Estate and Gift Taxes

Forms 706 and 709.

907 Information for Persons with Handicaps or Disabilities

Schedules A and R (Form 1040) and Form 2441.

908 Bankruptcy and Other Debt Cancellation

Forms 982, 1040, 1041, and 1120.

909 Alternative Minimum Tax for Individuals

Forms 6251 and 8801.

911 Tax Information for Direct Sellers

A direct seller is a person who sells consumer products to others on a person-to-person basis, such as door-to-door, at sales parties, or by appointment in someone's home. Information on figuring your income from direct sales and the kinds of expenses you may be able to deduct is provided.

Form 4562 and Schedules C and SE (Form 1040).

915 Social Security Benefits and Equivalent Railroad Retirement Benefits

Forms SSA-1099 and RRB-1099, Social Security Benefits Worksheet, Notice 703, Forms SSA-1042S and RRB-1042S.

917 Business Use of a Car

Form 2106.

919 Is My Withholding Correct for 1993?

Explains Form W-4 to help you make sure the right amount of tax is withheld from your pay.

Form W-4.

924 Reporting of Real Estate Transactions to IRS

This publication informs sellers of certain real estate about the information they must provide to the real estate reporting person in order that the reporting person can complete the *Form 1099-S* that must be filed with IRS.

925 Passive Activity and At-Risk Rules

Form 8582.

926 Employment Taxes for Household Employers

You may be a household employer if you have a babysitter, maid, or other employee who works in your house. This publication explains what taxes to withhold and pay, and what records to keep.

Forms W-2, W-3, W-5, 940, 940-EZ and 942.

929 Tax Rules for Children and Dependents

This publication describes the tax laws affecting dependents and certain children. It explains their filing requirement and the standard deduction amount for dependents. It also explains when and how a child's parents may include their child's interest and dividend income on their return, and when and how a child's parents are required to report part of their child's investment income on their return.

Forms 8615, 8814, and 8803.

936 Home Mortgage Interest Deduction

Form 1040 and Schedule A (Form 1040).

937 Business Reporting

This publication explains your tax responsibilities and reporting requirements if you have employees.

Forms W-2, W-4, 940, 941, and 1099-MISC.

938 Real Estate Mortgage Investment Conduits (REMICs) Reporting Information (And Other Collateralized Debt Obligations (CDOs))

This publication discusses reporting requirements for issuers of REMICs and CDOs. It contains a directory of REMICs and CDOs to assist brokers and middlemen with their reporting requirements.

939 Pension General Rule (Nonsimplified Method)

This publication covers the nonsimplified General Rule for the taxation of pensions and annuities, which must be used if the Simplified General Rule does not apply or is not chosen. For example, the nonsimplified method must be

used for payments under commercial annuities. The publication contains needed actuarial tables.

945 Tax Information for Those Affected by Operation Desert Storm

946 How to Begin Depreciating Your Property

This publication is for people who are depreciating property for the first time.

These publications can be ordered by calling IRS toll-free at 1-800-829-3676.

947 Power of Attorney and Practice Before the IRS

This publication explains who can represent a taxpayer before the IRS and what forms or documents are used to authorize a person to represent a taxpayer.

Forms 2848 and 8821.

950 Who Must File Gift or Estate Tax Returns

An easy-to-read publication that briefly outlines some of the topics covered in Publication 448, Federal Estate and Gift Taxes.

953 International Tax Information for Businesses

Covers topics of interest to U.S. citizens and resident aliens with foreign investments and nonresident aliens who want to invest in U.S. businesses.

1004 Identification Numbers Under ERISA

1045 Information for Tax Practitioners

1212 List of Original Issue Discount Instruments

This publication explains the tax treatment of original issue discount (OID) by brokers and other middlemen and by owners of OID debt instruments.

1244 Employee's Daily Record of Tips (Form 4070-A) and Employee's Report of Tips to Employer (Form 4070)

Forms 4070 and 4070-A.

1544 Reporting Cash Payments of Over $10,000 (Received in a Trade or Business)

This publication explains when and how persons in a trade or business must file a Form 8300 when they receive cash payments of more than $10,000 from one buyer. It also discusses the substantial penalties for not filing the form.

Form 8300.

TAX TIPS

AVOID THESE COMMON ERRORS

The most common errors taxpayers make on their *Forms 1040, 1040A* and *1040EZ* are explained below. Check your tax return carefully because these errors can delay any refund you may be expecting.

Checking the Age/Blindness box.

- If you are age 65 or older or blind, or your spouse is age 65 or older or blind, make sure you check the appropriate box(es) on *Form 1040* or *Form 1040A*.

Earned income credit not claimed.

- This is a special credit that can help some taxpayers who have a child and have incomes below a certain level. For more information on whether you qualify, get Publication 596, *Earned Income Credit* (available in Spanish).

Earned income credit is figured incorrectly.

- You may be entitled to a credit of up to $2,211 if your adjusted gross income is less than $22,370 and you have a qualifying child. *Schedule EIC* is in the *Form 1040* and *1040A* instructions and is used to figure the credit.

Social Security Tax, instead of Federal Income Tax Withheld, was entered on your tax return.

- *Form W-2* shows both the Federal Income Tax (Box 9) and FICA (Social Security Tax) (Box 11) withheld. Remember to use the amount in Box 9 on your return to calculate your total income tax withheld.

Omitting or making an incorrect entry for standard deduction amount.

- If you do not itemize deductions, use the correct standard deduction chart to find the right amount.

Incorrect refund or balance due.

- Verify your addition and subtraction. If your total payments are more than your total tax, you are due a refund. A "Balance Due" is figured when your taxes due are more than the amount you have already paid.

Incorrect tax entered from tax tables.

- First, take the amount shown on the taxable income line of your *Form 1040EZ, 1040,* or *1040A* and find the line in the tax table showing that amount. Next, find the column for your marital status (married filing jointly, single, etc.) and read down the column. The amount shown where the income line and filing status column meet is your tax.

Computation error when income amounts were totalled.

- Verify the addition of all income amounts on your return.

Incorrect entries for social security number and zip code.

- Check the preprinted address label that comes with your tax package and make any necessary changes on the label.

DOUBLE CHECK YOUR RETURN BEFORE MAILING

Take a moment to do the following:

- [ ] Check your return for math errors.
- [ ] Attach Copy B of all *Forms W-2.*
- [ ] Attach all required forms and related schedules.
- [ ] Put the preprinted address label on your return, and make any necessary corrections to your name, address, and social security number.
- [ ] Sign and date your return (on a joint return, both husband and wife must sign).
- [ ] If you owe additional tax, attach your check or money order payable to "Internal Revenue Service," not the "IRS." Remember to write your social security number, daytime telephone number, tax form number, and tax year on your check or money order.
- [ ] Make a copy of the return for your records.
- [ ] Use the envelope that came in the tax package to mail your return. If you do not have the preprinted envelope, address an envelope to the IRS Service Center for your state.
- [ ] Attach the correct postage.

CALL THE IRS WITH YOUR TAX QUESTION

If the instructions to the tax forms and our free tax publications have not answered your question, please call us TOLL-FREE. "Toll-Free" is a telephone call for which you pay only local charges, if any.

Choosing the Right Number

Use only the number listed on this page for your area. Use a local city number only if it is not a long distance call for you. **Please do not dial "1-800" when using a local city number.** However, when dialing from an area that does not have a local number, be sure to dial "1-800" before calling the toll-free number.

Before You Call

Remember that good communication is a two-way process. IRS representatives care about the quality of the service we provide to you, our customer. You can help us provide accurate, complete answers to your tax questions by having the following information available:

1. The tax form, schedule, or notice to which your question relates.

2. The facts about your particular situation (the answer to the same question often varies from one taxpayer to another because of differences in their age, income, whether they can be claimed as a dependent, etc.).

3. The name of any IRS publication or other source of information that you used to look for the answer.

Before You Hang Up

If you do not fully understand the answer you receive, or you feel our representative may not fully understand your question, our representative needs to know this. The representative will be happy to take the additional time required to be sure he or she has

Toll-Free Tax Help Telephone Numbers

Alabama
1-800-829-1040
Alaska
Anchorage, 561-7484
Elsewhere, 1-800-829-1040
Arizona
Phoenix, 640-3900
Elsewhere, 1-800-829-1040
Arkansas
1-800-829-1040
California
Oakland, 839-1040
Elsewhere, 1-800-829-1040
Colorado
Denver, 825-7041
Elsewhere, 1-800-829-1040
Connecticut
1-800-829-1040
Delaware
1-800-829-1040
District of Columbia
1-800-829-1040
Florida
Jacksonville, 354-1760
Elsewhere, 1-800-829-1040
Georgia
Atlanta, 522-0050
Elsewhere, 1-800-829-1040
Hawaii
Oahu, 541-1040
Elsewhere, 1-800-829-1040
Idaho
1-800-829-1040
Illinois
Chicago, 435-1040
In area code 708, 1-312-435-1040
Elsewhere, 1-800-829-1040
Indiana
Indianapolis, 226-5477
Elsewhere, 1-800-829-1040
Iowa
Des Moines, 283-0523
Elsewhere, 1-800-829-1040
Kansas
1-800-829-1040
Kentucky
1-800-829-1040
Louisiana
1-800-829-1040
Maine
1-800-829-1040
Maryland
Baltimore, 962-2590
Elsewhere, 1-800-829-1040

Massachusetts
Boston, 536-1040
Elsewhere, 1-800-829-1040
Michigan
Detroit, 237-0800
Elsewhere, 1-800-829-1040
Minnesota
Minneapolis, 644-7515
St. Paul, 644-7515
Elsewhere, 1-800-829-1040
Mississippi
1-800-829-1040
Missouri
St. Louis, 342-1040
Elsewhere, 1-800-829-1040
Montana
1-800-829-1040
Nebraska
Omaha, 422-1500
Elsewhere, 1-800-829-1040
Nevada
1-800-829-1040
New Hampshire
1-800-829-1040
New Jersey
1-800-829-1040
New Mexico
1-800-829-1040
New York
Bronx, 488-9150
Brooklyn, 488-9150
Buffalo, 685-5432
Manhattan, 732-0100
Nassau, 222-1131
Queens, 488-9150
Staten Island, 488-9150
Suffolk, 724-5000
Elsewhere, 1-800-829-1040
North Carolina
1-800-829-1040
North Dakota
1-800-829-1040
Ohio
Cincinnati, 621-6281
Cleveland, 522-3000
Elsewhere, 1-800-829-1040
Oklahoma
1-800-829-1040
Oregon
Portland, 221-3960
Elsewhere, 1-800-829-1040
Pennsylvania
Philadelphia, 574-9900
Pittsburgh, 281-0112
Elsewhere, 1-800-829-1040

Puerto Rico
San Juan Metro Area, 766-5040
Isla, 1-800-829-1040
Rhode Island
1-800-829-1040
South Carolina
1-800-829-1040
South Dakota
1-800-829-1040
Tennessee
Nashville, 259-4601
Elsewhere, 1-800-829-1040
Texas
Dallas, 742-2440
Houston, 541-0440
Elsewhere, 1-800-829-1040
Utah
1-800-829-1040
Vermont
1-800-829-1040
Virginia
Richmond, 649-2361
Elsewhere, 1-800-829-1040
Washington
Seattle, 442-1040
Elsewhere, 1-800-829-1040
West Virginia
1-800-829-1040
Wisconsin
Milwaukee, 271-3780
Elsewhere, 1-800-829-1040
Wyoming
1-800-829-1040

Hours of Operation:
Monday–Friday during regular business hours (may vary in your area).

Phone Help for Hearing-Impaired People with TDD Equipment
All areas in U.S., including Alaska, Hawaii, Virgin Islands, and Puerto Rico, 1-800-829-4059

Hours of TDD Operation:
8:00 a.m. to 6:30 p.m. EST (Jan. 1–April 4)
9:00 a.m. to 7:30 p.m. EDT (April 5–April 15)
9:00 a.m. to 5:30 p.m. EDT (April 16–Oct. 31)
8:00 a.m. to 4:30 p.m. EST (Nov.1–Dec. 31)

answered your question fully and in the manner that is most helpful to you.

By law, you are responsible for paying your fair share of Federal income tax. If we should make an error in answering your question, you are still responsible for the payment of the correct tax.

Should this occur, however, you will not be charged any penalty. To make sure that IRS representatives give accurate and courteous answers, a second IRS representative sometimes listens in on telephone calls. No record is kept of any taxpayer's identity.

☎ TOLL-FREE TELEPHONE NUMBERS ☎

WHAT IS TELE-TAX?

Recorded Tax Information includes about 140 topics that answer many Federal tax questions. You can listen to up to three topics on each call you make.

Automated Refund Information allows you to check the status of your refund.

Choosing the Right Number

Use only the number listed on this page for your area. Use a local city number only if it is not a long distance call for you. **Please do not dial "1-800" when using a local city number.** However, when dialing from an area that does not have a local number, be sure to dial "1-800" before calling the toll-free number.

Recorded Tax Information

Topic numbers are effective January 1, 1993. A complete list of these topics is on the next page.

Touch-tone service is available 24 hours a day, 7 days a week.

Rotary or pulse dial service is usually available Monday through Friday during regular office hours.

Select, by number, the topic you want to hear. **For the directory of topics, listen to topic no. 323.**

Have paper and pencil handy to take notes.

Call the appropriate phone number listed on this page.

- If you have a touch-tone phone, immediately follow the recorded instructions, or
- If you have a rotary or pulse dial phone, wait for further recorded instructions.

Automated Refund Information

Be sure to have a copy of your tax return available since you will need to know the first social security number shown on your return, the filing status,

Toll-Free Tele-Tax Telephone Numbers

Alabama
1-800-829-4477
Alaska
1-800-829-4477
Arizona
Phoenix, 640-3933
Elsewhere, 1-800-829-4477
Arkansas
1-800-829-4477
California
Counties of: Alpine, Amador, Butte, Calaveras, Colusa, Contra Costa, Del Norte, El Dorado, Glenn, Humboldt, Lake, Lassen, Marin, Mendocino, Modoc, Napa, Nevada, Placer, Plumas, Sacramento, San Joaquin, Shasta, Sierra, Siskiyou, Solano, Sonoma, Sutter, Tehama, Trinity, Yolo, and Yuba,
   1-800-829-4032
Oakland, 839-4245
Elsewhere, 1-800-829-4477
Colorado
Denver, 592-1118
Elsewhere, 1-800-829-4477
Connecticut
1-800-829-4477
Delaware
1-800-829-4477
District of Columbia
628-2929
Florida
1-800-829-4477
Georgia
Atlanta, 331-6572
Elsewhere, 1-800-829-4477
Hawaii
1-800-829-4477
Idaho
1-800-829-4477
Illinois
Chicago, 886-9614
In area code 708, 1-312-886-9614
Springfield, 789-0489
Elsewhere, 1-800-829-4477
Indiana
Indianapolis, 631-1010
Elsewhere, 1-800-829-4477

Iowa
Des Moines, 284-7454
Elsewhere, 1-800-829-4477
Kansas
1-800-829-4477
Kentucky
1-800-829-4477
Louisiana
1-800-829-4477
Maine
1-800-829-4477
Maryland
Baltimore, 244-7306
Elsewhere, 1-800-829-4477
Massachusetts
Boston, 536-0709
Elsewhere, 1-800-829-4477
Michigan
Detroit, 961-4282
Elsewhere, 1-800-829-4477
Minnesota
St. Paul, 644-7748
Elsewhere, 1-800-829-4477
Mississippi
1-800-829-4477
Missouri
St. Louis, 241-4700
Elsewhere, 1-800-829-4477
Montana
1-800-829-4477
Nebraska
Omaha, 221-3324
Elsewhere, 1-800-829-4477
Nevada
1-800-829-4477
New Hampshire
1-800-829-4477
New Jersey
1-800-829-4477
New Mexico
1-800-829-4477
New York
Bronx, 488-8432
Brooklyn, 488-8432
Buffalo, 685-5533
Manhattan, 406-4080
Queens, 488-8432
Staten Island, 488-8432
Elsewhere, 1-800-829-4477

North Carolina
1-800-829-4477
North Dakota
1-800-829-4477
Ohio
Cincinnati, 421-0329
Cleveland, 522-3037
Elsewhere, 1-800-829-4477
Oklahoma
1-800-829-4477
Oregon
Portland, 294-5363
Elsewhere, 1-800-829-4477
Pennsylvania
Philadelphia, 627-1040
Pittsburgh, 261-1040
Elsewhere, 1-800-829-4477
Puerto Rico
1-800-829-4477
Rhode Island
1-800-829-4477
South Carolina
1-800-829-4477
South Dakota
1-800-829-4477
Tennessee
1-800-829-4477
Texas
Dallas, 767-1792
Houston, 541-3400
Elsewhere, 1-800-829-4477
Utah
1-800-829-4477
Vermont
1-800-829-4477
Virginia
Richmond, 783-1569
Elsewhere, 1-800-829-4477
Washington
Seattle, 343-7221
Elsewhere, 1-800-829-4477
West Virginia
1-800-829-4477
Wisconsin
Milwaukee, 273-8100
Elsewhere, 1-800-829-4477
Wyoming
1-800-829-4477

and the **exact** whole dollar amount of your refund.

Then, call the appropriate phone number listed on this page and follow the recorded instructions.

The IRS updates refund information every 7 days. If you call to find out about the status of your refund and do not receive a refund mailing date, please wait 7 days before calling back.

- Touch-tone service is available Monday through Friday from 7:00 a.m. to 11:30 p.m. (Hours may vary in your area.)
- Rotary or pulse dial service is usually available Monday through Friday during regular office hours.

TELE-TAX TOPIC NUMBERS AND SUBJECTS

TOPIC NO. SUBJECT

IRS Procedures and Services
- 101 IRS help available—Volunteer tax assistance programs, toll-free telephone, walk-in assistance, and outreach program
- 102 Tax assistance for individuals with disabilities and the hearing impaired
- 103 Small Business Tax Education Program (STEP)—Tax help for small businesses
- 104 Problem Resolution Program—Help for problem situations
- 105 Public libraries—Tax information tapes and reproducible tax forms
- 106 1040PC tax return
- 107 The collection process
- 108 Tax fraud—How to report
- 109 Types of organizations that qualify for tax-exempt status
- 110 Organizations—How to apply for exempt status
- 111 Your appeal rights
- 112 Electronic filing
- 113 Power of attorney information
- 114 Change of address—How to notify IRS
- 911 Hardship assistance applications
- 999 Local information

Filing Requirements, Filing Status, Exemptions
- 151 Who must file?
- 152 Which form—1040, 1040A, or 1040EZ?
- 153 When, where, and how to file
- 154 What is your filing status?
- 155 Dependents
- 156 Estimated tax
- 157 Amended returns
- 158 Decedents

Types of Income
- 201 Wages and salaries
- 202 Tips
- 203 Interest received
- 204 Dividends
- 205 Refund of state and local taxes
- 206 Alimony received
- 207 Business income
- 208 Sole proprietorship
- 209 Capital gains and losses
- 210 Pensions and annuities
- 211 Pensions—The general rule and the simplified general rule
- 212 Lump-sum distributions
- 213 Rental income and expenses
- 214 Renting vacation property/Renting to relatives
- 215 Royalties
- 216 Farming and fishing income
- 217 Earnings for clergy
- 218 Unemployment compensation
- 219 Gambling income and expenses
- 220 Bartering income
- 221 Scholarship and fellowship grants
- 222 Nontaxable income
- 223 Social security and equivalent railroad retirement benefits
- 224 401(k) plans
- 225 Passive activities—Losses/credits

Adjustments to Income
- 251 Individual retirement arrangements (IRAs)

TOPIC NO. SUBJECT
- 252 Alimony paid
- 253 Bad debt deduction
- 254 Tax shelters

Itemized Deductions
- 301 Should I itemize?
- 302 Medical and dental expenses
- 303 Deductible taxes
- 304 Moving expenses
- 305 Interest expense
- 306 Contributions
- 307 Casualty losses
- 308 Miscellaneous expenses
- 309 Business use of home
- 310 Business use of car
- 311 Business travel expenses
- 312 Business entertainment expenses
- 313 Educational expenses
- 314 Employee business expenses

Tax Computation
- 351 Tax and credits figured by IRS
- 352 Self-employment tax
- 353 Five-year averaging for lump-sum distributions
- 354 Alternative minimum tax
- 355 Gift tax
- 356 Estate tax
- 357 Standard deduction
- 358 Tax on a child's investment income

Tax Credits
- 401 Child and dependent care credit
- 402 Earned income credit
- 403 Credit for the elderly or the disabled

General Information
- 451 Substitute tax forms
- 452 Highlights of 1992 tax changes
- 453 Refunds—How long they should take
- 454 Copy of your tax return—How to get one
- 455 Forms/Publications—How to order
- 456 Offers in compromise
- 457 Extension of time to file your tax return
- 458 Form W-2—What to do if not received
- 459 Penalty for underpayment of estimated tax
- 460 Recordkeeping
- 461 How to choose a tax preparer
- 462 Failure to pay child/spousal support and other Federal obligations
- 463 Withholding on interest and dividends
- 464 What to do if you haven't filed your tax return (Nonfilers)
- 465 Checklist/Common errors when preparing your tax return
- 466 Withholding on pensions and annuities
- 467 What to do if you can't pay your tax
- 468 Desert Storm

IRS Notices and Letters
- 501 Notices—What to do
- 502 Notice of underreported income—CP 2000
- 503 IRS notices and bills/Penalty and interest charges

Basis of Assets, Depreciation, Sale of Assets
- 551 Sale of your home—General
- 552 Sale of your home—How to report gain
- 553 Sale of your home—Exclusion of gain, age 55 and over
- 554 Basis of assets
- 555 Depreciation
- 556 Installment sales

TOPIC NO. SUBJECT

Employer Tax Information
- 601 Social security and Medicare withholding rates
- 602 Form W-2—Where, when, and how to file
- 603 Form W-4—Employee's Withholding Allowance Certificate
- 604 Employer identification number—How to apply
- 605 Form 942—Employer's Quarterly Tax Return for Household Employees
- 606 Form 941—Deposit requirements
- 607 Form 941—Employer's Quarterly Federal Tax Return
- 608 Form 940—Deposit requirements
- 609 Form 940/940-EZ—Employer's Annual Federal Unemployment Tax Return
- 610 Targeted jobs credit
- 611 Tips—Withholding and reporting

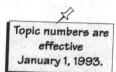

Topic numbers are effective January 1, 1993.

Form 1099 Series and Related Information Returns—Filing Magnetically or Electronically
- 651 Who must file—Originals and corrections
- 652 Acceptable media/Locating a third party to prepare your files
- 653 Applications, forms, and information
- 654 Waivers, extensions, and format deviations
- 655 Test files and combined Federal/state filing
- 656 Electronic filing of information returns
- 657 Information Returns Program Bulletin Board System

Tax Information for Aliens and U.S. Citizens Living Abroad
- 701 Resident and nonresident aliens
- 702 Dual-status alien
- 703 Foreign earned income exclusion—General
- 704 Foreign earned income exclusion—Who qualifies?
- 705 Foreign earned income exclusion—What qualifies?
- 706 Foreign tax credit

The following topics are in Spanish:
- 751 Who must file?
- 752 Which form to use?
- 753 What is your filing status?
- 754 Earned income credit
- 755 Highlights of 1992 tax changes
- 756 Forms and publications—How to order
- 757 Alien tax clearance
- 758 Refunds—How long they should take
- 759 IRS help available—Volunteer tax assistance programs, toll-free telephone, walk-in assistance, and outreach program
- 760 Social security and equivalent railroad retirement benefits

Tax Information for Puerto Rico Residents
- 851 Who must file a U.S. income tax return in Puerto Rico
- 852 Deductions and credits for Puerto Rico filers
- 853 Federal employment taxes in Puerto Rico
- 854 Tax assistance for residents of Puerto Rico

Service Center
Problem Resolution Offices

Correspondence should be addressed to:

Problem Resolution Office
Internal Revenue Service Center

with the appropriate address from the following list.

Andover Service Center
310 Lowell Street (Stop 122)
Andover, MA 05501

Atlanta Service Center
P. O. Box 48-549 (Stop 29-A)
Doraville, GA 30362

Austin Service Center
P. O. Box 934
(Stop 1005 AUSC)
Austin, TX 78767

Austin Compliance Center
P. O. Box 2986
(Stop 1005 AUCC)
Austin, TX 78768

Brookhaven Service Center
P. O. Box 960 (Stop 102)
Holtsville, NY 11742

Cincinnati Service Center
P. O. Box 267 (Stop 11)
Covington, KY 41019

Fresno Service Center
P. O. Box 12161
Fresno, CA 93776

Kansas City Service Center
P. O. Box 24551
Kansas City, MO 64131

Memphis Service Center
P. O. Box 30309 AMF
(Stop 77)
Memphis, TN 38130

Ogden Service Center
P. O. Box 9941
(Stop 1005)
Ogden, UT 84409

Philadelphia Service Center
P. O. Box 16053
Philadelphia, PA 19114

District
Problem Resolution Offices

Correspondence and facsimile transmissions should be addressed to:

Problem Resolution Office
Internal Revenue Service

with the appropriate address from the following list.

Aberdeen District
115 4th Ave. S.E.
Aberdeen, SD 57401
(605) 226-7278
FAX: (605) 226-7270

Albany District
Leo O'Brien Federal Building
Clinton Ave. & N. Pearl Street
Albany, NY 12207
(518) 472-4482
FAX: (518) 472-3626

Albuquerque District
P. O. Box 1040 (Stop 1005)
Albuquerque, NM 87103
(505) 766-3760
FAX: (505) 766-1317

Anchorage District
P. O. Box 101500
Anchorage, AK 99510
(907) 261-4228 or 4230
FAX: (907) 261-4413

Atlanta District
P. O. Box 1065
Room 1520 (Stop 202-D)
Atlanta, GA 30370
(404) 331-5232
FAX: (404) 730-3438

Augusta District
220 Main Mall Road
South Portland, ME 04106
(207) 780-3309
FAX: (207) 780-3515

Austin District
P. O. Box 1863 (Stop 1005)
Austin, TX 78767
(512) 499-5875
FAX: (512) 499-5687

Baltimore District
P. O. Box 1553 Room 620A
Baltimore, MD 21203
(301) 962-2082
FAX: (301) 962-9572

Birmingham District
500 22nd Street South
Stop 316
Birmingham, AL 35233
(205) 731-1177
FAX: (205) 731-0017

Boise District
550 West Fort Street
Box 041
Boise, ID 83724
(208) 334-1324
FAX: (208) 334-9663

Boston District
JFK P. O. Box 9103
Boston, MA 02203
(617) 565-1857
FAX: (617) 565-4959

Brooklyn District
G. P. O. Box R
Brooklyn, NY 11202
(718) 780-6511
FAX: (718) 780-6045

Buffalo District
P. O. Box 500
Niagara Square Station
Buffalo, NY 14201
(716) 846-4574
FAX: (716) 846-5473

Burlington District
Courthouse Plaza
199 Main Street
Burlington, VT 05401
(802) 860-2008
FAX: (802) 860-2006

Cheyenne District
308 West 21st Street
(Stop 1005)
Cheyenne, WY 82001
(307) 772-2489
FAX: (307) 772-2488

Chicago District
230 S. Dearborn Street
Room 3214
Chicago, IL 60604
(312) 886-4396
FAX: (312) 886-1564

Cincinnati District
P. O. Box 1818
Cincinnati, OH 45201
(513) 684-3094
FAX: (513) 684-2445

Cleveland District
P. O. Box 99709
Cleveland, OH 44199
(216) 522-7134
FAX: (216) 522-2992

Columbia District
P. O. Box 386, MDP-03
Columbia, SC 29202-0386
(803) 765-5939
FAX: (803) 253-3910

Dallas District
P. O. Box 50008 (Stop 1005)
Dallas, TX 75250
(214) 767-1289
FAX: (214) 767-2178

Denver District
P. O. Box 1302 (Stop 1005)
Denver, CO 80201
(303) 844-3178
FAX: (303) 844-4900

Des Moines District
P. O. Box 1337 (Stop 2)
Des Moines, IA 50305
(515) 284-4780
FAX: (515) 284-4299

Detroit District
P. O. Box 330500 (Stop 7)
Detroit, MI 48232-6500
(313) 226-7899
FAX: (313) 226-3502

Fargo District
P. O. Box 8
Fargo, ND 58107
(701) 239-5141
FAX: (701) 239-5644

Ft. Lauderdale District
P. O. Box 17167
Plantation, FL 33318
(305) 424-2385
FAX: (305) 424-2483

Greensboro District
320 Federal Place
Room 214B
Greensboro, NC 27401
(919) 333-5061
FAX: (919) 333-5630

Hartford District
135 High Street (Stop 219)
Hartford, CT 06103
(203) 240-4179
FAX: (203) 240-4023

Helena District
Federal Building
301 S. Park Avenue
Helena, MT 59626-0016
(406) 449-5244
FAX: (406) 449-5342

Honolulu District
P. O. Box 50089
Honolulu, HI 96850
(808) 541-3300
FAX: (808) 541-1117

Houston District
1919 Smith Street (Stop 1005)
Houston, TX 77002
(713) 653-3660
FAX: (713) 653-3708

Indianapolis District
P. O. Box 44687 (Stop 11)
Indianapolis, IN 46244
(317) 226-6332
FAX: (317) 226-6110

**Assistant Commissioner
(International)**
950 L'Enfant Plaza
Washington, DC 20024
(202) 447-1020
FAX: (202) 287-4466

Jackson District
100 West Capitol Street
Suite 504, Stop 31
Jackson, MS 39269
(601) 965-4800
FAX: (601) 965-5796

Jacksonville District
P. O. Box 35045
(Stop D:PRO)
Jacksonville, FL 32202
(904) 791-3440
FAX: (904) 791-2266

Laguna Niguel District
P. O. Box 30207
Laguna Niguel, CA
92607-0207
(714) 643-4182
FAX: (714) 643-4436

Las Vegas District
4750 West Oakey Blvd.
Las Vegas, NV 89102
(702) 455-1099
FAX: (702) 455-1009

Little Rock District
P. O. Box 3778 (Stop 3)
Little Rock, AR 72203
(501) 324-6260
FAX: (501) 324-5109

Los Angeles District
P. O. Box 1791
Los Angeles, CA 90053
(213) 894-6111
FAX: (213) 894-6365

Louisville District
P. O. Box 1735
(Stop 120)
Louisville, KY 40201
(502) 582-6030
FAX: (502) 582-5580

Manhattan District
P. O. Box 408
Church Street Station
New York, NY 10008
(212) 264-2850
FAX: (212) 264-6949

Milwaukee District
P. O. Box 386 Room M-28
Milwaukee, WI 53201
(414) 297-3046
FAX: (414) 297-1640

Nashville District
P. O. Box 1107 (MDP 22)
Nashville, TN 37202
(615) 736-5219
FAX: (615) 736-7489

New Orleans District
600 S. Maestri Place
(Stop 12)
New Orleans, LA 70130
(504) 589-3001
FAX: (504) 589-3112

Newark District
Problem Resolution Unit
P. O. Box 1143
Newark, NJ 07101
(201) 645-6698
FAX: (201) 645-3323

Oklahoma City District
P. O. Box 1040 (Stop 1005)
Oklahoma City, OK 73101
(405) 231-5125
FAX: (405) 231-4929

Omaha District
106 S. 15th Street (Stop 2)
Omaha, NE 68102
(402) 221-4181
FAX: (402) 221-4030

Parkersburg District
P. O. Box 1388
Parkersburg, WV 26102
(304) 420-6616
FAX: (304) 420-6699

Philadelphia District
P. O. Box 12010
Philadelphia, PA 19106
(215) 597-3377
FAX: (215) 440-1456

Phoenix District
2120 N. Central Avenue
(Stop 1005)
Phoenix, AZ 85004
(602) 379-3604
FAX: (602) 379-3530

Pittsburgh District
P. G. Box 705
Pittsburgh, PA 15230
(412) 644-5987
FAX: (412) 644-2769

Portland District
P. O. Box 3341
Portland, OR 97208
(503) 326-4166
FAX: (503) 326-5453

Portsmouth District
P. O. Box 720
Portsmouth, NH 03802
(603) 433-0571
FAX: (603) 433-0739

Providence District
380 Westminster Mall
Providence, RI 02903
(401) 528-4034
FAX: (401) 528-4646

Richmond District
P. O. Box 10113, Room 5502
Richmond, VA 23240
(804) 771-2643
FAX: (804) 771-2008

Sacramento District
P. O. Box 2900 (Stop SA 5043)
Sacramento, CA 95812
(916) 978-4079
FAX: (916) 978-5052

St. Louis District
P. O. Box 1548 (Stop 002)
St. Louis, MO 63188
(314) 539-6770
FAX: (314) 539-3990

St. Paul District
P. O. Box 64599
St. Paul, MN 55164
(612) 290-3077
FAX: (612) 290-4236

Salt Lake City District
P. O. Box 2069 (Stop 1005)
Salt Lake City, UT 84110
(801) 524-6287
FAX: (801) 524-6080

San Francisco District
P. O. Box 36136 (Stop 4004)
450 Golden Gate Avenue
San Francisco, CA 94102
(415) 556-5046
FAX: (415) 556-4456

San Jose District
P. O. Box 100
San Jose, CA 95103
(408) 291-7132
FAX: (408) 291-7109

Seattle District
P. O. Box 2207 (Stop 405)
Seattle, WA 98111
(206) 442-7393
FAX: (206) 442-1176

Springfield District
P. O. Box 19201 (Stop 22)
Springfield, IL 62794-9201
(217) 492-4517
FAX: (217) 492-4073

Wichita District
P. O. Box 2907 (Stop 1005)
Wichita, KS 67201
(316) 291-6506
FAX: (316) 291-6557

Wilmington District
844 King Street, Room 3402
Wilmington, DE 19801
(302) 573-6052
FAX: (302) 573-6309

National Office
1111 Constitution Ave., N.W.
Room 3003 C:PRP
Washington, DC 20224
(202) 566-6475
FAX: (202) 377-6154

Department of the Treasury
Internal Revenue Service

Catalog Number 10040G

Publication 1383
(Rev. April 1993)

The Correspondence Process (Income Tax Accounts)

Introduction

This publication explains what you need to do when the Internal Revenue Service (IRS) questions or examines your return by correspondence. It explains how to respond to our notice of proposed changes and ways you may avoid future notices. For information concerning your rights as a taxpayer, see Publication 1, *Your Rights As a Taxpayer,* enclosed or previously sent to you. The topics covered in this publication are:

- Responding to Our Notice
- Avoiding Future Notices

Responding To Our Notice

When we propose changes to your return by correspondence, your notice summarizes the changes and explains the reasons for making the changes. It is important that you understand the reasons for any proposed change. Please ask us about anything that is not clear to you. Once you understand the notice, you should:

1) **Review** the proposed changes and compare them with the information you included on your return.

2) **If you agree** with the changes, sign and date the consent form enclosed with the notice and return it to us using the envelope provided. If you pay any amount you agree you owe when you return the consent form, you will minimize further interest charges. Otherwise, we will bill you for the amount you owe plus additional interest when we receive you consent.

3) **If you agree but can't pay** the total amount due at this time, you still need to sign and return the consent form. Failure to do so will only delay resolving your tax matter and we may charge additional interest and penalty. You may include a partial payment when you return the consent. This will minimize interest charges on the part of the tax you do pay, although by law, we will continue to charge interest on the remainder until you pay it.

4) **If you don't agree** with our proposed changes or if any part of our notice is incorrect, write a statement explaining why you disagree, sign the statement and send it to us in the enclosed envelope. Be sure to include your social security number on the signed statement. Also, provide any additional information you would like us to consider and a telephone number where you can be reached during business hours with the best time to call if we need to reach you by phone. This is usually the easiest way to answer questions about your tax return and often lets us take care of the entire matter without further contact. You also may ask for an interview with an examiner. You should include your request for interview with your explanation of why you disagree with the proposed changes.

5) If you don't respond within 30 days, we will assume the proposed changes to your tax return are correct. We will send you a Notice of Deficiency of Tax followed by a final bill. You may contest the Notice of Deficiency of Tax in Tax Court within 90 days, if you believe you do not owe the additional tax.

6) If, after you respond to our notice, your tax matter hasn't been settled to your satisfaction, you have the right to appeal. In order to appeal, explain in a signed statement why you disagree with our findings and ask for a conference with an Appeals Officer. Please include your social security number and telephone number; send it to the IRS office in the envelope provided. An Appeals Officer will contact you. For additional information concerning your appeal rights, see Publication 1, *Your Rights As A Taxpayer*, enclosed or previously sent to you.

Avoiding Future Notices

Each year when you prepare your return, you should have a Form W-2 from each of your employers and a Form 1099 for each payer of interest, dividends, or royalties, and each person required to report securities sales or real estate transactions. In addition, you should receive Forms 5498, *Individual Retirement Arrangement Information,* for your IRA contributions and Forms 1098, *Mortgage Interest Statement,* for any mortgage interest paid. (Your bank may send you approved substitutes for these forms.) If you don't receive these forms, or they are incorrect, contact the person responsible for providing the form (such as your employer) and ask for an original or corrected form. You may avoid receiving unnecessary notices by making sure that your social security number (SSN) appears only on your accounts. In cases where income is paid and reported to you on behalf of another, you should issue a form 1099 to the party who really owns the income. Please contact IRS at 1-800-TAX-FORM (829-3676) to request *Instructions for Forms 1099, 1098, 5498, 1096, and W-2G.*

1. Table for Figuring Amount Exempt from Levy on Wages, Salary, and Other Income (Forms 668-W and 668-W(c)) 1993

(Amounts are for each pay period.)

Filing Status: Single

Pay Period	\multicolumn{6}{Number of Exemptions Claimed on Statement}	More Than 6
	1	2	3	4	5	6	
Daily	23.27	32.31	41.35	50.38	59.42	68.46	14.23 Plus 9.04 for each exemption
Weekly	116.35	161.54	206.73	251.92	297.12	342.31	71.15 Plus 45.19 for each exemption
Bi-Weekly	232.69	323.08	413.46	503.85	594.23	684.62	142.31 Plus 90.38 for each exemption
Semi-Monthly	252.08	350.00	447.92	545.83	643.75	741.67	154.17 Plus 97.92 for each exemption
Monthly	504.17	700.00	895.83	1091.67	1287.50	1483.33	308.33 Plus 195.83 for each exemption

Filing Status: Married Filing Joint (and Qualifying Widow(er)s)

Pay Period	Number of Exemptions Claimed on Statement						More Than 6
	1	2	3	4	5	6	
Daily	32.88	41.92	50.96	60.00	69.04	78.08	23.85 Plus 9.04 for each exemption
Weekly	164.42	209.62	254.81	300.00	345.19	390.38	119.23 Plus 45.19 for each exemption
Bi-Weekly	328.85	419.23	509.62	600.00	690.38	780.77	238.46 Plus 90.38 for each exemption
Semi-Monthly	356.25	454.17	552.08	650.00	747.92	845.83	258.33 Plus 97.92 for each exemption
Monthly	712.50	908.33	1104.17	1300.00	1495.83	1691.67	516.67 Plus 195.83 for each exemption

Filing Status: Unmarried Head of Household

Pay Period	Number of Exemptions Claimed on Statement						More Than 6
	1	2	3	4	5	6	
Daily	30.00	39.04	48.08	57.12	66.15	75.19	20.96 Plus 9.04 for each exemption
Weekly	150.00	195.19	240.38	285.58	330.77	375.96	104.81 Plus 45.19 for each exemption
Bi-Weekly	300.00	390.38	480.77	571.15	661.54	751.92	209.62 Plus 90.38 for each exemption
Semi-Monthly	325.00	422.92	520.83	618.75	716.67	814.58	227.08 Plus 97.92 for each exemption
Monthly	650.00	845.83	1041.67	1237.50	1433.33	1629.17	454.17 Plus 195.83 for each exemption

Filing Status: Married Filing Separate

Pay Period	Number of Exemptions Claimed on Statement						More Than 6
	1	2	3	4	5	6	
Daily	20.96	30.00	39.04	48.08	57.12	66.15	11.92 Plus 9.04 for each exemption
Weekly	104.81	150.00	195.19	240.38	285.58	330.77	59.62 Plus 45.19 for each exemption
Bi-Weekly	209.62	300.00	390.38	480.77	571.15	661.54	119.23 Plus 90.38 for each exemption
Semi-Monthly	227.08	325.00	422.92	520.83	618.75	716.67	129.17 Plus 97.92 for each exemption
Monthly	454.17	650.00	845.83	1041.67	1237.50	1433.33	258.33 Plus 195.83 for each exemption

2. Table for Figuring Additional Exempt Amount for Taxpayers at least 65 years old and/or Blind

Additional Exempt Amount

Filing Status	*	Daily	Wkly	Bi-Wkly	Semi-Mo	Monthly
Single or Head of Household	1	3.46	17.31	34.62	37.50	75.00
	2	6.92	34.62	69.23	75.00	150.00
Any Other Filing Status	1	2.69	13.46	26.92	29.17	58.33
	2	5.38	26.92	53.85	58.33	116.67
	3	8.08	40.38	80.77	87.50	175.00
	4	10.77	53.85	107.69	116.67	233.33

*ADDITIONAL STANDARD DEDUCTION claimed on Parts 3, 4, & 5 of levy.

Examples

These tables show the amount exempt from a levy on wages, salary, and other income. For example:

1. A single taxpayer who is paid weekly and claims three exemptions (including one for the taxpayer) has $206.73 exempt from levy.
2. If the taxpayer in number 1 is over 65 and writes 1 in the ADDITIONAL STANDARD DEDUCTION space on Parts 3, 4, & 5 of the levy, $224.04 is exempt from this levy ($206.73 plus $17.31).
3. A taxpayer who is married, files jointly, is paid bi-weekly, and claims two exemptions (including one for the taxpayer) has $419.23 exempt from levy.
4. If the taxpayer in number 3 is over 65 and has a spouse who is blind, this taxpayer should write 2 in the ADDITIONAL STANDARD DEDUCTION space on Parts 3, 4, & 5 of the levy. Then, $473.08 is exempt from this levy ($419.23 plus $53.85).

Department of the Treasury

★ U.S.GPO:1992-0-343-049/71933

Publication 1494 (Rev. 1-93)
Cat. No. 11439T

UNITED STATES TAX COURT

(FIRST)   (MIDDLE)   (LAST)

_____

(PLEASE TYPE OR PRINT)   Petitioner(s)

V.

COMMISSIONER OF INTERNAL REVENUE
                 Respondent

Docket No. _____

PETITION

1. Petitioner(s) disagree(s) with the tax deficiency(ies) for the year(s) _____ as set forth in the NOTICE OF DEFICIENCY dated _____, A COPY OF WHICH IS ATTACHED. The notice was issued by the Office of the Internal Revenue Service at

_____
(CITY AND STATE)

2. Petitioner(s) taxpayer identification (e.g. social security) number(s) is (are)

_____

3. Petitioner(s) dispute(s) the following:

Year	Amount of Deficiency Disputed	Addition to Tax (Penalty) if any, Disputed	Amount of Over-payment Claimed
_____	_____	_____	_____
_____	_____	_____	_____
_____	_____	_____	_____

4. Set forth those adjustments, i.e. changes, in the NOTICE OF DEFICIENCY with which you disagree and why you disagree.

_____
_____
_____
_____
_____
_____
_____
_____
_____
_____

Petitioner(s) request(s) that this case be conducted under the "small tax case" procedures to provide the taxpayer(s) with an informal, prompt, and inexpensive hearing. A decision in a "small tax case" is final and cannot be appealed to a Court of Appeals by the Internal Revenue Service or the Petitioner(s). If you do not want this case conducted as a "small tax case" place an "X" in the following box. ☐

_____ _____ SIGNATURE OF PETITIONER DATE	(PRINT) PRESENT ADDRESS-STREET CITY STATE ZIP CODE AREA CODE TELEPHONE NO.
_____ _____ SIGNATURE OF PETITIONER (SPOUSE) (IF NAMED IN A NOTICE OF DEFICIENCY) DATE	(PRINT) PRESENT ADDRESS-STREET CITY STATE ZIP CODE AREA CODE TELEPHONE NO.

_____
SIGNATURE, NAME, ADDRESS, TELEPHONE NO., AND TAX COURT BAR NUMBER OF COUNSEL, IF RETAINED BY PETITIONER(S)

UNITED STATES TAX COURT

```
.................................... )
        Petitioner(s)              )
                                   )
            v.                     )  Docket No.
                                   )
                                   )
COMMISSIONER OF INTERNAL REVENUE,  )
                    Respondent     )
```

DESIGNATION OF PLACE OF TRIAL

Petitioner(s) hereby designate(s) ....
as the place of trial of this case.   City and State


```
                    .................................
                    Signature of Petitioner or Counsel


          Dated: ........................, 19....
```

Election
of Small Tax
Case Procedure
& Preparation
of Petitions

United States Tax Court
Washington, D.C., November, 1990

CONTENTS

ADDRESS ALL MAIL TO:

United States Tax Court
400 Second Street, N. W.
Washington, D. C. 20217

ELECTION OF SMALL TAX CASE PROCEDURE AND PREPARATION OF PETITIONS

Introduction

Congress has provided for a simple and informal procedure in the United States Tax Court where taxpayers may dispute a deficiency in taxes claimed by the Commissioner of Internal Revenue in his **Notice of Deficiency.** This simplified procedure is limited to those cases where the amount in dispute is $10,000 or less and provides for their early trial in the United States Tax Court.

The United States Tax Court is a court of record and is not connected in any way with the Internal Revenue Service. The Tax Court decides whether a tax deficiency claimed by the Commissioner of Internal Revenue is correct.

If a **Notice of Deficiency** has been issued in which the amount of the deficiency, and additions to tax, if any, or the part of it you wish to dispute, is $10,000 or less (and you are not claiming an overpayment of more than $10,000) for any one year, you may use the simplified procedure for small tax cases described in this pamphlet.

The following instructions tell you how to proceed and how to complete the required forms. Use the Quick Checklist on page 8 to be sure you have given all the needed information.

You may file a petition with the Tax Court only after the Commissioner of Internal Revenue has sent you a **Notice of Deficiency,** sometimes called a "90-day letter." The **Notice of Deficiency** shows the year and the amount of any deficiency determined by

A simple printed form -- Petition, Form 2 -- is supplied by the Clerk of the Court, United States Tax Court, 400 Second Street, N. W., Washington, D. C. 20217. When completing the form, fill in all the information asked for. The information you must give (though not in this order) is: (1) the years for which the Commissioner of Internal Revenue claims a tax deficiency, (2) the disputed dollar amount of the deficiency for each year, (3) the dollar amount of any tax overpayment you are claiming for each deficiency year, (4) the city and State where the office of the Internal Revenue Service that issued your **Notice of Deficiency** is located, (5) your social security number (or other taxpayer identification number, if any), (6) a short statement of any change the Internal Revenue Service wants to make in your tax return that you do not agree with, and (7) why you do not agree with the change. Only the person or persons to whom the **Notice of Deficiency** is addressed may properly begin a case. If the **Notice of Deficiency** is addressed to only one person, only that person should enter his or her name in the blank space above the word "Petitioner[s]"; and sign and date the form. If the **Notice of Deficiency** is addressed to more than one person and both wish to dispute the deficiency then both names should be entered in the blank space above the word "Petitioner[s]"; and both should sign and date the form. Also show your present address and telephone number in the places indicated, and be sure to attach a complete copy of your **Notice of Deficiency** to the original and each copy of the petition you file. You should not attach anything else to the petition.

Electing the Small Tax Case Procedure

If your case meets the $10,000 test, you may elect to have your case handled as a small tax case under the simple, informal procedure. To do this leave blank the box at the end of your Petition, Form 2.

3

---

him and states that it is a **Notice of Deficiency**. It will tell you that the deficiency determined by the Commissioner of Internal Revenue will be assessed against you after 90 days from the date of mailing of the letter unless within that period of time you file a petition with the United States Tax Court. The date shown on the **Notice of Deficiency** is the date the notice was mailed to you.

Bringing a Case in the Tax Court

You may begin a case in the United States Tax Court by paying a filing fee and filing a proper petition with the Court in Washington, D. C. You must file your petition not later than 90 days after the **Notice of Deficiency** was mailed to you. (150 days if the notice is addressed to a person outside the United States.) Saturdays, Sundays, or local holidays in the District of Columbia are not counted as the last day. The date shown on the **Notice of Deficiency** is the date the notice was mailed to you.

To be timely filed, your petition must actually be received by the Court within the 90-day period, or received in an envelope addressed to the United States Tax Court, 400 Second Street, N. W., Washington, D. C. 20217 with a United States postmark showing a legible date within the 90-day period. If your petition is even 1 day late, your case must be dismissed for late filing because the law allows the Court to hear only those cases for which a petition is filed within the 90-day period. Please note that the period is 90 days and not 3 months.

For example, for a **Notice of Deficiency** mailed on April 10, 1990, the last day for delivering or mailing a petition would be July 9, 1990 -- 90 days later. It would not be July 10, 1990 -- 3 months later. By filing your petition early, you will insure your right to dispute in the Tax Court the claim made against you by the Commissioner of Internal Revenue.

2

Filing Fee and Case Identification

The fee for filing a petition is $60. If you are unable to pay the filing fee you may request the Court waive the fee. You must give reason as to why you are unable to pay the fee. The fee is payable when you file your petition. When you file your petition, the Clerk of the Court will assign to your case a special number, called a docket number. That number will be followed by the letter "S" if you select the special procedure. (For example: Docket Number 1627-85S.) Once you know your case's docket number you should put it on all documents or letters that you send to the Court.

Choosing the Place of Trial

You may select from the list below a place of trial in the city nearest you. The cities marked by asterisks (*) are those in which only small tax case trials are heard. In the other cities, both regular trials and small tax cases are heard. At the top of Form 4 (Designation of Place of Trial) that was sent to you, fill in your name (names of both husband and wife for a joint petition) above the word "[Petitioner[s]]". Choose the city nearest you in which you would like your trial held and enter it in the space provided on the form. Then, date and sign it and forward it with your petition to the Clerk of the United States Tax Court.

Places for Hearing Small Tax Cases

Alabama
Birmingham
Mobile
Alaska
Anchorage
Arizona
Phoenix
Arkansas
Little Rock

California
*Fresno
Los Angeles
San Diego
San Francisco
Colorado
Denver
Connecticut
Hartford

District of Columbia
Washington
Florida
Jacksonville
Miami
*Tallahassee
Tampa

Georgia
Atlanta
Hawaii
Honolulu
Idaho
Boise
*Pocatello
Illinois
Chicago
*Peoria
Indiana
Indianapolis
Iowa
Des Moines
Kansas
*Wichita
Kentucky
Louisville
Louisiana
New Orleans
*Shreveport
Maine
*Portland
Maryland
Baltimore
Massachusetts
Boston
Michigan
Detroit
Minnesota
St. Paul
Mississippi
Jackson
Biloxi

Missouri
Kansas City
St. Louis
Montana
*Billings
Helena
Nebraska
Omaha
Nevada
Las Vegas
Reno
New Jersey
Newark
New Mexico
Albuquerque
New York
*Albany
Buffalo
New York City
*Syracuse
Westbury
North Carolina
Winston-Salem
North Dakota
*Bismarck
Ohio
Cincinnati
Cleveland
Columbus
Oklahoma
Oklahoma City
Oregon
Portland

Pennsylvania
Philadelphia
Pittsburgh
South Carolina
Columbia
South Dakota
*Aberdeen
Tennessee
Knoxville
Memphis
Nashville
Texas
Dallas
El Paso
Houston
Lubbock
San Antonio
Utah
Salt Lake City
Vermont
*Burlington
Virginia
Richmond
*Roanoke
Washington
Seattle
Spokane
West Virginia
Charleston
Huntington
Wisconsin
Milwaukee
Wyoming
*Cheyenne

Mailing Petition and Other Papers

The petition (Form 2) is a four part form. You must submit to the Court the original and two copies of the petition. You should keep the last copy of the petition for your records. Remember to attach to each copy of the petition submitted to the Court a complete copy of your **Notice of Deficiency**.

You have also received with this booklet a Designation of Place of Trial (Form 4). You should submit an original and two copies to the Court.

You should also enclose a check or money order for your filing fee. Make your check or money order payable to the "Clerk, United States Tax Court."

You have been given an envelope for your use in mailing these various papers to the Court.

After your petition is filed, the Court will send a copy to the lawyer for the Commissioner of Internal Revenue.

Trial Calendar Assignment

Your case will be listed for trial at the next trial session regularly scheduled for the city you chose. Trial sessions will be announced and a notice of trial will be sent to you about 60 days before the trial date. The trial date will be set to give you a hearing as quickly as possible.

Removal of Small Tax Case Designation

At any time before trial the Court, on its own motion or on a motion filed by you or by the Commissioner of Internal Revenue, may remove the small tax case designation from your case and direct that it be handled as a regular case. After trial but before final decision, the Court may order proceedings as a small tax case discontinued if the disputed deficiency or claimed overpayment will exceed $10,000 and justice requires discontinuance, taking into account the inconvenience and expense for both parties that would result from taking such action.

Informal Trial Procedure

You may represent yourself or you may be represented by anyone you choose who is admitted to practice before the Tax Court. Most petitioners in small tax cases represent themselves. The trial will be conducted in an orderly manner, as simply as possible. Any evidence you offer which the Court thinks will have value as proof of your claim will be admissible.

If you have receipts or other papers or documents which support your claim, you should bring them with you when you come to Court for trial. The Court will try to help you develop the facts in your case through your testimony and that of other witnesses, and any receipts, papers, or documents which you bring with you to the trial.

Any information or documents which you have previously supplied to the Internal Revenue Service is not available to the Court and thus you must be prepared to present your oral information as testimony and to have available any necessary documents to be received in evidence at the trial. If you need documents which you have given to the Internal Revenue Service to support your claim, you should ask the Government lawyer to bring them to court for the trial of your case so that you can offer them in evidence as proof of your claim. Where original documents are lost or destroyed you may offer copies, if you have them.

Your testimony and that of any other witness will be recorded and you may order and pay for a transcript of the testimony if you wish. After you and any other witnesses have testified, you may argue your case orally.

Finality of Decision

If you elect to have your case tried as a Small Tax Case under the provisions of section 7463 of the Internal Revenue Code, the decision of the Tax Court is final and cannot be appealed. Thus, if the decision is in your favor, in whole or in part, the Government cannot appeal to a higher court to change the decision. On the other hand, if the Tax Court decides the deficiency claimed by the Commissioner of Internal Revenue is correct, in whole or in part, you cannot appeal.

Quick Checklist

(When you file your petition, be sure to include all the following information and attachments required.)

(1) Your full name (both names if the **Notice of Deficiency** was addressed to both and both wish to dispute the deficiency).

(2) The years of the claimed deficiencies.

(3) The name of the city and State from which the Internal Revenue Service sent your **Notice of Deficiency.**

(4) Your social security or other taxpayer identification number.

(5) (a) The year; (b) amount of the disputed deficiency; (c) amount of any disputed addition to tax (additional amount or penalty); and (d) for an overpayment, the amount claimed.

(6) A statement of the Internal Revenue Service's proposed changes with which you do not agree.

(7) Your reasons for disagreement with the proposed changes.

(8) Your signature, date, present address, and telephone number at the bottom of the petition.

(9) Your spouse's signature, date, present address, and telephone number if you are filing a joint petition.

8

(10) In your mailing to the Clerk of the Court include: (a) The original and two copies of your petition with a complete copy of your **Notice of Deficiency** attached to the original and each copy; (b) your filing fee in the form of a check or money order, payable to "Clerk, United States Tax Court"; and (c) your designation, Form 4, showing in which city you wish your case to be tried.

9

☆ U.S. GOVERNMENT PRINTING OFFICE : 1990 O - 279-745

Index

business taxes, 6/6
CP-500 notices, 6/5-6
delay, 6/6
individual income taxes, 6/5-6
offer in compromise, 6/25-35
advantages of, 6/30-31
disadvantages of, 6/31
future income agreements, 6/30
qualifying for, 6/26
rejection of, 6/34-35
appeal, 6/35
sample, 6/33
structuring, 6/30
submission of offer, 6/26-27, 6/31-34
property exempt from IRS seizure, 7/6
property seizure, service center, 6/6
protection of assets, 6/43-44
revenue officer, 6/10-25
collection interview, 6/11-13
divulging financial information, 6/12
expenses, defending to, 6/13
surprise visit by, 6/11
state of limitations, 6/4
state taxes, suspension of collection, 14/6
suspension of collection, 6/44
tax bill, 6/5-6
Company books, bringing to audit, 3/26
Complexity of income tax laws, and inefficiency of IRS, 1/6
Computer data sharing, state taxing authority, IRS, 14/2
Computer file, requesting copy of, 1/6
Computers, and inefficiency of IRS, 1/4
Confusion, and inefficiency of IRS, 1/6
Contact of friends/associates, by special agents, during criminal investigation, 10/8
Conviction, of fraud, 10/11-12
Correspondence audit, 3/13-14
Court system, interpretation of tax code, 1/7
CP-500 notices
delay, 6/6
of taxes due, 6/5-6
CP-2000 notice, 3/14-19
sample, 3/15-18
CPA. *See* Certified public accountant
Criminal charges
for late tax return filing, 2/7
for not filing returns, 2/2
Criminal investigation, 10/6-10
attorney-client privilege, 10/7
contact of friends/associates, 10/8
questioning by special agent, response to, 10/8-9
referral for fraud, 10/4-6

D

Death, tax issues, 9/7-9
Deductions, itemized. *See* Itemized deductions
Defense, against alleged fraud, 10/4
Delaying audit, 3/8
Delinquency, in filing returns, 2/2
Dependency exemption, 9/5
Designation, of tax payment, 12/8
DIF score. *See* Discrimination Function Score
Discrimination Function Score, 3/4
Dishonesty of spouse, in filing tax return, avoiding, 9/4
District offices, 1/3-4
Divorce, filing return, 9/3
Documentation
at audit, lack of, 3/27-28
to bring to audit, 3/26-27

E

Emergencies, Problems Resolution Program, 8/3
Employee, independent contractor, distinguished, 3/12, 11/2-6
Enrolled agent, 13/1-9
hiring for appeal of audit, 4/10-11
Escrow papers, bringing to audit, 3/27
Estate tax return
audit, 9/7-8
federal, 9/7
Evidence, tax court, small case, 5/8
Examination. *See* Audit
Examination report, from audit, 3/31-38
sample, 3/32-36
Expenses
calculation of, for proving fraud, 10/3
defending to revenue officer, at collection interview, 6/13
listing on Form 433, 6/14-21
listing on Form 433, checklist, 6/16
Extension
of audit, 3/30
for filing returns, 2/7-8

F

Federal estate tax, 9/7
joint ownership of property, 9/8-9
Fee, of tax professionals, 13/4-5
controlling, 13/5
Field audit, 3/11-13
asset sales, 3/12

CATALOG

...more books & software from Nolo

Your Rights in the Workplace

Attorney Barbara Kate Repa. Nat'l 2nd ed.

The first comprehensive guide to workplace rights—from hiring to firing. Covers wages and overtime, parental leave, unemployment and disability insurance, worker's compensation, job safety, discrimination and illegal firings and layoffs.

$15.95/YRW

How to Write a Business Plan

Mike McKeever. Nat'l 4th ed.

This book will show you how to write the business plan and loan package necessary to finance your business and make it work.

$21.95/SBS

The Partnership Book

Attorneys Denis Clifford & Ralph Warner. Nat'l 4th ed.

Shows you step-by-step how to write a solid partnership agreement that meets your needs. It covers initial contributions to the business, wages, profit-sharing, buy-outs, death or retirement of a partner and disputes.

$24.95/PART

The California Nonprofit Corporation Handbook

Attorney Anthony Mancuso. CA 6th ed.

Shows you step-by-step how to form and operate a nonprofit corporation in California. It includes the latest corporate and tax law changes, and the forms for the Articles, Bylaws and Minutes.

$29.95/NON

How to Form Your Own Corporation

Attorney Anthony Mancuso. CA 8th ed.

This book contain the forms, instructions and tax information you need to incorporate a small business yourself and save hundreds of dollars in lawyers' fees.

California $29.95/CCOR
New York $29.95/NYCO
Texas $29.95/TCOR

The California Professional Corporation Handbook

Attorney Anthony Mancuso. CA 5th ed.

Health care professionals, lawyers, accountants and members of certain other professions must fulfill special requirements when forming a corporation in California. Contains up-to-date tax information plus all the forms and instructions necessary.

$34.95/PROF

The Independent Paralegal's Handbook

Attorney Ralph Warner. Nat'l 3rd ed.

Provides legal and business guidelines for anyone who wants to go into business as an independent paralegal helping consumers with routine legal tasks.

$29.95 PARA

books with disk

How to Form a Nonprofit Corporation

Attorney Anthony Mancuso. Nat'l 2nd ed.

Explains the legal formalities involved and provides detailed information on the differences in the law among all 50 states. It also contains forms for the Articles, Bylaws and Minutes you need, along with complete instructions for obtaining federal 501(c)(3) tax exemptions and qualifying for public charity status. Includes incorporation forms on disk.

DOS $39.95/NNP

How to Form Your Own Corporation

Attorney Anthony Mancuso.

Step-by-step guide to forming your own corporation. Provides clear instructions and all the forms you need including Articles, Bylaws, Minutes and Stock Certificates. Includes all incorporation forms on disk.

Florida DOS $39.95/FLCO
New York DOS $39.95/NYCO
Texas DOS $39.95/TCI

Taking Care of Your Corporation, Vol. 1: Director and Shareholder Meetings Made Easy

Attorney Anthony Mancuso. Nat'l 1st ed.

This book takes the drudgery out of the necessary task of holding meetings of the board of directors and shareholders. It shows how to comply with state laws for holding meetings, how to prepare minutes for annual and special meetings, take corporate action by written consent, hold real or paper meetings and handle corporate formalities using e-mail, computer bulletin boards, fax and telephone and video conferencing. Includes all corporate forms on disk.

DOS $26.95/CORK

How to Form Your Own California Corporation With Corporate Records Binder & Disk

Attorney Anthony Mancuso. CA 1st Ed.

How to Form Your Own California Corporation is also available in a handy new format. It includes all the forms and instructions you need to form your own corporation, a corporate records binder, stock certificates and all incorporation forms on disk.

$39.95/CACI

The California Nonprofit Corporation Handbook

Attorney Anthony Mancuso. Version 1.0

This book with disk package shows you step-by-step how to form and operate a nonprofit corporation in California. Included on disk are the forms for the Articles, Bylaws and Minutes.

DOS $39.95 NPI
MACINTOSH $39.95 NPM

Software Development: A Legal Guide

Attorney Stephen Fishman. Nat'l 1st ed.

Clearly explains patent, copyright, trademark and trade secret protection and shows how to draft development contracts and employment agreements. Includes all contracts and agreements on disk.

DOS $44.95/SFT

software

Nolo's Partnership Maker

Version 1.0

Prepares a legal partnership agreement for doing business in any state. Select and assemble the standard partnership clauses provided or create your own customized agreement. Includes on-line legal help screens, glossary and tutorial, and a manual that takes you through the process step-by-step.

DOS $129.95/PAGI1

California Incorporator

Version 1.0 (good only in CA)

Answer the questions on the screen and this software program will print out the 35-40 pages of documents you need to make your California corporation legal. A 200-page manual explains the incorporation process.

DOS $129.00/INCI

audio cassette tapes

How to Start Your Own Business: Small Business Law

Attorney Ralph Warner with Joanne Greene. Nat'l 1st ed. 60 minutes

This tape covers what every small business owner needs to know about organizing as a sole proprietorship, partnership or corporation, protecting the business name, renting space, hiring employees and paying taxes.

$14.95/TBUS

Getting Started as an Independent Paralegal

Attorney Ralph Warner. Nat'l 2nd ed. Two tapes, approximately 2 hrs.

Practical and legal advice on going into business as an independent paralegal from the author of *The Independent Paralegal's Handbook.*

$44.95/GSIP

GOING TO COURT

How to Change Your Name

Attorneys David Loeb & David Brown. CA 6th ed.

All the forms and instructions you need to change your name in California.

$24.95/NAME

Represent Yourself in Court
Attorneys Paul Bergman & Sara Berman-Barrett. Nat'l 1st ed.

Handle your own civil court case from start to finish without a lawyer with the most thorough guide to contested court cases ever published for the non-lawyer. Covers all aspects of civil trials.
$29.95/RYC

Everybody's Guide to Municipal Court
Judge Roderic Duncan. CA 1st ed.

Sue and defend cases for up to $25,000 in California Municipal Court. Gives step-by-step instructions for preparing and filing forms, gathering evidence and appearing in court.
$29.95/MUNI

Everybody's Guide to Small Claims Court
Attorney Ralph Warner. Nat'l 5th ed. CA 11th ed.

These books will help you decide if you should sue in Small Claims Court, show you how to file and serve papers, tell you what to bring to court and how to collect a judgment.
National $18.95/NSCC
California $18.95/CSCC

Fight Your Ticket
Attorney David Brown. CA 5th ed.

Shows you how to fight an unfair traffic ticket—when you're stopped, at arraignment, at trial and on appeal.
$18.95/FYT

Collect Your Court Judgment
Gini Graham Scott, Attorney Stephen Elias & Lisa Goldoftas. CA 2nd ed.

Contains step-by-step instructions and all the forms you need to collect a court judgment from the debtor's bank accounts, wages, business receipts, real estate or other assets.
$19.95/JUDG

The Criminal Records Book
Attorney Warren Siegel. CA 3rd ed.

Shows you step-by-step how to seal criminal records, dismiss convictions, destroy marijuana records and reduce felony convictions.
$19.95/CRIM

audio cassette tapes

Winning in Small Claims Court
Attorney Ralph Warner with Joanne Greene. Nat'l 1st ed. 60 minutes

Guides you through all the major issues involved in preparing and winning a small claims court case—deciding if there is a good case, assessing whether you can collect if you win, preparing your evidence, and arguing before the judge.
$14.95/TWIN

THE NEIGHBORHOOD

Dog Law
Attorney Mary Randolph. Nat'l 2nd ed.

A practical guide to the laws that affect dog owners and their neighbors. Answers common questions about biting, barking, veterinarians and more.
$12.95/DOG

Neighbor Law:
Fences, Trees, Boundaries & Noise
Attorney Cora Jordan. Nat'l 2nd ed.

Answers common questions about the subjects that most often trigger disputes between neighbors: fences, trees, boundaries and noise. It explains how to find the law and resolve disputes without a nasty lawsuit.
$16.95/NEI

Safe Homes, Safe Neighborhoods:
Stopping Crime Where You Live
Stephanie Mann with M.C. Blakeman. Nat'l 1st ed.

Learn how you and your neighbors can work together to protect yourselves, your families and property from crime. Explains how to form a neighborhood crime prevention group; avoid burglaries, car thefts, muggings and rapes; combat gangs and drug dealing; improve home security and make the neighborhood safer for children.
$14.95/SAFE

FAMILY MATTERS

The Living Together Kit
Attorneys Toni Ihara & Ralph Warner. Nat'l 7th ed.

A detailed guide designed to help the increasing number of unmarried couples living together understand the laws that affect them. Sample agreements and instructions are included.
$24.95/LTK

A Legal Guide for Lesbian and Gay Couples
Attorneys Hayden Curry, Denis Clifford & Robin Leonard. Nat'l 8th ed.

This book shows lesbian and gay couples how to write a living-together contract, plan for medical emergencies, understand the practical and legal aspects of having and raising children and plan their estates. Includes forms and sample agreements.
$24.95/LG

Divorce:
A New Yorker's Guide to Doing it Yourself
Bliss Alexandra. New York 1st ed.

Step-by-step instructions and all the forms you need to do your own divorce and save thousands of dollars in legal fees. Shows you how to divide property, arrange custody of the children, set child support and maintenance (alimony), draft a divorce agreement and fill out and file all forms.
$24.95/NYDIV

Nolo's Pocket Guide to Family Law
Attorneys Robin Leonard & Stephen Elias. Nat'l 3rd ed.

Here's help for anyone who has a question or problem involving family law—marriage, divorce, adoption or living together.
$14.95/FLD

Divorce & Money
Violet Woodhouse & Victoria Felton-Collins with M.C. Blakeman. Nat'l 2nd ed.

Explains how to evaluate such major assets as family homes and businesses, investments, pensions, and how to arrive at a division of property that is fair to both sides.
$21.95/DIMO

How to Raise or Lower Child Support in California
Judge Roderic Duncan & Attorney Warren Siegel. CA 2nd ed.

Appropriate for parents on either side of the support issue. All the forms and instructions necessary to raise or lower an existing child support order.
$17.95/CHLD

The Guardianship Book
Lisa Goldoftas & Attorney David Brown. CA 1st ed.

Provides step-by-step instructions and the forms needed to obtain a legal guardianship of a minor without a lawyer.
$19.95/GB

How to Adopt Your Stepchild in California
Frank Zagone & Attorney Mary Randolph. CA 4th ed.

Provides sample forms and step-by-step instructions for completing a simple uncontested stepparent adoption in California.
$22.95/ADOP

Smart Ways to Save Money During and After Divorce
Victoria F. Collins & Ginita Wall. Nat'l 1st ed.

If you're going through a divorce, most likely you're faced with an overwhelming number of financial decisions. Here's a book packed with information on how to save money before, during and after divorce. It covers how to keep attorney's fees low, save on taxes, divide assets fairly, understand child support and alimony obligations and put aside money now for expenses later.
$14.95/SAVMO

California Marriage & Divorce Law
Attorneys Ralph Warner, Toni Ihara & Stephen Elias. CA 11th ed.

Explains community property, pre-nuptial contracts, foreign marriages, buying a house, getting a divorce, dividing property, and more. Pre-nuptial contracts included.
$19.95/MARR

Practical Divorce Solutions
Attorney Charles Sherman. Nat'l 1st ed.

Covers the emotional aspects of divorce and provides an overview of the legal and financial considerations.
$14.95/PDS

How to Do Your Own Divorce

Attorney Charles Sherman (Texas ed. by Sherman & Simons).
CA 19th ed. & Texas 5th ed.

These books contain all the forms and instructions you need to do your own uncontested divorce without a lawyer.

California $21.95/CDIV
Texas $17.95/TDIV

MONEY MATTERS

Stand Up to the IRS

Attorney Fred Daily. Nat'l 2nd ed.

Gives detailed strategies on surviving an audit, appealing an audit decision, going to Tax Court and dealing with IRS collectors. It also discusses filing delinquent tax returns, tax crimes, concerns of small business people and getting help from the IRS ombudsman.

$21.95/SIRS

How to File for Bankruptcy

Attorneys Stephen Elias, Albin Renauer & Robin Leonard. Nat'l 5th ed.

Trying to decide whether or not filing for bankruptcy makes sense? This book contains an overview of the process and all the forms plus step-by-step instructions you need to file for Chapter 7 Bankruptcy.

$25.95/HFB

Money Troubles:
Legal Strategies to Cope With Your Debts

Attorney Robin Leonard. Nat'l 3rd ed.

Essential for anyone who has gotten behind on bills. It shows how to obtain a credit file, negotiate with persistent creditors, challenge wage attachments, contend with property repossessions and more.

$18.95/MT

Simple Contracts for Personal Use

Attorney Stephen Elias & Marcia Stewart. Nat'l 2nd ed.

Contains clearly written legal form contracts to buy and sell property, borrow and lend money, store and lend personal property, release others from personal liability, or pay a contractor to do home repairs. Includes agreements to arrange child care and other household help.

$16.95/CONT

law form kits

Nolo's Law Form Kit: Power of Attorney

Attorneys Denis Clifford & Mary Randolph and Lisa Goldoftas. Nat'l 1st ed.

Create a conventional power of attorney to assign someone you trust to take of your finances, business, real estate or children when you are away or unavailable. Provides all the forms with step-by-step instructions.

$14.95/KPA

Nolo's Law Form Kit: Loan Agreements

Attorney Stephen Elias, Marcia Stewart & Lisa Goldoftas. Nat'l 1st ed.

Provides all the forms and instructions necessary to create a legal and effective promissory note. Shows how to decide on an interest rate, set a payment schedule and keep track of payments.

$14.95/KLOAN

Nolo's Law Form Kit:
Buy and Sell Contracts

Attorney Stephen Elias, Marcia Stewart & Lisa Goldoftas. Nat'l 1st ed.

Step-by-step instructions and all the forms necessary for creating bills of sale for cars, boats, computers, electronic equipment, household appliances and other personal property.

$9.95/KCONT

Nolo's Law Form Kit: Personal Bankruptcy

Attorneys Steve Elias, Albin Renauer & Robin Leonard and Lisa Goldoftas. Nat'l 1st ed.

All the forms and instructions you need to file for Chapter 7 bankruptcy.

$14.95/KBNK

Nolo's Law Forms Kit: Rebuild Your Credit

Attorney Robin Leonard. Nat'l 1st ed.

Provides strategies for dealing with debts and rebuilding your credit. Shows you how to negotiate with creditors and collection agencies, clean up your credit file, devise a spending plan and get credit in your name.

$14.95/KCRD

PATENT, COPYRIGHT & TRADEMARK

Trademark: How to Name Your
Business & Product

Attorneys Kate McGrath & Stephen Elias, with Trademark Attorney Sarah Shena. Nat'l 1st ed.

Learn how to choose a name or logo that others can't copy, conduct a trademark search, register a trademark with the U.S. Patent and Trademark Office and protect and maintain the trademark.

$29.95/TRD

Patent It Yourself

Attorney David Pressman. Nat'l 3rd ed.

From the patent search to the actual application, this book covers everything including the use and licensing of patents, successful marketing and how to deal with infringement. Includes all necessary forms and instructions.

$39.95/PAT

The Inventor's Notebook

Fred Grissom & Attorney David Pressman. Nat'l 1st ed.

Helps you document the process of successful independent inventing by providing forms, instructions, references to relevant areas of patent law, a bibliography of legal and non-legal aids and more.

$19.95/INOT

The Copyright Handbook

Attorney Stephen Fishman. Nat'l 2nd ed.

Provides forms and step-by-step instructions for protecting all types of written expression under U.S. and international copyright law. Covers copyright infringement, fair use, works for hire and transfers of copyright ownership.

$24.95/COHA

software

Patent It Yourself Software

Version 1.0

Patent It Yourself is also available in software. With separate tracks for novice and expert users, it takes you through the process step-by-step. It shows how to evaluate patentability of your invention, how to prepare and file your patent application and how to generate all the forms you need to protect and exploit your invention.

Windows $229.95/PYW1

HOMEOWNERS

How to Buy a House in California

Attorney Ralph Warner, Ira Serkes & George Devine. CA 3rd ed.

Effective strategies for finding a house, working with a real estate agent, making an offer and negotiating intelligently. Includes information on all types of mortgages as well as private financing options.

$24.95/BHCA

For Sale By Owner

George Devine. CA 2nd ed.

Everything you need to know to sell your own house, from pricing and marketing, to writing a contract and going through escrow. Disclosure and contract forms included.

$24.95/FSBO

Homestead Your House

Attorneys Ralph Warner, Charles Sherman & Toni Ihara. CA 8th ed.

Shows you how to file a Declaration of Homestead and includes complete instructions and tear-out forms.

$9.95/HOME

The Deeds Book

Attorney Mary Randolph. CA 3rd ed.

Shows you how to fill out and file the right kind of deed when transferring property. Outlines the legal requirements of real property transfer.

$16.95/DEED

LANDLORDS & TENANTS

The Landlord's Law Book, Vol. 1: Rights & Responsibilities
Attorneys David Brown & Ralph Warner. CA 4th ed.
Essential for every California landlord. Covers deposits, leases and rental agreements, inspections (tenants' privacy rights), habitability (rent withholding), ending a tenancy, liability and rent control. Forms included.
$32.95/LBRT

The Landlord's Law Book, Vol. 2: Evictions
Attorney David Brown. CA 4th ed.
Shows step-by-step how to go to court and evict a tenant. Contains all the tear-out forms and necessary instructions.
$32.95/LBEV

Nolo's Law Form Kit: Leases & Rental Agreements
Attorneys Ralph Warner & Marcia Stewart. CA 1st ed.
With these easy-to-use forms and instructions, California landlords can prepare their own rental application, fixed term lease, month-to-month agreement and notice to pay rent or quit.
$14.95/KLEAS

Tenants' Rights
Attorneys Myron Moskovitz & Ralph Warner. CA 12th ed.
This practical guide to dealing with your landlord explains your rights under federal law, California law and rent control ordinances. Forms included.
$18.95/CTEN

JUST FOR FUN

Nolo's Favorite Lawyer Jokes on Disk
Over 200 jokes and hilariously nasty remarks about lawyers organized by categories (Lawyers as Vultures, Nobody Loves a Lawyer, Lawyers in Love...). 100% guaranteed to produce an evening of chuckles and drive every lawyer you know nuts.
IBM PC $9.95/JODI
MACINTOSH $9.95/JODM

Devil's Advocates: The Unnatural History of Lawyers
by Andrew & Jonathan Roth. Nat'l 1st ed.
A hilarious look at the history of the legal profession.
$12.95/DA

Poetic Justice: The Funniest, Meanest Things Ever Said About Lawyers
Edited by Jonathan & Andrew Roth. Nat'l 1st ed.
A great gift for anyone in the legal profession who has managed to maintain a sense of humor.
$9.95/PJ

29 Reasons Not to Go to Law School
Attorneys Ralph Warner & Toni Ihara. Nat'l 4th ed.
Filled with humor, this book can save you three years, $150,000 and your sanity.
$9.95/29R

OLDER AMERICANS

Social Security, Medicare & Pensions
Attorney Joseph Matthews with Dorothy Matthews Berman. Nat'l 5th ed.
Offers invaluable guidance through the current maze of rights and benefits for those 55 and over, including Medicare, Medicaid and Social Security retirement and disability benefits, and age discrimination protections.
$18.95/SOA

Beat the Nursing Home Trap: A Consumer's Guide to Choosing and Financing Long-term Care
Attorney Joseph Matthews. Nat'l 1st ed.
Guides you in choosing and paying for long-term care, alerting you to practical concerns and explaining laws that may affect your decisions.
$18.95/ELD

REFERENCE

Legal Research: How to Find and Understand the Law
Attorneys Stephen Elias & Susan Levinkind. Nat'l 3rd ed.
A valuable tool on its own or as a companion to just about every other Nolo book. Gives easy-to-use, step-by-step instructions on how to find legal information.
$19.95/LRES

Legal Research Made Easy: A Roadmap Through the Law Library Maze
2-1/2 hr. videotape and 40-page manual.
Nolo Press/Legal Star Communications. Nat'l 1st ed.
Professor Bob Berring explains how to use all the basic legal research tools in your local law library with an easy-to-follow six-step research plan and a sense of humor.
$89.95/LRME

CONSUMER/REFERENCE

Nolo's Pocket Guide to California Law
Attorney Lisa Guerin & Nolo Press Editors. CA 2nd ed.
Get quick clear answers to questions about child support, custody, consumer rights, employee rights, government benefits, divorce, bankruptcy, adoption, wills and much more.
$10.95/CLAW

Nolo's Pocket Guide to California Law on Disk
This handy resource is also available on disk. With this new format you can rapidly search through California law by topic and subtopic, or by using the key-word index. The program tracks and saves searches, and allows you to save text to a file for later use.
Windows $24.95/CLWIN
Macintosh $24.95/CLM

Nolo's Pocket Guide to Consumer Rights
Barbara Kaufman. CA 2nd ed.
Practical advice on hundreds of consumer topics. Shows Californians how and where to complain about everything from accountants, misleading advertisements and lost baggage to vacation scams and dishonored warranties.
$14.95/CAG

Nolo's Law Form Kit: Hiring Child Care & Household Help
Attorney Barbara Kate Repa & Lisa Goldoftas. Nat'l 1st ed.
All the necessary forms and instructions for fulfilling your legal and tax responsibilities. Includes employment contracts, application forms and required IRS forms.
$14.95/KCHLD

How to Win Your Personal Injury Claim
Attorney Joseph Matthews. Nat'l 1st ed.
Armed with the right information anyone can handle a personal injury claim. This step-by-step guide shows you how to avoid insurance company run-arounds, evaluate what your claim is worth, obtain a full and fair settlement and save for yourself what you would pay a lawyer.
$24.95/PICL

Fed Up with the Legal System: What's Wrong and How to Fix It
Attorneys Ralph Warner & Stephen Elias. Nat'l 2nd ed.
Forty common-sense proposals to make our legal system fairer, faster, cheaper and more accessible.
$9.95/LEG

IMMIGRATION

How to Get a Green Card: Legal Ways to Stay in the U.S.A.
Attorney Loida Nicolas Lewis with Len T. Madlanscay. Nat'l 1st ed.
Written by a former INS attorney, this book clearly explains the steps involved in getting a green card. It covers who can qualify, what documents to present, and how to fill out all the forms and have them processed. Tear-out forms included.
$22.95/GRN

Como Obtener La Tajeta Verde: Maneras Legitimas de Permanacer en los EE.UU.
Attorney Loida Nicolas Lewis with Len T. Madlanscay. Nat'l 1st ed.
The Spanish edition of How to Get a Green Card.
$24.95/VERDE

ORDER FORM

Code	Quantity	Title	Unit Price	Total

Subtotal	
California residents add Sales Tax	
Shipping & Handling ($4 for 1st item; $1 each additional)	
2nd day UPS (additional $5; $8 in Alaska and Hawaii)	
TOTAL	

Name

Address

(UPS to street address, Priority Mail to P.O. boxes)

**FOR FASTER SERVICE, USE YOUR CREDIT CARD
AND OUR TOLL-FREE NUMBERS**

Monday-Friday, 7 a.m. to 6 p.m. Pacific Time
Order Line   1 (800) 992-6656 (in the 510 area code, call 549-1976)
General Information   1 (510) 549-1976
Fax your order   1 (800) 645-0895 (in the 510 area code, call 548-5902)

METHOD OF PAYMENT

☐ Check enclosed   ☐ VISA   ☐ Mastercard   ☐ Discover Card   ☐ American Express

Account #   Expiration Date

Authorizing Signature

Daytime Phone

**MAIL YOUR ORDER WITH A CHECK OR MONEY ORDER
MADE PAYABLE TO:
NOLO PRESS, 950 PARKER ST., BERKELEY, CA 94710**

VISIT OUR STORE

If you live in the Bay Area, be sure to visit the Nolo Press Bookstore on the corner
of 9th & Parker Streets in west Berkeley. You'll find our complete line of books
and software—all at a discount. CALL 1-510-704-2248 for hours.

ALLOW 2-3 WEEKS FOR DELIVERY. PRICES SUBJECT TO CHANGE.

TO ORDER CALL 1-800-992-6656   SIRS

Get your financial and legal affairs in order with books and software from Nolo

Plan Your Estate
by Attorney Denis Clifford
$24.95

Nolo's Personal RecordKeeper
Available for DOS and Macintosh
$49.95

Money Troubles
Legal Strategies to Cope with Your Debts
by Attorney Robin Leonard
$18.95

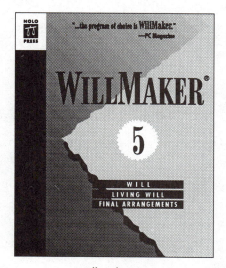

Willmaker 5.0
Available for Windows, DOS and Macintosh
$69.95

Please see the preceeding catalog pages for more information on these items

To order: Please use order form in catalog
or call: 1-800-992-6656 (in 510 area, call 549-1976)
or FAX: 1-800-645-0895 (in 510 area, FAX 548-5902)

GET 25% OFF
YOUR NEXT PURCHASE

RECYCLE YOUR OUT-OF-DATE BOOKS

It's important to have the most current legal information. Because laws and legal procedures change often, we update our books regularly. To help keep you up-to-date we are extending this special offer. Cut out and mail the title portion of the cover of any old Nolo book with your next order and we'll give you a 25% discount off the retail price of ANY new Nolo book you purchase directly from us. For current prices and editions call us at 1-800-992-6656.

This offer is to individuals only.

When you register, we'll send you our quarterly newspaper, the *Nolo News,* free for two years. (U.S. addresses only.) Here's what you'll get in every issue:

INFORMATIVE ARTICLES

Written by Nolo editors, articles provide practical legal information on issues you encounter in everyday life: family law, wills, debts, consumer rights, and much more.

UPDATE SERVICE

The *Nolo News* keeps you informed of legal changes that affect any Nolo book and software program.

BOOK AND SOFTWARE REVIEWS

We're always looking for good legal and consumer books and software from other publishers. When we find them, we review them and offer them in our mail order catalog.

ANSWERS TO YOUR LEGAL QUESTIONS

Our readers are always challenging us with good questions on a variety of legal issues. So in each issue, "Auntie Nolo" gives sage advice and sound information.

COMPLETE NOLO PRESS CATALOG

The *Nolo News* contains an up-to-the-minute catalog of all Nolo books and software, which you can order using our toll-free "800" order line. And you can see at a glance if you're using an out-of-date version of a Nolo product.

LAWYER JOKES

Nolo's famous lawyer joke column continually gets the goat of the legal establishment. If we print a joke you send in, you'll get a $20 Nolo gift certificate.

We promise *never* to give your name and address to any other organization.

Your Registration Card

Complete and Mail Today

STAND UP TO THE IRS   Registration Card

We'd like to know what you think! Please take a moment to fill out and return this postage paid card for a free two-year subscription to the *Nolo News.* If you already receive the *Nolo News,* we'll extend your subscription.

Name _____ Ph.( ) _____

Address _____

City _____ State _____ Zip _____

Where did you hear about this book? _____

For what purpose did you use this book? _____

Did you consult a lawyer?	Yes	No		Not Applicable			
Was it easy for you to use this book?	(very easy)	5	4	3	2	1	(very difficult)
Did you find this book helpful?	(very)	5	4	3	2	1	(not at all)

Comments _____
_____
_____
_____
_____
_____

THANK YOU   SIRS 2.2

[Nolo books are]..."written in plain language, free of legal mumbo jumbo, and spiced with witty personal observations."

—ASSOCIATED PRESS

"Well-produced and slickly written, the [Nolo] books are designed to take the mystery out of seemingly involved procedures, carefully avoiding legalese and leading the reader step-by-step through such everyday legal problems as filling out forms, making up contracts, and even how to behave in court."

—SAN FRANCISCO EXAMINER

"...Nolo publications...guide people simply through the how, when, where and why of law."

—WASHINGTON POST

"Increasingly, people who are not lawyers are performing tasks usually regarded as legal work... And consumers, using books like Nolo's, do routine legal work themselves."

—NEW YORK TIMES

"...All of [Nolo's] books are easy-to-understand, are updated regularly, provide pull-out forms...and are often quite moving in their sense of compassion for the struggles of the lay reader."

—SAN FRANCISCO CHRONICLE